JOHAN SVENDSEN

JOHAN SVENDSEN

The Man, the Maestro, the Music

Finn Benestad
Dag Schjelderup-Ebbe

English translation
William H. Halverson

Peer Gynt Press
Columbus

Originally published as
Johan Svendsen: Mennesket og kunstneren
© 1990 H. Aschehoug & Co. (W. Nygaard), Norway
Finn Benestad and Dag Schjelderup-Ebbe

Publication of the English translation was supported by a generous grant from
Anders Jahre's Humanitarian Foundation

Library of Congress Catalog Card Number:
95–67428

ISBN 0–9645238–0–9

Designed and typeset in Bembo
by John Delaine Design & Production.

Printed in the United States of America.

Printed with support from The Norwegian Cultural Council

9   8   7   6   5   4   3   2   1

Contents

AUTHORS' PREFACE

We are in Vienna, Paris or St. Petersburg, in Brussels, London, Stockholm or Copenhagen. An eager audience has filled the concert hall to see one of the greatest conductors of the day in action. Rumors have abounded regarding this Norwegian and his singular ability, both as an orchestra conductor and as a composer. Now they were about to see him in person.

Confident, anticipating another triumph, he mounts the podium. From the very first downbeat both orchestra and audience are spellbound. His whole being radiates power and strength, and the secure calm that is his hallmark is immediately conveyed to the musicians. Their tenseness is transformed into heightened concentration.

He has no need to make elaborate gestures to bring the musicians under his power. Even in his slightest movements they immediately understand his intentions. They watch his piercing eyes, and as their gaze meets his it is as if the space between them is electrified. Never have they met a conductor with greater rhythmical resilience and life—and never have they played better.

The loftiness and brilliance of his interpretations are also richly evident in his own vigorous, refreshing compositions, which shimmer with joy and festivity.

This is a typical account from the years around the turn of the century. Johan Svendsen was virtually idolized by those who were fortunate enough to meet him in person—as is evident from innumerable contemporary accounts, both oral and written.

This idealized picture of an emperor in the realm of music, flush with victories in concert halls from Moscow to Oslo, was our point of departure as we set about the task of writing the first biography of this great son of Norway. In the course of our work, however, a number of questions soon emerged. Was Svendsen really a child of fortune who always had the wind at his back? Was his professional life just one big party, as the music he wrote might seem to indicate? Did he never encounter the antagonism from his peers that is so common in the life of an artist? Were there no difficulties that he had to contend with during his childhood and youth, his years of professional study, or his struggle to improve the music life of his native Oslo? Was his 25-year tenure as conductor of the Royal Theater orchestra in Copenhagen a perpetual bed of roses? Were his many artistic triumphs on the podium in reality Pyrrhic victories that depleted his powers as a composer? Was he happy in his two marriages? What role did outward circumstances play with respect to his creative work? What was his attitude toward his great compatriot Edvard Grieg and his art?

After the strong cultural flowering that occurred in the first half of the 1800s, Norway produced several composers of international stature. The most important of these were Svendsen and Grieg, who during their lifetimes also towered above the composers from the other Nordic countries in the eyes of the rest of the world. During the twentieth century, however, Svendsen's music has unfortunately been overshadowed by that of Grieg. We think the time is ripe to stir up interest in him and his music once again.

In the course of our work we have had access to a wealth of previously unknown material about Johan Svendsen. The largest collection of Svendsen manuscripts is housed in the library of the University of Oslo, as are also a considerable number of important letters from the composer to his father, sister, and several Norwegian friends. The library also has a quantity of Svendsen material collected by Professor Olav Gurvin (1893–1974) during the period ca. 1930–60 for a projected biography. Included in this material is a fair copy of a 200-page handwritten manuscript tracing Svendsen's life and work up to ca. 1885. Professor Gurvin's manuscript is primarily biographical, but among his papers there are also some lengthy drafts of analyses of compositions.

Several important letters from Svendsen to Grieg are housed in the Bergen Public Library. The most valuable Svendsen material in the Royal Library in Copenhagen consists of manuscripts of a number of large works.

A large quantity of material has been preserved in the Musikhistorisk Museum Carl Claudius' Samling including music manuscripts, letters, telegrams, photographs, concert programs, and newspaper and journal articles and reviews. Most of this material was collected by Godtfred Skjerne (1880–1955). The museum has also taken over a rich body of material that Svendsen's late son, Eyvind Johan-Svendsen (1896–1946), an actor at the Royal Theater in Copenhagen, had in his possession. In addition, the museum owns a collection left by Victor Gandrup (1891–1966), who was for many years a violinist in the Royal Theater Orchestra. This collection includes not only memoranda and notes but a typewritten manuscript dealing with Svendsen's work in Denmark. Gandrup did not live to complete the book that he had planned to write, but he published some of the material in several articles.

There is also some important source material in the archives of the National Assembly (*Stortinget*) in Oslo, the Oslo diocesan archives, the Norwegian and Danish national archives, the archives of the Royal Theater, the Theater Museum in Copenhagen, and the National Archive for Zealand, Lolland-Falster and Bornholm in Copenhagen.

We are deeply grateful to all of these institutions and to the representatives of each with whom we dealt for their unfailing courtesy. Special thanks go to museum director Mette Müller and museum manager Ole Kongsted at the Musikhistorisk Museum Carl Claudius' Samling.

Dr. Dan Fog of Copenhagen has through the years assisted us by word and deed and has given us a considerable amount of relevant information. Professor Torben Schousboe of Copenhagen has read the passages in our book dealing with Carl Nielsen. We are indebted to both of them.

We also wish to thank Professor Harald Herresthal of Oslo for valuable information regarding Svendsen's youth. He willingly placed at our disposal two manuscripts, one dealing with the Philharmonic Society in Christiania [Oslo] during the years 1846–67, the other with Svendsen's violin teacher, Carl Arnold (1794–1863). Gulbrand Svendsen and Sven Moestue provided useful information regarding Svendsen's family history.

Our thanks go also to Inge Bergliot Benestad and Øivind Eckhoff, both of Oslo, who have read the entire manuscript and given valuable suggestions, and to Øyvin Dybsand of Oslo for preparing the music examples for publication.

For our research in Copenhagen and in Leipzig we received support from Fondet for dansk-norsk samarbeid (the Fund for Danish-Norwegian Cooperation), Universitetet i Oslo (the University of Oslo), Det Norske Videnskabs-Akademi (the Norwegian Academy of Science and Letters), Norges forskningsråd (the Norwegian Research Council) and Utenriksdepartementet (the Ministry of Foreign Affairs). We express our thanks to all of these institutions.

Special thanks are due to Professor Gurvin's daughter, Mrs. Solrun Opheim, who graciously allowed us to make use of the Svendsen material left behind by her father.

In the book we present, so far as possible, a strictly chronological account with brief discussions of Svendsen's compositions at appropriate points. The List of Compositions on pp. 379–401 includes essential bibliographical information about each work.

No date is given for critical reviews when they appeared the day after the concert. To spare our readers the distraction of an elaborate footnote apparatus, we have numbered each item in the bibliography and have given source references by number in the text of the book. The numbers in parentheses refer to the appropriate item in the bibliography and, in some cases, to the relevant page or pages.

Finn Benestad   Dag Schjelderup-Ebbe

TRANSLATOR'S PREFACE

It is surprising that so important and once celebrated a composer and conductor as Johan Svendsen (1840–1911) should have had to wait so long for his biography to be written. During his lifetime he was as highly regarded as his illustrious countryman, Edvard Grieg, and he was in great demand as a guest conductor in the music capitals of the world. Moreover, when he conducted the orchestras of London or Paris or Moscow or Vienna, it was primarily his own compositions that people wanted to hear—music that sparkled with the *joie de vivre* of a youthful Scandinavia even as it paid homage to the formal principles of late Romanticism.

Fortunately, this gap in the history of the music of the Romantic period has now been filled in an admirable way by this thorough study of the life and work of one of the most colorful figures in the musical world of his day. Finn Benestad and Dag Schjelderup-Ebbe, both professors in the Institute of Musicology at the University of Oslo, are already well known to serious students of Scandinavian music as the distinguished coauthors of *Edvard Grieg: The Man and the Artist* (Lincoln, University of Nebraska Press, 1988). *Johan Svendsen: The Man, The Maestro, The Music* is a worthy companion to that definitive work.

This book is for the most part an exact translation of the Norwegian original, *Johan Svendsen: mennesket og kunstneren*. The authors have, however, worked closely with the translator in the preparation of this new edition of their book and have used the opportunity to make a few small changes in the body of the work. Explanations of place names and historical and literary allusions have also been inserted in a few places for the benefit of non-Norwegian readers.

Two matters of a somewhat technical nature require a brief word of explanation. The Norwegian alphabet contains three vowels in addition to those used in English (æ, ø and å) that occasionally occur in proper names used in this book. The pronunciation is approximately as follows: æ is pronounced like the "a" in "man," ø like the "u" in "fur," and å like the "o" in "more." Secondly, the city known in ancient times and again today as Oslo was called Christiania from 1624 to 1877, at which time the spelling was changed to Kristiania. The original name, Oslo, was restored in 1925. To minimize confusion for non-Norwegian readers, the name "Oslo" is used whenever a reference to this city occurs in the body of the text. When the names "Christiania" or "Kristiania" appear in a direct quote, the name employed by the person being quoted is retained, followed by [Oslo] as a reminder. When "Christiania" or "Kristiania" constitute part of a proper name—as in Christiania Theater or Kristiania Artists' Society—the names are retained without further explanation.

The publication of this book was made possible with the help of generous grants from the Norwegian Cultural Council and from Anders Jahre's Humanitarian Foundation. Thanks are due also to Mr. Egil A. Kristoffersen of H. Aschehoug & Co., publisher of the Norwegian edition, who in the interest of scholarship granted world-wide English language rights in the book. Finally, and especially, I wish to thank Professors Finn Benestad and Dag Schjelderup-Ebbe, both of whom read my earlier drafts with meticulous care and made numerous suggestions that have improved the form as well as the accuracy of the final product.

William H. Halverson

1

A MUSIC TALENT
FROM THE HEART OF OLD OSLO

1840–62

TRADITION HAS IT that Johan Svendsen first saw the light of day in a little house in Oslo, just a few blocks from the Parliament Building. He was born prematurely, and it seemed likely that he would not survive. Fearing his imminent death, his parents had him baptized at home at the age of five days by Madam Inger Olsen (54). The first days were extremely critical; it is said that the little fellow was put in a box that was then placed on top of the stove in the kitchen to keep him warm!

The date of birth was September 30. The year was 1840, the very year that can be said to have heralded the beginning of a new era in Norwegian music. In many ways it marked the beginning of what is called the "golden age," a flowering of Norwegian music that led to Norway's achieving a place on the musical map of the world.

During the first four decades of the nineteenth century there had been little vitality in Norwegian music life. Serious economic problems had brought about the bankruptcy of a number of the wealthier families, whose musical interests and commitment had been the principal support of such activity. Without their support, music societies in several Norwegian cities had been forced to disband during the 1820s and 1830s.

Oslo's Music Lyceum was among the organizations that were forced to bow under the financial pressure of the times. This music society, which had been founded by Paul Thrane in 1810 and consisted for the most part of amateur musicians, had been a major cultural force in the capital for a generation. On December 22, 1838, however, *Den Constitutionelle*—the leading newspaper in the city at that time—wrote the organization's obituary in the ornate style of the day:

> Today the Music Lyceum sings its swan song. It is giving in to the pressure of the times and its creditors. . . . The Lyceum has bestowed upon most of us so many happy hours that we are obligated to shed a tear upon its grave. Despite the several organic defects under which we cannot deny that the society labored, doubtless each of us has a precious memory to treasure from these pleasant evening occasions, whether it was garnered while sitting with opera glasses in hand in one of the box seats or with a piece of pastry in one's mouth in the middle of the buzzing confusion at the formal tea. And no one who loves a lively dance will forget the many gay balls. . .

Underdevelopment in the field of music expressed itself in many ways. The level of both compositions and performances was with few exceptions purely amateurish. The audiences preferred simple, unpretentious music, and composers who today are almost totally forgotten dominated the programs.

One gleam of light in the musical darkness of the time was Waldemar Thrane, a son of Paul Thrane and the first Norwegian musician of international stature. Waldemar Thrane made an important contribution both as a violinist and as a composer. He also composed the first Norwegian comic opera, *The Mountain Adventure* (1825), some parts of which incorporate a distinctively Norwegian sound. Especially notable in this regard is *Aagot's Mountain Song*. Unfortunately, Thrane died in 1828 at the age of 38 and thus was not able to follow up this early example of genuinely Norwegian art music with other compositions of similar quality.

Such institutions as the Lyceum had been maintained by an exclusive circle of supporters from the upper stratum of the population. The masses lived in an oppressive poverty that severely limited their opportunities for musical expression. Musicality and the capacity for enjoying music were evenly distributed to the rich and the poor, however, and when musical talent manifested itself among the poorer classes it sometimes happened that they, too, made their mark. Such an occurrence, however, required a relentless tenacity that was reserved for the chosen few. Johan Svendsen was one of these.

1840: A MEMORABLE YEAR

In the year 1840, three young and very gifted musicians from various parts of the country gave notice that a new spring was about to dawn in Norwegian music. They were the bearers of fresh new impulses in widely different areas. Thirty-year-old Ole Bull, the world-renowned virtuoso violinist from Bergen, played his newest composition *Norway's Mountains*, the centerpiece of which was a genuine Norwegian folk-dance tune (a *springar*). Eight years later his enthusiasm for that which was distinctively Norwegian sprang into full flower in his masterpiece, *A Visit to the Seter*, in which *The Shepherd Girl's Sunday* is the loveliest blossom. Bull had by this time become a roving ambassador for Norwegian music all over the world.

The year 1840 also saw the publication by Ludvig M. Lindeman of the first folk melodies that he had collected. Lindeman, two years younger than Bull and a native of Trondheim, had been appointed the previous year as organist at Our Savior's Church in Oslo. Originally undertaken to supplement Jørgen Moe's collection of folk ballads, his work in transcribing Norwegian folk music was to prove epoch-making. In 1841 he published a collection entitled *Norwegian Mountain Melodies*, and this was followed by a multi-volume collection, *Older and Newer Norwegian Mountain Melodies* (1853–67). These publications became an important source of inspiration and musical material for generations of Norwegian composers. The foremost composer in this musical threesome was a native of Oslo, Halfdan Kjerulf. In 1840, after a productive stay in Paris, the 25-year-old student decided to abandon law in favor of music. Within a year he had published his first collection of original songs, one of which—*Water Sprite*—has a distinctively "folk" coloring. This emphasis on native idioms was carried further in the years that followed in piano and choral pieces and especially in a large number of songs. Indeed, as a writer of art songs Kjerulf ranks as one of the most gifted composers of his generation.

The 1840s marked the beginning of a pronounced economic upturn for Norway that was to continue for the next decade. A strong market in lumber that coincided with the beginning of the industrial revolution, and the ensuing increased activity for small industry, gradually produced better living conditions for the general populace. This in turn created possibilities for greater cultural expression, with positive consequences for the country's music life. The completion in 1839 of the Freemasons' Lodge, which contained a large assembly hall, also provided a more spacious venue for public concerts than any that had previously been available in Oslo.

Something else happened in 1840 that was to be of great importance for Norwegian music. In that year a number of professional German musicians arrived in Norway. The first of these was 31-year-old Friedrich August Reissiger, a versatile musician, who was appointed conductor of the Christiania [Oslo] Theater orchestra.

On May 24 of that year, Norway's first steamship, "Constitutionen," anchored in the Oslo harbor. On board was the "Harzmusikverein," an entire orchestra of German musicians about to undertake a tour to various cities and towns in Norway. One of these musicians was the hornist Carl Warmuth, who later came to mean a great deal to Johan Svendsen, both as his first Norwegian publisher and as his close friend. Reissiger saw in the "Harzmusikverein" an opportunity to strengthen the theater orchestra and negotiated an *en bloc* contract with the group effective until 1843. Thus they all made Oslo their home for at least three years, and several of them stayed there permanently. They significantly improved the quality of the orchestra and had much to do with the fact that during the next decade the Christiania Theater was able to produce no less than thirty-three operas. Of these, twenty—including Mozart's *The Marriage of Figaro*—were premieres in Norway.

In 1842 Reissiger established a singing school that became a predecessor of The Philharmonic Society, which was founded in 1846. He also presented a number of large oratorios during these years, including Haydn's *The Creation* and Mendelssohn's *St. Paul*.

The founder of The Philharmonic Society was the German-born cellist Georg Andreas Gehrman. The society depended primarily on amateurs, and the statutes specified that "Musicians *ex professo*" could not become members. Professional musicians could participate only as "paid assistants." In January 1847 the society had 219 paying members. The orchestra consisted of approximately twenty musicians, and the mixed chorus of some seventy singers.

Two names that appear frequently in the minutes of the society are those of Halfdan Kjerulf and L. M. Lindeman. The latter, who was "assistant instructor," functioned also as permanent accompanist and cellist. Kjerulf evidently helped out only now and then.

The Philharmonic Society gave its first public concert on February 1, 1847, when it presented Beethoven's first symphony. A major symphony by Haydn was performed in March, and in April some choral pieces from Mozart's *The Magic Flute*. "Paid assistants" were drawn as needed from Reissiger's theater orchestra.

In the autumn of 1847 Gehrman moved to Stockholm. Reissiger served as conductor of the Philharmonic Society orchestra for one season, and in 1848 he was replaced by another German-born musician, Carl Arnold, who remained in the position until 1863.

In 1850 Reissiger was compelled to give up his position as orchestra conductor at the Christiania Theater. Paolo Sperati, an Italian maestro, had brought his opera company to Oslo on tour and had created such a sensation in the city that the governing board of the Christiania Theater had summarily discharged Reissiger and engaged Sperati in his place. Reissiger became organist in the small town of Halden, where he made an important contribution as a composer as well as an organist.

The 1840s also saw significant development in the male chorus movement in Norway, which played an important role in Norwegian music during the so-called National Revival period (1840–70). Three large male choruses were established in Oslo during these years: the Norwegian Students' Male Chorus, the Merchants' Chorus, and the Craftsmen's Chorus. Men's singing immediately experienced a rapid growth, and singing contests that drew hundreds of participants became veritable folk festivals. Leading Norwegian composers got deeply involved in the male chorus movement. Halfdan Kjerulf, for example, composed many pieces in this genre, and in 1845 became the first director of the Norwegian Students' Male Chorus. Other musicians who played important roles in this movement were Johan D. Behrens and Johan G. Conradi.

Bull, Lindeman, and Kjerulf, each with his own distinctive emphasis, were in the vanguard of the National-Romantic movement and paved the way for the new musical threesome that would soon follow. For—remarkably—three men who would lead their countrymen into the "Golden Age" of Norwegian music were all born within a three-year period: Johan Svendsen (1840), Rikard Nordraak (1842), and Edvard Grieg (1843).

ROOTS

Virtually all of the native-born musicians whose names we have had occasion to mention thus far—Thrane, Bull, Lindeman, Kjerulf, Nordraak, Grieg—came from upper-class city families. Such, however, was not the case with Johan Svendsen. His parents were people without means who had come to Oslo in the hope of improving their fortunes.

His father's family history can be traced through many generations. The family was from Sandsvær, a small lumbering community about a hundred

Gulbrand Svendsen, Johan's father, who continued to perform as a musician in Oslo until he was in his 80s. (Universitetsbiblioteket, Oslo)

miles southwest of Oslo. In 1553 Gulbrand Strenge, one of his early ancestors, lived on a farm bearing the family name. In 1640 one of Gulbrand Strenge's descendants, Halvor, took over the Strenge farm. Halvor is referred to in the records as a "freeholder," which indicates that his family owned the farm. A daughter of Halvor married a man by the name of Torsten Rolvssøn Steg. Their son, Gulbrand Torstenssøn Sørby, is regarded as the progenitor of the musically gifted Meskestad family. His grandson, Gulbrand Haldorsen Meskestad—Johan Svendsen's great grandfather—had six children, all of whom were musical. The most talented of them, Svend Gulbrandsen (1795–1871), was reputed to be one of the foremost fiddle-players in Sandsvær. Several of his *slåtter*—distinctively Norwegian folk-dance tunes—are still being played in this district.

Svend was a shoemaker as well as a farmer, but his first love always was the fiddle. It is said that he was sometimes asked to play at as many as twelve weddings in a single summer, including some at places many miles away from his home community.

Svend's oldest son, Gulbrand Svendsen (1817–1900), also displayed special talent as a fiddler and began playing for dances as a young boy. De-

Pernille Marie Svendsen, Johan's
mother. She divorced Johan's father
in 1851 and moved to Øvre Rendal,
where she lived until her death.
(Universitetsbiblioteket, Oslo)

spite his evident talent, his father thought there was no future for him as a
fiddler and arranged for him to be apprenticed to a tailor. Gulbrand did not
take well to such sedentary work, however, so after a few months of desul-
tory struggles with needle and thread he left the tailor's shop for good and
fled to Oslo to become a musician. He was not to see his home community
again until forty years later (1871), when he returned to attend his father's
funeral.

At first, Gulbrand had little success finding work as a musician in Oslo.
He had hoped to become a military musician, but was turned down on his
first try because he was too short. Eventually, however, he won an appointment as a cornetist in the Second Akershus Infantry Brigade Music Corps.
After completing his period of compulsory military service, he continued
on as a "piper" (wind player) and some years later was promoted to the position of drum major. He played in the Music Corps for nearly thirty years,
and with his baton held high led the band on marches through the city and
up Karl Johan Street—the splendid avenue in the heart of Oslo that leads up
to the royal palace.

During his many years as a military musician, however, he did not give up playing the violin. Indeed, he took private lessons and in time became a competent violinist. After he left the Music Corps he worked as a private music teacher, in which capacity he continued to instruct violin students until he was eighty years old. He was a member of several orchestras, playing either violin or trumpet as needed, but in the orchestra of the Music Society in Oslo he played viola. When he retired from the latter organization, the board of directors awarded him a pension "on account of his zeal and love for art."

Gulbrand Svendsen was characterized by his fellow musicians as an outstanding colleague. He never thrust himself forward at the expense of others but, on the contrary, stood by them in good times and bad. In 1889 he joined Ernst Solberg in establishing the Kristiania Orchestral Musicians' Union (later renamed the Kristiania Association of Musicians), where during the first difficult years he served from time to time as chairman. Solberg and Svendsen were for many years the association's only honorary members.

Sometime during his first few years in Oslo, Gulbrand met his future wife, the temperamental and spirited Pernille Marie Jonasdatter Elg (1815–90). She had come to Oslo from Fåberg (near Lillehammer) to live with her sister, Rønnoug Marie, and her sister's husband, Hans Heinrich Struck. Struck, an immigrant from Schleswig-Holstein, was a well-known building contractor who played a role in erecting several of the stately buildings along Karl Johan Street. He also participated in the construction of the royal palace.

The Elgs were a family of coppersmiths who immigrated to the Fåberg district from Sweden during the eighteenth century. Tradition has it that the family also had some Gypsy blood in its veins. Jonas Jonasson Elg, Pernille's grandfather, was a coppersmith at Frederiksfoss Kobberhammer around 1770 and also a tenant farmer at the Sorgendal farm near Lillehammer. A probate document from 1772, when his first wife died childless, states that he had a net worth of 402 *riksdalers*—a substantial sum in those days. His second wife, Lisbet Pedersdotter Flugsrud, bore him two children. His son Jonas became a coppersmith and eventually established his own small factory. Among the products manufactured there were "post horns," an instrument without valves that resembles a miniature French horn. Horns made in Jonas Elg's workshop—and bearing his initials—can still be found in various parts of the country. Jonas the younger married Siri Valtin, who bore him seven children. Pernille, the second oldest, became Johan Svendsen's mother.

The Norwegian author Jacob B. Bull, who became acquainted with Pernille in the 1850s after she had moved to Øvre Rendal, has given a vivid characterization of her in her later years:

> It was especially in the community's primitive social life that she, with her lively artist's mentality and her boundless good humor, brightened things up and got things going. If there was a wedding, she had to be sent for immediately—to arrange everything beautifully, to help the bride with her dress and make-up, and to make sure that everything went festively and joyously. If there was a funeral, once again it was she who had to make the wreath and decorate the casket. A Christmas party with singing and dancing where she was not present just didn't seem quite right. She taught people new ballads and songs, sang with a clear, lovely voice, and imbued the dour mountain people with her *joie de vivre.*
>
> And what a story-teller she was! She told stories about things that had happened in Oslo, stories from strange milieus. And how her facial expression changed, how her eyes sparkled or became misty, all in concert with the content of her story! Always sympathy with those who suffered, always joy when something good happened to someone, always involvement in everything and with everyone in the valley!
>
> Johan Svendsen's mother, like Johan himself, was just music. It was at the center of her consciousness. How she loved to sing and to hear singing! How she got everything to *resound* and to *sing!* And how she *understood!* (20)

"Piper No. 2 of the First Company" Gulbrand Svendsen and Pernille Marie Elg were married in the military chapel at the Akershus Fortress in Oslo on May 19, 1840. The witnesses were Pernille's brother-in-law, Hans Heinrich Struck, and Gulbrand's fellow musician, French hornist Andersen.

AN UPBRINGING UNDER TIGHT REINS

The church records of the military chapel serving the personnel of the Akershus fortress list the Svendsen family's residence in April 1841 as "Vaterlands Section No. 4." No street address is given. Soon thereafter the family moved to Piperviken, a slum area near the harbor that had a very bad reputation. They lived in a tiny flat on Vinkel ("Angle") Street near where the City Hall now stands. It was also just a stone's throw from the home of "Mother Sæter," a locally well-known quack doctor, where Henrik Ibsen was lodging at the time. It was in the flat on Vinkel Street that Johan's sister Albertine Marie Fredrikke was born in 1842.

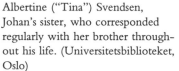

Albertine ("Tina") Svendsen,
Johan's sister, who corresponded
regularly with her brother throughout his life. (Universitetsbiblioteket,
Oslo)

During the first couple of years of their marriage, Gulbrand and Pernille apparently got along reasonably well. His income as a military musician was modest, however, and he often supplemented it by playing for dances and other social events. In the hope of further increasing his income he also tried his hand at something quite different from his principal line of work: in 1843 he sought permission to serve "distilled spirits," and the request was granted on the basis of his services as a member of the voluntary civil police.

Gulbrand had too little time to give proper attention to his fledgling sideline, however, and it did not go well. There was also a lot of competition: according to Odd Børretzen, in 1846 there were no less than 256 grocerymen, 90 small shopkeepers, and 141 open-air market vendors who had permission to sell hard liquor in the tiny city of Oslo!

Gulbrand found it increasingly difficult to pay the fees required to maintain his liquor license, and after five years it was permanently taken away from him. It was no doubt during these years that he developed an excessive taste for his own wares, and the problem plagued him for the rest of his life. Pernille is also said to have had "a certain liking for the strong stuff" (54).

Long before Gulbrand lost his license, however, the relationship between him and Pernille had begun to deteriorate. According to city records, as early as 1843 they took legal action to establish a period of separation. The terms of the agreement reached at that time specified that Gulbrand was to have custody of Johan while Pernille would be responsible for Albertine. Gulbrand was also to pay one *spesiedaler* per month in child support for his daughter. During the required period of separation prior to divorce, however, the parents reconciled, and in 1846 Pernille had a third child, Carl Martinus.

The reconciliation proved to be only temporary, however. On June 24, 1851, after the pastor of the military chapel had tried in vain to help them resolve their differences, they filed for divorce. The divorce decree states that they had two children, Johan and Albertine, and that Gulbrand accepted financial responsibility for both of them. In addition, he was to pay Pernille six *spesiedalers* per year for six years. The decree states matter-of-factly: "They own no furniture or household effects, so there can be no question of the division of a joint estate." They were required henceforth to live "separated from each other with respect to table and bed. . . . The parties were given to understand that the present decree does not give either of them the right to enter into a new marriage, but that such a right requires gracious permission from His Majesty."

Three weeks later Gulbrand appeared in divorce court again to dutifully report that because of a misunderstanding he had stated that he and Pernille had only two children. They actually had three:

> The reason for this being overlooked is that the child was conceived during the period in 1843 when the one parent was living apart from his wife . . . , which led to the conjecture that said child possibly should be counted as not conceived in wedlock and so should not be listed in the official document. That parent has since agreed that inasmuch as he has thus far exclusively paid for and arranged for this his youngest child's upbringing, in the same manner he will continue to regard this as incumbent on him.

That summer Pernille went to Øvre Rendal to live with her brother, Iver Elg, the coppersmith. She also lived for a time with Jacob Hårrset, but later moved frequently from one large farm to another. She supported herself as a seamstress, and part of the time her daughter lived with her. When Albertine became engaged and moved to Oslo, Pernille settled permanently in Øvre Rendal.

We know from several early letters from Johan to his mother that he often planned to visit her, but more often than not something came up to prevent him from doing so. Jacob B. Bull writes that "the few vacation days when her son was with her were the wonderful adventure of her life" (20). This presumably was during the years 1871–83. Thereafter, when his career required him to live in Copenhagen, he never saw her again. Indeed, he rarely wrote to her, so she was able to learn about his many achievements only through Albertine. He sometimes sent her a little money, but usually via his sister. It appears as if he almost avoided making contact with his mother. Perhaps he felt guilty because of his continuing close association with his father, with whom he stayed in contact through personal visits and frequent exchanges of letters.

On November 11, 1856, Gulbrand became father to yet another daughter, Elise Henrikke. In the church records, the mother's name is given as "unmarried girl Maren Hansdatter." Elise, who grew up with the other children, had exceptional musical talent. She became a professional singer and appeared in concerts in Oslo, Copenhagen, London and elsewhere.

The family's poverty was a dominant factor during Johan's childhood. There was little to eat, and the young boy, who later would become a husky fellow, was thin and ungainly during his growing years. He was often sickly, but his father made a deliberate effort to toughen him. One result of this approach was that Johan learned to endure pain without complaining. He has told of one occasion when, at the age of five, he got a serious bone-marrow infection that required surgery. Without giving him an anesthetic, the surgeon made a deep cut and dug clear into the bone. Then he plunged a stick of silver nitrate into the open wound, and through it all the little boy did not utter a sound. His father, on the other hand, could not hold back his tears. As a reward for his stoic behavior, Johan was allowed to go with his father to the stately funeral of Henrik Wergeland, Norway's great national poet—an experience that he never forgot (54).

At home, Gulbrand maintained an almost military discipline. Johan, as the oldest child, bore the brunt of his father's severity. He was required, for example, to get up at five in the morning during the summer and at six in the winter. He first had to sweep the sidewalk in front of the house, then chop wood, brush his father's clothes and shine his shoes. Usually he then practiced his violin for half an hour before mustering in military fashion to report that everything was now in order. When his father had then verified that his ears, neck, and fingernails were clean he could finally leave for school. The afternoons were mainly spent in homework and music lessons, so there was little time for fun and games.

Johan became the acknowledged leader of the throng of ruffians with whom he grew up. In later years he told about some of their childhood pranks. He described, for example, how the little pranksters in the evenings would sometimes put bloated fish on a line that was then strung across the narrow alleys in such a way that pedestrians would bump into them. The sounds of the fish splattering against the cobblestones would then reverberate throughout the neighborhood. The boys sometimes also "borrowed" boats and engaged in mock sea battles on the fjord.

If anyone complained about Johan—the "Svendseboy" as he was called—his father was quick to use the whip. This was especially the case if he had the temerity to disobey his father's moral commands. One summer day, for example, Johan and some of his friends had gone swimming. They made a bet about who dared to dive from the highest point. Johan won, of course, but unfortunately in his haste he had forgotten to take off his woolen shirt—the only one he owned. He didn't have time to dry it properly, so when he got home his father smelled the sea-water. Johan made an inexperienced attempt at lying, but to no avail: his father forced him to tell the truth, whereupon he got a spanking that he would long remember (54).

Gulbrand's intentions in enforcing such strict discipline were good. He had noticed Johan's unusual musical talent when the boy was very young, and he believed that it could be developed only through discipline and hard work. He himself began to give his son systematic instruction in violin before he was nine years old. In a letter to Catharinus Elling dated May 12, 1901, Svendsen wrote concerning his father, "At an early age he impressed upon me a feeling for pure intonation and rhythmic clarity."

Gulbrand would not tolerate carelessness. Every lesson was to be learned perfectly. At first, practicing was a struggle, but Johan soon became so adept at playing the violin that it became almost a game. His father also gave him thorough instruction on flute and clarinet when he was quite young, and the musical training that he thus received during his formative years proved to be invaluable to him later on.

No doubt the father also had an ulterior motive in all of this, viz. that as a musician the boy could earn a little money for the perpetually strained family coffer. Even as a ten-year-old he joined his father in playing for parties and dances. The frequency of such engagements increased little by little, though it never resulted in any pocket money for the young musician himself.

Johan also began to compose during his childhood years. At age eleven he wrote a little march for violin, and a few years later he produced both marches and dances for orchestra. To Johan's dismay, his father reacted negatively to such activity because he considered it a waste of both time and expensive note paper. His "honorarium" for each new piece was a spanking (136).

The earliest composition about which we have any knowledge today is the *Anna Polka*, which was published by Carl Warmuth in Oslo in 1883— almost thirty years after it was written. It is strange that Svendsen would permit this piece to be published so late in his career, but for safety's sake he placed the words "Composed in 1854" on the title page to show that it was a musical memento from his fourteenth year. The polka was published in three different arrangements: for violin and piano, for piano, and for piano four-hands.

Polkas are also among Nordraak's and Grieg's very earliest compositions. Grieg wrote his so-called *Larvik Polka* when he was fourteen, and Nordraak had three polkas published as "Opus 1" in 1859. Nordraak exhibits the most striking melodic talent of the three, while Grieg is the most daring with respect to harmony. Svendsen's polka does not have any really distinctive feature, though it demonstrates technical skill and a sure sense of form. One thing that all three of this youthful trio had in common is that none of them had as yet received any formal instruction in harmony when they wrote their early polkas.

At the time when Johan wrote the *Anna Polka* he was about to be confirmed, and there is a touching story about the relationship between father and son that dates from this period. Confirmation is an important "rite of passage" in Norway, a time when young people don their best clothes and stand before their local congregation to be formally inducted into the adult community. Gulbrand did not see how he could afford to buy his son a new outfit for his confirmation, and Johan quietly resigned himself to this unpleasant fact. There was just one thing that he begged his father to get for him: a new pair of shoes. To stand in front of the church in his shabby old shoes would, he thought, be too much of an embarassment. But Gulbrand refused: there was no money for shoes either. The night before the big event, Johan cried himself to sleep. The next morning, however, just as they were about to leave for church, Gulbrand presented him with a brand new pair of shoes. Johan reported many years later that this was the happiest moment his father had ever given him (54).

THE MILITARY BANDSMAN

In 1856, at the tender age of fifteen and a half years, Johan enlisted in the army with the intention of becoming an officer. If the discipline at home had been strict, that which he now experienced was even stricter. As a result, he had far too little time to do what he wanted most—to play his instruments. Soon after enlisting, therefore, he requested a transfer to the brigade music corps. The request was granted, and on April 11, 1856, he was transferred to his new unit. Playing in a music corps was nothing new for him, for as a boy he had often accompanied his father to rehearsals. The other musicians had long since taken a liking to the energetic and musical "Svendseboy."

The conductor of the band was Paolo Sperati, who served from 1854 to 1882. Johan was assigned to the clarinet section, and in a short time was appointed principal clarinetist. He later told about the first rehearsal following his promotion:

> Due to the departure of many members of the corps, I advanced so rap-
> idly that one fine day I became principal clarinetist—very young. Our
> director, old Sperati . . . , found that a little hard to swallow. He didn't
> really like me, though he had respect for me. During the first hour of the
> rehearsal following my promotion, he called for the pieces containing the
> longest clarinet solos in our entire repertoire, with cadenzas and all sorts
> of figurations. We played, and I played quite well—well enough to be
> above criticism. Sperati just muttered something unintelligible. He
> couldn't scold me—and he didn't want to praise me. But I had also prac-
> ticed many hours a day just to achieve a beautiful, clear, and genuine
> clarinet sound (71).

After serving for some time as a clarinetist he switched to flute, but he also mastered several other instruments including trombone and snare drum. In a pinch, therefore, he could make a contribution in any of several places in the ensemble. Such versatility was not unusual among corps members: most, if not all, also played one or more string instruments. This experience playing many instruments would later prove of inestimable value to Svendsen both as a conductor and as an orchestrator.

Sperati had exceptional ability as a band director and guided the ensemble to a high level of excellence. In July, 1858, he took the group to Axvalla, Sweden, and for this occasion Svendsen composed an *Axvalla*

March (F major). During the course of this tour he also wrote another little march in E-flat major. The Norwegian musicians acquitted themselves well; indeed, their Swedish colleagues were absolutely astounded when the bandsmen from Oslo demonstrated their diverse talents by producing from their ranks a competent string orchestra.

Notwithstanding his proficiency on clarinet and flute, however, the violin remained Johan's first love. In the late 1850s, having outgrown his father's ability to teach him further, he began to take lessons from Fredrik Ursin, who had studied in Brussels with the well-known violinist Hubert Léonard. The dream of a future career as a soloist began to take form.

For the moment, however, his finances were even more in need of improvement than his violin artistry. To earn a little extra money, he played for dances in his spare time and also held a temporary position as a musician at a school for dance. The pupils at this school sometimes heard some rather peculiar dance music, for he did not limit himself to the standard fare but amused himself by transforming several of the Kreutzer etudes and Paganini caprices that he was working on into polkas and waltzes.

Johan also gained experience as a violinist at the Norwegian Theater, and it is possible that he also played in the orchestra at the Christiania Theater. Haakon Zappfe reported in the Oslo daily *Morgenbladet* (October 4, 1930) that Svendsen and Zappfe's brother received the paltry sum of one *spesiedaler* a month at the Norwegian Theater—for which sum they were expected to attend rehearsals and to participate in three performances each week:

> They were promised more, but they never got it. So one evening they
> didn't show up at the usual time. Somebody was sent out to look for
> them, and eventually found them, but when they came they announced
> that they would no longer play for one dollar a month. They were
> offered two, but they said no, they wanted three. I think they finally
> got three.

Zappfe's recollection probably is somewhat mistaken, however, for according to Harald Herresthal's historical account of the Philharmonic Society during the years 1846–67, the regular musicians usually had a salary of three or four dollars per *week*. Understandably, the youngest players were sometimes paid less because their participation was a kind of learning experience for them.

Sperati, who also conducted the Norwegian Theater orchestra, could

Paolo Sperati, the versatile Italian-Norwegian musician who was conductor of the military band in which Svendsen played during his youth. (Universitetsbiblioteket, Oslo)

boast that as a young pianist he had even accompanied the great Paganini. As a conductor, he displayed a Mediterranean temperament. Svendsen thought he was excessively preoccupied with what today would be called "music for easy listening." The programs for his many concerts in Oslo's Tivoli amusement park show, however, that he also performed music by the great masters. Not infrequently he presented overtures by Mozart, Beethoven, Mendelssohn and Wagner. In band music, too, he showed his support for serious music by performing numerous arrangements of Classical and Romantic works.

Sperati was popular with the concert-going public, not least as a composer of pieces in the popular genre. But he also had his critics. A letter to the editor that appeared in *Morgenbladet* on March 21, 1874, stated that his compositions were "[merely imitations of] Offenbach as well as his imitators, transmuted into dances, marches, potpourris, etc. and then presented in such a tasteless manner that Offenbach himself would have been appalled."

Like most musicians, Sperati was constantly looking for paying jobs in order to augment his income. Sometimes his zeal had comical results, as Svendsen once reported with amusement:

He collected musical jobs like a dog collects bones. Then the best organist position in Kristiania [Oslo]—the one at Trinity Church, the largest
Protestant church in the city—became vacant. Sperati was the first person to apply for the job.

"But my dear Mr. Sperati," said the pastor, "this is absurd. Surely
you're Catholic, aren't you?"

"Me go over to Luthair!" Sperati said quickly and tersely. But his
readiness to convert was of no avail (71).

In 1856 Sperati became organist among his fellow believers at St. Olaf
Catholic Church. There may be some question about how seriously he
took his work as a church organist, however. It is said that at the service
installing him as organist "during a moment of silence the congregation
suddenly heard two voices up in the choir loft: 'Skoal, Metz!' – 'Skoal,
Sperati!'" (35:70).

The young Svendsen presumably received from Sperati some encouragement to compose, and it seems likely that some of the waltzes he wrote
were specifically intended for Sperati's concerts.

Several of Svendsen's earliest compositions are lost, but the waltz cycle
At the Seter (1856) has been preserved. Sperati presented it at an orchestra
concert in the Oslo Tivoli amusement park on June 10, 1863. Like the
Anna Polka, it was published in 1883 by Carl Warmuth in three different arrangements: for violin and piano, for piano, and for piano four-hands. Both
pieces were sent to the Copenhagen newspapers for review, and the December 18 number of *Berlingske Tidende* contained the following brief statement: "They are capable works from the composer's youth that show his
versatile talent."

The title page of the printed edition of *At the Seter* states that it was composed in 1856. Svendsen also orchestrated the waltz cycle, but the score has
unfortunately been lost. Handwritten parts for some instruments are still extant, however.

Simple though it is, *At the Seter* is competently worked out and testifies
to a feeling for quality—this despite the fact that in the middle 1850s the
youthful composer, still in his teens, had not yet received any theoretical
training. No doubt the 1883 version reflects a few changes, however, for
Svendsen had written to the publisher in a letter dated August 6, 1883, that
it was essential for him to have the proofs so that he could have the arrangements presented "in the form that I consider most desirable."

The composition consists of five short waltzes with tuneful melodies in the popular style of the time. The waltzes are framed by an extended introduction and an elaborate conclusion—a pattern that clearly owes much to the example of the waltz king, Johann Strauss the elder.

The most interesting feature of *At the Seter* is the inclusion of elements drawn from Norwegian folk music. In the introduction we hear the folk ballad, "I know a little maiden." There is also a *lokk* motive—i.e., a snatch of melody of the type used to call farm animals—that is somewhat similar to the one used by Waldemar Thrane in *Aagot's Mountain Song*. The piece also contains an audacious-sounding *halling*, which is perhaps the most distinctively Norwegian-sounding type of folk dance. The finale employs a waltz that clearly imitates the style of another type of Norwegian folk dance—the *springar*—as well as a new *lokk* motive.

Svendsen obviously had gotten the idea of using folk-like material from C. P. Riis's comic opera *At the Seter*, which premiered at the Christiania Theater in 1850 and subsequently became very popular. The music had been arranged by Reissiger, who had borrowed a number of folk tunes (including *I know a little maiden*) from Ludvig Lindeman's collections. Svendsen certainly knew this work from beginning to end, and it is obvious that he wanted to ride further on the wave of national-romantic sentiment that surrounded *seter* life—i.e., life on the mountain dairy farms.

Svendsen's *halling*, which has the distinctive flavor of music intended for the Hardanger fiddle, is transcribed in the violin edition with a sure sense for the two-part polyphony that is so characteristic of this type of music. Whether the sixteen-year-old composer wrote it himself or borrowed an existing *halling* is not known. He did not borrow it from Lindeman, in any case, for his collections contain no dance tunes for the Hardanger fiddle. Svendsen may have been familiar with Ole Bull's *A Visit to the Seter*, which contains imitations of Hardanger-fiddle music. It is also possible that he had heard the famous Hardanger-fiddle player Torgeir Audunsson—affectionately known to Norwegians as "Myllarguten" ("The Miller Boy")—who in 1854 gave several public concerts in Oslo. Olav Gurvin thinks it can be shown that Svendsen's *halling* is similar in some ways to the dance tunes played by Myllarguten and transcribed by Carl Schart in the late 1850s. The Schart transcriptions were not published until almost ten years later, however.

Undoubtedly Johan received some exposure to folk music at home, but Gulbrand played his folk-dance tunes on an ordinary violin, not a Hardanger fiddle, so the young man can scarcely have received any direct help regarding the *halling* from his father. It is more likely that friends in the theater orchestra were his principal sources of information. Several of them, including Fredrik Ursin and Johan's good friend Anders Heyerdahl, had personally transcribed Hardanger-fiddle dance tunes. Ursin was in close contact with both Myllarguten and Ole Bull, and Heyerdahl's composition *Nissespel* ("Pixie Play") made prominent use of Hardanger-fiddle dance tunes. Indeed, folk music enjoyed wide popularity in Oslo during the 1850s.

A MUSICAL AWAKENING

The year 1857 became a decisive turning point for Johan, for it was then that he became fully conscious of his calling as a serious artist. The immediate stimulus of his new awareness was his first hearing of Beethoven's *Fate* symphony.

In autumn 1857, Halfdan Kjerulf and Johan G. Conradi launched a series of subscription concerts in competition with the Philharmonic Society. Kjerulf was responsible for rehearsals of the chorus while Conradi, who had just returned from two years of study at the Leipzig conservatory, conducted the orchestra. The core of the latter consisted of twenty-five professional string players from the two theater orchestras. Oslo was about to experience for the first time a classical symphony played as it was intended to be played.

The opening concert was scheduled for December 14, and the main number on the program was Beethoven's *Fifth Symphony*. The anticipation was great. Two weeks before the event was to occur, Kjerulf wrote to his friend Dr. Julius Nicolaysen in Stockholm:

> Here in Oslo we are attacking Beethoven's No. 5—and God help us so that the whole thing doesn't fall apart and the 700 [listeners] get up and leave saying, "No, thanks a lot, but now we've had more than enough." I tremble for this first concert. I tremble for my colleague, Conradi (74:168).

Six days after the concert, however, a relieved Kjerulf was able to give Nicolaysen a positive report:

> Our first subscription concert is now happily over. In and of itself the performance was only so-so, and yet it was so completely different, espe-

cially as regards the orchestra, from what people here are used to that we have certainly won the battle. The big-wigs in the Philharmonic Society, who right up to the dress rehearsal hoped for the worst, are now utterly crestfallen. Several of them have whispered in gossipy ears that we won, and that they themselves have lost. More and more of them are defecting to us, and their acknowledged leader, old Arnold, came clear across the street to tell me that he had been very interested to hear what he had heard that evening—that the concert was well planned, well rehearsed, and that everything went better than he had thought it would based on his opinion of the players and the general situation (74:174).

One person who experienced the whole thing—not as a listener, but as one of the players—was Johan Svendsen. After an interview with the composer, Svendsen's biographer Aimar Grønvold wrote as follows about the seventeen-year-old's first encounter with symphonic music:

> Now his ears were filled for the first time with a stream of sounds whose power over the young mind was so overwhelming that he left the concert giddy with enthusiasm, filled with an undefined and undefinable ecstasy, a jumble of thoughts and plans concerning which only one thing was clear: he had never before known what real music was. He didn't *know* it now either, but he *felt* that it was something beyond what he had experienced thus far. Long after the concert was over, the beating of the wings of the mighty genius continued to reverberate in his ears. He heard them amidst the ever-changing tumult of life, urging and enticing—but years would pass before the awakening that occurred that evening would manifest itself in action (51:76).

Johan continued to play under Conradi's baton until 1859, when the subscription concerts ceased for lack of public support. It meant much to him to have contact with someone who not only made stern demands but also had the ability to share his considerable knowledge. Conradi was unreservedly committed to quality, and this was evident in his selection of repertoire as well as in other ways.

Of even greater significance for Johan at this juncture was his meeting with a musician of the old school, the German pianist and composer Carl Arnold (1794–1873). According to Arnold's biographer, Harald Herresthal, Arnold and his son came to Norway in 1848 on a concert tour that had previously taken them to such cities as Warsaw, St. Petersburg, Stockholm, and Gothenburg. Their public concerts in Oslo created a great deal of interest

Carl Arnold, a prominent
German-Norwegian musician.
As a teacher he had an important
influence on Svendsen's early
musical development. (Universitetsbiblioteket, Oslo)

and a number of people encouraged Arnold to make his home in the Norwegian capital. Some influential people suggested the possibility of a position in music at the university, but nothing came of this. In 1859, Professor
O. P. Monrad tried to get him a personal instructorship similar to the one
given to the author Andreas Munch, but that also did not work out.

Nonetheless, Arnold made the best of the situation and remained in
Norway for the rest of his life. Shortly after his arrival in Oslo he succeeded
Reissiger as leader of the Philharmonic Society. He also became organist at
Trinity Church. His great musical ideal was Beethoven. It is said that he
once studied with the great master himself, but there is no reliable proof of
this. It is possible that he met him on a concert tour to Vienna in 1817, and
it is known that he was in personal contact with some of Beethoven's students in the course of his work in Berlin in 1824–35. As a pianist he performed Beethoven's *Piano Concerto No. 3* at various places in Scandinavia,
and he also played trios and other things with his son, Carl Jr., and Ole Bull.
He was a productive and highly regarded composer as well, influenced by
Beethoven and the early Romanticists. His extensive pedagogical efforts
had a stimulating effect on a number of students including Halfdan Kjerulf,
who thought very well of him.

Svendsen began to feel at this time an increasingly insistent need to study harmony and music theory, and he began to take private lessons from Arnold. This learned man quickly perceived that his new pupil was a young man of great ability, but he seems to have had the greatest confidence in his future as a violinist. He, therefore, went through the most important violin literature with him; together they played, among other things, all of Beethoven's violin sonatas and many of Mozart's. In a letter to Catharinus Elling more than forty years later, Svendsen gave his teacher a beautiful tribute:

> I took instruction from Arnold for about one and a half years in 1860–61, though less in harmony than in performance . . . , and since he was an inimitable master performer—the finest I have ever known—both practically and with respect to his insight, I learned from him a considerable part of that which became fundamental for my entire artistic future (May 12, 1901).

Svendsen joined one of the string quartets that Arnold had formed. According to Professor Gurvin's notes he was active in this quartet from 1858 to 1862, on occasion also playing solo parts at concerts of the Philharmonic Society under Arnold's leadership.

The association with a highly cultured man such as Arnold must also have had a stimulating effect on Svendsen in other ways as well. His formal schooling up to this point had been exceedingly sparse, but during this time of maturation he acquired the desire to widen his horizons. He developed a love of reading and began to devour both novels and lyric poetry. His favorite kind of reading, however, was historical literature, and he retained this interest for the rest of his life. He began also to study German and French on his own, as if he had a premonition that he would be spending important periods of his life on the continent.

On June 17, 1859, Svendsen and some of his young musician friends established an orchestral association called the "Christiania Norwegian Music Society." It is possible that the inspiration for this undertaking came from Ole Bull's idea of an orchestra composed solely of Norwegian-born musicians. Bull had, in fact, assembled such a group for a concert in Oslo in December of the previous year. In the newly established orchestral society, Svendsen wielded the baton, thus for the first time trying out his skills as a rehearsal conductor. As far as we know, though, he did not conduct any public concerts with the orchestra, and after he went abroad in 1862 the ensemble apparently ceased to exist. There was, however, a concert by a group called the "Christiania Norwegian Orchestra" in the Oslo Tivoli amusement park on September 11, 1863, and it is quite possible that this group was a continuation of the orchestra founded by Svendsen and his friends.

Svendsen visited Trondheim in 1860, when the military band of which he was a member played for the coronation of King Carl XV and Queen Louise in the famous Nidaros Cathedral. As a violinist he also played in a coronation cantata written by Carl Arnold for the occasion.

After the coronation festivities, band director Sperati returned to Oslo by land while the musicians went by ship. They made a stop at the western coastal city of Bergen, and arrangements were made for the band to give a concert. The band members all agreed that Svendsen should take Sperati's place on the podium, even though he was one of the youngest members of the ensemble. Thus it was that Svendsen had his first public appearance as a conductor.

Quite a few of Svendsen's compositions from these youthful years are extant. In the Musikhistorisk Museum in Copenhagen, several orchestral parts for a number of pieces of dance music are preserved. The Norwegian Music Collection in the library of the University of Oslo contains not only instrumental parts but a number of complete scores, most of them dated and signed. In addition, Svendsen made simple arrangements for string quartet of such things as twenty-seven short pieces by Beethoven, Paganini, Mendelssohn, Meyerbeer, and several other composers.

In February 1859 Svendsen composed three short etudes for string quartet. They are unpretentious, well-written pieces, all with a slow introduction in minor followed by a fast section in the relative major key.

The dances that Svendsen wrote at this time were primarily waltz cycles with female names for titles: *Catharina, Caroline, Antonia, Elise,* and *Albertine.* He also wrote a bolero, the salon polka *Klingenberg,* and two marches. Little is known about these early compositions. One lone comment from Svendsen occurs in a letter to his sister Albertine dated September 25, 1861. Here he mentions that he had composed the waltz *Antonia* and the march *The Ninth of November,* and that both pieces had been "favorably judged by my colleagues—I mean by those who understand anything."

All of the waltzes were cut from the same pattern as *At the Seter*: a cycle in the form of an introduction, five separate waltzes, and a concluding section. They are all solidly constructed, well orchestrated, and sound quite spirited. They call for an orchestra of Vienna-classical size, with strings, complete winds, and percussion. Some of the waltzes are quite extensive, with scores running to as many as forty pages.

The likelihood of getting these compositions published was virtually nonexistent, but getting them played was another matter. Several of the manuscripts show evidence of having been used a number of times. The pieces seem to have served three purposes: they were practical exercises in instrumentation, they provided good musical fare at dances and on festive occasions, and they could also be used as popular music in the concert hall.

Formal dances played an important role in the social life of the day, and Svendsen's waltzes were in part a response to the constant demand for dance music. It is not unreasonable to think that the many "young women" waltzes were commissioned by wealthy citizens for social events of one kind or another, and that the composer earned a little extra money in this way.

The instrumentation suggests that Svendsen may have intended these works primarily for the concerts that Sperati gave from time to time in the Tivoli amusement park. It was mentioned earlier that the waltz cycle *At the Seter* was on the program on June 10, 1863. We also know that the *Caroline Waltz* was played on July 7 of that year and one of the marches on November 30.

In the midst of this large quantity of dance music, another piece of quite a different sort appeared in the summer of 1859: *Farewell,* a fantasia for violin and piano, labelled "op. 10." The piano accompaniment was also arranged for string quartet. The fantasia, which is dedicated to Svendsen's contemporary and fellow musician, the violinist Gudbrand Bøhn, was probably a farewell greeting to Bøhn as he was leaving for Brussels to study with Hubert Léonard, a more eminent teacher than any that Norway could offer him.

We do not know of any public performance of *Farewell.* Svendsen did not include it in his final opus list and never mentioned the piece in any of his writings. It was, however, his first compositional effort in a new genre. The fine-sounding solo part has a touch of virtuosity, with melodious passages alternating with faster ones. The over-all effect is somewhat reminiscent of Gypsy music. The harmony is in the facile style of the time, with no personal touches. Strangely enough, the piece concludes with the same folk-tune-like *lokk* motives as those used in the waltz cycle *At the Seter,* played with harmonics. If one compares these two compositions, however, the difference is striking. The waltz cycle has an elegance that is not present in the fantasia.

Early in the winter of 1859, Svendsen had personal contact for the first time with his great artist-ideal, Ole Bull. In a letter to his mother dated January 4, 1860, he wrote: "You may be sure that I have recently made many good acquaintances. I have even spoken with Ole Bull. What an honor for me, the poor, insignificant musician, to be able to say that I have shaken the hand of that great man."

This meeting remained vivid in his memory almost half a century later. In an interview with Charles Kjerulf reported in the Copenhagen daily *Politiken*, he is quoted as saying:

> He was a wonderful man and a wonderful artist. Never have I been so thrilled as I was the first time I met him. My God, how handsome and charming he was in his tight-fitting clothes and with this toss of the head. We talked, of course, about violin-playing, and I was already so advanced that I was able to talk with some authority—yes, I even contradicted him on some points—he became agitated—grabbed the violin and the bow (this big, heavy, heavy bow that almost no one else could use)—and then he played . . . in such a way that one could almost go mad—double harmonics or a simple, sustained melody amidst a welter of pizzicato . . . absolutely insanely difficult, but like child's play—and *so* beautiful! (71)

His final two years in Oslo were not an easy time for Svendsen. During autumn and winter 1859–60 he was ill and had to be placed on sick leave from the music corps for an extended period of time. In the January 4, 1860 letter to his mother he wrote:

> Recently I have been very ill and for that reason have not been able to carry out my military duties. Now, though, I am steadily recuperating and hope with God's help that I will soon be fully healthy again. . . . Let me now see that you immediately write to me and tell me how you are getting along and how you have celebrated Christmas. I don't have to tell you how I have celebrated it, for you know that the lot of the poor musician is to work while other people are amusing themselves.

It was both illness and financial problems that were burdening him, for his meager monthly salary as a military musician was barely sufficient for the absolute necessities. From the money he earned playing for special occasions he tried whenever possible to send a little to his mother—something he continued to do as long as she lived. Rikard Nordraak, who understood clearly the miserable conditions under which Svendsen was living, lamented in a letter to his father dated November 14, 1861, "that a talent such as violinist Johan Svendsen must remain in Norway, starving."

A letter dated September 25, 1860, from Johan to his sister Albertine, who at that time was living with their mother at Øvre Rendal, provides a first-hand glimpse of how hard up he was. They had requested many times that he send them a photograph of himself. Finally he went to the photographer and had his picture taken—but he couldn't afford to pick it up: "My portrait is ready," he wrote, "but I must still wait awhile because I don't have any money." Two months later he was finally able to send them the photograph.

After serving for more than four years as a military musician, Svendsen began to do some careful forward planning for a career as a serious artist. In an application to the Ministry of Church and Education dated July 24, 1860, he noted that his period of enlistment as a military bandsman would be up the following spring, and in that connection he was requesting a travel grant that would enable him to go to Brussels "in order, by studying for some time at a regular music institute, to further prepare myself in my field." Specifically, he wanted to study violin with Hubert Léonard. He enclosed with his application two letters of support—one from his violin teacher, Fredrik Ursin, the other from bandmaster Paolo Sperati. Sperati's letter stated in part, "He plays violin very well, and on the whole gives evidence of a more than ordinary talent for music and especially for composition."

Despite the accolades from his mentors, however, Svendsen did not get the grant, and in spring of 1861 he felt that he had no choice but to re-enlist for another year. He also continued to work as a theater musician, and during the 1860–61 season he participated in the large orchestral concerts of the Philharmonic Society under the leadership of Carl Arnold.

During the summer of 1861 he began to experience a deep depression. In a letter to his sister dated September 25, 1861, he gave her a glimpse of what he was struggling with:

> All summer I have had an enemy to contend with. If you knew how many dark hours this struggle has cost me—me who at the same time (like a good actor) has had to smile in the midst of it all—perhaps you would feel sorry for me instead of accusing me. The nature of this enemy—who now, thank God, is conquered—is a secret that I would not reveal for anything in the world.

By spring of 1862 it was six years since he had entered the military, and he could not bear the thought of continuing as a military musician. He wanted to devote himself to violin-playing and composition, not to continue as "bandsman No. 9" for miserable pay. The receipts issued upon his discharge indicate that his salary—excluding uniforms, room and board—for forty days of service was just one *spesiedaler!* According to the University of Oslo Coin Cabinet, a *spesiedaler* in 1860 had approximately the following purchasing power: you could hire a day laborer (who paid his own living expenses) for three days, or you could buy two liters of cognac. A plow cost nine-and-a-half *spesiedalers*, a one-way ticket to America cost thirty-six.

Upon leaving the military, Svendsen received a formal letter of discharge. The letter is dated April 11, 1862, and is signed by battalion commander Nicolai E. Hoff:

> Johan Svendsen, age 21½. 65½ inches tall, dark hair, blue eyes, slender build, has served in the 3rd and 1st companies of the corps since April 11, 1856, as an infantryman and bandsman, and during that time has deported himself as is appropriate for a brave soldier. Since he now has completed his period of enlistment and does not desire to remain with the corps any longer, he is hereby granted an honorable discharge from military duty. It should be mentioned that he has never been given any kind of punishment.

A notation from the battalion physician, Thorvald Willum, attested that Svendsen was "free of any sign of contagious illness."

In spring of the same year something happened that was to be of decisive significance for Johan, but nobody—neither his family nor his friends—had any idea what it was all about. He had promised to visit his mother and sister during the summer, but instead of doing so he sent each of them a letter. Both letters were dated Midsummer Eve, 1862. To his mother he wrote:

> Man proposes, God disposes. Never have I felt the truth of this proverb more strongly than now. An event that I had never dreamed of has suddenly upset all my plans and calculations and is also to blame for the fact that I cannot fulfill my most cherished promise this summer either. Your beautiful dream of a reunion and embrace is shattered. The reality is that I must travel a road quite different from that which leads to you. Do not worry, dear mother; don't think for a minute that something terrible has happened.

He was not willing to confide his plans to his sister either, and the letter to her is equally cryptic: "Circumstances that I cannot very well tell about now force me to go away. . . . You must not let on that I have not come to visit you, for it is extremely important that everyone here in the city think that I am staying in Østerdalen."

His closest friend of these years, Theodor Løvstad—who also was told nothing about Svendsen's travel plans—has provided a vivid account of their last time together that summer:

> Then came an evening when the two friends had walked homeward
> together farther than usual, and the conversation had been more hectic
> and perhaps a little more serious than before. They finally paused in front
> of a place called "Prindsestalden"—where St. John's Church now
> stands—about midway between their respective homes, and there they
> agreed to part.
>   "Tell me, do you ever pray to God?" asked the older one.
>   "Why do you ask about that?"
>   "Well, if you do—pray for me tonight!"
>   "Is something wrong?"
>   "Oh no, not yet."
>   "Yes, but—"
>   "Let's not talk about it any more."
>   "Tomorrow, then. Good night!"
>   After they had gone a few steps they turned around and looked at each
> other—something they didn't usually do.
>   The next day, at about seven o'clock in the evening, the younger of
> them ran faster than usual up Rådhus Street, down Piperviks Hill and up
> to the garret on the fourth floor where his friend had his little room. He
> knocked. Nobody answered. He knocked again. Same result. Finally a
> woman came out of the room next door.
>   "Is it Svendsen you want to talk with?"
>   "Yes."
>   "He left this morning."
>   "*Johan Svendsen* left? Where did he go?"
>   "That I don't know."
>   The young man went down the stairs more slowly than he had gone
> up. He paused in the stairway and prayed for his departed friend (82).

Four years later (August 6, 1866) Svendsen gave Albertine a few hints about what had happened, but in such general terms that one still cannot understand why his departure had to be kept a secret: "I need not assure you that I am an artist heart and soul. For art's sake I endured a six-year mind-consuming existence as a dance musician and military bandsman in the city of my birth; for art I rashly undertook a trip abroad with just ten *spesiedalers* in my pocket."

Whatever may have been the reason for his sudden departure, it effectively jolted Svendsen out of his more or less miserable life in Oslo and prompted him to take his chances on a future as a serious artist. Filled with a spirit of adventure, he left Oslo on Midsummer's Day, 1862. He was not to see his home city again until five years later.

THE YOUNG MUSICIAN SETS OUT TO SEEK HIS FORTUNE

It was not exactly with seven-league boots that the young man from Oslo set forth on his journey toward the distant peaks of success and fame. With his violin under his arm he boarded the Swedish steamship *Excellencen Toll* early in the morning of June 24, 1862, and journeyed southward. The ship made stops at several towns along the Oslofjord, arriving at Gothenburg (Sweden) at 11:30 in the evening.

Johan was so embarrassed about his hasty departure that he did not communicate with his family until the following spring, when he was in Germany. On April 23, 1863, he wrote to his mother from Hamburg: "A truly bad and wayward son am I, who thus without explanation goes away and doesn't write for ten whole months."

He wrote to his sister the same day, giving a somewhat fuller account of his journey: "Last June, then, I went to Gothenburg, where I remained for two months. From there I went to Halmstad and Malmö. At the latter, where I also stayed for two months, I was offered an appointment as an orchestra conductor, but since I wanted to travel farther I turned it down. From Malmö I came by way of Copenhagen to Hamburg."

He lived from hand to mouth, playing for dances at cafés and taverns, personally "passing the hat" to patrons to collect a few coins to buy food and lodging. He also earned a little as a violin teacher, but he gave no public concerts during this period in either Sweden or Denmark.

He did do some composing, however, writing—as before—dance music for orchestra. We know from the dates in the scores that the fair copy of the *Adéle Waltz* was completed in Gothenburg on September 4. On September 16 he arrived in Halmstad, where he put the finishing touches on the *Julie Galop*. The *Johanne Galop* was completed in Malmö, where he had arrived on September 30. The *Hedwig Waltz*, his last composition in the waltz-cycle genre, was written in December.

In Hamburg he joined a small orchestra attached to a traveling theater company. The orchestra went to Lübeck to give some concerts, but soon thereafter the group disbanded. Svendsen returned to Hamburg, where he tried in vain to find regular employment as a performing musician. He nonetheless remained there until shortly before Christmas 1862, when he returned to Lübeck. There, he wrote to Albertine in a letter dated April 23, 1863, "I lost all my earnings, and thus stood helpless among foreigners." He had an abiding optimism, however, and a firm belief in his calling as an artist. This is evident from a letter written to his sister three years later (August 6, 1866): "All the privation and humiliation that filled my life at this time I have borne with serenity and devotion, for I felt something deep within me that whispered 'courage' and drove me forward."

When he found himself one day absolutely penniless, however, it was clear that the situation called for something more substantial than cheery optimism. His only hope seemed to be to appeal to the Norwegian consul in Lübeck for enough travel money to get him back to Norway.

The consul received a report about the young musician's troubles and about his plans to study at a German music conservatory—preferably the one in Leipzig, where several of his countrymen had previously studied. Now it appeared that all avenues were closed to him. He knew that he had ability as a violinist and sought permission to show what he was capable of. The consul requested that he come back the following day, for since he had little understanding of music he wanted to seek the advice of experts who could better judge the young man's achievements.

The authorities called in for the occasion were impressed with Svendsen's playing, and to his great good fortune one of them was an employee of the Swedish-Norwegian royal family. He was Queen Louise's secretary, court councilor Schüssler, who would soon play an important role in advancing Svendsen's career.

The Swedish-Norwegian consul general in Lübeck was Carl F. Leche, a highly cultivated person. He rekindled the embers of hope in the young Norwegian's breast and became an invaluable source of support for him for some time thereafter. From March through December, 1863, the consul even let him live in his home. They became very good friends; Leche sometimes went so far as to call Svendsen his "foster son."

Svendsen's feelings toward his benefactor were marked by a moving devotion. He expressed this in a letter to Albertine written on Christmas Eve: "I have been very fortunate. . ., among foreigners have found a man who with the most selfless motives accepted me. . ., a man who has treated me like his own son."

Two years later he dedicated his first symphony to Leche, placing these words on the title page: "Seinem väterlichen Freund und Gönner Herrn Dr. Leche in Lübeck königl. schwedisch-norwegischem Generalkonsul, Ritter mehrerer hoher Orden etc. in tiefster Dankbarkeit und Hochachtung gewidmet" ("Dedicated in deepest gratitude and esteem to my fatherly friend and patron, Dr. Leche in Lübeck, royal Swedish-Norwegian consul general, knight of several high Orders, etc.")

In Lübeck, Svendsen proceeded once more to compose, but now his creative efforts moved in some new directions. In the space of four days in February 1863 he wrote three short pieces: the songs *Ich stoß auf des Berges Spitze* (*I reached the top of the mountain*—Heine) and *Dæmring* ("Dawn"— Chr. Molbech) and a piece for male chorus entitled *Guds fred* ("God's Peace"—B. S. Ingemann). The two songs, which represent his first efforts in this genre, sound rather ordinary and have no distinguishing features. The captivating male-chorus piece is more broadly conceived but lacks the childlike innocence that has made the beautiful setting of this text by A. P. Berggreen (1841) a national favorite in Norway.

In March 1863 Svendsen began working on a larger work for orchestra with solo violin obligato. The piece, entitled *Caprice,* was completed on July 21. It was the most ambitious composition he had attempted up to that time, with a score encompassing no less than 41 pages. The point of departure is the technically demanding violin style of the fantasia *Farewell,* written four years earlier. In the *Caprice,* however, the virtuosic element is further emphasized with advanced figurations and double-stops. Several of the two-voiced sections are somewhat reminiscent of the technique used so elegantly by Mendelssohn in the second movement of his *Violin Concerto* in E minor. Svendsen's piece calls for a large orchestra, and it is obvious that it was written by an able orchestrator. The principal weakness of the composition lies in the joining of the several sections. Svendsen had no experience writing a long, unified work, and when he tried to apply ideas derived from the mosaic structure of the waltz cycle to the new genre the resulting organization undeniably became somewhat loose. A year later, when the piece was premiered at the Leipzig conservatory, Svendsen himself realized that it was not completely successful. In a letter written later he excused himself on the grounds that at that time he had not yet "studied musical form."

In the 1860s, Lübeck—a lovely old Hanseatic city on the German coast of the Baltic Sea—had a quite diverse cultural life. The city's venerable music society gave a series of subscription concerts that included classical symphonies and large choral works, and operas were regularly presented in the local theater. There was also a great deal of interest in chamber music among both professional musicians and amateurs. Each year eight public concerts devoted to chamber music were given, and they were well attended.

Svendsen, who little by little gained a certain foothold in the music life of the community, assisted in several concerts both in Lübeck and in the nearby town of Travemünde. In Lübeck he participated in August 1863 in a "Musikalische und dramatische Soirée" at which he, as a violinist, upstaged the man who was giving the concert, the pianist A. Wohlgeboren. A local newspaper reviewed the performance:

> The assisting violinist, Mr. *Svendsen* from Christiania [Oslo], could re-joice even more than the concert-giver himself over the unequivocal recognition of those in attendance. . . . The liveliest applause was given to him. His playing distinguishes itself by a beautiful tone and a sensitive and refined cantilena as well as by impressive technical skill—although the latter is not yet perfect in all respects. If Mr. Svendsen is equally successful in the further development of his considerable talent, he will bring honor to his homeland—which, indeed, in the person of Ole Bull has given us one of the most renowned violin virtuosos—and one dares to predict for him a brilliant career as an artist (53).

As early as spring of 1863 Consul Leche set about trying to get a grant for Svendsen from the Swedish-Norwegian government. On April 4 the Norwegian Prime Minister in Stockholm, Georg C. Sibbern, wrote to the ranking government representative in Oslo, First Minister Frederik Stang:

> From our consul in Lübeck, Herr Leche, whom I know to be a very agreeable and good man, I have received the enclosed letter regarding a young Norwegian, Mr. Svendsen, who is said to be equipped with rare musical aptitude and has already achieved considerable proficiency on the violin. I ask the honorable Minister to take under favorable consideration whether something should be done for this young artist in the form of a travel grant. . . (78).

The well-known Hungarian-German violinist Joseph Joachim was scheduled to give a concert in Hamburg at the end of April, and Consul Leche saw this as an opportunity to strike a blow for his young Norwegian friend. He put him on the train, and April 23 Johan wrote glowingly to his mother:

> This evening I am going to hear one of the world's greatest artists. He is a young man by the name of Joseph Joachim; he plays in such a way that people sit quite anxiously lest he stop playing. There is something wonderful about such a man, who can so entrance people with his violin.

The consul had more ambitious plans for the Hamburg visit, however, namely, that Svendsen should demonstrate his violin-playing ability for Joachim. He did so, whereupon the brilliant violinist gave him the following recommendation:

> Mr. Svendsen played for me an etude of Léonard and the first movement of a concerto by Bériot. Requested to express my opinion regarding the said gentleman's proficiency, I dare say with a clear conscience that Mr. Svendsen has good qualifications for violin playing and under able instruction can certainly become a useful performer. Mr. Svendsen's playing, though not distinguished, yet has at the least the stamp of healthiness and uncorruptedness. Thus I can in this connection recommend him to the favor of music-loving friends.

This recommendation, which is preserved in the State Archives in Oslo, certainly was not particularly glowing, but Leche—who had more confidence in Joachim's fame than in the content of the recommendation—thought it could have great significance for his protegé. On May 7, therefore, he wrote to Prime Minister Sibbern:

> As well as enclosing Joachim's testimonial, allow me to mention that in addition to several other friends and countrymen who heard Svendsen here, court councilor Schüssler . . . was so enthralled by his playing that in his letter to H[er] M[ajesty] the Queen—dispatched from here the same day—he ventured a humble recommendation for the young artist. . . .
> Your Excellency, be assured that Svendsen will in a perhaps not so distant future redeem the bank note that is drawn on his talent! Joachim advised him to choose Dresden for further musical education.

With Leche's encouragement, on May 31 Svendsen drafted a formal request for a grant. The request was addressed to King Carl XV:

The undersigned, who is 22 years old, humbly petitions for a grant in order to undertake a journey abroad.

I have since my childhood concerned myself with music, and now for several years have been a member of the Second Akershus Infantry Brigade's Music Corps. But since this provides little opportunity for experience on my real instrument, the violin, I have constantly had to seek private teaching as well as instruction regarding technical skills and theory of composition. Since my present teachers have all attested to the fact that I possess musical talent, and moreover, since it is my deepest desire to study this art as thoroughly as possible, I have resolved, insofar as it is within my power to do so, to perfect the art as fully as my abilities allow.

Consequently, I have, with the help of my friends, now undertaken a trip to Germany so that under the guidance of a capable teacher I can continue my studies, especially the theory of composition, although I also will try to further develop my technical skill.

But since, owing to financial circumstances, the present trip can only be a short one, I humbly venture to approach Your Majesty with a petition for support such that I could be enabled to continue my studies for a somewhat longer time. In support I humbly venture to enclose six of my own compositions.

There followed an anxious period of waiting during which Svendsen's spirits were put to the test. He also began to question his own abilities, as is evident from a June 28 letter to Albertine:

You wish me well in view of the fact that I now stand at the portal of my sacred abode. Yes, yes, that is true, but unfortunately I still only stand *outside* the portal. Will I ever get in? I have posed this question more than a thousand times, and the unresolved doubt that each unanswered question leaves behind is at times about to kill me. It is terrible to doubt oneself. I now understand for the first time how much I have to learn before I rightly dare consider myself a worthy priest in Apollo's temple. It would be awful for me to be compelled to give up the fulfillment of all the beautiful dreams that I have had.

On July 3 the designated grant committee sent its proposal to the ministry. All the documents regarding Svendsen's application, including the letter from Leche and the recommendation from Joachim, were available to the committee. They did little good, however, for Svendsen was but one of eight talented musicians who were seeking grants. The committee—

consisting of Carl Arnold, M. J. Monrad, and Halfdan Kjerulf—recommended four candidates prioritized as follows: Gudbrand Bøhn, Just R. Lindeman, Rikard Nordraak, and Edvard Grieg. The other four, including Svendsen, were not mentioned by name in the committee report although the committee indicated in general terms that the remaining candidates should not be regarded as undeserving of a grant.

As was usually the case, only the first two names on the list were given serious consideration. The somewhat lukewarm statement from Joachim was no doubt more of a boomerang than the bull's-eye Leche had anticipated, especially when Bøhn was able to support his application with a glowing recommendation from Hubert Léonard in Brussels. That Trondheim composer Just Lindeman was ranked above Nordraak and Grieg may have been due in part to geographical-political considerations. Grieg was especially shocked by the decision: he had been so confident of getting a grant that he had borrowed money in advance.

Svendsen was in good company, then, but that was of small comfort to him. Though the first battle had been lost, however, Consul Leche was not ready to concede defeat. During a visit to Stockholm in late summer 1863 he discussed Svendsen's plight with Prime Minister Sibbern. Sibbern, in a letter to First Minister Stang dated September 4, once again raised the grant question:

> Tell Mr. Riddervold that Consul Leche from Lübeck has come up to see me and strongly recommended the Norwegian violinist Svendsen, who is seeking a grant. Leche speaks of his talent with enthusiasm, and as proof of his sincerity it may be noted that Mr. Svendsen is even living in Dr. Leche's house. If it is possible to do something for this talent in the way of a grant, please do it!

Stang answered on September 11; the ministry could not do anything because it felt bound by the committee's recommendation:

> It pains me that it was impossible to get Svendsen recommended for a grant, since one could not take a grant away from the other musicians, who were favorably recommended, while Svendsen was not recommended by the authorities here. The matter was considered with great care by the cabinet, but the thing proved to be impossible.

Svendsen was very discouraged by this setback, as is evident from a letter written to his sister on October 30:

You ask me if I think that Consul Leche will be able to get something for me. We have now made a final effort—but to be honest, I have little confidence in it and I presumably am going to have to try to get along on my own. May God give me strength and good fortune so that I don't buckle under in the struggle with the trivialities of life. It is no easy task to preserve one's musical taste pure and unadulterated when as a dance musician, teacher etc. one is obliged to endure so many repugnant sounds and so many unesthetic thoughts.

The "final effort" to which Svendsen referred was a new application, this time directed personally to Carl XV via Sibbern. And this time Leche succeeded. The king made the decision himself, and a travel grant was awarded to the promising young musician from Norway.

Before an answer had been received from the king, however, friends in Oslo led by Svendsen's former teacher, Fredrik Ursin, had taken steps to collect some funds for him. On November 27 a long item in support of the ingathering appeared in *Aftenbladet*, one of Oslo's principal daily newspapers. It actually came too late, however, for as it was stated in a postscript:

After this was already written we received word that our royal family recently has awarded Mr. Svendsen the substantial amount of 200 *spesiedalers*; but we have been advised nonetheless to take up the collection described above, since a course in Leipzig takes three years, and the young artist will, therefore, need some private help in order to maintain himself abroad for such a long period.

What results were produced by this appeal is not known, but with a royal grant in his pocket Svendsen could in any case confidently seek admission to the famous Leipzig conservatory that he had long dreamed of attending. Another young Norwegian—19-year-old Edvard Grieg—had just completed his studies there the previous year.

According to conservatory records, Svendsen was accepted as a student on December 5, 1863, and it is specifically mentioned that he had support from the Swedish king. By Christmas Eve he was able to tell his sister Albertine that he had long been "fully occupied—playing violin, reading figured bass, and hearing lectures about music and music history."

2

THE LEIPZIG YEARS

1863–67

SVENDSEN'S YOUTHFUL DREAM had come true: he was in Leipzig, one of the most important cities in the world of music. Judged by the standards of the day, Leipzig was a large city. In 1858 it had a population of 74,000, and by virtue of the industrialization that was in process at this time it was growing rapidly. In the realm of music the ancient traditions were being preserved, and new ones were being created as well. The heritage from Bach was carefully guarded, not least by the Thomaner choir in St. Thomas Church. The city could boast two symphony orchestras: the famous Gewandhaus Orchestra, founded in 1781, which Mendelssohn had taken to great heights, and *Euterpe,* which was more of a forum for the younger composers. The townspeople were also justly proud of the local opera company, which was ranked among the finest in Germany.

Leipzig was like a magnet for the leading musicians of the day. This was especially the case during the internationally famous trade fair, held semiannually, when the city was seething with life and activity.

The city was the headquarters of several world-famous music publishers, most notably Breitkopf & Härtel and Edition Peters. It was also the home of two of Europe's leading music journals, in whose pages musicological issues were subjected to lively debate: *Allgemeine musikalische Zeitung,* which was strongly conservative; and its opposite, *Neue Zeitschrift für Musik,* started by Schumann in 1834, which waged a prodigious struggle against the reactionary "philistines" in music.

Ferdinand David, the eminent German violinist who was Svendsen's principal instructor in violin and conducting at Leipzig. (Det kgl. Bibliotek, Copenhagen)

The verbal strife between old and new reflected differing tastes in the leading music circles of the city. The orchestral and opera repertoires by and large showed great respect for time-honored traditions, yet there was a certain openness to new trends as well. Leipzig audiences suffered no lack of opportunities to hear music written by their contemporaries.

A "FRESHMAN" AT THE LEIPZIG CONSERVATORY

The excitement in Leipzig's music life naturally had an impact on the conservatory, the latest bud on the city's luxuriant musical stem, which had been founded by the classical-leaning Mendelssohn in 1843. Mendelssohn had been tolerant of differing musical orientations, however, and had worked in cooperation with the temperamental "agitator" Robert Schumann, whom he had engaged as a teacher of piano and composition. The conservatory had opened its doors on April 2, 1843, with 22 students and six teachers. The latter had included, in addition to Mendelssohn and Schumann, such notables as the violin virtuoso, Ferdinand David, and the choral director at St. Thomas Church, Moritz Hauptmann. During the late

1840s this small group had been expanded to include such renowned figures as the pianist Ignaz Moscheles, the composers Niels W. Gade and Carl Reinecke, and the distinguished contrapuntalist Ernst F. Richter.

The conservatory's reputation grew rapidly and its standards soon reached a level that was legendary. Students poured in, not only from Germany but from the Slavic countries, Scandinavia, England and America. For Norway the conservatory became a kind of musician hatchery: during the first fifty years of its existence it had no less than 198 Norwegian students— ten times as many as it had from Denmark. Among the Norwegians who preceded Grieg and Svendsen at Leipzig were Halfdan Kjerulf, Johan G. Conradi, Martin A. Udbye and Otto Winter-Hjelm. Many of the men who were to become leaders in the music life of Norway came later, including Eyvind Alnæs, Johan Halvorsen, Iver Holter, Johannes Haarklou, Sigurd Lie, Ole Olsen, Johan Selmer, and Christian Sinding.

One of the conservatory's main goals was that the students should get a solid technical foundation within the context of Classical-Romantic principles of style. But new ideas also found their way into the curriculum, so the students were by no means forced into a strait jacket. Each of them found opportunities to develop his or her special talent.

Both Grieg and Svendsen profited from the conservatory's strict, tradition-based standards and from the teachers' tolerance and openness to the more progressive currents in the music of the day. It is hard to understand why Grieg, toward the end of his life, disparaged the instruction he had received there. His more or less questionable statements on this subject have been disproven in various ways including studies that have been made of his exercise books and compositions dating from this period (104). Moreover, Grieg was only fifteen years old when he came to Leipzig and just eighteen when he graduated. There is no doubt that he received solid training and a secure foundation on which he could build further as his skills developed.

While Grieg's artistic nature was most akin to that of the full-blooded Romantic composer Robert Schumann, Svendsen was more attracted to the refined classicism of Mendelssohn. He was a conservatory student for the same length of time as Grieg, but he came to Leipzig as a 23-year-old with considerable experience as a performer on several different instruments. Moreover, he had by this time done quite a bit of composing, especially of orchestral works. He was far more mature than Grieg had been

when he came to Leipzig and was much better prepared to make immediate
practical use of what the conservatory had to offer. For these reasons he was
able even during his student years to compose large works that attracted international attention.

Unlike Grieg, Svendsen's interests were not focused primarily on harmonic innovations. He was more interested in an elegant voice-leading
within the context of a plastic, balanced form. His feeling for timbre manifested itself first and foremost in the realm of instrumentation, where he
demonstrated an almost dazzling brilliance.

Svendsen came to the conservatory with great expectations. Some years
later (on August 6, 1866) he wrote to Albertine that he had wanted to realize his highest wish: "to study my divine art under the renowned teachers in
Leipzig. From this time onward everything changed; I went forward unhin-
dered on the path I had chosen, and every step was accompanied by good
fortune and joy."

He began his studies immediately after his arrival in December 1863,
which is to say in the middle of the academic year. Soon thereafter—on
January 12, 1864, in "Inscript No. 1096"—he was identified as an honor
student in the official records of the conservatory. The violinists Ferdinand
David and Felix Dreyschock wrote, "he has great talent for violin playing,
and with hard work and zeal can become a very good violinist." By spring
there were further testimonials. M. Hauptmann, professor of music theory
and composition, wrote, "Mr. Svendsen is very industrious and is making
good progress." C. Reinecke stated matter-of-factly that "Mr. Svendsen has
attended my class only once, but he has turned in a reasonably good composition." E. F. Richter attested that he was "industrious and made quite good
progress." Piano teacher R. Papperitz noted that he had made "a good beginning," while the two aforementioned violin teachers issued a joint statement that Svendsen "is very industrious and is making excellent progress."

It is clear that Svendsen concentrated primarily on the violin during the
first months, for his ambition was to become a concert violinist. In Ferdinand David, one of Europe's leading virtuosos, he had an outstanding
teacher. David gave special attention to the technical aspects of violin playing, so Svendsen had to struggle with demanding etudes by Kreutzer,
Fiorillo, Rode, and David. He made a thorough study of David's and
Spohr's violin concertos and Bach's solo sonatas. David was frequently away
on concert tours, and in his absence the instruction was given by Felix

Dreyschock, assistant concertmaster of the Gewandhaus Orchestra. Soon Svendsen also began to play chamber music and became a member of the conservatory orchestra, of which David was conductor.

With respect to the theoretical disciplines (harmony, figured bass, counterpoint, and form), Svendsen felt—despite his background as a composer—so untrained that he insisted on starting at the very beginning. In a short time, however, he was placed at a more advanced level.

The composition that Reinecke characterized as "reasonably good" presumably was the *Caprice* for solo violin and orchestra that Svendsen had written in Lübeck the previous year. It was premiered at the conservatory in December, 1864, probably with the composer himself as soloist and conductor. He described his debut in a letter to his father dated December 12. He had had ten rehearsals with selected students:

> Everyone regarded the matter with the greatest interest. As you presumably know, I had already composed the above-named piece during my stay in Lübeck, and for that reason it does not have any traditional form since at that time I had not yet studied the theory of form. This very circumstance has resulted in the composition having a certain peculiarity that makes the dry theoreticians shake their heads with a disbelieving smile. They can't fathom the idea that imagination can be clothed in forms different from those bequeathed to us by Haydn, Mozart, and Beethoven. It is high time that composers learn to understand that one cannot always hang on to the old forms when one wishes to set forth new ideas. . . . The *Caprice* was a roaring success with the large audience.

Despite the success he experienced with the work, he later had to agree with "the dry theoreticians" that the piece was loosely constructed. When Gudbrand Bøhn played it at Svendsen's introductory concert in Oslo on October 12, 1867, Grieg, too, observed that "despite the talent to which it bears witness, it comes across as somewhat formless." Halfdan Kjerulf noted tersely in his diary: "The weakest piece was the *Caprice*, which began better than it ended." This performance in Svendsen's home city proved to be the piece's swan song. The composer allowed it to fade from memory and did not include it in his opus list.

Svendsen threw himself fully into the conservatory environment. His fellow student Hans von Ende later wrote a biographical article in which he told of his Norwegian friend's popularity:

He won the hearts of all of the more awakened conservatory students by virtue of his forthright nature and his infectious jocularity. . . . He was the most gifted student among us, and his inexhaustible humor and incomparable amiability made him everybody's favorite. Whenever there was an artistic plan to be implemented, it was always done his way (33 and 122).

As the acknowledged leader among the students, Svendsen participated in the founding of the "Euphonia" student association and served as its first president. On one occasion he wrote a humorous overture based on the drinking song *So leben wir,* which aroused great enthusiasm among the members. The student association became the scene of heated debates regarding the issues of the day—musical, literary, and political. Svendsen was no narrow specialist, but was vitally concerned with what was going on in the wider world. He was captivated not only by the masters of classical literature—Goethe and Schiller—but also by Jean Paul, Schumann's favorite author, and by Norwegian poet Henrik Wergeland.

He also made frequent visits to the university, where he often attended the lectures of cultural historian Eckhardt. Here he became acquainted with some newer artistic trends—George Sand and Heinrich Heine in literature, Wilhelm von Kaulbach in painting, Schumann and Wagner in the field of music.

During this entire period in Leipzig, however, what proved to be of greatest significance for him was the musical experiences, especially the orchestral concerts. On October 9, 1864, he reported in a letter to his father that during the most recent trade fair he had attended excellent concerts in three different locales: in "Schützenhaus" there was a good 25-piece orchestra, in Central-Halle one of 60, and Benjamin Bilse's famous ensemble had played in Hotel de Pologne:

> Bilse's Orchestra was worth more than the other two combined. Everything was so precise that even the most complex modulations were always clear and understandable. Crescendos, *fz* and sudden transitions from *forte* to *piano,* and vice-versa, were accomplished with a mastery and a precision that enchanted the harshest critics. . . . At the twelve concerts that I attended I did not once see a player using fingering or bowing different from the others. As I said, the guiding principle of these musicians was unity expressed in the little things as well as the big ones. With respect to purity and precision, Bilse's Orchestra is far superior to the famous Gewandhaus Orchestra.

In comparing the two orchestras he knew whereof he spoke, for he himself played "first-stand violin" in the Gewandhaus.

But there were also "serious things to write about." He had recently received a financial jolt that threatened to thwart all his plans:

> The local Norwegian-Swedish Consul, Mr. Schulz, from whom I have
> been receiving money during my stay in Leipzig, has informed me that the
> sum provided for me by the king will soon be exhausted. The money that
> remains (about 40 *thalers*) will supply my needs for a couple of months. I
> wanted, therefore, to find out if I can count on any help from Norway.
> Otherwise I must try to find a job, for I *can't* go home without having
> reached the goal toward which I have been striving. It would surely be a
> shame if I were now to be compelled to forsake my studies and to resume
> the struggle to make a living without being prepared in such a way as to be
> able to make a success of it.

Throughout his life Svendsen had trouble managing his finances. He never learned to be frugal; as soon as he had money in his pocket it seemed to disappear. The royal grant should have been adequate to see him through his conservatory studies—but it wasn't. The money slipped through his fingers. His father was shocked when he heard that the grant had been used up so quickly, so Johan tried in his next letter (June 6, 1865) to explain where the money had gone: "You ask me if it is true that I have used 500 *spesiedalers* (from December 1863 to February 1865). *No!*" During this entire period he had only spent "500 *thalers* (354 *spesiedalers*)," including 80 *thalers* paid to the conservatory, 20 for violin repair, plus various amounts to purchase books and music and for two trips to Dresden. "So you can figure out approximately how much that leaves for food, drink, lodging and clothes; I certainly have not been living in the lap of luxury."

He did manage to get through this first financial crisis. In response to his father's pleas, Gudbrand Bøhn and Fredrik Ursin managed to get him a loan, and he himself raised some money by giving lessons and playing in various groups.

More ominous, however, was a nervous disorder that developed in his left hand. It first appeared in February, 1865, but it was not until the letter of June 6 that he told his father about it:

> It looks almost as if fate itself is opposed to the idea of my becoming a
> violinist. Just think: everything was going wonderfully, and I had decided

not to worry about the stage fright in order at David's urging to perform at one of the conservatory's evening programs, when I suddenly noted a sharp pain in my left little finger when I played. I couldn't figure out what was wrong with it myself, so I went to one of the most renowned doctors. He explained to me that it was a nervous disorder for which there is no known cure, and that I would simply have to wait patiently until it went away by itself. He forbade me to play—a directive that I promptly disobeyed by playing in a quartet that very day; but I got a real scare when I noted that the little finger grew worse and that two of the other fingers also began to hurt. This happened in February, and unfortunately I still see no sign of improvement.

It must have been a very severe form of occupational neurosis, and it would not go away despite various attempts at treatment, including "electricity and Spanish flies." The idea of a career as a concert violinist had to be abandoned. His violin teachers commented wistfully on what had happened. On April 15, 1865, they wrote: "Mr. Svendsen was, to begin with, very industrious and made significant progress. More recently, owing to pains in his hand he has been unable to take lessons. He is an outstanding quartet and orchestra player." Ferdinand David's final assessment, dated May 20, 1867, was as follows: "At the beginning he took lessons and demonstrated great talent; illness prevented him from preparing himself to be a good violinist."

It is natural at this point to pose a few questions. Did Svendsen really feel it as a catastrophe that he had to give up the idea of a career as a violinist? Is it unreasonable to assume that as a 25-year-old he had a clear premonition that he had no chance of becoming a first-rank concert violinist? Time was running out. Joseph Joachim's evaluation some years earlier may have sown some doubt, and the statements from Ferdinand David, who really thought well of his student, were also quite restrained. The "stage fright" mentioned in the letter to his father may also have played a role in deterring him from a career as a soloist. One is tempted to think that he may have realized early in his conservatory period that his greatest opportunities lay in other directions—i.e., as a conductor and, even more, as a composer. A clear indication of this assessment of himself appears as early as December 12, 1864, in a letter to his father: "You want to know how it is going with my violin playing. To tell the truth, I am much more interested in composition than in playing, though you must not think that I have laid the violin totally aside."

The expressed interest in composition soon was manifest in a splendid way in his first chamber-music work: the *String Quartet* in A minor, op. 1.

THE STRING QUARTET

As the finger problem progressed, Svendsen was able to concentrate more and more on composition. Early in the spring of 1865 he set to work on a truly demanding task, the writing of a string quartet. At the conservatory this was an assignment usually given to the advanced students. Grieg, for example, had studied for three years before he was assigned to such a task; the quartet in D minor which he produced at that time, and which was performed in Bergen in 1862, was later rejected by the composer and apparently destroyed.

Svendsen, who had been a conservatory student for only one year and who was, moreover, the youngest member of the composition class, had the advantage of having played both violin and viola. He could, therefore, tackle the compositional problems with a completely different experiential background than Grieg, and the writing of a quartet was for that reason a challenge that was right down his alley.

Carl Reinecke, the principal teacher in composition, was the imposing conductor of the Gewandhaus Orchestra. An acclaimed composer, he was of a conservative bent, with both feet firmly planted in the Mendelssohn-Schumann tradition. Reinecke had considerable influence on Svendsen, especially during the first two years, and helped to develop his understanding of the classical forms. He regarded the young man from Norway as one of his most gifted students: "Rarely have I met a student who has developed as quickly as Svendsen. After some quite ordinary student exercises he wrote in rapid succession his *String Quartet*, op. 1, the *String Octet*, op. 3, which has become very well known, and the *Symphony No. 1*, op. 4, etc.—all of which are works that were written with great skill" (97).

Aimar Grønvold has given an amusing account—based on conversations with Svendsen—of Reinecke's involvement in the writing of the quartet. After reading through the manuscript of the first movement for the first time, Reinecke said:

> "It's very good, sir, very poetic; but it could of course be made far more musical and contrapuntally interesting—for example, here and here"—Reinecke pointed out a couple of places where such changes could be made.
>
> Svendsen took his manuscript home and revised it from beginning to end, paying careful attention to all the rules of composition and the

professor's suggestions. Some time later he brought the new manuscript to his teacher.

"Very good, but it could of course be done much more freely and poetically—for example, here and here"—whereupon Reinecke pointed out some possible changes that would restore the composition to roughly the form it had had in the beginning.

That was all Svendsen needed. He retained his first draft and wrote the remaining movements in the same manner, and soon thereafter he let his classmates rehearse his op. 1, the quartet, without Reinecke's knowledge (51:85).

The conservatory concluded each academic year with a public graduation concert, where some of the best student compositions were performed. Svendsen submitted the quartet to the faculty committee, which unanimously accepted it for performance at the Gewandhaus on May 21, 1865.

He recruited the best quartet players at the conservatory, and they had "twelve real rehearsals." On June 5 he wrote exultantly to his sister that the performance was a complete success and that "in addition to the generous applause after each movement I was rewarded after the concluding movement with a triple curtain call."

The faculty, too, expressed their enthusiasm. Ferdinand David said the composition was "the most significant one of all." Reinecke had taken the unusual step of presenting his gifted student with a copy of the score of Beethoven's string quartets "in honor of this for me so auspicious debut as a composer." That particular expression of gratitude was the perfect gift for a man who was known by his fellow students as "the score-gulper."

It is easy to understand the faculty members' enthusiasm, for the first mature fruit of Svendsen's conservatory period is a well-written work, free of superficial clichés. Formally, it follows traditional patterns, but one could hardly have expected anything else from a conservatory student. He employs sonata form with a sure hand in three of the quartet's four movements, manipulating the material easily and elegantly, without a trace of the roughness that one might expect in a student composition. The instruction in counterpoint that he had received from Richter had demonstrably given him a solid basis upon which he could express himself within the confines of a Mendelssohnian quartet texture. His broad experience as a string player enabled him to mould the material for the performers in a striking way.

It is interesting that in this early composition we find a manner of

expression and a style that is not significantly different from that of
Svendsen's later works. The light, optimistic tone is a hallmark: he seems to
be smiling even when he is writing in a minor key. It is also worth noting
that the quartet is the only one of his multi-movement works that contains
movements in a minor key. Several of the themes also exhibit a pulsating
rhythm marked by sharply dotted notes—another special characteristic of
his music.

If this composition cannot be placed on a level with other particularly
notable quartets—for example, Grieg's *String Quartet* in G Minor, op. 27—
the reason is that the melodic material, pleasing though it is, does not have
the same potency.

The harmonic richness of Svendsen's quartet, on the other hand, gives
it a certain personal character. Svendsen clearly is building on Schubert's
characteristic abrupt changes between third-related keys, but he does so in
surprising ways, often in connection with advanced chromaticism. A typical
example occurs in the following measures from the second movement:

Example 1   *String Quartet,* op. 1, 2nd movement

The fearless aggressiveness in this passage shows that the composer dares to
venture outside the conservatory's main thoroughfare. In the 1860s this
probably sounded like "music of the future" to the traditionalists, and it

would have been interesting to see Svendsen's reaction when he read the review that appeared following the premiere—the first public review that he ever received as a composer. It appeared in *Leipziger Nachrichten* on May 23, 1865: "The most interesting piece for us was a string quartet by Svendsen. Here we encountered an unmistakable talent, which, however, needs much purification. Mr. Svendsen must be especially careful to avoid the so-called super-brilliant harmonic devices employed by Wagner so that his fine compositional disposition, which is already capable of creating a coherent whole, does not get choked by the weeds of affectation."

The first movement, *Allegro*, greets us with a graceful and lively principal theme. An ingratiating subsidiary theme in the relative key of C major provides an effective contrast. This is one of the places where Svendsen employs a series of third-related changes of key, a stylistic feature that also marks the development section of the movement.

In the lyrical second movement, marked *Andantino*, Svendsen approaches Schubert's emotional world. There are associations with the *Rosamunde* music. In the recapitulation the principal theme is assigned to the cello's *cantilena* register while the first violin plays a decorative role.

The third movement, *Allegro scherzando*—the only movement that is not in sonata form—is a free rondo in which all the episodes are derived from the rondo theme. A long, modulating middle section with the rondo theme in augmentation has the character of a development. The movement absolutely sparkles with musical brilliance, clearly inspired by Mendelssohn's *Canzonetta* (from the E-flat major quartet).

The last movement, *Finale. Allegro assai con fuoco*, incorporates dance rhythms in a furious tempo. Augmented intervals derived from Gypsy music are also prominent in this movement.

The A-minor quartet is much more than a conservatory student's "proof of competence." It is a mature work by a brilliant young composer; it is as surprising as it is regrettable that it has not retained a place in the international repertoire.

EXPLORING GERMAN CULTURE

Svendsen, who was by nature inquisitive, made use of every opportunity to broaden his experience. He did not isolate himself in Leipzig but tried to get as complete a picture of German culture as he could within the confines of his limited financial resources.

Toward the end of May, 1865, he and some of his fellow students attended a music festival in Dessau focused primarily on modern trends. The festival gave him an opportunity to become better acquainted with the New German school, Liszt and Wagner, and with orchestral virtuoso Berlioz. Many years later, in a conversation with Didrik Grønvold, Svendsen talked about this trip and its effect on his relationship with his teachers at the conservatory. It seems that at that time it took a certain independence—indeed, courage—for a conservatory student to attend such a "New Music" festival. But Svendsen was richly endowed with such qualities: "I remember that sort of thing in Leipzig many years ago, when I disagreed strongly with my teachers—often was absolutely inconsiderate of them—argued with them during lesson periods and more often than not insisted on having the last word" (53). Returning to Leipzig after the festival he discovered that several of the professors, not least Reinecke, were offended by the students' trip to Dessau. Hauptmann, however, displayed a more receptive attitude, calmly asking Svendsen what he thought of the new music. "I knew exactly what I thought and told him what I liked and what I didn't like. Then the old man said, 'Well, since so many of the young people go crazy over this music, I guess there must be something to it. We teachers are too old.' That's something I can really appreciate—an urbanity of that sort" (53).

Of the various teachers he had at the conservatory it was the gentle and amiable Hauptmann to whom Svendsen felt the closest bond. The same was true for Grieg. The illustrious professor had a unique ability to get along with students—to such an extent, in fact, that a kind of friendship developed between them. Hauptmann was by this time old and frail and often had to do his teaching in his own home. In that setting, however, he would sometimes sit for hours with his young students and talk to them about music. What he especially encouraged them to do was to cultivate the well-balanced classical ideals of form. Svendsen took this advice to heart.

A rather different kind of teacher was the more rigorous Ernst F. Richter, who had responsibility for giving instruction in counterpoint. Grieg, who by nature was no contrapuntalist, had regarded assignments on such strict formal techniques as canon and fugue as pure drudgery. Svendsen, on the other hand, was right at home with Richter's stringent requirements, and in a short time he was busily at work writing fugues. It is clear from the annual teacher evaluations that the professor was especially pleased with what Svendsen accomplished. It is also evident from his later work that the insight and preparation he acquired in counterpoint was not mere theory for Svendsen, but a vital stimulus that enriched everything he wrote thereafter.

One unexpected occurrence at the Dessau music festival was a chance meeting with Ole Bull, who, as Svendsen wrote to his father on June 6, "looked very good, and was very friendly to me." Just a year earlier Ole Bull, whose dominating idea was that the compositions of a Norwegian composer should exhibit a marked national profile, had played an important role in launching Grieg on the path he was to take—a role so important that Grieg later characterized Bull as "my rescuer."

Ole Bull's ideas quickly took root in Svendsen's mind. In the above-mentioned letter to his father he wrote, "Isn't it possible to get *Older and Newer Norwegian Mountain Melodies* collected and published by Ludvig Lindeman for a fairly reasonable price?" So it is evident that he wanted to develop a first-hand acquaintance with this part of Norwegian musical culture. After he got the Lindeman volumes, national characteristics began to appear in his compositions—for example, in the string octet and the first symphony, on which he was working in the autumn of 1865.

Late in the summer of 1865 Svendsen set out on another trip, this time in the company of eight friends. Their first destination was Schiller's home in Weimar, Thuringia, in the heart of cultural Germany. On December 20 he wrote a long and beautifully composed letter to his father in which he told of some of their experiences:

> Just think that this great man, who through his immortal works succeeded in reaching the hearts of his people, and who can therefore be justly re-garded as the teacher of the entire nation, lived and died in poverty. It was with feelings of awe that I entered this humble abode from which so many brilliant rays have emerged to enlighten and inspire the world. A famous thinker has characterized the relationship of the German people to their great poet in the following words: "While the poet was living, you refused to give him bread; after his death you gave him a stone." When, after having seen Schiller's modest house, one observes the huge statue of him that his countrymen erected after his death, one realizes the poignant truth of these ironic words.

Several letters from this period make it clear that he was also reflecting on the role of the artist. On April 25, 1865, he wrote to his sister about the privations a creative artist had to be willing to accept in a materialistic world. He emphasized the fact that his studies of German masterworks "are for me ample recompense for the joys that the so-called fashionable world could give me, and which I cheerfully leave to those who don't know anything better."

From Weimar, Svendsen and his friends proceeded to Wartburg: "Afterwards we marched over numerous mountains and rivers, past many castles and rural villages to the shrine of the entire Protestant world—I mean the Wartburg fortress, where Luther translated the Bible and wrote several of his pithy protests against the tyrannical acts of the Pope."

They returned to Leipzig by way of Köthen, where Bach had once lived and worked. A rollicking folk festival—called "Kermes" (or Kirmsen)—was held there each summer. Peter Jessen, a Norwegian student who had been one of Svendsen's traveling companions on this trip, later reported that when he first heard the scherzo movement of his friend's first symphony the thought immediately came to him: "That is for sure the trip to Kirmsen." Svendsen, according to Jessen, had been "the liveliest, most active, and wildest one of the bunch. He was the life of the party with his jokes and wisecracks, and at Kirmsen he danced as if he had never done another thing in his life. . . . I may be wrong, but there is no doubt about the fact that the scherzo resounds from beginning to end with the sounds of Kirmsen and its dancing" (64).

Jessen was absolutely right, for Svendsen was indeed working on his first symphony at this time. On September 20 he wrote to his father, "Composition is going well: for Dr. Hauptmann I'm writing fugues, and for [Professor] Reinecke I have started a symphony that I think is going to be good."

In the same letter he mentioned that the big Leipzig trade fair was in full swing and that "during the four weeks that the fair lasts a lot of different music ensembles have the privilege of torturing people's ears." They made a "dreadful racket that I can't avoid hearing." Bilse's orchestra concerts were, however, "a great compensation for these monstrosities—so great that one could almost wish that the fair (with its many unpleasantries) would last forever, for of course when it is over Bilse also leaves."

At the conservatory, he wrote, the violin playing was going badly, but "[Professor] David is treating me with the greatest kindness. Very often he lets me conduct rehearsals of the conservatory orchestra in his place. That's an honor that during the time I have been here has not been given to any other student."

In November of 1865 Svendsen had an exciting visit from home. Edvard Grieg was back in his old haunts. He was enroute to Italy, having said goodbye in Berlin to Rikard Nordraak, who lay on his deathbed. Grieg was in Leipzig to perform his *Violin Sonata in F Major*, and Svendsen now met him for the first time. This meeting became the beginning of a lifelong warm friendship between two artists who by nature and musical bent were opposites, but who perhaps for that very reason would complement each other in such an effective way.

They quickly discovered that they were on the same wave-length; it was as if a magnetic field had sprung up between them. Svendsen was ecstatic about the new music that had caught his fancy, especially Berlioz's works, and he did his best to get Grieg interested in the French master of instrumentation.

Grieg was at this time at the peak of his enthusiasm for the national element, and he spoke at length about Ole Bull's and Rikard Nordraak's visions of an independent Norwegian music and about how he himself, in his first larger works—the *Humoresques*, the *Piano Sonata in E Minor*, and the *Violin Sonata in F Major*—had tried to integrate folk-music elements in accordance with the musical views so vigorously defended by Bull and Nordraak. Svendsen, with fresh impulses from his own recent encounter with the virtuoso violinist—"the Norwegian Norseman from Norway" as Bull proudly called himself—could report to Grieg that he, too, was working with material with a national tinge in his new string octet. When they parted on November 12 he wrote a few measures from the first movement of the octet in Grieg's autograph book "as a friendly reminder" of the visit.

At this time Svendsen put the finishing touches on his second opus, *Two Songs for Male Chorus*. These were settings of texts by King Carl XV, who dabbled in poetry. This work was published in spring of 1866, presumably with financial support from Sweden, by "Componistens Förlag" ["The Composer's Press"] on consignment to Breitkopf & Härtel in Leipzig. The title page has the following grandiose dedication (in Swedish): "Poems by C★★★ composed for men's voices and His Majesty Carl XV, King of Sweden and Norway, dedicated with deepest gratitude and humble respect." The score was sent to the royal palace. It soon elicited a letter of thanks, dated Stockholm, April 6, 1866, and signed by the queen's secretary, court councilor Dr. Schüssler, whom Svendsen had gotten to know in Lübeck.

The two songs for male chorus contrast sharply and make a nice pair.

The first, *Till Sverige* (*To Sweden*), in a pompous male-chorus style, is developed almost like a cantata, with several passages for solo quartet. A lively tempo and dotted rhythms give the song a pithy character. In *Aftonröster* (*Evening Voices*) an idyllic nature lyricism is combined with a dream-like, elegiac mood. Both songs reveal Svendsen's skill as a melodist and document a significant harmonic inventiveness in both daring chromaticism and colorful modulations.

That Svendsen set these poems and also got them published may have nourished the strange rumor that was spread about Leipzig to the effect that the young man from Scandinavia was of royal blood, indeed, an illegitimate son of the Swedish king. This was one of the many priceless anecdotes from his student days that Svendsen could share with friends at parties in later years. He also reported that the presumption of his royal birth was further strengthened during the cholera epidemic in Leipzig when the authorities secured for him the use of a stately residence where he could safely avoid infection.

One result of the rumor that Svendsen was of royal blood was that he gained entry to the city's leading social circles. Also among those who knew full well that this young man from Norway was not a real prince, however, Svendsen was a welcome guest. For two summers, for example, he was invited to live at the summer home of the Norwegian-Swedish consul, Dr. Friedrich Gustav Schulz. This was in the town of Connewitz, where wealthy residents of Leipzig often spent their vacations. Consul Schulz supported Svendsen in Leipzig in many of the same ways that Consul Leche had done in Lübeck.

People's good will sometimes also produced hard cash, which was fortunate for someone like Svendsen, who was perpetually short of money. One such case is reported in a letter to his father dated January 11, 1866. The preceding December the first movement of his octet had been played at the conservatory and had been well received by both his fellow students and his teachers. Svendsen wrote:

> A rich man was present, and the next day I received from him a very gracious letter in which he expressed his satisfaction with my composition and moreover asked that I not refuse the enclosed 50 *thalers* [which he desired me to use] for a vacation trip during the Christmas holiday. The same day I received a friendly letter from the consul in Lübeck inviting me to spend the holiday with him. The letter was signed by the whole family. What a day. So I have spent Christmas very happily in Lübeck.

Svendsen returned from Lübeck by way of Berlin. There he met the Norwegian pianist Edmund Neupert, with whom he had had some spirited correspondence.

Back in Leipzig, working in his simple lodging at Universität-Straße 11, Svendsen completed his first major work, the *String Octet*.

THE STRING OCTET

Svendsen's decisive breakthrough as a composer occurred in spring of 1866. The *String Octet*, op. 3, was completed on February 20, 1866, and was played for the first time at a private conservatory concert a few days later.

Strangely enough, he had composed this work completely on his own, without help of any kind from his composition teacher, Professor Reinecke. This is clear from something he wrote to Grieg many years later (in a letter dated December 15, 1878): "The *Octet* was written, rehearsed and performed before Reinecke got to see a single note . . ."

At the end of April he again saw Grieg, who had come from Italy on his way to Berlin to visit Nordraak's grave. In his diary Grieg mentions that they had dinner together on April 29. Svendsen was able at that time to show him his new compositions: the *Octet* and the first movement of the *Symphony No. 1* in D Major. Grieg presumably was present at one of the many rehearsals of the *Octet*, which was to be performed at the conservatory's public graduation concert at the Gewandhaus on May 9. The first movement of the *Symphony* was also to be performed at this concert.

The premiere of the *Octet* was an overwhelming triumph. Johan wrote to his father on May 24:

> I was awarded the conservatory's first prize. A few days before this happened, I was unanimously elected president of the Conservatory Society. The *Octet* . . . has now been publicly performed; under my own leadership, of course. When I tell you that we had a total of 14 rehearsals for this performance, you can well imagine that the performance was exemplary in every respect. Each movement was rewarded with generous applause; indeed, the second movement (Scherzo) had to be repeated twice, and after the conclusion of the Finale I had to make four curtain calls. The *Symphony* movement was equally successful; thus I have publicly proven that I am not altogether unworthy of the honor bestowed on me in the awarding of the prize. Two days after this very fortunate experience as a composer and conductor I got a letter from Breitkopf & Härtel offering to publish the *Octet*. Naturally I accepted this offer.

For a conservatory student to receive such an offer from the famous Leipzig publisher was nothing less than sensational. The work was in need of some further polishing, however, and it was not until September 11 that Svendsen was able to deliver a fair copy of the manuscript to the publisher. In a later interview he told of an amusing episode in connection with the piece:

> One day I came up to the head of the big publishing house Breitkopf & Härtel. He was up to his ears in—well, to put it bluntly, a piece of awful musical trash. I said something to that effect, and do you know what he answered? "It's because of this trash that once in awhile we can publish a little octet by, for example, somebody like you!" (133)

The *Octet*, which was dedicated to Queen Louise "in deepest gratitude and veneration," received laudatory reviews in the Leipzig press. Yuri von Arnold wrote in the May 12 issue of *Leipziger Tageblatt* of "the rich imagination that in the *Octet* is developed into a highly interesting tone painting with the help of a national (Norwegian) coloration." He found "a hint of genius" and asserted that Svendsen "had started his artistic career on a level that many others do not even reach at the end of their lifework." *Neue Zeitschrift für Musik* (May 13) underscored the work's richness of musical ideas and its "genuine French *esprit* and Romantic, national color." The critics in *Deutsche Allgemeine Zeitung* and *Dresdner Telegraph*, exponents of broadmindedness who sought to further Schumann's ideas of openness toward new music, were equally enthusiastic.

But there were also a few "philistines" among the reviewers, soreheads who reacted grouchily to everything new and unfamiliar. No one, to be sure, could deny Svendsen his indisputable skill as a composer, but some raised a warning finger against what they regarded as unsightly growths on the solid classical stem. The conservative *Leipziger Allgemeine Musikalische Zeitung* wrote on May 16 that the octet revealed a composer who had launched out upon "questionable paths in a quest for superficially brilliant effects. The young man would undoubtedly do well to compose works in which a search for effects is absolutely out of the question—for example, string quartets."

After the octet was published, the same journal (on October 30, 1867) printed a detailed analysis—six pages long and with eleven music examples—written by the editor, Selmar Bagge. The general tone of this review was more positive than that of the earlier one but it, too, was fairly critical. Some parts of the work seemed to Bagge to be aimless, with "excessive harmonic artificialities and confusion." The changes of key were altogether too abrupt and the harmonic turns "unclear, risky and ugly."

Svendsen's youthful composition is a milestone in Nordic chamber music. Every single movement is bursting with captivating material, and elements with a national tinge are integrated into this exciting sound world in a natural way. Svendsen employed polyphony to a much greater extent than Grieg ever did, but he did so with such elegance that his expertise never comes across as mere technical competence. The eight instruments are handled with striking imagination. A more vibrant piece of chamber music has perhaps never been written by a Norwegian composer.

What sources of inspiration did Svendsen have for a work for eight independent instruments (four violins, two violas and two cellos)? Of the famous composers there were only two who had ventured to create works in this demanding form. Mendelssohn composed his brilliant octet in E-flat major when he was just 16 years old. Niels W. Gade, who clearly was influenced by Mendelssohn's example, was 31 when he wrote his octet in F major. Moreover, it is interesting that the few notable composers who have since written in this genre have all been young: Georges Enescu and Dmitri Shostakovich were each 19 when they wrote their string octets.

Mendelssohn's octet undoubtedly was important to Svendsen, but it was not a direct model for his work. The differences between them are too great for that to have been the case. The most important similarity is in the area of general mood: a light, optimistic, life-affirming undertone is prevalent in both. Mendelssohn, strangely enough, is much freer in his handling of the traditional classical forms, but Svendsen evens things up by displaying a more aggressive harmonic boldness. Both strive for an orchestral sonority. But while the first violin part in Mendelssohn's work incorporates a certain soloistic virtuosity, Svendsen has integrated it more fully into the work as a whole.

The most conspicuous difference results from the folkloristic elements in Svendsen's octet. Svendsen, moreover, employed related motivic-thematic material, derived from the opening theme, in all of the movements, thereby making a deliberate effort to create unity in a manner common among Romantic composers.

The first movement, *Allegro risoluto ben marcato*, is in sonata form and begins with a unison eight-measure theme. It has animated, dotted rhythms and a melodic arch that moves by means of broken triads all the way up to the leading tone before the tension is released in a passage that moves steadily downward in a more or less stepwise manner. Captivating material such as this was to become typical of Svendsen as a melodist:

Example 2   *String Octet,* op. 3, first movement

This theme contains motivic seeds that are employed in a new main theme. The same motivic seeds also determine the character of the subsidiary themes, both of which begin in E minor, and the epilogue theme, which is a version in the major mode of the first subsidiary theme. The harmonic foundation for the initial, boldly modulating subsidiary theme contains a number of smooth chromatic progressions, a characteristic feature of Svendsen's harmony:

Example 3   *String Octet,* op. 3, first movement

Of the melodic material of this movement, it is the second subsidiary theme that, owing to its Aeolian coloration, has the most distinctively Norwegian sound. Svendsen clearly was familiar with Lindeman's transcriptions of Norwegian folk-dance music (*slåtter*), but he did not merely imitate those models. Rather, the folk-music material was filtered through his own artistic faculty.

In the tightly knit development section all of the themes are handled with great cleverness. Effortlessly and playfully the composer moves as far away from the home key as it is possible to go—to E-flat major—and just as nimbly he returns to the starting point.

The recapitulation, which is markedly different from the exposition, contains several sections that are developmental in character. In this respect Svendsen was different from Grieg, who nearly always wrote recapitulations that were more or less identical to the exposition. The expansive coda is characterized by colorful, abrupt turns of key, and the whole movement is brought to a grandiose conclusion in a unison restatement of the opening motive in augmentation.

In the second movement, *Allegro scherzoso* (E major), Svendsen has fun with some amusing musical materials as the music swirls around in a mood of infectious joy. In this movement he also gives free reign to his newly awakened enthusiasm for Norwegianness. The opening theme with its bouncy triplet figures reminds one in many ways of a genuine Norwegian folk dance (*springar*). The second theme also has something of a national coloring. The melodic seed consists of the so-called "Grieg formula"—a descending minor second followed by a major third—and the continuation is surprisingly similar to the theme later used by Grieg as the subsidiary theme in the first movement of his string quartet in G minor (1877–78):

Example 4   Johan Svendsen, *String Octet*, op. 3, second movement

Example 5   Edvard Grieg, *String Quartet*, op. 27, first movement

Because of its development-like sections, the scherzo is similar in many ways to a sonata movement. It is more like a rondo, however. The composer's effervescent inventiveness expresses itself in varied rhythms and refined instrumental effects including a sophisticated use of pizzicato.

The third movement, *Andante sostenuto* (C major), which is characterized by wide melodic phrases, is also permeated by inspiration. The opening section is marked by a Schubertian use of suspensions, but the noble melodic content soon comes to the fore with a G-major theme that is clearly related to the second theme of the scherzo. The movement is cast in a freely handled sonata form in which the middle section—after 18 measures that provide barely a hint of development—introduces a completely new theme which, however, does not alter the movement's basic character. The biggest contrast occurs in the recapitulation, where Svendsen amuses himself by suddenly restating in a rapid tempo a couple of short thematic snippets from the principal theme of the second movement.

The Finale has a slow introduction, *Moderato*, which anticipates the principal theme in the fast part, *Allegro assai con fuoco*. The character is for the most part similar to that of the first movement, with which it has a certain rhythmic and melodic similarity. Both the principal and the subsidiary themes have typical dotted notes and melodic lines in broken chords. The structure, which follows the classical pattern of sonata form, is terse and concise. The development section contains a little canon. Toward the end of this section there is a short quotation from the beginning of the third movement. The *più mosso* with which the coda concludes begins triumphantly with the first three measures of the principal theme of the first movement—as if the composer wanted here, too, to emphasize the unity of the work.

With his *con amore*-like string octet, Svendsen had achieved a level of mature mastery and had found a style that would open the way to major international triumphs.

THE LAST YEAR IN LEIPZIG

Johan had planned a trip to Norway during the summer of 1866 to visit his family, but in a letter to his father dated June 28 he wrote that unfortunately he would not be able to come. He could perhaps have scraped up enough money for a one-way ticket, he wrote, but that was all. And then the worst might happen, "the possibility of being compelled to remain in Norway . . . because I lack the means to return to Germany." He continued:

You presumably will think that I have become absolutely infatuated with Germany since I regard it as something bad to remain in Norway. Don't you think that it is absolutely necessary for a composer to get his works published and paid for and performed? And do you think this can happen in Norway? That, of course, is the reason why all of the capable composers who live in Norway produce so little, and why what they do produce nearly always consists of small—not to say insignificant—works. The fault consists first and foremost in the fact that there is no proper musical organization capable of giving a creditable performance of larger works. From this it follows that there is a lack of public interest; for one can hardly blame the public for not taking an interest in things it knows nothing about, and the only way one could acquaint them with good music is public performances—which, as you yourself know, is an impossibility.

Under such circumstances I, like so many others, would soon lose all desire to continue my efforts as a composer and little by little degenerate into a nonentity. This is more or less how I see things, and it is the reason why my homeland unfortunately is not the place where I want to stay unless the conditions up there have changed considerably.

Svendsen didn't get to Norway on this occasion, but neither did he spend the whole summer sitting and moping in his humble room at Universität-Straße 11. He received a welcome invitation from Consul Schulz to stay with him at his summer home in Connewitz during June and July. Here he was able to work at a leisurely pace as he prepared the string octet for publication. He also made arrangements for symphony orchestra of Norwegian composer Johannes Steenberg's well-known *Minuet* and Schumann's large piano composition *Faschingsschwank aus Wien*, op. 26.

On March 8 he had sent to the Norwegian National Assembly (Stortinget) a lengthy application for "a grant of 300 *spesiedalers* from the funds available to support foreign travel by scientists and artists—so that I may remain abroad for about two more years to study classical music and composition." Three years earlier he had been refused when he sought the same grant, but now he could support his request with excellent recommendations from such teachers as David, Hauptmann and Reinecke. Reinecke wrote of his significant talent as a composer and stated that he had made "eminent progress" in his studies. He stated further that Svendsen's talent for conducting was "most extraordinary."

The committee responsible for distributing the available funds consisted of three people who had also been on the committee on the previous occasion—Carl Arnold, Halfdan Kjerulf, and O. P. Monrad—plus Ludvig M. Lindeman. On May 19 the committee unanimously recommended Svendsen, cellist Hans Nielsen, and pianist Erika Lie for one-year grants of 300 *spesiedalers* each, and on July 28 the National Assembly concurred.

That autumn, however, Svendsen's money problems became steadily more acute when bureaucratic inertia led to a delay in sending the first installment of his grant. He wrote despairingly to his father on October 1: "I haven't had a shilling for several months, and without the help of the local Norwegian consul I really don't know what I would have done. . . . The money that I have used for music, books, paper, clothes, theater tickets, concerts etc. I earned during the first part of the summer giving lessons, but this source has dried up for the moment because all my pupils have fled to escape the cholera, which is absolutely pandemic here. About 50 or 60 people are dying each day." On October 17 he wrote: "Forgive me for not paying the postage, but I haven't got a penny. Dear, good father, please do what you can for your J. Svendsen."

Meanwhile, in Oslo his friend Fredrik Ursin had collected the sum of forty *spesiedalers* to enable Johan to pay off a debt he had run up in Norway the year before. Johan asked his father to arrange for this money to be sent to him as soon as possible, for "since my creditors are all people in comfortable circumstances whereas I, on the other hand, am in dire need of this money, I don't think I'll be committing a sin by making them wait a while longer." He had definite plans for the use of the big grant: "Since I wanted to save as much as possible and not touch the grant until everything else was used up, so that I might be able to go to Paris or Rome next year, you can understand how important it is to me to get the 40 *spesiedalers* Ursin has for me." Ursin, however, was not willing to go along with Svendsen's proposal, and the grant money did not reach Leipzig until November 29.

Financial worries did not put a damper on Svendsen's enthusiasm for creative work during this autumn, however. On October 19 he completed an orchestral version of Liszt's *Hungarian Rhapsody No. 2.* Two days after the premiere of this work at Svendsen's introductory concert in Oslo on October 12, 1867, Grieg reviewed it very positively in *Aftenbladet*:

> The concert concluded with a flourish; Liszt would have been very happy to hear his *Hungarian Rhapsody* handled so brilliantly. Here Svendsen has not been sparing in his use of the resources, and rightly so; piccolos and the big drum constitute the outer limits, and between these Svendsen has with

the most brilliant skill created something so fantastic that even a Berlioz could not have done it better.

More importantly, however, he completed the large composition that he had been working on for a year and a half: the *Symphony No. 1* in D major, op. 4. This milestone was reached in December, 1866, and he set to work immediately to prepare a fair copy, presumably with a view to publication. The title page of this score is dated January 1867.

Svendsen participated enthusiastically in the concert life of Leipzig during this winter and spring. On April 9, 1867, he wrote to his father that in addition to all the recitals at the conservatory there had been more than 40 public concerts that he "had to devour this winter. Fortunately I have a good digestive apparatus, so I have stomached this fare very well." Among the artists he heard were the violinists Leopold Auer, Joseph Joachim, and August Wilhelmy as well as the pianists Clara Schumann and Karl Tausig, "whose equal would be difficult to find."

On April 10 he sent a report to the Ministry concerning his use of the grant, mentioning among other things that some of his works had been performed in the Gewandhaus: "The unanimous applause that I received from the public as well as the local musical authorities justifies my belief that I have not labored in vain and has encouraged me to continue forward with undaunted steps along the path so happily begun."

Svendsen's studies at the conservatory were concluded on May 20, 1867, and he received a laudatory final report in which all of his teachers witnessed to his talent. David wrote that he had developed considerable confidence and breadth as a conductor. Reinecke mentioned that he had often been absent during the last months, but other than that had always been very industrious and possessed extraordinary talent for composition. Hauptmann observed that the young man from Norway was not particularly punctual, but he had been extremely diligent. Richter noted that although he had not spent much time on his theoretical studies, his work had always exhibited competence and talent.

Heinrich Conrad Schleinitz, Director of the conservatory, wrote in his concluding remarks that in spring 1866 Svendsen had received the conservatory's first prize "as one of the institution's most outstanding and deserving students." He also emphasized that "his moral behavior has always and in every way been exemplary."

The Director could not have known that just a month earlier the unmarried conservatory student had secretly become the father of a child, Johann Richard, who was born on 'March 19. The mother, Johanne Henriette Rudolph, who was then 19 years old, had been a maid in the home where Svendsen had his lodging. In the situation in which they found themselves, neither of the young parents could undertake the raising of a child. Fortunately, Johanne Henriette had a childless brother and sister-in-law who were willing to take the child, so the boy grew up on their farm in Schladebach.

This intermezzo in Svendsen's life was kept a strict secret, not least from his family in Oslo. However, later in life he did not seek to evade his responsibility: even though he was under no legal obligation to do so, he regularly sent money to his son and assisted him in getting training as a tanner. Such a problem was not an easy one for a composer with scant resources to deal with, but for Svendsen it was a matter of honor and he felt obliged to do what was right.

Johann Richard was given his mother's family name. After completing his training as a tanner he worked for some time in Paris and London, then married and settled down in Leipzig. In 1899 he had a daughter, Martha Margrethe. In an undated letter to her half-aunt Sigrid, Johan Svendsen's daughter in Copenhagen, Martha Margrethe has given a detailed account of the circumstances of their family in Germany. She also visited Sigrid in Copenhagen; Sigrid served as a source for Olav Gurvin, who mentions in his notes that Johann Richard once visited his father in Copenhagen during Svendsen's tenure there. The son died in Leipzig in 1933. Martha Margrethe (whose married name was Hardtmann) had a daughter Ellen (married name Gläser) in 1927. Ellen has two daughters, Gabriela (b. 1950) and Kirsten (b. 1952), who are, therefore, Svendsen's great-great-granddaughters.

His feelings of honor were not so great, however, as to prevent Svendsen, immediately after the birth of Johann Richard, from ingratiating himself with another young lady, Ida Böhme, whom he had met in Weimar the previous summer and with whom he had exchanged letters. Immediately after completing his conservatory studies he took another trip to Weimar to visit her. He was very enamored of her, as is evident from a letter to his sister Albertine written January 1, 1868:

> In one of your letters you asked me to get you a picture of a certain lady in Weimar. I am very pleased at this time to be able to fulfill your request.

She was very happy about the interest you showed in her by requesting her picture and asked me to greet you many times.

You will hardly get an accurate idea of her appearance from the enclosed photograph, as it is not a very good picture, and besides, she has many beautiful qualities that can't really be photographed. Since I am now writing about her, I must not fail to disabuse you of a mistaken idea that you have as to the relationship between her and me. She is still only my girl friend, albeit a very special friend. For example, we address each other as "du" rather than "Sie"—indeed, our intimacy is such that we keep few secrets from each other, but we are not engaged.

If I were to get a job that would put me in a position to offer a woman a carefree and comfortable existence, I would consider it a singular joy to be able to see her as the queen presiding over my house. Until this is possible, I consider it my duty not to obligate her, although I think that she will not under any circumstances have anyone else—at least she has already turned down several eligible suitors.

The two young people stayed in contact with each other until the spring of 1868, but after a letter from Ida dated April 17 she disappeared without comment from the Svendsenian saga.

In the midst of his paternity and romantic problems, Johan also celebrated a new artistic triumph. On May 17, 1867—Norway's Constitution Day—his latest work, String Quintet, op. 5, was premiered at the first concluding graduation concert at the Gewandhaus. Twelve days later, at the second such concert, he conducted the last three movements of his first major orchestral work: the Symphony No. 1 in D major, op. 4.

THE FIRST SYMPHONY

The D-major symphony, which Svendsen completed in December 1866, was not a work that he dashed off in a hurry. He had gotten it under way in the summer of 1865 and continued working on it at the same time that he was writing the octet. Aimar Grønvold reports that in February 1866, when Svendsen showed Reinecke the completed string octet, his composition teacher was almost flabbergasted:

"Next time I suppose you'll bring a symphony, Mr. Svendsen," he added half ironically.

Ah, he of course did not know that it had already been written! A

few days later Svendsen knocked on the professor's door and walked
in with a big manuscript under his arm.

"What have you there?"

"You wanted a symphony, sir. Here it is" (51:86).

No doubt this story is more amusing than true, for at this point in time only
the first movement was complete. But Reinecke must have liked what he
saw, for this movement as well as the string octet were placed on the program for the conservatory's public graduation concert at the Gewandhaus
on May 9, 1866.

Dresdner Telegraph wrote on May 14: "The symphonic movement, in
which both the clear form and the wealth of imaginative ideas created the
liveliest interest, surprised us even more than the octet. Virtually nobody
can have any doubt about Johan Svendsen's bright future . . . , not least because he also seems to be a born conductor."

The reviewer in *Leipziger Nachrichten* (May 13) was surprised by the
charming formative power, the richness of the instrumentation, and the
confidence of the detail: "When one looks at the development of our most
accomplished masters and compares it with that of Johan Svendsen, we are
convinced that Svendsen will reach the great heights and be counted among
those who will bring honor to our time."

The music journal *Signale für die musikalische Welt* (May 17) characterized Svendsen as "a most talented and promising composer." *Neue Zeitschrift
für Musik* (May 18) was somewhat more guarded: the reviewer stated that
the symphonic movement seemed to be on the one hand aphoristic and disjointed, on the other hand nimbly and brilliantly orchestrated, albeit with
long and excessively loud parts in the trumpets. The national tinge was as-
sessed positively: "Svendsen's style can, indeed, often be similar to that of
Mendelssohn and Gade, occasionally also to that of Beethoven or Wagner,
but it contains a refreshing element that is distinctively Norwegian. The
composer often employs this with seductive coquetry and ardor, and he also
displayed his skill as a conductor in a similar manner by his free and inspiring
leadership of the orchestra."

These reviews provided a strong incentive for Svendsen to get to work
on the remaining three movements of the symphony. He felt, however, that
this first symphonic work needed time to ripen, and he also felt a need to
polish his skills as an orchestrator. The latter was probably one of the reasons
why he spent the summer and autumn of 1866 orchestrating some large piano works by Schumann and Liszt.

It is not known what role Professor Reinecke played in the final development of the symphony, but everything would seem to indicate that Svendsen worked very freely and independently—a fact that is also corroborated by the examination papers.

Why, then, was the entire D-major symphony not premiered at Svendsen's graduation concert at the Gewandhaus on May 29, 1867? One possible explanation is that since the first movement had already been played the year before, the conservatory faculty chose on this occasion to be content with just the remaining three movements. It is also possible, however, that Svendsen himself wanted to reserve the premiere of the work as a whole for his home city, where he had plans to give an introductory concert that autumn.

The symphony's first movement, *Molto allegro*, is a genuine Svendsenian sonata movement with close ties to the Vienna Classicists' handling of form. The opening, as Øivind Eckhoff aptly describes it, "throws us right into the whirling allegro tempo and the bouncy rhythm of the principal theme with no hesitation or preparations of any kind." Eckhoff continues: "Unabashed joy and youthful energy united with authority and confidence exude from this principal theme" (28:174):

Example 6   *Symphony no. 1*, op. 4, first movement

The rhythmic pithiness and simple construction of this theme remind one of the opening theme of the string octet, but it strikes one as being more breathless. Note that measures 4 and 8 are exact repetitions of measures 3 and 7 respectively, as if the composer is determined to force the theme into a strict four-measure pattern. This tenacious insistence on four-measure symmetry dominates much of the movement.

The thematic material may be simple, but Svendsen makes up for it in the area of harmony. In the continuation of the theme he moves rapidly through an intense passage in *ff* into G-sharp minor. By way of several measures of vague tonality he then comes to rest on a C-major chord. A peaceful transitional section, in which the subsidiary theme is suggested in the clarinet and oboe, leads to a new tranquil section; thematic material from this is later employed in the development. A modulation to A major ends with the solo horn's short but very expressive subsidiary theme, which positively steals in, supported by the strings. Its descending, "sobbing" melody has a character as of resignation and stands in sharp contrast to the energetic principal theme.

The development section is bursting with technical compositional subtleties, but the ingenuity never becomes obtrusive. The music has a natural flow that doesn't stop. What is especially exciting is that in the midst of all the tumults Svendsen, in a very smooth way, works in a contrasting section of no less than 56 measures. This section, which is related motivically to the subsidiary theme, both begins and ends in the remote key of D-flat major. One would think that such a long cantilena at the end of the development would come across as an alien element in the otherwise so "classical" formal pattern, but it doesn't. It functions more as a welcome release of tension, thus preparing the way for the ensuing strong intensification just before the recapitulation.

The recapitulation, which is constructed along traditional lines, ends unconventionally in *ppp*. The coda, which makes dazzling use of motives derived from the principal theme and is brilliantly orchestrated as well, further enhances the happy, light, festive mood of the movement.

After this robust first movement it is obvious that Svendsen felt a strong need in the second movement, *Andante*, to calm the music down. The result was one of the most beautiful evidences of his ability to create long, substantial melodic arches. He has molded the symmetrical pattern into a freer type of melody in which such features as syncopation and suspensions play a role in determining the character of the music. Whereas in earlier works— in the string quartet, for example—he had "smiled in a minor key," it is as if the tears are not so far away in this somewhat melancholy movement in A major.

Once again he finds sonata form to be suitable for his purposes, but in this case he gives it a Romantic stamp. There is a clear demarcation between the several sections, with a hint of ternary form, but the music nonetheless glides forward in an unbroken flow. In the exposition the themes really contrast only in tonality, not in character, and in the development the dramatic explosions that one expects to find there are for all practical purposes nonexistent. What actually creates excitement in the second movement is a richly faceted, strongly chromatic harmony and the dynamic climaxes that in this movement are reserved for the varied recapitulation.

In the third movement, *Allegretto scherzando* (G major), Svendsen reaches an early pinnacle as a symphonist. The music is built around two tuneful themes, both of which are somewhat folk-like in character. In the case of the first theme one wonders if Svendsen might not have been thinking of Haydn's folkishness, for it is quite reminiscent of the principal theme in the first movement of the Viennese master's *Symphony No. 88* in G major. In these measures Svendsen also seems to anticipate in a remarkable way—melodically, harmonically, and even with respect to instrumentation—the beginning of the overture in Tchaikovsky's *Nutcracker* ballet music from 1892.

The second theme is introduced already in measure 12, but somewhat surprisingly in B minor, without modulation. Here the Norwegian flavor is clearly evident, with *halling* rhythms so authentic that one could think the music had come right out of a genuine folk dance. These two themes continue to appear and reappear in new forms and exciting combinations. The conservatory student excels in sophisticated compositional tricks, but the whole thing nonetheless comes across as a lighthearted game. It is a bit like hearing a Mendelssohn scherzo clothed in a Norwegian costume!

The playfulness is further strengthened by an instrumentation that has the same shining, transparent clarity as that of Berlioz at his best. Svendsen frolics between strings and winds, often employing solo instruments in a high register, and achieves stunning effects.

The structure of the movement is nontraditional. Viewed from the outside it is an eight-part, very free rondo with two *ritornellos*, but it also reveals clear elements of sonata form both in its extensive use of advanced development techniques and in its varied recapitulation.

The composer's odyssey into the realms of remote keys is one of the most astonishing aspects of this scherzo. Øivind Eckhoff has clearly pinpointed the audacity of Svendsen's achievement: "It is unlikely that in pure instrumental music written before 1870 one could find its equal in this area: a movement that immediately after the presentation of the principal theme abandons the home key, and does not return to it—indeed, doesn't so much as hint at it—until three-fourths of the movement is over!" (28:174).

While Svendsen wanted to express himself in freer forms in the inner movements of the symphony, he returned to tradition in the *finale*, marked *Maestoso. Allegro assai con fuoco.* Here he again emphasized his foundation in the formal structures of classicism as he fashioned a concise, orderly movement in sonata form in which he engages in no experiments of any kind. Melodically and harmonically, however, he is a full-blooded Romanticist.

The slow, majestic introduction has a somewhat pensive mood by virtue of its fluctuation between major and minor keys. The opening theme returns as a subsidiary theme in the *Allegro*—a procedure not unlike that used by Grieg in the first movement of his string quartet in G minor. As a matter of fact, the principal theme of the *Allegro*, which is also anticipated in the introduction, is somewhat Griegian in character in that it incorporates chains of the so-called "Grieg formula."

The development section, which opens with the principal theme in augmentation, is very concentrated and demonstrates the composer's mastery of the technique of metamorphosis as he presents a series of transformations of the motivic material. In the middle of all this there is a long passage that echoes something of the atmosphere of Mendelssohn's *Hebrides* overture.

One also notes the motivic-thematic connection between the principal themes in the first and last movements, in line with the idea of uniting the movements of a symphonic work in such a way as to create a cyclic whole.

How does the style of this work compare to Wagner's music? In melody, rhythm, and form he stands far removed from the German music dramatist. Many of Svendsen's contemporaries, however—including Grieg—pointed out that his harmony showed a certain influence from Wagner, not least in some chromatic passages. This is correct as far as it goes. It should be added, however, that at this point in time Svendsen was familiar only with the early Wagner operas; he had never heard *Tristan and Isolde* or the *Ring* series, where the Wagnerian chromaticism comes most sharply to the fore. It is understandable that Svendsen, in his admiration for Wagner, was not able to free himself totally from the magic spell of his music. Nonetheless, despite this deep admiration he succeeded, even during his conservatory period, in putting a pronounced personal stamp on his often bold harmonies through such things as audacious, abrupt turns to remote keys.

The freshness that permeates the D-major symphony was very appealing to Svendsen's contemporaries. Thus the symphony did much more than the octet to lay the foundation for Svendsen's international renown.

THE STRING QUINTET

Svendsen's second composition marking the conclusion of his studies in Leipzig was the *String Quintet* in C major, op. 5, which was premiered at the Gewandhaus on May 17, 1867, at the conservatory's first public graduation concert offered that spring. Once again the composer received favorable reviews in the local press.

Neue Zeitschrift für Musik stated (May 31), "Mr. Svendsen manifests an unmistakable musical talent and great artistic seriousness." Yuri von Arnold wrote in *Leipziger Tageblatt* (May 20) that one might indeed have desired a bit of "polishing" of technical aspects here and there, but nonetheless the quintet in its present form inexorably gripped the hearer "deep in the soul, and that is the best proof of the young composer's singular and thoroughly original talent."

The string quintet was performed a number of times during the ensuing years. As late as 1911 the Danish composer Fini Henriques wrote enthusiastically, "The quintet has just one defect: that it is not a quartet; then all of the quartet ensembles in the world would vie to spread its fame. For me it is the epitome of what constitutes chamber music. Its simple, lucid form and thematic conciseness make it an aristocrat among the long-winded but insubstantial plebeian compositions of our day" (60:69).

Since Svendsen's death, however, the quintet has been almost totally forgotten. This is due primarily to the fact that in our view the composer failed to ride further on the wave of inspiration that had carried him forward in his first four opuses. The quintet certainly is ably written for the five instruments (two violins, two violas and cello), the musical handiwork is flawless, and the musical style is in many ways typical of the composer. There are also a few distinctively Norwegian elements, but for the first time in Svendsen's music they do not seem to be organically integrated; they are more like spices added to a movement that in other respects is continental in character.

The principal criticism of the quintet lies, nonetheless, in another area: it lacks to some extent the melodic appeal and substance that can make a work live. It has something of the character of an academic exercise, without the spark of brilliance that was so evident in the octet and the symphony.

The quintet has just three movements, which is unusual for a work of this kind. The outer movements are in sonata form, the second movement is a theme with variations—the only such movement in a cyclic work by Svendsen.

The first movement begins with a short, slow introduction, *Andante*, in which the principal theme of the ensuing *Allegro* is foreshadowed. Svendsen

had used a similar procedure in the last movement of the D-major symphony. The themes can hardly be said to be especially memorable. The subsidiary theme is perhaps even less distinctive than the principal theme,
despite the fact that toward the end Svendsen introduces something of a
Norwegian flavor with some spirited triplet passages.

In the second movement, *Moderato quasi Andantino*, we get a theme
consisting of eight + eight measures which is then presented in seven contrasting variations. The original theme is then restated in a coda, with which
the movement concludes. This expansive movement abounds in pleasing
sonorities, but one's interest tends to wane from time to time.

The finale, *Allegro*, is unquestionably the quintet's best movement. The
jocular, humorous principal theme, which is first presented by the second
violin, contrasts sharply with the blander thematic material of the second
movement. As the movement progresses this theme sparkles in a series of interesting turns that carry us all the way to the coda. Here, so briefly as almost
to escape notice, there is a quotation from the principal theme of the first
movement. It is not enough to create an impression of cyclic unity.

The string quintet was published by E. W. Fritzsch in Leipzig in 1868
and is dedicated to court councilor Dr. Schüssler, who for several years had
been the intermediary between Svendsen and the Swedish-Norwegian
royal family.

3

A PERIOD OF MATURATION

1867–72

THE DOORS OF the conservatory closed behind Johan Svendsen in the spring of 1867. The time had come for him to proceed on his own and begin his lifework as a professional musician. He had received the best training available for a young artist at that time, so he was well prepared. The ensuing five years—until he settled down in Oslo in autumn 1872—became a time of further maturation both musically and personally. It brought experiences of many kinds: interesting trips to such places as Iceland and the United States; marriage to an American-born woman; a short visit to Oslo and a two-year stay in Paris; long visits to various music centers in Germany including Bayreuth, where he became a friend of Richard and Cosima Wagner. Most important of all was the major triumphs he achieved during this period as a composer and conductor.

JOURNEY TO ICELAND

The trip to Norway that Svendsen originally planned for the summer of 1866 finally occurred the following year, and it came about in connection with a longer trip that proved to be something of an adventure. He spent two months visiting Denmark, Scotland, the Faroe Islands, Iceland and England before arriving at last in Oslo.

He had received the final installment of his government grant on May 24, 1867, so his wallet was comfortably filled when he left Leipzig the following week. In a letter to his father written from Reykjavik on June 22, he wrote of the surprising turn of events that led to the trip:

73

> The final exams at the conservatory in Leipzig were nearly finished, and I
> had just begun to toy with the idea of finally taking a trip home. Then
> bookseller Brockhaus got the blessed idea of inviting me to go with him
> on a trip to Iceland. As you can well understand, I didn't hesitate for one
> minute before accepting the invitation.

Heinrich Brockhaus was a prominent Leipzig publisher with six hundred
employees. His main hobby was taking long trips. During two earlier visits
to Norway he had learned to read the Scandinavian languages and was,
among other things, a great fan of Bjørnstjerne Bjørnson's tales of peasant
life. He was also very interested in music and was a shirt-tail relative of
Wagner through his brother, who was married to one of Wagner's sisters.

Both Brockhaus and Svendsen kept detailed diaries during the trip. Six
years later Brockhaus's memoirs were published (17), and his account of the
trip to Iceland comprises 133 pages. Svendsen's diary for the period from
May 31 to August 2, 1867, is also extant and consists of 161 small handwritten pages. The diary, which is preserved in the University Library in Oslo, is
a colorful document that provides a number of fascinating glimpses of the
trip. Though he perhaps was not exactly the world's most accomplished
writer, the young composer nonetheless wielded a nimble pen and did not
forget to season his reports with lively bits of humor and a few sentimental
descriptions of the scenery. His terse accounts are highly consistent with
Brockhaus's extremely detailed and much more effusive descriptions.

Traveling north from Leipzig, Svendsen used the opportunity to pay a
visit to old friends in Lübeck, but unfortunately Consul Leche was away at
the time. Brockhaus arrived in Lübeck on June 1, and after a 24-hour voyage on the Swedish steamship *Najaden* they checked in at the Phoenix,
Copenhagen's most luxurious hotel.

They remained in Copenhagen for a week, and on June 5 Svendsen
tried to meet Niels W. Gade, "the lion of Danish music." His first attempt
was not successful, but as a calling card he left a printed copy of his string
octet. This was undeniably a rather daring thing to do, for apart from
Mendelssohn, Gade himself was the only other composer who had ever
written a similar work. Thus Svendsen was venturing right into the "lion's"
den. He wrote about it in his diary:

> Around noon I again went to see Gade, and I not only met him but I was
> received by him and treated in such a gracious manner that I could hardly
> bring myself to leave him. After a conversation that lasted about two

Svendsen in his rain gear during the trip to Iceland. (Det kgl. Bibliotek, Copenhagen)

hours I finally tore myself away from this man, whom I have always
regarded so highly as an artist and who has now also made such a positive
impression on my hard-to-please mind as a human being.

Brockhaus knew Gade well from the time when the Danish composer had
lived in Leipzig, and two days after meeting Svendsen, Gade invited the two
travelers to dinner at his summer house in Klampenborg. Svendsen wrote in
his diary, "While Brockhaus took a nap after dinner, Gade and I went for a
walk during which we talked at length about our wonderful art and he expressed his views on the matter, which are as correct as they are beautiful."

A few years earlier, Gade had exchanged views about music with
Edvard Grieg and had seen a few of his compositions. Upon meeting a new
talent from the far north, he was undoubtedly surprised that provincial Norway had been able to produce two young composers of such outstanding
promise.

And as luck would have it, on June 8 Svendsen ran into Grieg at Hotel
Phoenix. Grieg, he wrote, "surprised me with his visit. He has come down
here for his wedding." Svendsen was not able to attend the wedding on
June 11, however, because the little steamship *Arcturus* that would take him
and Brockhaus to Iceland was lifting anchor on June 9.

The usually hardy Johan had his problems with the turbulent Skagerrak:

Woke up about 7 A.M. (June 10) and noted to my great fright that the ship
was rocking in a very unsettling manner. Nonetheless, I got up to have
breakfast, but found it necessary to leave the dining room because of seasickness. I dashed up to the deck and vomited terribly and hurried to my
cot and didn't leave that wretched place for the rest of the day.

The weather did not improve, and he stayed in bed most of the next day as
well. By June 12 his zest seemed to have returned:

Several signs that I have already become somewhat adapted to the sea. . . .
This afternoon I took out my violin and, accompanied by the sound of
the waves and the howling wind, have been playing Norwegian and
Swedish national melodies for a very large and grateful audience. Later
we drank champagne.

The following day the boat docked at Grangemouth, Scotland, and that afternoon Svendsen and a young Danish student took the train to Edinburgh,

where they spent the night. Neither of them knew English, but Svendsen made himself understood "by doing pantomimes, which went very well, for in this way we got all of our wishes taken care of."

On June 17 they arrived at Thorshavn in the Faroe Islands: "The sight of these majestic mountain peaks thrusting out of the sea in their Nordic barrenness is indescribable." The very first evening several of the passengers were invited to a party at the home of one of the town's most prominent citizens, a merchant named Hansen. Among the guests was Svendsen, who "gladly played for an appreciative audience."

The next morning Hansen offered to take his guests on a sightseeing trip to the ruins of Kirkabø. Transportation was via an open boat rowed by eight Faroe Islanders. Among the sights, Svendsen reported, was "the cave where our brilliant and valiant King Sverre was born."

During the voyage, Brockhaus and Svendsen became acquainted with three people who were prominent in Iceland's cultural life: Jón Sigurdsson, president of the Icelandic legislature; Vilhjálmur Finsen, an attorney; and Consul Carl Siemsen. When the *Arcturus* reached Reykjavik on May 21, Siemsen graciously invited them to stay in his home.

Svendsen was of course interested in familiarizing himself with Iceland's music and music life, and on June 25 he visited the country's leading organist, Pitur Gudjónsson. At Svendsen's urging, Gudjónsson wrote down three melodies from his homeland which Svendsen preserved in his diary. However, it was not these melodies that he used in 1874 when he arranged *Two Icelandic Melodies* for string orchestra, op. 30. According to a later report (October, 1885) in *Nordisk Musik-Tidende*, in op. 30 he used instead some folk melodies that he himself had transcribed during the trip.

After the visit to Gudjónsson's, Svendsen went to a choir rehearsal at the Latin school. He wrote: "Their singing gave evidence of a good sense of pitch and rhythm, but with respect to enunciation and spirited interpretation it left much to be desired. A young man who was said to be musically gifted led the performance."

If Svendsen had felt that Oslo was a musical wasteland, the conditions in Reykjavik were far worse. But there were some talented people, and it soon became apparent that the 19-year-old choir leader—Sveinbjørn Sveinbjørnsson, a theological student—was one of them. Svendsen became aware of his talent when he talked further with him.

The difficult circumstances under which the fatherless Sveinbjørnsson was living made a deep impression on Svendsen. It is evident from his moving diary entry of June 26 that he found definite similarities with his own situation in his youth:

> Sveinbjørnsson is a 19-year-old with an outward appearance that is both intelligent and attractive. I could tell by his piano playing that he has excellent musical talent. It was difficult to get him to express himself regarding this or that, as his modest reserve was such as to border on cowardliness. The reason for this cowedness in his demeanor no doubt lies in the unfortunate circumstances in which he lives. The poor young man presumably is consumed by longing to get away and study music, which reportedly is the only thing that interests him, but since he is poor he can see no way to do this. How many talented people—yes, even geniuses—go to their graves after a life filled with longing for a goal that they never reach. It must be frightening to feel the ability within oneself and yet, because of outward circumstances, be obliged to give up. I did what I could to be friendly to him and eventually persuaded him to join me in some music-making.

Young Sveinbjørnsson did indeed have considerable talent and was to become Iceland's first renowned composer. It probably was Svendsen's belief in his talent that led to the decision of the Reykjavik authorities to take a chance on him, for the very next year he was given a grant that enabled him to go to Copenhagen to study music. Later he went to Leipzig, where he studied with Svendsen's former composition teacher, Carl Reinecke. For Iceland's millenial celebration in 1874 he wrote the hymn "O Gud vórs lands," which soon thereafter was adopted as the Icelandic national anthem.

On June 20, Svendsen and Brockhaus attended a big party that also included officers from a French warship. Svendsen wrote: "I plied them with Ole Bull's *A Visit to the Seter.* I was greatly amused to see what a powerful impact these melodies had on the Frenchmen."

At Eyrarbakki they visited the Thorgrimsson family, which was deeply interested in music. Svendsen had not brought his violin, but fortunately a Danish amateur violinist was living there—a cooper by the name of Holm—who willingly put his instrument (such as it was) at the visitor's disposal. Svendsen performed several pieces as best he could to the great delight of those present. He felt, in fact, that the violin responded quite well, noting in his diary: "Later I picked up my violin and played for over an hour without feeling the slightest pain in my fingers. If this trip to the north really has had such a beneficial influence on my nervous system, that will be a great gain."

July 1 they were invited by President Sigurdsson to attend the ceremonial opening of the national legislature. Svendsen wrote: "By and large this ceremony made a favorable impression. Everything came off with a kind of dignified peace and order."

The visitors had many opportunities to enjoy the renowned Icelandic hospitality. On July 7 Svendsen confided to his diary: "There doesn't seem to be a lack of champagne any place in Reykjavik, for that is what one is offered everywhere. Also at Gudjónsson's I poured down a considerable quantity of this drink fit for the gods."

And it was to get worse. On July 27 Svendsen wrote an amusing account of how he got himself out of a jam: "We began to drink 'Faroe soda water' (which is what Carl Siemsen called the wonderful champagne), and I soon found myself in a condition that made me wonder whether I dared to present myself to the chief administrative officer." But with the help of a cold rubdown he soon was in shape to go to the appointed place: "Here there was a big party, and I had to be very careful to avoid getting so drunk that I wouldn't be able to stand up when dinner was over. I filled all of my glasses with water, to which I added a couple drops of red wine, and this is what I used for all of the skoaling."

Poor weather delayed a trip eastward until July 10, when they set out with a "caravan" consisting of four people and eleven horses. The four people were Svendsen, Brockhaus, their driver—a man named Olafur—and his helper, Grimur. Their destination the first day was Thingvellir, but since they didn't get started until well into the afternoon, and, Svendsen wrote, "since it is impossible to get Brockhaus to ride fast, we had to be content to go just half of the way." They spent the night in a tent "on a tiny little grassy area that was surrounded on three sides by a flowing brook, which after our modest evening meal lulled us to sleep."

Arriving in Thingvellir the next day after a seven-hour ride, they took lodging in "a little wooden church which the pastor had pointed out to us as a dwelling. We made ourselves as comfortable as possible, and after an excellent meal—thanks to the kindness of the pastor—we went happily to sleep, having decided to remain for a day at this beautiful and interesting place."

The pastor, Simon Bech, had promised to drink a glass of punch with them, but the next day he sent a message saying that he was ill. "Presumably," Svendsen wrote, "he has misgivings about carousing in God's house. We, however, did not refrain from enjoying the drink." But although the pastor would not imbibe with them in the church, he did treat them to boiled trout.

Svendsen took a walk on his own to Lovberget and "enjoyed from that vantage point the beautiful sight of this wonderful valley, which in the marvelous light of the setting sun appears more and more beautiful... I tore myself away from this enchanting sight and wandered back to the church, where Brockhaus was already snoring."

As they continued their journey on horseback over "really dangerous paths through lava and more lava" enroute to Geysir, Brockhaus fell off his horse. Svendsen was on the point of disgracing himself when he saw "the oddly ludicrous expression he had after getting back on his feet—an expression in which fear, irritation, surprise and shame produced a comic effect that almost made me laugh out loud."

Geysir, unfortunately, was not especially cooperative, but on July 17 they finally observed "the long-awaited show . . . , a gusher of water 80 feet high illumined by the morning sun. According to Olafur, the eruption, which lasted for about 10 minutes, was not a particularly big one; indeed, he claimed that he had never seen such a puny one as this one. We were nonetheless mightily impressed with what we saw."

The following day they reached Haukadal, where the farmer's wife demanded nine *riksdaler* for hay for the horses and milk for the travelers. Brockhaus thought this was somewhat excessive, but when he observed that the woman had seventeen children he gladly paid it. Brockhaus and Svendsen were invited into the house, where according to Brockhaus's diary they encountered "the awfullest smell." "From an artistic point of view," Brockhaus observed, "these green huts are exceedingly beautiful, but inside they are really loathsome."

Svendsen recorded in his diary that on July 21 they came to "a farm situated in the middle of this desert; here we stayed overnight. Cleanly people, pretty girls, good food." The following day they reached Krisurvik, where "the sulfur springs make the place a veritable hell."

But a couple of weeks of rugged outdoor life were more than enough: "Despite the fact that our trip had been so interesting and as auspicious as possible in every way, it was nonetheless indescribably pleasant to think that tomorrow we can return to Reykjavik."

Upon returning to Reykjavik, they were invited to have lunch with the governor, but Svendsen became alarmed at his opinions: "He is a very pleasant man, but he has a really astonishing contempt for Iceland and the Icelanders. He is Danish."

The time for them to leave Iceland was approaching. Throughout their journey Svendsen had been apprehensive about what awaited him at home. As early as June 24 he had written: "How will I find my home city and the many colleagues and friends whom I know so well? But let me not dwell on these thoughts, which so easily lead to melancholy misgivings. He only reaches the goal who boldly and bravely moves steadily forward on the pathway that lies before him."

ARTISTIC TRIUMPH IN OSLO

On August 1, 1867, Brockhaus and Svendsen boarded the *Arcturus* along with two Danish merchants and a hundred Icelandic horses. The weather was so bad, however, that for a time they were obliged to remain in port. The last page of Svendsen's diary (dated August 2) has the following entry: "Yesterday's storm has developed into a hurricane, and according to the captain there is little likelihood of getting under way any time soon. This delay makes me very depressed, for if I get to Oslo too late all of my happy plans will come to naught."

Despite the continuing gale, however, they were able to get under way the following day—but they were plagued by stormy weather and seasickness all the way to the Hebrides. They did not reach Liverpool until August 10. Three days later the two travel companions parted company.

Svendsen travelled from Hull to Hamburg on the English steamship *Leopard*. From there he went by train to Copenhagen and then by ship to Norway, arriving in Oslo on August 17.

Nobody was waiting at the pier to welcome him home again. Indeed, it would not have been easy to recognize the sturdy and well-dressed fellow with full beard who strode ashore that day. Svendsen told later of the meeting with his father, whom he met not at home but in the Tivoli Amusement Park. Gulbrand had no idea who this handsome fellow was, and the mischievous Johan jumped at the chance to play a trick on him. He said that he had recently met Johan Svendsen, who had asked him to bring greetings to his father. Gulbrand became very excited and wanted to hear news about his son. As the questions became more and more probing, Johan ended the

ruse, saying "But do you really not recognize your own son?" Thereupon
followed "[the first hug] that the son could remember ever having received
from this stern, imposing fellow whose joy and pride in the young man who
stood before him now found expression in what for him was a totally
unique way" (106:125).

As a composer, the young musician was pretty much an unknown
quantity in Oslo. He was not totally unknown, however, for on May 11
Gulbrand had arranged for a premiere performance of the string octet at an
"Extra-Soirée for Chamber Music" at Hotel du Nord. The work had been
extensively reviewed in *Morgenbladet* by music critic Otto Winter-Hjelm,
who wrote:

> It is a great pleasure for us to call the public's attention to this young
> countryman, who in the present work demonstrates that in natural ability
> and professional competence he is one of our most outstanding artists
> whom it would be a pleasure to welcome home. The octet, as we have
> said, reveals both considerable talent and study, and it contains so many
> piquant and entertaining passages that even a large audience could not
> fail to find it interesting. These fine qualities are as much a result of the
> youthful freshness and originality that radiate from the piece as of the
> composer's mastery of the instrumental aspects.

However, Winter-Hjelm did not conceal his misgivings about the fact that
Svendsen was so markedly influenced by modern stylistic tendencies, which
to a much too high degree "contained certain fallacies originating in Leipzig
and Weimar—mistakes that often enough sacrifice the beautiful means of
expression and forms prescribed by clear logic in order to allow the brilliant
whim of the moment to create a momentary effect. Our ground for asserting that Svendsen by his own choice subscribes to this modern tendency is
that one finds in his compositions instrumental effects that are indeed very
striking, but that spring up outside the normal structure and take the place of
motivic development—despite the fact that in all of the movements there
are numerous indications that he has the ability to develop his motives in a
consistent manner."

Now Winter-Hjelm was not just a run-of-the-mill music critic. Three
years older than Svendsen, he himself had studied composition in both
Leipzig (1857–58) and Berlin (1861–63). He had already composed two
fine symphonies of his own (B-flat major, 1861, and B minor, 1863). The
latter work, as a matter of fact, included elements borrowed from Norwe-

gian folk music—for example, a Norwegian ballad is used as one of the themes in the last movement.

In July, Grieg had completed his second violin sonata (G major, op. 13) and had dedicated it to Svendsen. On July 30 he wrote to Gottfred Matthison-Hansen in Copenhagen that he looked forward to hearing the sonata when Svendsen came to Oslo: "He is the only one to whom I dare to give it. The other violin players all hate me, probably out of envy. . ." So it was a happy day for both Grieg and Svendsen when they met in Oslo once again.

Svendsen immediately began making preparations for a concert of his own works, including the symphony. The task proved to be more difficult than he had anticipated, however, for the orchestral resources left much to be desired. He wanted to play for high stakes, so he engaged the Christiania Theater orchestra and supplemented it with "so many amateur players that the number of musicians was much larger than people here are accustomed to"—as it was reported in *Aftenbladet* on October 4.

Svendsen began rehearsals in September, but there were problems from the outset with nerve-wracking sick leaves for several of the principal players in the orchestra. Fortunately, there were also many expressions of encouragement. Grieg, who was present at one of the last rehearsals, was astounded at the quality of the *Symphony No. 1* in D major. On October 8 he wrote to his friend Gottfried Matthison-Hansen in Copenhagen:

> Today I attended a rehearsal for Johan Svendsen's concert and heard his
> symphony. That was really something! The most scintillating genius,
> boldest national flavor, and truly brilliant handling of an orchestra.
> Where he has gotten this from the gods only know, but I think it is from
> Berlioz, about whom I unfortunately know too little to venture to affirm
> a strong influence here. But be that as it may, when I heard the sym-
> phony I was completely jolted. Everything had my fullest approval and
> forced itself upon me with irresistible power.

Svendsen's concert took place on October 12 in the Freemasons' large auditorium—the best concert venue in the city. Unfortunately, the attendance was rather disappointing: just 400 people, of whom 250 had received free tickets. The program was as follows:

1. *Symphony No. 1* in D major, op. 4.
2. Johannes Steenberg, *Minuet*, arranged for orchestra by Svendsen, who had also composed a *finale*.

3. *Theme with Variations* (second movement of the *String Quintet*, op. 5).
4. *Caprice* for violin and orchestra.
5. Franz Liszt, *Hungarian Rhapsody No. 2*, arranged for orchestra by Svendsen.

The soloist in *Caprice* was Gudbrand Bøhn, who was joined by H. Zappfe, F. Ursin, M. Hansen and J. Hennum in the performance of the second movement of the string quintet.

This concert was a topic of conversation for a long time. People had never heard such a big orchestral sound, nor had they ever before seen such an outstanding and inspiring conductor. The enthusiasm of the audience in the concert hall was tremendous, and the critics used every superlative they could think of to describe what they saw and heard. A standard had been set by which future orchestral performances would be measured.

Regarding the compositions, Winter-Hjelm (in *Morgenbladet*, October 16) once again expressed serious reservations about the modern tendencies evident in Svendsen's music, but he, too, made no attempt to conceal his admiration for the young composer: "Mr. Svendsen possesses a talent that must not be underrated. His ideas, which are often of great and pregnant beauty, bear as well the mark of the thought's boldness and daring, of having been born in a flash of inspiration."

Halfdan Kjerulf, an "old guard" Norwegian composer who was present at the concert, also had strong opinions about Svendsen's music. His views were not published, but his diary contains the following entry dated October 12:

> Svendsen is undoubtedly a major talent in his command of the orchestra, and as a composer he has fresh ideas and good technical competence. New influences have an impact on him, but S. is too strong a person to merely copy these influences. Life, demonstrative power, surprising orchestral shifts abound. Now and then, perhaps, his works are too vague and unclear—for example, in the *Andante* of the symphony. The *Scherzo* was enchanting—a broadly conceived, national tone picture, melodious and humorous. The principal theme of the first movement [of the symphony] is very energetic; the last movement is more delicate and piquant. The orchestra, which was enlarged substantially (3 double basses, 8 first violins, etc.), was led by S. with great competence. It aroused a great deal of attention that everything went as well as it did.

Edvard Grieg (*Aftenbladet*, October 14) used even stronger words in support
of his composer friend:

> Today Norwegian art has celebrated one of its triumphs. For triumph it
> must be called when a musically unenlightened audience—an audience
> of only a few hundred people—is so carried away by that which is
> absolutely new and great that it forgets its archenemy, the symphony—
> "that artificial music," as it is called—and breaks out in enthusiastic ap-
> plause. . . . The concert opened with Svendsen's *Symphony in D major*, a
> work that provides insight into an individuality that is so great that it
> would be easier to write books about it rather than pages. What first
> comes across as so pleasant in this symphony—unconsciously, of course,
> to a non-musician, but to a musician in such a way that throughout the
> symphony he preserves a sense of comforting calm—is the perfect bal-
> ance between the musical ideas and the technical dimension. Svendsen
> makes great demands on his audience. He takes you with him into the
> fantastic, the humorous, the enchanted land of Romanticism—but he
> doesn't let each person decide whether or not he wants to go along: he
> forcibly abducts the audience, so to speak, simply by virtue of knowing
> how to hit the nail on the head in his employment of the technical de-
> vices. In this way he takes his audience by storm even in those places
> where his ideas are so lofty that it would appear impossible for the aver-
> age hearer to understand him. Svendsen's instrumentation is as perfect as
> any to be found. It is this successful transformation of ideas into sound
> that has enabled him to capture not only the imaginative listeners but
> even those who in this respect are less well endowed.

Grieg compared Svendsen's instrumentation with Gade's and contrasted
"the generally soft coloration" of Gade's music with the sharp contrasts of
Svendsen's. That Svendsen employed greater contrasts had its natural origin
in the fact that he belonged to a more modern time, "and we could not see a
striving for effect—for example, in the piquant *Scherzo*, where the soft mur-
mur of *pizzicato* is organically employed."

The subsidiary theme in the first movement was in Grieg's opinion
"distinctly Wagnerian, but the unique way in which he later develops it in
conjunction with the principal theme causes any thought of reminiscence
to vanish."

Grieg found the most pronounced national coloring in the *Scherzo*,
which contained "the most inspired and humorous combinations." He

continued: "The composer demonstrates that gigantic powers slumber within him in the introduction to the *Finale*, where he boldly reintroduces the principal theme. There is grandeur in this rising tension, which in combination with the canonical art that Svendsen reveals at this precise point, warrants the prediction of a great future for him." Grieg concluded his review with a bold declaration:

> That an artist such as Johan Svendsen, after such meager financial rewards, will pack his bags and leave as quickly as possible, is only to be expected. But it will be a shame if something is not done to keep him here among us. We have only a few national talents—enough, however, that through their mutual effort a true artistic life might be established. We are convinced that Johan Svendsen would not have left us if the public's reception had not forced him to do so. It is a sad thought, but it must nonetheless be expressed, that if the public consistently goes on treating the best of our own people in this way, it will not be long before Norwegian music here at home will be nothing but an empty phrase, whereas abroad—especially in enlightened Germany—it will find the recognition it deserves. Svendsen intends to leave as early as next week, presumably for Leipzig.

Svendsen gave a farewell concert in the Freemasons' large auditorium on October 22. The program was the same one presented at the first concert except that the *Andantino* movement of the string quartet was inserted in place of the *Caprice* for violin and orchestra. *Morgenbladet* reported that the compositions were received "with loud applause, especially the symphony, the *Scherzo* of which the audience demanded to hear again—and they did. Mr. Svendsen will be returning to Leipzig in a few days, but we hope that in the future he will find occasion to visit his homeland and allow it to share in his activity."

Three weeks later Svendsen bid farewell to the city of his birth, and once again he was to be away for five years.

A SELF-STYLED "SAD HERMIT IN THE MODERN BABYLON"

In the autumn of 1867 Svendsen had hoped that it would be possible for him to make a living in Oslo, but he quickly realized that for the time being the greatest opportunities for him as an artist lay abroad. The city that especially beckoned to him at the time was Paris.

Johan Svendsen in the late
1860s. (Universitetsbiblioteket,
Oslo)

It had been his good fortune to receive another travel grant, not from
the Ministry but from the estate of a Mr. Schæffer, who had been a customs
official. The grant, which was in the amount of 216 *spesiedaler* and was to last
from January 1, 1868 to June 30, 1869, was later extended for another six
months with the addition of 60 *spesiedaler*. Svendsen sent a letter of thanks to
Prime Minister Sibbern on November 29, 1867: "For this kind gesture I
take the liberty of conveying my sincere thanks, for I hope by further study
in Paris to achieve the goal toward which Your Excellency's goodness
charges me to work."

The following day he parted from his family and friends and boarded
the Danish steamship *Uffo* for Copenhagen. The weather was terrible; a hurricane in the Skagerrak was so ferocious that a number of ships sank, and
Uffo was forced to take shelter at Fredrikshavn, Denmark. Svendsen spent
the night at an inn where he, ever appreciative of the fair sex, observed "a
delightful waitress."

He got to Copenhagen on December 4 and remained there for a few
days renewing contacts with friends and acquaintances. The day after he

arrived he looked up Gade and showed him the score of his symphony, which the old man perused and praised highly. That same evening he went to the Royal Theater to see a "masterly performance" of Ludvig Holberg's famous comedy *The Busybody*.

He travelled "through blowing snow and storm" on the steamship *Halland* to Lübeck, where Leche received him with open arms. In a letter to his father written on New Year's Eve, Svendsen wrote: "[Leche] did me the honor of 'drinking brotherhood' with me, thereby indicating that he regards me as his eldest son." By this time, however, Svendsen had been in Leipzig for some time and had found new lodgings in Johannisgasse 29, where he lived for two months.

His friends at the conservatory surprised him with a performance of the string quintet, and he was received by the student association *Euphonia* with loud applause. Despite the warm welcome, however, he felt lonely. He was no longer a part of the pulsating student milieu where he had formerly been the acknowledged leader.

The *String Quartet*, the *Symphony No. 1* in D major, and the *String Quintet* were published by C. W. Fritzsch at this time, but "without much of an honorarium for such large works."

On February 14, 1868, filled with great expectations, he took the train to Paris. The exciting cosmopolitan city, a center of art and science—and locus of an aggressive political milieu—immediately took him by storm. On March 12, 1868, he wrote to his father: "The first impression is magnificent. I stared and stared until I almost lost my mind, but now I have begun to get accustomed to these varied and stirring surroundings."

With an almost insatiable hunger for music, he sought out the Paris conservatory in order to study the works of the old French masters. Soon after his arrival he learned about the popular concerts conducted by Jules Pasdeloup. Each Sunday an audience of as many as six thousand gathered in Cirque Napoléon to hear a hundred-piece orchestra, and Svendsen was extremely impressed with the performances. The programs included works from Bach and Handel to Berlioz and Wagner.

His regard for some French conductors fell to a very low level, however, when he himself was appointed first violinist in *Concert Mussard*, a small Parisian orchestra. The solo cellist was Svendsen's boyhood friend Hans Nielsen, who had arranged for Svendsen to get the job. Johan wrote to his father on June 28:

> The conductor here is the biggest blockhead I have ever seen with a
> baton in his hand. Although there are some excellent players in the or-
> chestra, he is unable to get anything to go well. And then there's all this
> poor music that he has us play! It's enough to make one go mad!

Somewhat later he became a member of the orchestra at the Odéon The-
atre, and here he was able to use his talents more fully. Among other things,
he was given the task of arranging the music for François Coppée's play *Le
Passant* (*The Wayfarer*), in which Sarah Bernhardt played the leading role.
He himself had a solo passage that went well, but this was to be his only solo
performance in Paris.

Svendsen was obliged to take these tedious orchestra jobs for financial
reasons, for the Schæffer grant was far from sufficient to cover his expenses.
As early as spring 1868 he had made an effort to get further help from Norway. His friend Alexius Ræder made a request on his behalf to Thomas J.
Heftye, a wealthy patron of the arts, but without success. In a letter to his father dated August 6, Svendsen hinted at the reason for the turn-down: "If in
order to get support I am forced to let others decide what I am going to do,
then I would get into a dependency relationship that would be as hard to
bear—and perhaps a lot more confining—than that of poverty. I am not at
all inclined to sell my freedom of action for such a price, not even to
Heftye."

In autumn of 1868, Ræder sent a request to the National Assembly for a
permanent composer's grant for Svendsen in the amount of 300 *spesiedalers*
per year. In support of this request he enclosed a summary of Svendsen's
testimonials from the Leipzig conservatory, where the young composer's
incontrovertible talent and achievements were unambiguously affirmed
(112a).

On November 2, Ræder's petition was brought up in the National Assembly, but in the committee dealing with such matters none of his arguments had been accepted. It was firmly asserted that in granting a total of
2,000 *spesiedalers* to enable scientists and artists to travel abroad, the National
Assembly had "done enough for this cause":

> Composer Svendsen, like anyone else who assumes that he ought to be
> considered when these funds are distributed, must, therefore, apply to the
> government in connection with this matter, for the committee assumes

that the fact that he has already received such a grant once before does not in and of itself imply that he is absolutely ineligible to receive another one (112b).

When the matter was discussed in a plenary session in March of 1869, the committee's negative proposal was approved and Svendsen had no choice but to accept the decision. Immediately afterwards, therefore, he asked to be considered for some of the funds allocated for "scientists' and artists' travels abroad." The committee dealing with the matter placed him in the third position on the list of eligible candidates, but when the matter came up for a vote his name was stricken. Grieg, on the other hand, had the pleasure of receiving 400 *spesiedalers* for a trip to Rome.

Svendsen continued to slave away in Paris. At one point he was forced to generate a little income by working as a music copyist—undeniably a dreary occupation for a creative artist. He wrote dejectedly to his father on July 20, 1869: "What bothers me most is that this desperate struggle to earn a living makes it impossible to compose anything." There were times when cold and hunger were his daily companions. On February 2, 1869, he wrote to Grieg:

> [I have been leading] a dog's life, and yet a quite natural feeling restrains me from revealing the complete wretchedness of my existence. This much is certain, that if it were not so important to me to learn French and a few other things that I think I could most easily acquire here, I would long ago have returned to Germany, where I have prospects of being able to live fairly respectably. I feel almost like a sad hermit in the modern Babylon.

Just how discouraged he was is also reflected in an unsigned article in the Ohio newspaper *The Cincinnati Commercial* (124), written by one of his fellow students from Leipzig:

> As Berlioz had done, he lived in an attic room in an unlit street in the Latin Quarter, and like Berlioz he often didn't know where his next meal was coming from.
>
> About two months before we met he had really been in the most desperate straits, completely without either food or money. He hadn't eaten for two days, and there were only two possibilities: either to steal or to starve to death. In complete desperation he wandered through the streets, and finally, almost without realizing it, he found himself in a little

eating place on Rue Monsieur le Prince. There he ordered coffee, milk, and bread. But instead of paying for it, he just made a very courteous bow as he left the cafe.

Since, however, he had the impression that the cafe proprietor had given him a friendly, understanding look, he repeated the same experiment a number of times until at last he became almost a regular patron at the cafe, without ever paying a cent. Nor was he ever asked to pay.

Right down to the day that brought us together he remained indebted to this extraordinary restaurateur, and the only thing he ever did to pay down his debt (which was never mentioned) was that he gave short, free concerts on his violin for a very small and select audience—never more than six people.

Toward the end of 1868 friends and acquaintances in Leipzig had strongly encouraged him to return to Saxony. "Yes," he wrote to his father on February 2, 1869, "a rich man has even offered to take care of me if I will promise to stay in Leipzig, but since I am not at all inclined to give up my personal freedom I have turned down the offer."

It is clear that the stay in Paris nourished his longing for freedom and helped him tear himself loose from all authorities. In Leipzig he had been more or less under the guardianship of the conservatory for nearly four years, and the moral escapades that he engaged in toward the end of his time there can perhaps be viewed as part of his effort to liberate himself. This effort sometimes made his life difficult and led to a troublesome nervous condition. To be sure, he had exhibited certain depressive tendencies earlier as well, but during the summer of 1869 the depression returned with a vengeance. Fortunately, he found a doctor who was able to help him. On August 6 he wrote to his sister, Albertine:

I am very fortunate to have met a doctor who is not only competent but also humane. He understood immediately that my illness had its root in spiritual problems, and after I had bared my soul to him he treated me with commendable insight. He made a special effort to awaken my own moral strength, proving with powerful words how strong a person can be if he has the will to desire it. If I now have regained my peace of mind to some extent, it is owing more to the confidence in my own strength that he inspired in me than it is to the medicine he gave me. Moreover, it appears that I have won this man's broad interest: he treats me like a loving father treats his son, and rarely does a week go by that he does not visit me, and very often I am invited to his home.

Svendsen was learning a lot from philosophical and political literature at this time. He immersed himself in the works of Auguste Comte and Ernest Hamel and glowed with enthusiasm for Louis Blanc's history of revolutions. He lived in the Latin Quarter, first at 29 Rue de Tournon, later at 41 Rue d'Aboukir. Thus he was right in the middle of the revolution-minded student milieu, where he could constantly feel the pulse of the ongoing debate that exposed the profound disagreements between the old and the new France. The new political ideas, which included elements of socialism and communism, were attractive to him, and in view of his own class background it was natural for him to identify with the radicals.

The strength of his political awakening is reflected in a series of letters to his family. He had nothing but contempt for Emperor Napoleon III, whom he called (in a letter to his father dated September 26, 1870) "this scoundrel who for over ten years has oppressed France and chased its best men into exile." The same day he wrote to his sister: "Seldom has a person so sullied by crimes and villainy sat upon a throne, to say nothing of his political tyranny. . . . The dastardly act on the night of December 2, where despite his sacred oath he betrayed the republic with a bloody coup and had himself proclaimed emperor. . . ."

The radical views are most pronounced in the letters to his father. An open and sometimes aggressive tone replaced the deferential one that had characterized his earlier letters. He also minced no words in expressing his opinion about conditions in Norway, making derogatory remarks about the ultraconservative Norwegian press that was totally behind the establishment. In a letter dated August 6, 1869, he lashed out at the Norwegian police force with fiery intensity:

> Old free Norway! I never hear this boastful phrase without blushing with shame, for I can't help but think of the many acts of tyranny which the Christiania [Oslo] police, for example, commit. Yes, even the first and best oaf of a constable can insult whomever he will with impunity, and woe to him who gives any indication that he will not tolerate such behavior: without further ado he is forced to go with him to the police station, where the officer in charge summons all of his impressive sophistry to extract from the "criminal" a fine (as big as possible)—usually for interfering with a law enforcement officer.
>
> As you know, I speak from experience. [There was one] time when— unwilling to tolerate a constable's violence, which was as brutal as it was

unjustified—I forcibly resisted him and had to pay a fine of 2 *spesiedalers*. Since that time, I have lost all faith in the reality of a principle that is highly praised in Norway: the principle of equality before the law, the corollary of the freedom of the citizens that is guaranteed by law. For I experienced on that occasion that it is regarded as an offence to defend yourself against any brutalities a constable may get it into his head to commit.

A letter to Grieg on February 2, 1869, contained a number of interesting remarks about the relationship between artists and the general public. Henrik Wergeland, Norway's great national poet and champion of national independence in the first half of the nineteenth century, had succumbed in the struggle against his more or less unworthy opponents—and now, Svendsen wrote, it appears that there is nothing that some prominent people will not do to silence the poet Bjørnstjerne Bjørnson, the new voice of freedom in Norway:

I mention these two men particularly because I regard them as the principal factors in our spiritual development and because at root they have fought the same fight, namely that of genius against mediocrity, and lastly because this wretched struggle unfortunately characterizes all too accurately the conditions in Norway at the present time.

I suppose I don't have to tell you that if people—I mean people in general, in Norway as well as Germany—were given direct access to art through such means as inexpensive editions of poetry, popular concerts, etc., and thus not compelled to remain totally passive (as is really the case in Norway), all such controversies would end with the triumph of the things that are really good. Because people who are not blinded by sophistic theories, but with childlike naiveté almost always instinctively make the right judgment, would unhesitatingly side with those who were striving for beauty.

The best proof of the truth of what I have just stated is the complete triumph that Wagner has achieved in the face of his many opponents in Germany. In Norway, the decision in all such matters is left to what is called the audience, and it is no wonder that this audience—which on the one hand does not have the positive knowledge and on the other hand lacks in varying degrees the naiveté without which one cannot discern the poetic element in a work of art—lets itself be led by these aesthetes who easily make themselves understood for the very reason that they are speaking on behalf of mediocrity.

With idealistic views such as these, it was painful for Svendsen to see the extent to which a crass materialism had placed its stamp on the Parisian art world. He became aware of the fact that if he wanted to make a future for himself as a performing artist and composer in France, he had to be willing to compromise his own principles: to pay special attention to reporters—indeed, to virtually buy column space for himself and his music in the local press. His moral integrity rebelled against any kind of bribery; this commitment to principle is presumably also the reason why he would not make use in Paris of the important letters of introduction that he had brought with him from Leipzig.

He did, however, receive help from his Norwegian composition student, legation secretary Fredrik Due, who introduced him to a number of prominent people in the art world. He became acquainted with George Sand, whose poetry had made a strong impression on him even when he was living in Leipzig. Among the well-known musicians that he met were the violinists Henri Vieuxtemps and Hubert Léonard and the composer Georges Bizet. In Camille Saint-Saëns he found a kindred soul with whom he quickly felt on the same wave length. In the summer of 1869 they collaborated in a private evening program that included Grieg's second violin sonata. His own string quintet and string quartet were performed at two other private programs. Both Vieuxtemps and Léonard participated in the performance of the quartet. So far as we have been able to determine, however, he did not succeed in getting his compositions performed at any public concert in Paris.

Svendsen got along best of all with the younger French composers. Through the 20-year-old Henri Duparc he came in contact with Vincent d'Indy, who was only 17 years old at the time. Many years later Gustav Hetsch told (61) about a conversation he had had with d'Indy in which d'Indy talked about what an impression Svendsen had made on the young French composers:

> If he remembered him! Of course! It was in his early youth, but he remembered it vividly. And it was to this very building, the one in which we were now sitting—no. 7 Avenue de Villars, just a few steps away from the Hotel Invalide—that Svendsen had come almost every day. Because this was where both Duparc and d'Indy lived as young men, one on each floor. And they took turns gathering friends for evening music programs where they showed each other their compositions long before they were presented to the public—if, indeed, they ever were, for some were just tucked away in a desk drawer.

Here people discussed music with passion and youthful enthusiasm. Svendsen made his important contribution to both the performances and the discussion, and it was always received with interest. He was, after all, a few years older than the French friends, and by the time he got to Paris he had already produced a number of very important compositions: the quartet in A minor, the quintet, the octet, the symphony, etc. For that reason alone he was a musician whom the others looked up to. And we quickly learned to enjoy this foreigner's works, which were so transparently clear in form and so genuinely human in content, simultaneously warm-blooded and chaste, at one moment sparkling with humor, at another permeated by controlled passion.

As a matter of fact, d'Indy became so interested in Svendsen's music that in the 1880s he arranged two of his songs for piano four hands: *Quel prodige, ó fille accorte*, op. 23 no. 3, and *Le bouleau et l'étang*, op. 24 no. 2.

The young French musicians were entranced by Wagner, and Svendsen's enthusiasm for the master was heightened when, shortly after the premiere of *The Mastersingers of Nuremberg* in 1868, he "was lucky enough to get hold of a piano score and studied it assiduously." He wrote to his father on February 2, 1869, that he was spellbound by its "beautiful melodies and marvelous harmonies."

Enthusiasm for Wagner was something that he shared with his countryman Johan Selmer, also a composer, who in 1869 had come to Paris to study composition with Ambroise Thomas at the conservatory. From time to time Svendsen also was with Thomas Tellefsen, a native of Trondheim and a student and close friend of Chopin. Tellefsen had been living in Paris for a number of years and had made something of a name for himself both as a pianist and as a composer.

Svendsen's efforts to compose music were not very productive. He made a few sketches of an orchestral fantasy based on the *Marseillaise*, but it was never finished. He also created an arrangement for full orchestra of Schubert's work for piano four hands, *Divertissement à la hongroise*, op. 54. His main achievement, however, was the *Violin Concerto*, op. 6, which for the most part was written in Paris.

One can be puzzled about the fact that Svendsen composed so little during these two years. Illness and difficult financial circumstances have not always been a decisive hindrance for creative artists. An important reason in this case, in our opinion, is that at this time he was forced to deal seriously with stylistic tendencies with which he was not intimately familiar. Already during his years at the conservatory he had been fascinated by Berlioz's

instrumentation. Now, in his association with the young French avant-
garde musicians, he was brought into close contact with the program-music
movement. The confrontation between the tradition-bound and the new
created an artistic dilemma for him. His outstanding ability to create large
works within the confines of the established forms came into conflict with a
growing desire to launch out into the new, in keeping with the ongoing
spiritual liberation that he was experiencing. Tradition won the first round,
as evidenced by the classically oriented violin concerto. His first forays into
the realm of program music—the symphonic poems *Sigurd Slembe* and *Carnival in Paris*—would have to wait for a couple of years.

We know from letters to his family that continuing financial difficulties
forced him to bid farewell to Paris before he was really ready to leave. In autumn of 1869 the directorship of *Euterpe* was open in Leipzig, and Svendsen
was encouraged to apply for the position. He declined at that time, but the
following spring when he was offered the position of concertmaster and assistant conductor of the same orchestra he felt that he had no choice but to
accept. The ground had already been prepared for his work in Leipzig, for
on February 8 *Euterpe* had performed his first symphony in its entirety for
the first time in Germany.

In March, 1870, Svendsen left for Leipzig with the fervent hope that he
would some day return to Paris.

THE VIOLIN CONCERTO—"A COMPLETE SYMPHONY"

The last page of the original manuscript of the *Violin Concerto*, op. 6, contains the notation, "Leipzig, June 1870," but for the most part the work was
written in Paris. As early as October 9, 1868, he had mentioned to Grieg
that he was thinking strongly of writing such a concerto, some ideas for
which he had been mulling over for a long time.

Scandinavia produced very few violin concertos during the Romantic
period. Ole Bull's two concertos were really the only ones that became internationally known, and even these were kept alive only by his own magic
bow. Not a single violin concerto was written in Norway between Bull and
Svendsen.

An American who had been a fellow student of Svendsen at Leipzig
told in *The Cincinnati Commercial* (124) about an 1869 banquet in Paris to
which he had invited the penniless composer. Svendsen was hard at work
on his violin concerto at the time, and "as he swallowed oysters and drank

champagne, he sang themes from all three movements and described for me in detail what he himself thought was new and original in the work, illustrating the technical subtleties with his arms and fingers. He became more and more excited. . . ."

What, then, was new and original in this work, and what was the composer trying to achieve with it?

In a letter to Grieg dated September 22, 1871—after he had tried out the concerto with a full orchestra—Svendsen emphasized that it absolutely had to be handled like a symphony, "but if this done, it will really sound like a symphony." Grieg, in a letter to August Winding of January 3, 1872, reiterated this point: "Svendsen's concerto is actually a complete symphony."

When Svendsen lays such stress on the symphonic aspect of his violin concerto, he may have gotten the idea both from Berlioz's *Harold in Italy*, where the solo viola plays a decisive role, and from Brahms's first piano concerto. In any case he proceeds with a remarkably sure hand within the symphonic framework. Paradoxically, however, the very thing that was conceived as the principal virtue of the piece became also the cause of its downfall. In the process of strongly emphasizing the symphonic element, the traditional virtuosic aspects were deliberately neglected. The result was a concerto that lacked both the performing appeal to the virtuosos and the roguish courting of the audience that might have won it a place in the international violin repertoire.

The symphonic character of the piece is most evident in the first movement, where nearly a third (152 of 471 measures) is played entirely by the orchestra—an exceptionally large portion considering that the orchestra is very active in the rest of the movement as well. The music sounds like a veritable protest against the Romantic virtuoso concerto of the type pioneered by Paganini and brilliantly copied by such composers as Bériot, Vieuxtemps, and Ole Bull.

Often in a solo concerto the most technically demanding passage for the soloist is the cadenza that occurs near the end of the first movement. Typically, the cadenza is an opportunity for the soloist to display his virtuosity at its dazzling best. Not so in Svendsen's concerto. With sovereign disdain for outward effects, he wrote a cadenza in which parts of the principal theme constitute a bass melody in a series of broken chords, supported by the orchestra. In and of itself this is an acceptable idea, but the cadenza lacks the feeling of vibrancy that could have made it into an instrumental challenge.

The thematic material of the concerto is quite beautiful. The last movement, especially, has something both audacious and mischievous about it. As a whole, however, the melodies sound more anonymous than Svendsenian.

The concerto was dedicated to Svendsen's violin teacher, Ferdinand David. For the premiere performance at the Gewandhaus on February 6, 1872, it was not David but one of his earlier students, Robert Heckmann, who played the solo part. Svendsen himself wielded the baton. Moreover, the program on which it appeared was not an ordinary Gewandhaus concert but one arranged by Universitäts-Gesangverein zu St. Pauli.

A review (signed O.B.) in *Neue Zeitschrift für Musik* (February 22) was fairly reserved. The piece was said to be "sensitively orchestrated" and rich in "noble ideas," but despite competent handling of thematic details the composer had not yet reached full maturity. The February 20 issue of *Signale*, however, carried an extremely negative review by Eduard Bernsdorf, who wrote that the concerto "did not show itself to be worthy in any way of the loving care with which Heckmann performed it."

The Oslo premiere of the piece was given in the large auditorium of the Masonic Lodge on November 30 of the same year with Gudbrand Bøhn as soloist. Svendsen was once again the conductor. A review in *Aftenbladet* two days after the concert characterized it as remarkable and imaginative. August Fries performed the last two movements of the concerto in Bergen on February 18, 1873. The February 20 issue of *Bergens Tidende* contained a lengthy review which, however, dwelt not so much on the composition itself as on the evidences of modernity in the work. The reviewer mentioned that Svendsen's music undeniably had encountered energetic resistance: "What we have here is neither more nor less than a complete break with the traditional model for such a work, not only with respect to form but really also with respect to the emancipation of mind and thought that gave rise to the work." It was seen as significant that a young composer adopted a standpoint representing the avant-garde:

> For it is nothing other than these very ideas that underlie the so-called
> "music of the future"—ideas which, as everyone knows, were formerly
> the objects of universal scorn and bitter persecution but have recently
> won the artistic approval of countless enthusiastic adherents. These ideas
> have found in Johan Svendsen one of their talented apostles.

The concerto was well received in the United States when, on January 7, 1876, it was performed in Baltimore at a Scandinavian concert given under the leadership of a Danish conductor, Asger Hamerik. *The Baltimore Bulletin* wrote: "It is a superb work, as richly instrumented and as elaborately treated as a symphony, and the solo part written by a man who evidently is a master of the violin in all its resources"

With respect to form, the first movement, *Allegro moderato ben risoluto*, follows for the most part the established Mozart-Viotti-Beethoven-Spohr tradition. However, the finely chiselled principal theme is not announced until measure 83 after a long introduction, with preparatory thematic work in the orchestra and a solo part having the character of an improvisation. The most interesting feature of the movement consists in the symphonic development of the thematic material (7).

The second movement, *Andante* (E major), exhibits via a simple ABA form the composer's ability to create light, melodic music despite the fact that it has a certain elegiac character. This movement also provides a striking example of a stylistic device that is characteristic of Svendsen's works, namely artistic combinations of two dissimilar melodies.

The third movement, *Finale. Allegro giusto* (A major), is a free sonata rondo with marked elements of sonata form. This is the movement in which the composer comes closest to the traditional form, and the solo part calls for more virtuosity than do the preceding two movements.

In keeping with the ideals of Romanticism, Svendsen attempted to give this work a feeling of unity by employing motives from the first movement in the two succeeding movements.

Within the orchestra the strings have the most important assignments. Comparing the concerto with the first symphony, however, one can see that Svendsen is enroute toward a freer, more individual handling of the woodwinds. He clearly has benefitted from his study of French orchestral music, especially Berlioz.

Svendsen must have realized quite soon that the violin concerto was not the international trump card that he had hoped it would be. It was played occasionally during his lifetime and usually was received with approval, not least in the press. It continues to be played from time to time today, but it has not had sufficient appeal to win a prominent place in the international repertoire.

BACK TO GERMANY

On March 26, 1870, Svendsen wrote to his father: "Well, I'm finally back in old Leipzig, where I once spent many wonderful and happy days and

where I had so many marvelous friends. I don't have to tell you that everything seems rather tame after my visit to Paris, but I hope to soon acclimate
myself to conditions here once again." But it is evident from a letter to his
sister written six months later that the readjustment process was not altogether painless. Leipzig was the same, "only I had changed." The "almost
brutal change" that he had experienced in Paris was so radical that "everything contributed to completely reshape the artist as well as the man in me."

On May 28 he had the honor of having his string octet placed on the
program at a big music festival in Weimar. The ensemble included some of
the most illustrious performers of the day, including violinists Ferdinand
David, Robert Heckmann and Joseph Helmesberger and cellist Friedrich
Grützmacher. During the festival, Svendsen met Franz Liszt, whom he had
once briefly encountered in Leipzig. But Svendsen's impression of him was
not very positive. On September 26 he wrote to his father: "This famous
and brilliant man unfortunately has a fault that makes him absolutely unbearable. He is as vain and conceited as an old coquette, and he appears to be
happy only so long as people shower him with flattery."

But Svendsen's joy over his success in Weimar was soon overshadowed
by the outbreak of war between Germany and France in July, and he was
merciless in his criticism of the political game being played between the two
countries. In a letter to his father he stated his views as follows:

> The tyrant and liar in the Tuileries [palace] insults the crowned fat-head
> in Berlin, and the result is that two nations that claim to be the standard-
> bearers of civilization slaughtered one another. They are indeed two
> "nice bunnies" to die for . . . When will people finally get smart enough
> to tell the priests and princes to go to hell!?

In a letter to his sister he wrote in greater detail about the tragic circumstances:

> I understand that people's sympathy goes out to the amiable French, but
> one must not be unjust. The Germans didn't want this war; until the last
> moment they hoped for a peaceful diplomatic solution. Finally the
> French declared war, and then it was as if a wildfire spread throughout
> the whole country: "War is inevitable; let us wage it with all our
> strength." "Victory or death" was the battle-cry. It was also about time
> that Germany put a stop to allowing itself to be treated like a stupid child.

As for France, now that it is rid of its crowned monster I hope that it will use its strength and intelligence to carry out the internal reforms that are so badly needed.

The war disrupted Svendsen's work with *Euterpe* when the entire 1870–71 concert season was canceled, and he suddenly found himself without the employment that he had come to Germany to undertake. This turn of events did, however, give him more time to compose. The fruit of this effort was the *Cello Concerto*, op. 7, which was completed in November 1870.

The D-major symphony was published in 1868, but it took some time before it began to appear on German concert programs. After a very positive review in *Neue Zeitschrift für Musik* on June 24, 1870, however, two leading German orchestras found it worthy of performance. The first ensemble to perform it was the royal orchestra of Dresden on January 10, 1871. B. Pohl, who reviewed the concert in *Neue Zeitschrift für Musik*, wrote: "Freshness, vitality, confidence, and an occasionally gentle charm characterize the work in a very propitious way." Just two days after the Dresden concert, Svendsen himself conducted the symphony at a subscription concert by the Gewandhaus Orchestra. Each movement was followed by enthusiastic applause, and most of the Leipzig critics were effusive in their praise and called the concert a tremendous success for the composer. A January 18 article in *Deutsche Allgemeine Zeitung* characterized the symphony as a model work, the product of a "clear artistic consciousness and a noble feeling for the beautiful forms." Two days later, *Musikalisches Wochenblatt* wrote that the brilliant elements that permeated the work really hit home with the audience. Svendsen's qualifications as a conductor were praised even more highly: "We have never before seen anyone perform so difficult a task with such total confidence and grace."

But Svendsen learned that he had to take the bitter with the sweet when he read Eduard Bernsdorf's review of the concert in *Signale*. This reactionary critic made it abundantly clear that he was a sworn enemy of Norwegian music—as both Svendsen and Grieg were to find out on numerous occasions. On January 16, 1871, he wrote that the *scherzo* movement in Svendsen's symphony evoked in him the thought of "a brooding box or a dovecote." The composer tried to conceal the limitations of his talent, partly with Scandinavianisms and affinities to Wagner and Liszt, partly through "dashes of dazzling instrumentation." That the symphony, despite these shortcomings, achieved a "modest success" was something Bernsdorf was neither able nor willing to explain.

But Svendsen had more than music to think about at this time. The stay in France had placed a radical stamp on his political consciousness. In late spring he reacted strongly when the Communard uprising in Paris was brutally suppressed by the reactionaries, as is evident from a letter written to his father on July 5:

> I am greatly surprised that the communists in Paris have been judged so unjustly, not least here in Germany. Reading the newspapers here, one is tempted to think that all they were interested in was to loot and plunder. Having been in written communication with various people in Paris throughout this time, I can assure you that at least 95% of the evil that has been attributed to the Commune and its leaders is malicious invention and that the Commune has in fact been well regarded and respected in Paris. The people there knew enough to evaluate what the Commune was trying to achieve—to ensure the existence of the republic, to destroy the priestly authority, and by radical reforms in the system of public education to increase enlightenment among the lower classes. As I see from the newspapers, several of my dearest comrades in Paris have been shot."

THE CELLO CONCERTO—AN EXPERIMENT IN FORM

After Svendsen had finished the violin concerto in June of 1870, he began work on a new composition in the same genre—the *Cello Concerto* in D major, op. 7. Completed in November, it was dedicated to a friend and former fellow student, the German cellist Emil Hegar. Hegar played the solo part when the work was premiered at a subscription concert of the Gewandhaus Orchestra on March 16, 1871. The conductor was Ferdinand David.

Despite the exemplary performance, the premiere was only a modest success. In *Allgemeine musikalische Zeitung*, the principal organ of the "philistines," the reviewer thundered at the circle of young hotheads who "saw in Svendsen a star of the first rank in our future musical heaven and rallied around him as their hero and leader." It was this young clique that had gotten this "completely unfinished work" performed in the Gewandhaus:

> We are greatly astonished that the board of directors—which let it be clearly known even during the rehearsals that the composition was seri-

ously inadequate—didn't eliminate it before the actual concert. . . . This boring and insignificant composition gave the audience's patience a severe test. . . . All things considered we can say that the work was not created on the basis of an inner necessity but is rather a manifestation of outward sensationalism; it lacks intellectual content as well as heart and soul. Hence its deadly monotony.

This was indeed a severe blow to the aspiring young composer. Nor was he much more heartened by the review in the progressive *Neue Zeitschrift für Musik*. Here it was stated that the work did indeed contain some beautiful passages, but its weakness lay in the fact that the most beautiful, singable sections were given to the orchestra and treated symphonically while the cello got only a few cantilenas and for the most part moved about on rather insignificant phrases.

Before publication of the work later that year, Svendsen made a number of changes, and in *Musikalisches Wochenblatt* on January 5, 1872 it was given a somewhat more positive review. The reviewer, A. Maczewski, noted that in contrast to the violin concerto's profusion of interesting details, the cello concerto exhibited a refreshing artistic restraint. His main complaint was with the introduction, which struck him as flawed: one shouldn't put a long section having the character of a development in the place where the orchestral exposition is supposed to go! Maczewski also thought the piece was not very rewarding for a virtuoso cellist, but he nonetheless recommended it for cellists who were more concerned about musical content than outward effects.

The negative remarks in these three reviews contain some important observations. The monotony mentioned by one of the reviewers results not least from the fact that the concerto is so lacking in contrast: the music moves languidly along in a continuous, somewhat colorless melodic flow. It is of little help that the outer movements are marked *allegro* when the note values are so long that the tempo sounds more like an *andante*. The thematic material is marked by sameness from beginning to end. If one could say that the themes in the violin concerto sometimes lacked appeal for the general public, the same was even more true of the cello concerto.

What was the main compositional idea underlying this work? In line with the tendencies that we found in the violin concerto, Svendsen's aggressive attitude toward the existing conventions is here expressed even more clearly. He has completely renounced all virtuosity; the concerto does not even have a solo cadenza. Indeed, one could almost interpret the composition as an orchestral fantasia with cello obligato. Svendsen's progressive ideas are most clearly evident, however, in his experimentation with the structure of the work—both the structure of the whole and that of the constituent parts. The concerto is constructed as a unity: the three movements are played without interruption. The fragmentary sonata form of the first movement is evident in the fact that the development section is very short. The motivic-thematic development of the material is instead woven into the expanded exposition. The missing recapitulation appears in the third movement, where we find the traditional change of key of the subsidiary theme. This movement contains no other thematic material of its own.

The second movement, an *Andante* (in G major) in ABA form, contains some new thematic material but provides very little contrast to the other two movements. It, too, is marked by homogeneity.

The composition as a whole could also be described as a one-movement work in sonata form with a slow middle section interpolated between the development and the recapitulation.

Bjarne Kortsen has discussed several of the features mentioned above in his analysis of the concerto (75). He has also pointed out that Liszt's first piano concerto (E-flat major, 1857), with its one-movement structure, must have been a model for Svendsen, and that the cello concerto probably is the first Nordic composition to make use of this structural principle.

While Svendsen's violin concerto sometimes sparkles with charming chord progressions, the cello concerto, strangely enough, contains no harmonic experiments commensurate with the boldness of the form. For once in his life inspiration in this area seems to have failed him.

Like the violin concerto, the cello concerto has in recent times failed to find any proponents in the concert hall, but it has been used from time to time as instructional material at conservatories in Europe.

MARRIAGE IN "THE NEW WORLD"

The USA was not a particularly inviting destination for European composers during the 19th century. Dvořák's stay here in 1892–95 is a well-known exception. But two Norwegians were here before Dvořák. Ole Bull, after many triumphant tours as a virtuoso violinist, virtually became an American himself. And Johan Svendsen came to New York for two months during the summer of 1871—to get married.

During his stay in Paris, Svendsen had fallen in love with an American singer, Sarah ("Sally") Levett, whose brother David had been one of his fellow students at Leipzig. She was the daughter of Morris Levett, a well-to-do dentist in New York who had achieved success by making some important discoveries in his field.

Sally, who was the same age as Johan, had already been married once to a rich American, Lewi Schmidt. Upon her divorce from him she had been granted custody of their 3-year-old son. In spring of 1871 she went to Leipzig, both to visit her brother and to see Johan again, and early in May they announced their engagement.

They had been attracted to each other by their contrasts. She was a cultured and sophisticated woman of the world from a well-to-do family in a large city; he was a man of limited means from underdeveloped Norway, a dynamic personality whose political awakening had taken a radical turn. What they had in common was a pleasing appearance: she, dark-haired and Mediterranean-looking; he, brawny and Nordic.

Johan wrote to his father on June 5 that his wife-to-be was not just beautiful, "she also possesses all of the intellectual qualities that I in my dreams have always wanted to find in my life companion." She had a singular poetic and musical nature and was "completely conversant with French and Italian opera music, and her understanding of the great classical masters from Bach all the way to Wagner is incomparable. Under such circumstances it goes without saying that I am happy and content."

They had hoped to be able to marry in Germany, but because Sally was Jewish a church wedding was unthinkable and a civil ceremony difficult in view of the fact that they were both foreigners. The obvious solution was to go to the United States and get married there.

In mid-June, therefore, they left for New York aboard the German steamship *Main*. On July 24 Johan wrote to his father that upon their arrival a month earlier they had gone directly to the courthouse, "without taking time to change clothes," and the ceremony had been performed by none other than "New York's presiding judge himself."

Sally's father was one of the witnesses at the ceremony. Johan immediately felt on the same wavelength with this "old, handsome, and friendly man." Some years later he dedicated *Two Swedish Folk Melodies*, op. 27, to him.

Their wedding night was spent at one of New York's leading hotels—St. James—but two days later the newlyweds moved to a boarding house.

Johan Svendsen in New York City,
1871. (Universitetsbiblioteket, Oslo)

During the honeymoon Johan wrote blissfully to his father that his chosen
one was "indescribably gracious and kind." The same day he wrote to Grieg
that "since the woman of whom I dreamt, after innumerable hardships and
obstacles, is now mine, I have regained my balance."

It did not take long for Svendsen to get a foot in the door of New
York's music life. It helped greatly that several of his former fellow students
had settled there and occupied good positions. Sally's influential family also
had connections that gained him entry into the city's cultural circles, and

Dr. Levett made every effort to attract attention to his son-in-law and his music. Aware of the power of the press, he allied himself with the editor of *Watson's Art Journal*. This prominent publication, which later received the name *American Art Journal*, became almost a public relations organ for Svendsen. Over a period of several years it published a number of laudatory articles about his artistic triumphs as a composer and conductor both in Scandinavia and on the continent.

As early as July 15 this journal carried an introductory article containing detailed biographical material about the newly discovered star in Europe's firmament of composers. The following month there was another long article under the title, "Two Afternoons with Svendsen, the Composer." Here the author told in flowery language of the conversations he had recently had with the composer, "a few precious hours of pure, unadulterated pleasure, snatched from the commonplace of our daily life" (123).

The first meeting occurred in Morris Levett's home, the second at the home of one Mr. Ward on 46th Street in Manhattan. Ward, one of Svendsen's former fellow students, had gathered several of their common music acquaintances from Leipzig. They combined their talents to perform Johan's three chamber-music works: the string quartet, the string octet, and the string quintet. As if that were not enough, Mr. Wenzel Kopta then played the composer's violin concerto "almost sight-reading, with true artistic feeling," accompanied on the piano by Mr. von Inten.

The author of the article, who wrote with obvious musical expertise, gave detailed and exceptionally positive evaluations of all the compositions. After having declared that "Mr. Svendsen is, beyond dispute, a man of genius," he concluded with the following bold assertion: "[We believe] that in Svendsen the world will gain a man worthy to continue the art-glories which have descended to us from Haydn, Mozart, Beethoven, and Mendelssohn. Their follower in faith, but the creator of his own manner."

Especially important for Svendsen was his friendship with the prominent German-American conductor Theodore Thomas, who two years later would present both the *Symphony No. 1* in D major and *Sigurd Slembe* in New York. Johan wrote to his father that this colleague, who was five years older than he, was "as clear-sighted and impartial in his artistic views as he is skillful and energetic in his conducting." During the summer months Thomas presented a series of concerts in Central Park with a 60-piece symphony orchestra. The orchestra "compared favorably with the best ensembles in Europe with respect to performance, but is vastly superior to them when it

Johan Svendsen with Sarah (Sally) and her son Sigurd in Leipzig in spring of 1872. (Universitetsbiblioteket, Oslo)

comes to richness of programming. [At these concerts] I heard many pieces that until then I had known only through reading the score."

Svendsen thought that a solid foundation had now been laid for public music life in America: "What I have seen and heard here of a musical sort is, though but a beginning, such as to raise great expectations for the flowering of our glorious art here." The young nation had until now had enough to do just to deal with its political problems, "but I am confident that when the Americans once begin to seriously concern themselves with art, they will surpass their current superiors in this area as well." He was especially impressed with the extensive freedom of American society, which had "a constitution that allows each person to develop according to his own ability—in both a material and intellectual sense."

Svendsen also found time to compose in New York, and followed up his earlier success with the orchestration of Liszt's second *Hungarian Rhapsody* by orchestrating the sixth rhapsody. The manuscript is dated "New York July 1871". He also began work on two original orchestral works: *Sigurd Slembe* (op. 8) and *Carnival in Paris* (op. 9), both of which were completed after his return to Europe.

The newlyweds also followed the American tradition of taking a trip to Niagara Falls, traveling by boat and train to view this natural wonder. At the beginning of September, Sally and Johan bid farewell to their American family and friends and boarded a ship to return to Europe. But the trip was not without some unpleasantries. After two days enroute, the ship developed mechanical troubles and had to return to New York. They then got berths on another ship, and after a stormy voyage they arrived in Bremen at the end of September. From there they proceeded directly to Leipzig.

ASSOCIATION WITH WAGNER AND LISZT

After the conclusion of the Franco-German war in March 1871, music life slowly returned to normal. In Leipzig, the *Euterpe* music association resumed activities. Svendsen served as concertmaster for the ten subscription concerts that were given during the 1871–72 season.

In a letter to his father written on December 31, 1871, Svendsen reported that he conducted the orchestra "for all instrumental solos, such as violin, piano, and cello concertos. In the symphonies I play first chair violin." Everyone agreed that in every way the concerts had been "better than ever before."

At the fourth subscription concert on December 12, 1871—a big festival concert given in honor of King Johann of Saxony's 70th birthday—Svendsen conducted the premiere of his new work, *Sigurd Slembe*, op. 8, which "was played with zeal and power and came off well."

As usual, *Allgemeine musikalische Zeitung*, in its issue of December 14, vented its anger against the newfangled music. This music, they declared, showed that *Euterpe* was going down a road that "we can only characterize as a sick and harmful offspring of our own time." Svendsen's *Sigurd Slembe* was thoroughly savaged, but on one point the reviewer could not conceal his enthusiasm: "We admired only the composer's talent as a conductor, who managed so effectively to drill the mediocre orchestra in these startling effects."

On the same date, however, both *Leipziger Tageblatt* and *Leipziger Nachrichten* published highly positive reviews of the concert. Indeed, these critics had nothing but praise for both the music and the conductor.

At Christmas, 1871, Johan and Sally were invited to visit Consul Leche in Lübeck. There was a very special reason for this invitation: early in November Svendsen had been informed that King Carl XV had awarded him a distinct honor, namely the gold medal for science and art (*Litteris et artibus*). Leche had the pleasure of presenting this medal to his protegé during the Christmas season.

The winter and spring of 1872 were spent in hectic musical activity in Leipzig. In addition to serving as concertmaster of *Euterpe*, Svendsen played in the 22 concerts given by the Gewandhaus Orchestra.

Svendsen also had the pleasure at this time of the company of two fellow musicians from Oslo, namely the composer Johan Selmer and the pianist Erika Lie. Selmer, who had been forced to interrupt his studies in Paris and flee the country because of his participation in the Communard uprising, had come to Leipzig to take lessons at the conservatory. In January and February of 1872, Erika Lie scored great triumphs in Leipzig. "I have really not heard for a long time anything as excellent as her playing," Johan wrote to his sister on January 28. On February 22 Erika Lie was soloist with the Gewandhaus Orchestra in a performance of Grieg's A-minor concerto. This was the first performance of the concerto in Germany, and it was an enormous success. Only the fanatical opponent of new music, the *Signale* reviewer Eduard Bernsdorf, achieved unenviable notoriety by characterizing the work as "that hopeless Grieg piano concerto."

The city was absolutely bursting with musical events at this time.

Nearly all of Wagner's operas were on the program of the local opera company. Large choral works were also being performed, including Berlioz's *Requiem*, which made a powerful impression on Svendsen when he heard it for the first time on May 8. Despite Leipzig's rich music life and the progress Svendsen was making as both composer and conductor, however, he realized that it would not do as a permanent home. His unconventional music made him an implicit challenge to the conservatives who dominated the music life of the city, and opposition and intrigues simply drove him away. His words to Grieg on May 25 were bitter:

> You talk about the philistines back home and think things are better in Leipzig. If I didn't like you so much I would be tempted to wish that you might go and live there for a year in order to be thoroughly convinced of your error. Leipzig is wonderful during one's student days, but if you try to earn a living there you soon run into such a lot of dirty tricks that you can't take it any more. And now these Signalers and Gewandhausers who use the most dastardly means to thwart every forward step, ridicule every ideal, and almost systematically embitter the existence of every artist— no, no, a thousand times no! No place is worse than Leipzig in this respect. I doubt that by next winter I will have anything more to do with Leipzig and *Euterpe*.

At the conclusion of the concert season in the middle of May, Svendsen left the city that had meant so much to him. He wrote to Grieg on May 9 that his plan for the summer was to settle down "in some valley or other in Bavaria, primarily for financial reasons, as it will be very cheap to live there." The family went, therefore, to Bayreuth, where they felt at home and spent the whole summer.

Svendsen went to Bayreuth not only in the hope of getting personally acquainted with Wagner, who lived there, but also because he had been offered a position as first violinist in the big orchestra that was to participate in celebrations honoring Wagner's birthday on May 22. After laying the cornerstone for the new concert hall that was about to be built, Wagner himself was scheduled to conduct a huge orchestra in the old opera house in a program featuring the premiere of his *Emperor March*, written for the occasion, as well as Beethoven's *Symphony No. 9*. Wagner had stipulated that the 120-man orchestra should consist of the best musicians that could be found. The 20-piece first violin section included such well-known performers as August Wilhelmy and Edmund Singer, and Svendsen shared a stand with his former fellow student, Robert Heckmann. Curiously enough, the timpani and triangle were played by the famous Wagnerian conductor Hans Richter of the Budapest Opera House.

Plans for the laying of the cornerstone in the morning were ruined by a violent downpour. According to a letter from Svendsen written to his sister three days later, however, the Beethoven performance in the afternoon made a most powerful impression: "With respect to both size and composition, the orchestra was in a class by itself . . . Add to this maestro Wagner's enlivening and inspired leadership and you may get some idea of what an impression Beethoven's imposing work evoked."

Friedrich Nietzsche and other prominent visitors from Germany and elsewhere had come to Bayreuth, and Svendsen made a number of new and interesting acquaintances. Among them were Countess Elisabeth von Krockow, "one of Europe's wittiest and most charming women," and composer and poet Peter Cornelius, Wagner's best friend, "a splendid and warm-hearted man."

The high point, however, was meeting the great man himself. On July 5 Svendsen wrote to Grieg that it was almost impossible to get next to Wagner, and that "only an unexpected conjunction of various fortunate circumstances prevented him from turning me away as he has so many others. He is the embodiment of niceness and has totally won me over."

Wagner's new home, *Villa Wahnfried*, was under construction at this time. He and his wife Cosima, Liszt's daughter, and their three children were living in the meantime at the castle hotel *Fantaisie* in Donndorf, a tiny village just outside Bayreuth. And as luck would have it, the Svendsen family, which had been staying at the nearby *Golden Peacock Inn*, moved in July to *Fantaisie*. The two families soon became well acquainted. Cosima quickly found a kindred spirit in Sally, who was her age, and Sally's son played with the Wagner children—Isolde, Eva, and Siegfried. Cosima's diaries (117) contain a number of entries about the Svendsen family—about walks together and other shared experiences during the period June 10 to August 25. The Svendsens, she wrote on June 16, "are thoroughly nice people," and in July she reported that the two composers had had several long conversations about Nordic sagas.

Svendsen later told his friend, the poet John Paulsen, that Wagner and he often went on walks together and that they usually ended their walks with a "happy hour" at a tavern that was famous for its beer (93 and 95). Wagner talked about his great interest in Norway, an interest that had been awakened in the course of a boat trip from Riga to London in 1839 when they had been forced to seek refuge from a storm at a port in southern Norway. The legends he heard there and the storm itself provided the inspiration for *The Flying Dutchman*, and he cocksurely asserted that the heroine's name, Senta, was typically Norwegian—which it is not.

Svendsen used this golden opportunity to make a careful study of Wagner's music. The master was at that time engaged in the orchestration of *Twilight of the Gods*, and it must have been a singular experience for Svendsen when Wagner went through the entire *Ring* cycle with him as one of his few chosen followers.

In April, while he was in Darmstadt, Svendsen had written an orchestral arrangement of Wagner's song *Träume* (*Dream*, text by Mathilde Wesendonck), one of the famous preliminary studies for *Tristan and Isolde*. He presumably got Wagner's approval of the arrangement, but it was not printed until 1893, when it was published by Wagner's own publishing house, Schott & Söhne, in Mainz. Svendsen premiered the work in Oslo on October 26, 1872.

Fate decreed that Svendsen would play a most unusual role in the life of the Wagner family at this time. It came about as follows. After her marriage to Wagner in 1870, Cosima, who was Catholic, decided in 1872 to convert to Protestantism. This decision came as a real shock to her father, who was zealously Catholic, and it led to a chilling of the relationship between Liszt and Wagner. A few days before the festivities in Bayreuth were scheduled to begin, Wagner nonetheless sent a cordial invitation to Liszt: "You were the first one who ennobled me with your love. . . . Now I say to you: Come!" Liszt expressed hearty thanks but replied that he unfortunately had other engagements.

It was Svendsen who brought about a reconciliation between the two. At the end of June he was invited to conduct *Sigurd Slembe* at the big music festival at Kassel arranged by the *Allgemeiner deutscher Musikverein*. Liszt was there as an honored guest in connection with the performance of his oratorio, *The Legend of St. Elizabeth*.

Since Svendsen had told the Wagner family of his acquaintance with Liszt in Weimar two years earlier, Wagner thought that his Norwegian friend might be the ideal person to carry a letter of reconciliation to the angry father-in-law. During the music festival, Svendsen found an opportune moment to deliver the letter, and Liszt was very moved by its content. The result of Svendsen's successful diplomatic mission was that in September the

Wagner family visited Liszt in Weimar. It was the first time they had been together in more than two years.

The performance of *Sigurd Slembe* at the festival concert in Kassel on June 28 was another major triumph for Svendsen. He wrote to Grieg a week later that the 100-piece orchestra had played "with a will" and that the work was "received with enthusiasm." In an April 27, 1875, letter to Kristian Winterhjelm, a journalist who had requested some biographical information, Svendsen reported that "Liszt spoke very flatteringly about both my composition and my conducting."

In Oslo, the August 13 issue of *Aftenbladet* carried a long article on the music festival. It was written by "one of the participants," probably Johan Selmer, who according to the article had been in Kassel at the time. *Sigurd Slembe* had "aroused considerable interest and lively applause even among the concert-goers who profess to be less supportive of the new trend in music, which Svendsen has also adopted as his own." It was further reported that B. F. Siebold, the principal speaker at the concluding banquet, had thanked Svendsen for his "splendid" composition.

Svendsen, however, was not present to hear these words of praise or the threefold "hurrah" that followed, for he had returned to Bayreuth on July 4. On July 7 Cosima wrote in her diary that she and Richard had visited him and heard "all kinds of nice things from Kassel."

The walks with Wagner had to be temporarily interrupted because of a foot ailment that required Svendsen to remain housebound at *Fantaisie*. He used the opportunity to continue working on his new orchestral composition, *Carnival in Paris*. He later told his Danish composition student, Hakon Børresen, that Wagner had dropped in one day while he was busy composing. The master looked briefly at the score, grunted with satisfaction and said, "that looks like a lot of fun!"

It was just as well, however, that Svendsen didn't hear Wagner's ill-tempered and rather uncharitable evaluation of *Sigurd Slembe* reported in Cosima's diary on July 22, which shows that Wagner did not at all like this newfangled program music without accompanying words:

> During the evening Richard unfortunately did not feel well. . . . A composition by Mr. Svendsen provoked R. to talk about the revolting characteristics of the new music: grimaces, bizarre effects, absence of calm human expressions, odd rhythms are used to produce themes that appear to be powerful but whose melodies do not remain in one's mind. And everything exceeds the boundaries of instrumental music because one is

compelled to pose questions about the subject and the situation in order to understand all the murders and the massacres."

Wagner in such a sputtering mood was not easy to deal with. But Cosima, Svendsen once told John Paulsen, "kept her husband totally under control. . . . Wagner was by nature extremely vehement, but a quiet admonition from her (*Aber, lieber Richard!*) was enough to immediately calm him and get him to make an apology."

At his best, however, Wagner was the epitome of sociability, and it presumably was thus that Svendsen usually saw him. He loved being surrounded by admirers and winning new followers. Cosima's conversion to Protestantism was a triumph for him, and now he saw an opportunity to make some new converts: Sally and her son should convert to Christianity, and he and Cosima would be godparents at the baptism.

Sally in fact let herself be persuaded to take this step, and the baptismal ceremony took place on August 15, 1872. Cosima's diary states, "To town early this morning, 10 a.m. baptism with Mrs. Svendsen and her boy, R. and I (sponsors) were deeply moved. Weeping, R. said that each time the words 'This is my body' etc. are uttered, one's heart is literally torn to pieces." Sally and her son were given Nordic-sounding names, Bergljot and Sigurd, both of which were associated with characters in the writings of Svendsen's compatriot Bjørnstjerne Bjørnson, whom he greatly admired. The festive occasion concluded with a big dinner party given by Svendsen at the hotel, after which Wagner took his Norwegian colleague to see and admire Villa Wahnfried, which was nearing completion.

Some weeks later the summer stay in Bayreuth was over, and the Svendsen family returned to Leipzig. From there they went to Oslo via Copenhagen.

TWO PROGRAMMATIC WORKS:
SIGURD SLEMBE AND CARNIVAL IN PARIS

Sigurd Slembe, op. 8, and *Carnival in Paris*, op. 9, marked a new departure in Svendsen's compositional work. In all of his earlier works other than the two compositions for male chorus he had restricted himself to the established musical types: three large chamber-music works, a symphony, and two concertos. Now he was getting tired of these traditional genres. In the concertos, especially the cello concerto, he had engaged in some experimentation, but he obviously must have felt that this had taken him down a blind alley. He did not find there the freedom for which he was seeking. For that reason he now chose to take an even more radical step, namely to try his luck at writing music in a programmatic vein. Only once thereafter would he write anything employing any of the strict classical forms: the *Symphony No. 2* in B-flat major, op. 15 (1876).

It was during his Paris years, when he became enamored of modern French music, that he had begun to toy with the idea of employing some of the more contemporary musical forms. In a letter to Grieg dated September 22, 1870, he wrote that for a long time he had been thinking of writing music for Bjørnson's *Crippled Hulda* and *Sigurd Slembe*, but that he didn't want to interfere with any plans that Grieg might have to do this. But Grieg's collaborative work with Bjørnson was of a different kind, so Svendsen was free to go ahead with music for *Sigurd Slembe*. He did not get around to it, however, until the following summer when he was in New York. *Watson's Art Journal* reported on August 12 that the composer was at work on two big concert overtures; one was a composition illustrating a poem based on Norwegian sagas, the other—presumably *Carnival in Paris*—was a composition celebrating an anniversary. According to *American Art Journal* (125), during his stay in New York Svendsen visited a Scandinavian art exhibit where he took special notice of a large painting, *The Battle of Hafrsfjord*, by Oslo painter Ole Peder Hansen Balling (1823–1906). The painting made a deep impression on him and prompted him to get to work on *Sigurd Slembe*. Balling later became one of his good friends.

Bjørnson's saga-based play was written in 1862, but the only person who had previously set any part of the text was Rikard Nordraak, who had set *Kaare's Song* (from Act 2) for baritone solo, chorus and orchestra. The play is loosely based on actual historical events from the beginning of the 12th century:

> After Sigurd learns from his mother that he is an illegitimate son of King Magnus Barfot, he has no peace. He will seize the crown that is rightfully his. Returning from a crusade, he seeks out his half brother, King Harald Gille, to share the throne with him.
>
> At first the indecisive Harald accepts him as co-king, but on the advice of his powerful vassals he has Sigurd imprisoned. But Sigurd manages to escape and kills his half brother. He has to flee to northern Norway, where he falls in love with a Sami (Lapp) girl. Despite her warnings he resolves to return to the south to try once again to reclaim his kingdom.
>
> According to Snorre [the Icelandic historian and poet who wrote

down some of the sagas], Sigurd is taken prisoner by his enemies in the battle of Holmengrå and is tortured to death. Bjørnson lets the play end with a scene in which Sigurd again meets his mother, who has become a nun. She begs him once more to give up his claim to the throne and become a man of peace. But he cannot do it, despite a premonition of defeat. Fate compels him to complete the struggle for justice, and with the crusader's song *Beautiful Savior* on his lips he goes confidently into battle. Death will release him.

Bjørnson's blending of Adam Oehlenschläger's elaborate narrative style and Snorre's terse manner of expression gives the work a hyper-Romantic aura that probably would have little appeal today, but according to an article by John Paulsen in the February 23, 1908 issue of *Verdens Gang*, Svendsen apparently was enthralled with it. The meeting between Sigurd and the Sami girl in Act 3 "struck him as one of the best things he had ever read." It was as if the Sami girl "embodied in her being and talk the mystic and fascinating beauty of the entire Northland."

We do not know if Svendsen had plans to write music for the entire play, but in the "symphonic introduction," as he calls the overture, he in a way incorporates the essence of the whole. It is program music without any accompanying words. The interpretation is left to the hearers.

Following the premiere of the piece in Oslo on October 26, 1872, the *Aftenbladet* reviewer gave the following programmatic account of the content:

> The mother's gentle voice in the opening measures, which the ear wants so much to dwell upon a bit longer, must immediately yield to Sigurd's pale, nervous, restless character, which is not at peace throughout the entire composition but is stirred up again and again, even by the Sami girl's alluring speech near the end, and one cannot but be reminded of the girl's words to Sigurd: "No place in the world can ever again give you peace."

For foreign listeners, who knew nothing about Bjørnson's play, it undoubtedly was difficult to find any meaning in Svendsen's composition without a description to give them some idea of what to listen for. After the premiere performance in the Gewandhaus, the reviewer in *Allgemeine musikalische Zeitung* (December 14, 1871) confessed that he simply didn't understand the piece. He characterized it as "a piece of program music that incorporates a virtuosic handling of the orchestra and that has been called *Sigurd Slembe* only to divert attention from the paucity of content by giving it a foreign-sounding title."

Other critics were inclined to regard the piece as "pure music" without a programmatic content, and their estimate of the piece was more favorable. *Leipziger Tageblatt* (December 14), for example, averred that this new gift from Svendsen's muse was a further proof of his rich talent and of his skill in employing the musical forms. *Leipziger Nachrichten* wrote that "the work promises something new and original, something independently creative that can be brought forth only by one whom nature has endowed with a fortunate gift."

After the music festival in Kassel, the Viennese newspaper *Neue Freie Presse*—one of Europe's leading papers—affirmed in its issue of July 3, 1872, that the piece witnessed to a "genuine, thoroughly warm-blooded, energetic natural gift that indeed is still in the midst of a most tempestuous period of turbulence." *Neue Zeitschrift für Musik* (July 12) stated that the overture "captivated the audience by its unique harmonic color even if everyone perhaps did not feel sympathetically moved by this musical introduction to the play about the deranged Sigurd." The piece was played abroad a number of times in the years that followed, usually with very positive reactions. In our day it has, undeservedly, been all but forgotten.

The melodic material in *Sigurd Slembe* is more striking than that of the cello concerto, and the sonority is somewhat more Wagnerian than that of any of his previous works. There is a spirited drive in the symphonic handling of the material within the context of a free but skillfully crafted sonata form. The distinctive character of the piece results not least from its daring modulations.

The introduction to the overture contains some melodic features that are rarely found in Svendsen's music—such things as major sevenths, tritones, and minor and major ninths. These intervals are undoubtedly intended to picture the restless Sigurd. Next comes a subdued, calm section with motives derived from what has preceded it. It depicts the mother and her attempt to calm her son. The exposition that follows has an agitated principal theme with pounding rhythms and chords. It represents Sigurd in battle and in flight. The subsidiary theme, resigned in character, portrays the fascinating and mystical traits of the Sami girl. In the development section the various motives are ingeniously interwoven, and in the coda the music drives relentlessly toward a powerful climax. Sigurd goes bravely forth to meet his cruel fate.

The next composition, *Carnival in Paris*, which was given the subtitle *Episode for Large Orchestra*, stands in contrast in every way to the intensely serious *Sigurd Slembe* overture. Here Svendsen abandons himself to humor and *joie de vivre*, cavorting as an orchestral virtuoso in a festive display of rhythms and sounds. It is evident that he had not totally confined himself to the life of "a sad hermit" in Paris, but had also tasted deeply of the unbridled carnival gaiety of this "modern Babylon." It is happy memories of these good times that are vividly portrayed in *Carnival in Paris*. It is another example of program music without an accompanying text, this time also without any connection to a literary theme.

While Wagner did not think well of *Sigurd Slembe*, it is not surprising that the infectious joy and opulent instrumentation of *Carnival in Paris* struck a responsive chord with him. Happier music has perhaps never been written in Scandinavia; indeed, this composition is comparable to the best of Berlioz's works. It contains no "bizarre grimaces" or "odd rhythms," just a spontaneous celebration of life in a torrent of melodies that stick in one's memory.

Carnival in Paris, completed in Bayreuth in August of 1872, was premiered under the baton of the composer in Oslo the following October 26. It won the immediate approval of both the audience and the critics. Grieg, who was present for the performance, was quite overwhelmed by the brilliant orchestral garb in which Svendsen had clothed his sparkling ideas. One is absolutely dazzled by the handling of the woodwinds, which seem almost to emit sparks. But the string parts, too, are replete with brilliant effects.

The festive material is framed by a clever structure in which Svendsen's creative imagination as a master of form scores new triumphs. The basic structure is a large ABA' form which, however, is fused with a sonata rondo in a quite original way.

In the introduction, it is as if the wild rhythms are opening the window on the carnival's events. Then the *ritornello* theme springs happily into view. It constantly receives new disguises along the way, as if a series of carnival figures is passing in review. Even the slow middle section is rooted in the *ritornello*.

The A-section has several contrasting episodes, but most striking is a theme that is built on a rhythmic motive in the Introduction:

Example 7   *Carnival in Paris,* op. 9

What one's ear picks up here is not only the descending chromaticism in the voices carrying the melody but also the harmonic underlay: real sequences extending over two measures with ascending minor thirds which are then transposed down a fourth. After the first eight measures, which start out in C-sharp minor, the tonality shifts to E minor. The recapitulation and coda also abound with lively notions and transformations of the *ritornello*.

After having written four works of minor importance (opp. 5–8), in *Carnival in Paris* Svendsen succeeded in getting everything to work together. This composition stands as one of the finest works of his early period.

4

PRODUCTIVE YEARS IN OSLO

1872–77

IN SEPTEMBER 1872 Svendsen returned to Oslo, where he quickly established himself and became the center of the city's music life. He busied himself with a wide range of activities, not least as the inspiring conductor of the newly established Music Society orchestra. He remained in Oslo for five years, and these years proved to be the most productive period of his life as a composer. He wrote no less than eleven large works during this period, including several of his most important compositions. It was also at this time that he began to achieve international fame both as a composer and as a conductor.

COLLABORATION WITH GRIEG

It must have been a singular experience for Svendsen finally to return to his homeland after having been away for so long. Now, after a decade of training and practical experience abroad, he was going to settle down and participate in the task of building up the music life of the city in which he had spent his childhood and youth. This was a challenge that appealed to his very best instincts. But why, one might ask, was Svendsen willing to risk his professional life on such an uncertain future in musically undeveloped Norway? O. P. Monrad has suggested some of the reasons:

> It is also remarkable that at just this time Svendsen longed to go home—
> to Oslo!—with its empty seats [in the concert hall] and miserable music
> conditions. I think that in this longing we can see a . . . deep and abiding

proof of a genuine love of the homeland in Svendsen's soul. Something had to be done back home, no matter what it might cost. For that reason he would take time at this point, just as his career was in its ascendancy— indeed, he longed to do it, for there was no one else who needed music's soothing breath of fresh air so much as his countrymen (84/I:37).

Svendsen would by no means be alone in this endeavor, however, for Grieg was going to share in the work. Their ever growing friendship as they worked together would enrich them both.

After going to Oslo in 1866, Grieg—by sheer hard work and despite many difficulties—had managed to create a firm position for himself, not least through the establishment of the Music Society in the autumn of 1871. He became conductor of the Music Society orchestra, which at this time was the only one giving regular concerts in the city. In the summer of 1872 it occurred to him that he could further strengthen the organization if he could persuade a man like Svendsen to share the leadership with him. No doubt he entertained the further hope that such a move would also unburden him to the extent that he could devote more of his time to composition.

In several letters to Grieg, Svendsen had clearly anticipated what such a collaboration between them might be like. As early as January 1, 1868, he wrote, "It really would be wonderful—I daresay for both of us—if we could soon work together. Basically we are pursuing the same goal, and although our inclinations and opinions on some matters are not identical, I know that our personal friendship—combined with the artistic universal humanity that more or less distinguishes every genuine artist—is more than enough to hold us together." He expressed similar thoughts in a letter from New York dated July 14, 1871:

> You wouldn't believe how happy and proud I am about every evidence of friendship that I receive from you, my magnificent, unbiased, and brilliant friend. . . . It is regrettable for me, perhaps for both of us, that we are so far apart. How stimulating and, therefore, fruitful a close association with you would be.

Grieg, for his part, wrote to Aimar Grönvold—Grieg's first biographer— about what the collaboration with Svendsen meant to him:

> I am increasingly attracted to Svendsen's art despite the fact that nothing could be more different than our respective artistic bents. He has taught

me to believe in myself and in the power and justification of the individual. There was a time in Kristiania [Oslo] when to be an individual was considered tantamount to being a criminal. But then Svendsen came, and he was also an individual—and then the miracle happened: from then on I, too, was tolerated. There are, therefore, few artists to whom I feel such a debt of gratitude as I do to Svendsen. When he came [to Oslo] in 1872, there were a few people who would have liked to see us end up as enemies. But, thanks to our mutual loving concern for our art, the plan totally failed. (Letter of April 25, 1881.)

It was their integrity and mutual respect that made it possible for them to work together without the slightest hint of jealousy. To the contrary: they supported one another and stood together through good times and bad. As early as 1867, when he first heard Svendsen's D-major symphony, Grieg realized that his friend was superior to him as a composer for orchestra, and Svendsen's later compositions only strengthened this view. Nonetheless, there was no sense of rivalry. Svendsen, for his part, was well aware that Grieg's special strength lay in writing chamber music, piano music, and songs.

The concluding concert of the Music Society in May of 1872 included Svendsen's *Sigurd Slembe*. This was the first time Grieg conducted one of Svendsen's compositions. In a letter to Gottfred Matthison-Hansen of April 29, 1881, he characterized it as "a brilliant, powerful piece," although he missed the Nordic element.

Svendsen put *Sigurd Slembe* on the program again at a concert of new compositions in Oslo on October 26, 1872—the first such concert he had given in five years. As in 1867, the concert was presented in the Freemasons' large concert hall with full orchestra. The core of the orchestra consisted of the musicians from the Christiania Theater, but Svendsen had also rounded up a number of the city's other foremost performers. And all of them were persuaded to play with no honorarium!

The concert offered eight selections never before heard by a Norwegian audience, including two first performances in Oslo and no less than six world premieres. Among the latter were three orchestral arrangements by Svendsen of works by other composers: Liszt's *Hungarian Rhapsody No. 6,* Schumann's *Abendlied,* and the Wagner song, *Träume (Dreams).* The remaining world premieres were Selmer's *Nordens Ånd (The Spirit of the North)* for male chorus and orchestra and Svendsen's own two latest compositions: the colorful *Carnival in Paris* and the *Funeral March for King Carl XV.* The

Oslo, 1872 (l. to r.): Hilda Elisabeth Neupert, Nina Grieg, Edvard Grieg, Edmund
Neupert, Johan Svendsen, Sarah (Sally) Svendsen. (Troldhaugen)

last-mentioned composition had been written shortly after the death of
Svendsen's royal patron on September 20. It was a mere occasional piece,
and it has had a sad fate: the publication rights, which were sold to Oslo music publisher Carl Warmuth for three hundred crowns, were later conveyed
to C. F. Peters in Leipzig. The piece was never printed, however, and it apparently has not been played at a public concert since 1872.

The solemn, rather unimaginative funeral march was the opening number on the program and was followed by *To Sweden,* op. 2, No. 1—the piece for male chorus written in 1865 to a text by King Carl XV—performed by a large chorus of student singers.

The reviewers were for the most part enthusiastic about the new examples of Svendsen's work even if the musical language seemed at times to be somewhat too vehement. *Aftenposten* reported as follows on October 28:

> We do not doubt that Svendsen's music was too powerful for a few sensitive ears, and that some cannot abide his style and general tendency. But no one can be blind to the richness of ideas, the boldness, the power that reveal themselves in his compositions, and everyone will agree that his orchestration is absolutely superb. Overall, he has managed to create a brilliant sonority that contributes mightily to add luster to his compositions without, however, laying himself open to the charge of creating mere empty effects. Of the pieces on the program we would call attention to the *Funeral March,* which was dignified and effective, as well as the *Carnival in Paris,* which sparkled with life and gaiety.

Aftenbladet remarked that the concert was not only a triumph for Svendsen personally but a joyous occasion for his countrymen as well. From the very first measures, they reported, one felt that one was in the presence of something great that was of one's own flesh and blood: "One heard through the different and most striking harmonies and rhythms—which abounded in both *Sigurd Slembe* and *Carnival in Paris*—the deep fundamental tone of our national core, and yet the composer's independence did not for a moment seem to be constrained by the echo of those indigenous sounds."

Morgenbladet characterized Svendsen the conductor as an absolute virtuoso, but the reviewer did not think he was in a position to give the compositions their full due. It is not so easy, he said, to "give an intelligible account of the intricacies of the music of the future. The whole concert was interesting, but left, perhaps, a desire to hear also some older, classical orchestral works under Mr. Svendsen's masterful leadership."

Grieg made some interesting comments in a letter to his Danish friend August Winding written on the day of the concert:

> I wish you were here this evening and could go along to Svendsen's concert, which includes some truly brilliant things. I am sending you the program, which shows that we do indeed have some talent up here. The

Carnival in Paris is the best. Here rhythm and harmony vie with an instrumentation that is not only masterful but often entirely new. For this occasion Svendsen has managed to put together an enormous orchestra (and
for once the musicians are donating their services; the Music Society,
which has to pay its musicians, simply can't compete). He conducts splendidly, so for once we can indulge completely in pure enjoyment of the
music. You should hear his orchestration of Liszt's *Rhapsody* [No. 6]! In his
arrangement, the piano passages turn into the most original and imaginative orchestral play . . . , and I won't now talk about the dynamic level.
Here it is as it should be, but sometimes in the other pieces it assumes such
dimensions that I—once the initial surprise is over—become almost numb
and then weak, unreceptive to everything, no matter how wonderful it
may be. . . . But as I said, we have talent up here—and better to have
something demonic that is kept under control than that German morbid-
ity that isn't capable of vigorous development.

Once the concert was over, Svendsen was able to turn his attention to other
tasks. He had gained a foothold in his home town, and he thrived in the en-
virons that were so familiar to him. His stepson Sigurd enrolled in the local
school and soon began to feel quite at home. For Bergljot, however, it was
not easy to make the adjustment from "the good life" in the major cities and
music centers of Europe and America to the dull routine of life in a provincial city like Oslo.

Marital strife soon reared its ugly head. Bergljot, who came from a
wealthy family, was accustomed to luxury and found it difficult to adjust to
her situation as the wife of a penniless composer. She wanted to continue
living in the manner to which she was accustomed, and to that end she
made frequent shopping trips to the finest stores in town. The bills that followed drove her husband to despair. He found it necessary to take out loan
after loan, and the debt he thus incurred was such that it took him twenty
years to fully pay it off. Another and even more serious point of contention
between them was Bergljot's tendency to jealousy—which, in view of
Johan's weakness for the fair sex, was not totally unwarranted.

One bright spot in Svendsen's life at this time was his association and
collaboration with Grieg. In temperament and artistic bent the robust and
extroverted Svendsen was almost the direct opposite of his often sickly and
hypersensitive friend. They complemented each another in a remarkable
way: where Svendsen was strong, Grieg was weaker—and vice versa.

In their work together in the Music Society, which was to continue for a year and a half and become more and more comprehensive, they shared the responsibility in a completely amicable way. Under the joint leadership of two such talents, the Society entered a period of growth that led to a series of outstanding performances of both older and newer works. Grieg assumed responsibility for the more administrative duties.

At the general meeting of the Music Society in October, 1872, the Society was reorganized and new by-laws were adopted. As part of the reorganization, a board consisting of fourteen members was created. The board included such wealthy men as Consul Thomas J. Heftye, Professor Julius Nicolaysen, and Supreme Court Justice Peder Lasson but also such well-known music people as L. M. Lindeman and piano manufacturer Karl Hals. The November 3 issue of *Morgenbladet* told of the Society's plans to perform major works by Beethoven, Mendelssohn, Gade, and Liszt.

The season opener on November 30 was well attended. Grieg conducted Beethoven's fifth symphony and premiered his own latest work, *Before a Southern Convent*. Svendsen wielded the baton for the Norwegian premiere of his *Violin Concerto*, op. 6, with fellow Norwegian Gudbrand Bøhn as the soloist. The critics were effusive in their praise, noting especially Svendsen's "brilliant" leadership of the orchestra. The foundation appeared to have been laid for further triumphs to come.

THE CORONATION MARCH AND FESTIVAL POLONAISE

After the smashing success of the autumn 1872 concert, Svendsen entered upon a two-year period that proved to be both demanding and rewarding. There were problems aplenty, but he overcame them and bit by bit began to feel that his work was beginning to show results.

In January 1873 he planned to present another orchestral concert on his own, but unforeseen problems arose that required him to postpone it just a few days before the scheduled performance. He revealed his disappointment in a January 22 letter to his publisher, E. W. Fritzsch in Leipzig, telling of difficulties so numerous that they threatened to rob him of his courage to go on:

> The musical conditions here are anything but encouraging. There is no complete orchestra, there are no singers, not a single choir, and worst of all: no true interest on the part of the audience in real music. You cannot

imagine how hard I have worked to arrange a concert. If circumstances require that I continue working here, I feel that the artist in me will die. It is, therefore, my firm decision to get away as soon as possible—where and when, the gods only know.

But it was contrary to his nature to give up, and on February 18 he was able to present his concert to a packed house with an orchestra composed of "both local theater instrumentalists and other professional musicians and amateurs."

The concert was enormously successful. King Oscar II, who was in Oslo on his first-ever visit to Norway, added luster to the event and, according to *Morgenbladet,* "participated in the enthusiastic applause that accompanied each number and each movement."

The program included Svendsen's D-major symphony, his violin concerto, the prelude to Wagner's *Lohengrin,* and Svendsen's own arrangements of Schumann's *Abendlied* and Liszt's *Hungarian Rhapsody No. 2.* Also on the program was the world premiere of Svendsen's arrangement for string orchestra of Ole Bull's *The Shepherd Girl's Sunday.* In Svendsen's arrangement this wonderful melody, which in Bull's original version was given only a sparse chordal accompaniment, was clothed in colorful harmonies that raised it to new heights.

This was the second performance of Svendsen's violin concerto in Oslo, and this time the reviews were even more favorable. *Aftenposten* wrote that it "abounded with great musical ideas, while the symphonic treatment of the motives bears both beautiful and powerful witness to the composer's poetic sense of beauty with respect both to the larger whole and to the details."

Svendsen astonished the audience by conducting the entire concert from memory—an unheard-of feat in Norway at that time—and *Aftenposten* concluded its review by saying that he had convincingly demonstrated that he deserved "the significant rank, which he was accorded abroad long ago, among the most brilliant orchestral leaders of our time."

The concert triumph restored Svendsen's courage. He realized that he could not desert his hometown, for he had truly experienced at first hand that there was understanding both for him personally and for "real music." Despite the burdensome financial problems, therefore, he decided to stay in Oslo and continue the work that he had begun.

In order to make ends meet, however—at least to some extent—it was not enough just to give an occasional concert. On March 6, 1873, an advertisement appeared in *Morgenbladet*: "Johan Svendsen will accept students in harmony, orchestration, free composition, violin, and ensemble playing for piano students." Grieg had carried on similar kinds of private instruction for several years, for the music academy that he had established in collaboration with Winter-Hjelm had lasted for only two years. Grieg and Svendsen became, therefore, friendly rivals for the same "student market." The rivalry was not totally without complications, however. The two friends had agreed that they would charge three crowns for each lesson, but Svendsen soon insisted that the fee be doubled. According to Svendsen's second wife, Juliette, who recounted the story many years later, "Grieg was dismayed—they would lose all their students! Who in this poverty-stricken town would pay six crowns for a music lesson? But it went all right." Mrs. Svendsen added that this was perhaps the only time in his life that her husband displayed any financial sense, for "he sold all of his compositions outright without ensuring for himself a royalty for each new edition" (136).

Svendsen, by virtue of his winning personality and cheerful disposition, quickly became a popular teacher, and he soon had almost more students than he could handle. Among the Norwegian musicians who studied with him were Iver Holter, Per Lasson, and Per Winge. Later he also had several foreign students, including Robert Kajanus, a Finn who studied with him in Paris in 1879–80, and such Danish students as Hakon Børresen, Fini Henriques, and Alfred Tofft, who studied with him in Copenhagen. Many of his students later told of the strong and lasting impression made on them by his inspiring teaching. His capacity for empathetic understanding and his sensitivity for his students and their compositions enabled him to bring out their best.

During the winter season of 1872–73 the Music Society presented three large evening orchestral programs, all led by Grieg. The second subscription concert (December 21) included Norwegian premieres of two Danish works: Niels W. Gade's *Symphony No. 4* and August Winding's *Nordic Overture*. Norwegian pianist Edmund Neupert also appeared as piano soloist in Beethoven's *Emperor Concerto*. The subscription concert on January 4 was devoted to chamber music, the performers being Gudbrand Bøhn, Edmund Neupert, Hans Nielsen, and a chorus directed by Johan D. Behrens. On January 11 Schubert's C-major symphony was performed and Agathe Backer appeared as soloist in Schumann's piano concerto. On

March 11 the Christiania String Quartet (G. Bøhn, E. Kortoe, F. Ursin, and H. Nielsen) presented a program of chamber music in which Svendsen's string quartet was played in its entirety for the first time in Norway. The Music Society's last orchestral concert, which was postponed several times, finally occurred on April 26, with Mendelssohn's *Elijah* leading the program.

According to the April 23 minutes of the board of The Norwegian Student Society, Svendsen had just taken over the leadership of the Student Society orchestra, which had maintained a somewhat fragile existence for about fifty years. According to Erik Hagtun, who has studied the history of this organization (25), the orchestra at this time consisted of some thirty players, and its principal task was to assist in theatrical productions of the Student Society. How much Svendsen had to do with this organization is not known, but it apparently was not much. His name appears in the minutes just this one time, and he himself never mentioned anything about his work with the students.

Meanwhile, Svendsen's music was beginning to win an international audience. On April 29 his string quintet was played in Cologne and on May 6 the string octet became the first of his large works to be performed in Denmark. The Copenhagen daily *Dagbladet* wrote, "The composer, who is said to be a young Norwegian educated in Germany, gives the impression of being a gifted musician, and his octet is heard with interest although it has a somewhat extravagant stamp." The reviewer in *Berlingske Tidende* found the octet to be rather strong fare: "In addition to unmistakable brilliance of inventiveness and evidence of significant skill in the development of the musical material, there is throughout the composition's several sections a tendency toward abrupt transitions and baroque turns that casts a certain feverish disquiet over several sections and hurts the overall effect."

On July 10 the D-major symphony was performed at an outdoor concert conducted by Theodore Thomas in New York's Central Park. *Watson's Art Journal* (July 12) was outspokenly positive: "The work strikes us as fresh in thought, vigorous and delicate in imagination and broad in treatment." The *New York Daily Tribune* (same date) stated, "the harmonic progressions are occasionally unduly difficult." Thomas also presented *Sigurd Slembe* at concerts in November 1873 and February 1874. *The World* (November 24) wrote that on the basis of the Svendsen compositions that had been played in New York up to that time the Norwegian would have to be regarded, not least with respect to his orchestration, as one of the foremost composers of the day: "His technical mastery of the resources of the modern orchestra is as complete as that of Liszt and Berlioz but unlike these composers, that mastery is with him a means, and not as with them, it seems to us, an end. These tumultous and strident effects which are in their works are in his also, but Svendsen rides his whirlwinds, whereas the whirlwinds of Liszt and Berlioz ride them."

That autumn Svendsen's music was for the first time the subject of a serious discussion in a Parisian publication. Adolphe Jullien wrote a long article, "La musique en Norvège," in *Le Ménestrel*, wherein he stated that Svendsen's orchestral works suffered to some extent from excessive use of short motives and phrases, but that by and large the music was skillfully written and artistically well developed. "The themes in the *scherzo* and *allegro* movements are graceful and charming," he wrote, "and the orchestration abounds with piquant effects; there is a felicitous use of contrasts whereby there is an alternation in the same movement between powerful outbursts of emotion and ingratiating melodies" (67).

During the summer of 1873 Svendsen composed two occasional works: *Coronation March,* op. 13, and *Festival Polonaise,* op. 12. The former was written for the coronation of King Oscar II and Queen Sophie at the Nidaros Cathedral in Trondheim on July 18. As the coronation parade marched up the main street toward the cathedral, Svendsen's new work was played by an ensemble consisting of no less than four military bands. Unfortunately, however, this first performance of the piece proved to be a musical disaster, for the several bands had been placed so far apart that they were unable to hear each other. The result, of course, was sheer cacophony. The Swedish composer Gunnar Wennerberg, who was present, said it sounded "[like a] cry of distress from beginning to end."

The orchestral version of the *Coronation March* was performed abroad sporadically during the following decade. On October 18, 1874, it was the opening number at a large matinee concert at the Gewandhaus in Leipzig. The ensemble, conducted by Carl Reinecke, included musicians from both the Gewandhaus and opera-house orchestras. Two months later Theodore Thomas presented it at one of his philharmonic concerts at Steinway Hall in New York, and *Watson's Art Journal* (December 19) asserted that it ranked with Wagner's *Emperor March* and must be regarded as "one of the most significant marches in the music repertoire of the entire world." Two years later it was played in New York again at a big concert of Scandinavian music. The reviewer for *The World* (October 21, 1876) wrote that the piece "reveals an orchestral mastery exceeded only by that of Wagner. With respect to sound, power, and variation there are few pieces in this format with which it can be compared." After a performance at the Crystal Palace in London on October 16, 1880, *The Musical Standard* (October 23) characterized it as "one of the finest occasional compositions ever written." Svendsen himself presented it at a concert in Stockholm on May 8, 1883. Thereafter, however, it disappeared from the repertoire, and deservedly so, for it really cannot bear comparison with such other well-known Norwegian marches as Grieg's *Homage March,* Halvorsen's *Entrance of the Boyars,* or Johannes Hanssen's *Valdres March.* In melodic appeal it is inferior to all of these, and even the most elegant orchestration cannot conceal this fact.

Some weeks after the coronation festivities in Trondheim the royal couple was scheduled to visit Oslo, and elaborate plans were made to properly welcome the celebrated guests. Svendsen was given the honor of being asked to write a festival polonaise to be played at the opening of a "public ball" on Saturday, August 6—a gigantic folk festival held under the open sky in a large city square. The local newspapers waxed rhapsodic in their reports of the gala event. The thrones had stood beneath an ermine-trimmed drapery, with the crowns and royal coat-of-arms displayed on a red-bedecked dais. *Morgenbladet* reported that the king "led the polonaise . . . , for which Johan Svendsen had composed some stately music."

The task of writing music for an event such as this was tailor-made for Svendsen, who loved parties, and the piece was finished in a very short time. The result—*Festival Polonaise,* op. 12—fairly sparkles with infectious joy, bubbling as it is with melodies that quickly etch themselves into one's memory. Here is the opening theme:

Example 8   *Festival Polonaise,* op. 12

An important new theme enters in G major, and soon it is combined with a countermelody derived from the opening theme—a typical Svendsen maneuver that is used here with marvelous effect:

Example 9   *Festival Polonaise,* op. 12

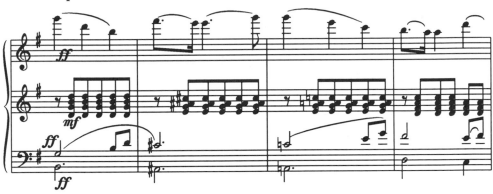

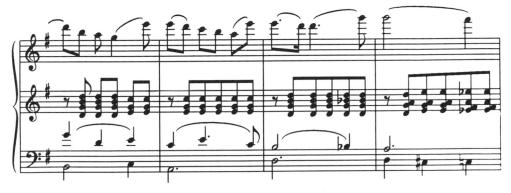

The structure is ABA. In the middle section Svendsen adds a Norwegian touch to this Polish dance form in a series of short motives that clearly reflect the characteristics of Norwegian folk dance music. The piece is brilliantly orchestrated and sounds wonderfully fresh and bright.

Svendsen's is undoubtedly one of the finest festival polonaises ever composed, and one can only wonder why it has thus far failed to find its rightful place in the orchestral repertoire outside Scandinavia. It is, to be sure, occasional music, but occasional music of the very finest kind. Perhaps it will one day be "discovered" by the rest of the world.

The 1873–74 concert season of the Music Society got off to a surprisingly slow start. Not until November 26 could the newspapers report that there would, indeed, be a series of concerts once again. Svendsen and Grieg's friends Julius Nicolaysen and Alexius Ræder had headed up a successful drive to raise enough money to underwrite a 16-concert subscription series. It did not actually prove possible to put together that many programs in the time remaining, but from December to May there were eleven. Of these, eight were orchestral concerts and three were devoted to chamber music. Three of the orchestral concerts also involved choirs, and Grieg conducted these. Svendsen conducted the five purely orchestral concerts and was responsible for the chamber music programs. He also played viola at some of the latter.

One might have expected that the two young composers would use this opportunity to feature their own compositions, but this did not occur. They evidently did not want to open themselves to the charge of blowing their own horn.

The programs consisted largely of works by the old masters—Bach, Haydn, Mozart, Beethoven, Schubert and Schumann—though some space was also given to such then-contemporary composers as Liszt, Wagner, and Brahms. Among the Scandinavian composers whose works appeared on these programs were J. P. E. Hartmann and Niels W. Gade—both Danes—and Johan Selmer, a Norwegian. The principal reason for this cautious choice of repertoire was financial: as a private organization the Music Society received no public funding and was, therefore, heavily dependent on good concert attendance to balance its budget. Economic wisdom dictated that nothing be done to scare audiences away.

Nonetheless, the season did not proceed without some friction. Two "letters to the editor" tell much about what the conductors had to contend with. One indignant man wrote to *Morgenbladet* (January 18, 1874) complaining about the fact that the Music Society had the audacity to offer concerts on Sunday forenoon. He also fretted about the large number of concerts being offered: "Neither one's time nor one's purse can tolerate so many. One can see that in arranging so many concerts the Music Society is doing the exact opposite of what it intends, which is to maintain and strengthen the awakening musical interest." A few weeks later (March 31) the following little complaint from an "unmusical" patron appeared in *Aftenposten*:

> We are equally mystified by Mr. Johan Selmer's *Scène funèbre* and by Mr. Johan Svendsen's *Coronation March*. . . . We are bored by these *classical* concerts that some people make such a pretentious fuss about here— concerts where one hears compositions that drag on for an hour and in which one must be happy if one finds one single beautiful melody which, like the gospel in a sermon, is as easy to understand as the sermon is te-

dious and incomprehensible. Moreover, most people are not musical in the sense that they enjoy this classical music. The vast majority even of those who attend the concerts during the winter—among other reasons, because (as one lady innocently explained) "Mama wants me to go because it is cultured"—are terribly bored with many of them. One can see it clearly in the uninterested and distracted faces of ladies as well as gentlemen, young as well as old—who find insufficient comfort in the assurance that the music is classical.

The Music Society also had to compete with other musical events for the available audience. The city had grown considerably by this time, increasing from ca. 30,000 inhabitants in 1845 to double that number in the mid-1860s and over 100,000 by 1874. Oslo was no longer a small town but a large and growing city with big ambitions in music as in other areas. Many concerts of various kinds were given in several different locations. The Christiania Theater was the principal home of operas, operettas, musical comedies, and dramatic productions with incidental music. Møllergadens Theater competed with Christiania Theater for audiences desiring the lighter musical fare, and during the summer months the Klingenberg Theater in the Tivoli amusement park also offered operettas and musical comedies.

When one compares Svendsen's and Grieg's work in the Music Society it is clear that the musicians were more comfortable under Svendsen's baton than under Grieg's. The latter's musicality and selfless commitment obviously won their respect, but he never became popular. The intense preoccupation with details sometimes struck them as arrogance, and the musicians often became irritated at his bad habit of going over selected passages again and again without explaining clearly what he was trying to accomplish. O. M. Sandvik relates that at one rehearsal the musicians had more of this than they could stomach, and when Grieg, after endless repetitions of this sort, finally said, "All right, now we will take the whole thing over once again," the concertmaster, Fredrik Ursin, replied, "Yes, let's do that!" and struck up a fast popular dance tune for solo violin. Everybody laughed, and Grieg bowed and said: "Yes—well, that will be all for today!" And with that the storm was over (99/II:165).

Svendsen, on the other hand, was practically idolized by the musicians, both because of his infectious joy in making music and because of his unique leadership abilities. Professor O. P. Monrad, who played cello in the orchestra, tells of one revealing episode. Svendsen was conducting the first rehearsal of a large orchestral work containing a virtuoso solo passage that was to be played by the first clarinetist. The soloist had not yet learned the part, however, but Svendsen, unperturbed, simply sang the entire passage in falsetto (84/II). On another occasion when Grieg was conducting the rehearsal, the timpanist was absent. "Now comes this lovely passage where the timpani comes in, but we'll have to get along without it today," Grieg said sadly. But when the passage arrived the timpani boomed out as it was supposed to, for Svendsen had surreptitiously slipped in behind the timpani. Grieg could barely discern the good-natured smile on his friend's face (135).

Svendsen's leadership ability found expression not least in his warm humanity and good psychological sense. Monrad reports:

> A poor second violinist might sit well hidden as far away as possible and play, say, a simple F too high or too low. You couldn't fool Svendsen. He heard it, but didn't make an issue of it at the time. But you may be sure that in due course the offending player got what he deserved: later, when they were alone, Svendsen might quietly raise an eyebrow mischievously, smile wanly, and ask, "Say, whatever happened on that F?" (84/II).

Monrad also reported that the members of the orchestra regarded Svendsen as one of themselves, even though they didn't dare to call him by his first name. Moreover, he was a master at explaining what he wanted. "It was purely and simply a pleasure to listen to him," Monrad wrote. "Having worked hard to acquire his broad musical knowledge, he knew how to explain things in such a way that anyone hearing him would grasp the heart of the matter. It was as if he, in his own quiet way, knew how to add just enough salt to make the admonition palatable." The musicians sat as if spellbound when he alternated between "a sudden, biting malice which he immediately chased away with a smile" and a "fresh, witty remark that he just *couldn't* hold back." But he also had a rare capacity to express himself "in words of sterling, powerful value" (84/II).

Doctor of medicine F. G. Gade, an amateur violinist who played under Svendsen, reported that "Johan Svendsen had an exceptional ability to get the most delicate *pianissimo* out of the orchestra. In this connection I remember one rehearsal when he gave the following general instruction: 'When it says *ppp*, every single player must hear the rest of the orchestra better than he hears his own instrument. When it says *fff*, one should only be able to hear oneself.' And one could never forget this delightful overstatement; one became vigilantly aware of changes in the dynamics" (138).

When Svendsen was on the podium the orchestra always felt secure. He for his part knew what he could reasonably expect out of his players. He knew their strengths and their weaknesses and knew how to get each of them to do his very best. But slovenliness was anathema to him. He was a strict disciplinarian, but he exercised his discipline in such a way that no one felt unjustly treated. Gade wrote about the orchestra's first rehearsal of Svendsen's second symphony in 1876:

> There were plenty of mistakes at this sight-reading rehearsal, but Svendsen immediately zeroed in on the places where his sharp ears noted errors. [The problem sections] were repeated again and again, and finally it began to take shape. The most dangerous moment during this rehearsal occurred when that lovely bassoon solo at the end of the *scherzo* was handled so badly by the bassoon player that the whole orchestra spontaneously burst into laughter. That made the bassoonist angry, so he began to put away his instrument and was about to leave. It took all the charm and persuasive ability that Svendsen could muster to calm the man down and get him to stay for the rest of the rehearsal.

Many stories are told about Svendsen's skill in repartee. On one occasion he stopped the orchestra during a rehearsal to correct an error. The offending player, a highly experienced musician known for his obstinacy, muttered to himself: "O kiss my a--!" Svendsen, overhearing the remark, shot back: "Sorry, there isn't time—we must go on!"

GRIEG AND SVENDSEN ARE AWARDED ANNUAL STATE GRANTS

In February of 1874, in the midst of the Music Society's most active season, Grieg and Svendsen sent a joint application to the National Assembly (*Stortinget*) seeking annual grants in the amount of 400 *spesiedalers* each. This amount would not in and of itself constitute a living wage, but it was a considerable sum of money. The National Archivist, for example, earned a full-time annual salary of 1,000 *spesiedalers*. The application, which was written in Grieg's hand, argued as follows:

> Since our economic circumstances compel us to spend nearly all our time in routine teaching, which totally destroys the creative power that we feel is necessary to proceed successfully on the path that we have chosen, we venture to send forward the present request.
> We want to call your attention to the way in which provision is made

for musicians in other countries. In the larger countries artistic activities abound: there are sinecures, positions for artistic consultants under a wide variety of forms and titles, all of which exist exclusively to give creative talents an opportunity to develop and thereby enrich their country. But in the smaller countries, with which the comparison in our case perhaps is most appropriate—and restricting ourselves to Scandinavia, and especially Denmark—all the outstanding creative musicians have public annual grants. And we would especially stress that such an arrangement must appear even more necessary here in our developing artistic environment, where we still have none of the things that in other countries have a stimulating effect on the artist's imagination; for we lack the foundation that is to be found in a national opera with an orchestra and a chorus corresponding to the requirements of art and of our time. Finally, we venture to call attention to the fact that, in accordance with our talents, we have worked for the advancement of our art here in Norway, and with respect to the essential facts about our circumstances we refer to the enclosed biographical summaries (33 and 112c).

Neither Grieg nor Svendsen was particularly optimistic about the outcome of this request, for when Alexius Ræder had sought a composer's grant for Svendsen five years earlier it had been denied. The reason given then was that the National Assembly was already providing 2,000 *spesiedalers* annually to support travel abroad for scientists and artists, and that was all that could reasonably be expected of it!

By 1874, however, the political circumstances had changed. The Left Party (*Venstre*) had won the national election, and Grieg hoped that the newly elected representatives might be more inclined to provide public support for the arts. Bjørnson wholeheartedly supported the application in a warm letter of recommendation to his friend Johan Sverdrup, president of the National Assembly, arguing strongly that Norway should recognize this decisive opportunity and act accordingly.

Nonetheless, an affirmative decision did not come easily. The budget committee was evenly divided on the matter, with five members in favor and five opposed to the proposal. According to the rules of the National Assembly, however, the committee chairman had a double vote, and fortunately the chairman, B. L. Essendrop, favored the proposal. Thus the committee supported the proposal by a single vote and sent it to the National Assembly with the following comments:

> Five members of the committee, including the chairman, now wish to support the petition. They assume that the great importance of music for

our cultural development is generally recognized and that art no less than science warrants public assistance. They consider that under present circumstances the most practical way to work toward this end is to support, by personal grants, those who have been endowed with a higher talent along this line. That those whose application we are considering possess such talent has been recognized also in foreign lands in recent years.

They cannot imagine that anyone would suggest that the 2,000 *spesiedalers* appropriated for travel support for artists and scientists constitute such support and they do not fear the implications, since the proposal has to do only with supporting composers who have demonstrated their creative talent. These members assume, however, that the petitioners will dedicate their abilities to the furtherance of music in their homeland (112 d).

The debate in the National Assembly went smoothly, with only two speakers dissenting from the majority recommendation. O. T. Lindstøl maintained that one should not "get into grants of that sort," and P. Jensen told his fellow legislators that if they were to approve such a grant they would "start down a slippery slope and you never know where you can get a foothold." The majority faction was well prepared, however. A. O. Sæhlie had on his own initiative secured a statement of support from the governing board of the Music Society; it was signed by C. Lasson, L. M. Lindeman, J. Nicolaysen, and A. Winge. This statement, which was read aloud during the debate, averred that "both these artists have brought and will bring honor to our country, and they are fully deserving of public financial support."

Johan Sverdrup made a strong statement, emphasizing that the country should now be past the almost "overwhelming work of absolute necessity" that had absorbed the minds and muscles of the entire nation since the political separation from Denmark in 1814. The nation's development now required efforts on other fronts, not least in the area of its cultural life: "It would give us self-respect and the respect of others." The National Assembly had earlier, and rightly, appropriated funds for the gathering of a rare treasure of national melodies, which lay on a shelf gathering dust. It was time that they be appropriately dealt with by well-trained artists. By giving composers' grants to Grieg and Svendsen they would take an essential step forward to advance art music in Norway and at the same time would make the two young composers "men of high rank" in the development of their country's cultural life. Sverdrup acknowledged that he himself had voted against the proposal to give Svendsen a similar grant in 1869, but now, he said, the situation was entirely different. Both Grieg and Svendsen had completed their professional studies long ago and had convincingly demonstrated mastery of their art. Therefore, he concluded, it was appropriate to reach a helping hand to these two rare artistic talents.

The committee's proposal carried on a roll-call vote by a margin of 61 to 44. Each composer was awarded the sum of 400 *spesiedalers* annually "until the National Assembly decides otherwise" (112 e). It was a high honor, placing them in the company of such literary giants as Bjørnstjerne Bjørnson, Henrik Ibsen, and Jonas Lie.

The following year the government recommended that all the annual artists' grants be increased by 200 *spesiedalers* each. The responsible department had found it desirable to extend recognition to these artists "to a somewhat greater extent than had been the case heretofore, provided that the State's resources and due regard for other demands on those resources do not make such an increase inadvisable." This amount, it was pointed out, was in line with the grant given to the linguist Ivar Aasen to further his scientific work, and there was no reason to treat the authors and composers differently (112 f).

Once again the committee was divided, with five members favoring the increase and four opposed (112 g). When the matter was brought before the National Assembly, two separate votes were taken. The first was on a proposal to increase annual grants to authors. This proposal failed by a vote of 54 to 42. The recommendation to increase the grants to Grieg and Svendsen was then quickly defeated, with just 15 votes in support of the increase. Music was clearly not held in the same regard as literature in Norway—yet.

THE NORWEGIAN ARTISTS' CARNIVAL

In 1873 Svendsen became a member of the Artists' Association, the principal gathering place in Oslo for party-loving artists of all types. The major focus of the activity of the Association was the annual festivals, which each year had a special theme and motto. In 1874 Svendsen was elected president of the organization. The motto for the festival that year was "Prince Carnival's Marriage to the Daughter of the Mountain King," and Svendsen decided to write a large orchestral work for the occasion.

The festival, which took place in the Freemasons' Lodge on March 17, was supposed to depict the affinity between the cold North and the warm-blooded South. The North was represented by the Mountain King and his daughter (clearly inspired by Ibsen's *Peer Gynt*), trolls, dwarfs, and other figures drawn from Norwegian folk fairy tales. Representing the South were such characters as Prince Carnival, Bacchus, Columbine, Harlequin, and Pierrot.

The guiding spirit behind the festivities was the painter Knut Bergslien, who skillfully organized the whole event in such a way that the preparations for the festival became a kind of party as well. His appreciation for the grotesque found expression in colorful decorations and costumes, and he himself played the part of the Mountain King with great effect. Bergslien's young colleague Gerhard Munthe, who played the part of Harlequin, later described the dress rehearsal:

> [Under Svendsen's guidance], 80 players rehearsed the music, sometimes individually and sometimes together, making such a racket that we had to shout instead of speaking. . . . The little hall was painted to represent a covered balcony with a view toward the Jotunheimen mountains. The innermost room was the place where the Mountain King kept his valuables. There stood 'the chest containing rare things. . . .' Some things [during the rehearsal] were done well and beautifully, other things were unnecessarily poor, but the party itself was a rousing success! (108:219)

Aftenbladet reported the day after the festival proper that as Svendsen conducted his new work "the grotto in the background opened for the attendants of the Mountain King . . . , whereupon the master of ceremonies withdrew to welcome Prince Carnival and his retinue and to escort them into the hall."

The merriment reached its peak when the portly Bergslien, alias the Mountain King, performed as a tight-rope walker! He had placed a plank between two sawhorses—but all that could be seen from the auditorium was the edge of the plank, which he had painted to look like a real rope. The audience gasped at the sight of the rotund troll king swaying from side to side as he negotiated the perils of his "rope."

As president of the Artists' Association, Svendsen threw himself heart and soul into preparations for the festival, and the orchestral work that he wrote for the occasion was a perfect fit. The antics appealed to his sense of humor, and just as Bergslien painted in colors so he did the same thing in sound.

The work begins with a lively folk-dance tune (a *springar*). It clearly is intended to depict the bride, the Mountain King's daughter. The tune, which is Svendsen's own, demonstrates that he was no less adept than Grieg at creating melodies with a distinctively Norwegian stamp.

The bridegroom, Prince Carnival, is characterized by means of a Neapolitan melody—*Te voglio bene assai (I am very fond of you)*—written by Raffaele Sacco in 1835. The piece had become extremely well known in Italy in an arrangement by Donizetti.

The third theme is a bridal march from Sogn (No. 476 in Lindeman's large collection of folk tunes). This was the first time Svendsen had made use of a genuine folk-dance tune in a composition, but since the work in which he was using it had something of the character of a polonaise in 3/4 time he had to alter it somewhat to adapt it to his purposes.

The climax of the composition is the actual "nuptials" of the Mountain King's daughter and Prince Carnival. With his brilliant ability to combine dissimilar themes, Svendsen managed to bring together the *springar* theme (in flutes, clarinets, and violins) and the Mediterranean melody (in horn and trombones), both in slightly altered forms. The most striking effects have to do with the rhythm. While the *springar* proceeds in triple time as before, the Neapolitan melody—though it is notated in 3/4—clearly comes across as if it were in duple time (6/8). The result is an exciting confrontation between two opposing rhythms. It is a meeting of opposites:

Example 10   *Norwegian Artists' Carnival,* op. 14

Svendsen had called the composition *The Wedding on Mt. Dovre,* and in 1881, when it was to be published as op. 14 by C. F. Peters in Leipzig, this was the title on the manuscript. Max Abraham, director of the Peters firm, recommended that the title be changed to *Nordic Carnival.* In a letter dated June 7, 1881, Svendsen suggested some other possibilities: *Norwegian Artists' Carnival* or *Festival Prelude.* He added that the latter title was "most correct and not so demanding . . . , but since it has to do with a piece of program music it may be a matter of some importance that the piece be given an accurately descriptive title." *Norwegian Artists' Carnival* was the eventual choice.

Later this same year Svendsen wrote another but much shorter work for the Artists' Association: *Purple Nose March.* At the Association's "birthday party" on December 13, 1873, the group had founded "The Ancient and Honorable Order of the Purple Nose." Candidates for membership were blindfolded and subjected to secret operations, and the next time they saw each other they discovered that they had been given bright red noses. Svendsen was slated to become a knight of this order at the party in December of 1874, whereupon he would receive his official ribbon with corkscrew and purple nose "on an (aqua-)white [aquavit] background". The *Purple Nose March,* written for this occasion, was later included in Svendsen's opus list as op. 16 under the title *Humorous March.* It was not published during Svendsen's lifetime, however, and all that has been found is a few pages of a score for strings and piano four-hands. In 1916, however, the march was published by Skandinavisk Musikforlag, Copenhagen, in an arrangement for piano trio by G. Tronchi. Here it was given the title *Paraphrase sur des chansons populaires du Nord.* This sounds more exciting than it is, however, for it turns out that it is nothing more than a march based on a well-known Scandinavian children's song the words of which are the nonsense syllables "Ritsj, ratsj fillibombombom!"

ZORAHAYDA—A MUSICAL DEPICTION OF A MOORISH LEGEND

After Grieg left the city for good in the summer of 1874, Svendsen was deprived of a valued colleague, and it is clear that he felt deeply the absence of his friend. On July 21 he wrote to Grieg:

> I cannot tell you how beautiful it is here just now. The view from the
> house where I live seems to me to grow more beautiful day by day, but

even so I do not feel particularly contented. Except for puttering with my flowers, which are now in full bloom, I have a strange aversion for all activity, especially music. So I don't do anything, and this makes me irritable and dispirited. The best thing for me would be if I could go abroad again. Unfortunately, at the moment there seems little likelihood that I can.

On November 11, in another letter to Grieg, he complained about how hard it was to find enough musicians to give his concerts, and he intimated that the season would be a meager one. The musicians were so tied down with rehearsals for new productions of operas at Christiania Theater that they didn't want to participate in "other undertakings." The operas he was referring to were Mozart's *Don Giovanni* and Gounod's *Faust*.

Svendsen's gloomy prediction proved to be correct, for during the autumn season not a single concert was given at the Music Society. On October 3, however, he managed to put on a concert on his own initiative in the gymnasium of the Akershus fortress. Agathe Backer appeared as soloist in Schumann's piano concerto; otherwise the program was devoted entirely to Svendsen's compositions: *Festival Polonaise* and *Coronation March* as well as premieres of *Zorahayda*, *Two Icelandic Melodies*, and *Last Year I Was Tending the Goats*. The last two were compositions for string orchestra.

The attendance at the concert was good, but even though the musicians played without compensation the profit amounted to only a small sum (fifty *spesiedalers*). In order to make ends meet, therefore, Svendsen was obliged to go further into debt. His constant debt weighed heavily on him during these years—a fact of which he took note in a letter to Grieg dated April 15, 1875: "It is not a pleasant life that I am living. Plagued by debt and other related miseries, I am seldom content, and as a result I am seldom in a mood to compose." The state grant had clearly not made his daily existence as free of care as he had hoped it would.

Zorahayda, which has the subtitle *Legend for Orchestra* and was dedicated to King Oscar II, was finished in August, 1874. A month after its premiere—in a letter to Grieg dated November 11— Svendsen described his new work in a remarkably deprecatory way: "Except for a minor orchestral piece (*Zoraidée*)—which, moreover, is a failure—I haven't written a thing since you left Oslo, and I'm afraid there won't be anything either until I get out of my present situation." He later revised the work, and on February 15, 1879, he wrote to Grieg: "Despite the fact that I am not at all pleased with this opus, I have sold it to Warmuth. What a coward one becomes through lack of money!" Three years later, however—in a letter to Grieg dated June 22, 1882—he expressed himself somewhat more positively: "I am glad that you find some pleasure in *Zorahayda*, which despite the many faults I can now see has nonetheless become dear to me."

It is hard to understand Svendsen's ambivalence regarding *Zorahayda*, for it must be ranked as a very successful example of program music from the Romantic period. The only explanation we can imagine is that he, with his firm anchoring in the classical forms, felt uncomfortable about the looser structure of this "legend for orchestra." It is our opinion that in *Zorahayda* Svendsen has convincingly transported a literary program into a world of sound of surpassing beauty without allowing the music to become episodic in the slightest degree. At the same time, the music is so melodic and sonorous that it is capable of standing on its own, totally independent of the "program" that was the occasion for its coming into being.

Zorahayda was well received by the critics. *Morgenbladet* wrote on October 8, 1874, that the composition "is without doubt a brilliantly inspired work, full of feeling and character, but it is not easily understood and can hardly be properly evaluated until one becomes more familiar with it."

As the nineteenth century drew to a close, *Zorahayda* was perhaps the orchestral work by Svendsen that became most popular internationally. After a performance in Copenhagen on December 4, 1880, Charles Kjerulf wrote in *Dagsavisen* that this composition contained some of the most graceful and poetic music written by any composer of that day. Indeed, he continued, it was one of the best proofs available of the legitimacy of program music.

Zorahayda is based on material created by the American writer Washington Irving. During the 1820s Irving lived in Granada, Spain, where he gathered and recounted Moorish legends. In 1832 he published *Legend of the Rose of the Alhambra,* which was widely acclaimed for its poetic qualities. Svendsen's orchestral composition was inspired by the story of "the three beautiful princesses," and for the first and only time in his life he included a literary program (in French) in the score. The program is as follows:

> One bright and clear summer night Jacinta is sitting beside the alabaster fountain in a courtyard in Alhambra. She is weeping. The tears stream down over her cheeks and her breast, and some of the tear-drops fall into the pool near her feet.

Little by little the crystal-clear water begins to stir. Out of the mist surrounding the alabaster fountain emerges a pale, dream-like figure in the form of a beautiful young woman. In her hands she holds a silver lute and her clothes sparkle with precious jewels.

"Why are you so sorrowful, Jacinta?" asks a melodic, mild voice. "Why do you cloud my pool with your tears? Why do your sobs disturb my restless, wakeful nights?"

"I weep for my beloved, who has left me!"

"Your sorrow will soon be ended. . . . Listen to me! I am the unhappy Zorahayda, like you unhappy in love. A Christian knight from your family won my heart. I promised to follow him to his homeland and to adopt his faith. But I lost my courage, I hesitated too long and was detained as a prisoner in this palace. Therefore the evil powers were given authority over me until a true Christian overcomes the magic power and breaks the spell that keeps me here. You can free me! . . . Will you?"

"Yes, I will!" Jacinta answered.

"Come closer, and be not afraid! Dip your hand in the water from the fountain, pour it over me and baptize me in the customary way in your own faith. My soul will then return to its eternal resting place."

Jacinta went closer, filled her empty hand with water and poured it over the pale figure, whose face beamed in a smile of indescribable loveliness. The silver lute slipped from Zorahayda's hands and came to rest beside Jacinta's feet. The vanishing figure placed her white arms over her breast in the form of a cross, and with a look of inexpressible tenderness she disappeared in a cloud of mist. . . .

Jacinta thought she had been dreaming, but when she saw the silver lute beside her feet all doubt vanished and she rejoiced at the thought that Zorahayda's prediction would soon be fulfilled.

In addition to this descriptive text, Svendsen included supertitles at six points in the score where the principal elements of the story are repeated.

One might wonder why Svendsen—this jovial music-maker who was so much at home at parties and festivals—was attracted by a heart-rending, hyper-romantic story like this. It may have had something to do with what was going on in his life at the time. He himself had married a woman who was raised in a different faith and had participated in a similar baptismal event, i.e., when his own wife had submitted to Christian baptism, with Cosima and Richard Wagner as godparents.

Zorahayda begins quietly (in G minor) with muted strings and a horn sounding longingly in the distance. A tender passage in the oboe becomes a kind of framing melody that recurs later in the piece, including near the end. Jacinta's sadness is depicted by the clarinet with a chromatically colored descending motive, which is taken up and further developed by the flute and oboe:

Example 11   *Zorahayda,* op. 11

This central motive reflects the Oriental atmosphere of the piece. The vision of Zorahayda's sudden appearance in the fountain is illustrated by means of quivering *pizzicato* strings while her telling of her story and conversation with Jacinta are expressed via solo violin supported by the orchestra. This part constitutes the major portion of the composition (in B-flat major).

The section depicting the "baptismal ceremony" consists of simple triads played by the strings (in C major). A certain modal tinge underscores the religious character of what is transpiring at this point.

Zorahayda's subsequent disappearance is accompanied by trills and *pizzicatos* played by an 8-part violin group. Jacinta's joy is then expressed in a broad melody, first in the oboe, then in the first violin and clarinet (in G major) in a strong *crescendo*. The framing melody near the end appears as Jacinta's formerly melancholy motive is transformed from lamenting minor to exultant major.

As always, one is fascinated by Svendsen's exquisite instrumentation. The exotic atmosphere of the text is skillfully reflected in the magical sounds of the orchestra; it is evident from this work that Svendsen's mastery as a composer was not limited to festival music and symphonic form. Special attention was given to the strings, with a sophisticated use of *pizzicato* and the extensive division of players within the different groups.

Some of the same expressive intimacy is to be found also in the sonorous variations for string orchestra on the Norwegian folk tune *Last Year I was Tending the Goats.* Here the smooth chromaticism, so typical for Svendsen, has called forth exquisite nuances.

His arrangements of the two Icelandic folk tunes that he himself had transcribed during his visit to Iceland in 1867 were far less Romantic in character. In these works, which also reflect the hand of a master, he chose an archaizing style with simple, sometimes modally tinged, chord progressions.

ALONE ON THE RAMPARTS

From the very beginning the Music Society had had problems assembling an adequate orchestra. The string section was strongest, with ten first violins, ten seconds, six violas, four cellos, and four double basses. Among these were a number of fine players, including the excellent concertmaster Gudbrand Bøhn. The woodwinds were weaker. Typically there was just one oboe, and if they weren't able to borrow a second oboist from the Christiania Theater orchestra they had to substitute a C-clarinet instead. The bassoons posed an even bigger problem; often the part had to be played by a tenor trombone. There was, however, a good supply of competent flute and clarinet players. An occasional shortage of horn players was covered by adding a couple of alto saxhorns to the French horn section. O. M. Sandvik has given a vivid description of the conditions:

> The French horn players were musical enough, but a little slow on the uptake, so in Beethoven's fifth symphony Grieg had to wait patiently for their introduction of the second theme in the first movement. The Swede Johanson, an excellent performer on the natural (valveless) horn, was only rarely willing to be a guest performer with the orchestra. He preferred to go around in the city backyards to make money, playing solo!
>
> Only a few of the players were professional musicians. It was necessary to depend on interested amateurs. Many of these were also fine players.
>
> Eventually it became impossible to manage with the available woodwinds. The conductor always had to go around to the cafés and haggle with them to get them to participate (99/II:171).

Such were the conditions that Grieg and Svendsen had to contend with. After Grieg left to go abroad in 1874, Svendsen had to carry on by himself. The results he achieved under such wretched conditions were, therefore, remarkable.

Prior to the beginning of the 1874–75 season he tried very hard to organize a concert series under the auspices of the Music Society. Despite his persistent efforts, however, the musicians were unresponsive. Many of them were busy with other musical activities and were reluctant to spend their efforts on symphonic music. A number of the most faithful musicians, especially some of the older string players, had by this time left the orchestra. Concertmaster Gudbrand Bøhn had more or less had to give up his career because of a finger malady. New, inexperienced players had to be recruited and whipped into shape.

A surprising number and variety of musical activities were going on in Oslo at this time. During the 1874–75 season, for example, the Christiania Theater gave no less than 55 operatic performances (including Mozart's *Don Giovanni* and *The Marriage of Figaro* and Gounod's *Faust*), 15 performances of operettas and comic operas (including Waldemar Thrane's *The Mountain Adventure*), and 20 performances of plays requiring incidental music (including Bjørnson/Grieg's *Sigurd Jorsalfar*). During the 1875–76 season the number of operatic performances was nearly doubled! In addition to all of these performances at the Christiania Theater, there were the performances at the other two theaters in the city as well as a goodly number of concerts given by both local and visiting artists.

In the face of such competition, the Music Society had trouble getting an adequate number of either subscribers or capable musicians. The result was that the first subscription concert of the season did not take place until January 30, 1975.

Toward spring a total of four orchestral concerts were given. To make the programs more attractive to a broader public, some lighter numbers were included—such things as songs and short orchestral pieces. Each program included at least one major work, however—a symphony or a concerto. That Svendsen's first symphony was included in the program for May 1 was owing not least to the following notice—signed by several subscribers—that appeared in the city's major newspapers on April 8:

> Mr. Johan S. Svendsen. We hereby take the liberty of encouraging you to allow your wonderful symphony to be played at the next concert of the Music Society. In so doing you would satisfy the wishes of many people even as that thoroughly interesting and magnificent composition would contribute mightily to bringing the present season's series of concerts to a worthy conclusion.

Morgenbladet wrote glowingly of the event: "The curtain calls that ensued for Mr. Svendsen after the conclusion of the symphony were not only to honor the composer but also to thank him for the remarkable way in which he has managed to keep the Music Society going this winter."

Svendsen did not do any further composing at this time, however. In an August 10 letter to Johan Selmer he explained his lack of productivity: "I am too preoccupied with pecuniary woes for my imagination to develop as it should, and the result is that I don't write anything. If only I could have paid off my debt!"

The autumn season of 1875 was heavily dominated by the German musician W. Zogbaum, who had come to Norway in 1859. Zogbaum was the conductor of the military orchestra in Horten, a town about fifty miles south of Oslo, but also came to Oslo from time to time to give concerts "for winds as well as string instruments." Zogbaum had contact with many musicians in his homeland, and as a result of his efforts Norway experienced a veritable invasion of German musicians at this time. *Zogbaums Kapel* absolutely bombarded Oslo's concert-going public, giving no less than 36 concerts in the course of just two months. Most of these were of the popular variety, but a few of them included demanding classical works—for example, Beethoven's *Emperor Concerto*, with Erika Lie as soloist.

The Music Society obviously was affected by the competition from Zogbaum, but Svendsen also realized that he could benefit from the services of the best of the German musicians. The musicians, for their part, were interested in earning a little extra money, so a mutually beneficial collaboration developed. But when the Music Society orchestra was to play Beethoven's *Eroica* at the third concert of the season (March 25, 1876), an acute problem arose. The Germans demanded double pay as a condition of their participation in the playing of this piece, and the Music Society could not agree to that. When the musicians were told at the dress rehearsal that their demand had been rejected, they walked out. "Svendsen was white with rage, and the episode affected him so deeply that after the rehearsal he was spitting blood. Some quick changes were made in the instrumentation, and they got along with the players that remained" (99/II:167). Several of the musicians, however, ended up playing parts at the concert that they had not had an opportunity to practice!

Aftenbladet praised Svendsen for having succeeded in putting on the concert under such trying circumstances, concluding with the following expression of concern: "It is easy to see that the task of putting together an

Johan Svendsen in 1875. (Universitetsbiblioteket, Oslo)

orchestra under these and other current painful circumstances is extremely
difficult. . . . We are left once again with an orchestra situation that ranks
somewhere between miserable and worrisome."

Throughout the spring season the Music Society had to compete with
the magnificent *Peer Gynt* performances at the Christiania Theater, which
were playing to a packed house. It became evident that a complete symphony orchestra could not be assembled for the last subscription concert of
the season, scheduled for May 20. The bulk of the program, therefore, consisted of chamber music that would appeal to a wide audience—including
such works as Handel's *Concerto Grosso* in G minor and Schumann's *Piano
Quintet.*

This concert, too, was a total success—despite the fact that on the very day of the concert *Aftenbladet* published an article chastising Svendsen for his "perhaps too great willingness to include modern compositions on the program." After the concert, however, the newspaper encouraged him in its lead article not to lose courage because of the dismal orchestral resources but, on the contrary, to redouble his efforts to continue his great and important work.

We have two statements from Svendsen during this period that shed light on his view of the role of the composer and the artist's lot. On February 28, in response to an inquiry from his young pupil, Iver Holter, he wrote:

> You are well aware that with respect to matters affecting free composition it is impossible to establish rules that apply to every circumstance, for the circumstances are so various and often of such an unanticipated character that it would be folly to try to control them by setting up rules in advance. In circumstances such as these, the composer himself is the highest authority, and I can therefore only advise you on such occasions to consult your own good sense. It is, when all is said and done, the surest [source of good advice].

Three months later Holter, who was trying to decide between a career in medicine and one in music, asked for Svendsen's advice. Svendsen replied in a very candid letter dated May 24, 1876:

> Do you feel that you have the strength to seriously begin a long and difficult course of study? And finally the chief point: Are you so committed to art that you—without regard to the material rewards that a successful exercise of it might possibly bring you—are ready to offer *everything* in its service? The physician's ideal task is indeed to help his fellows, the task of art is to ennoble, gladden, and inspire them; and I daresay that neither of these is inferior to the other in worth—provided that one is equal to the chosen task.

In the midst of all the annoyances with the orchestra, in the spring of 1876 Svendsen managed to find the strength to complete his largest work: the *Symphony No. 2* in B-flat Major, op. 15. He was also at work at this time on a composition in a totally different genre: the "Fantasia for Orchestra," *Romeo and Juliet*, op. 18, which was finished in September. He also turned his attention once again to folk music, making arrangements of two Swedish folk melodies: *Den sörjande* (*The Mourner*) and *Allt under himmelens fäste* (*Everything under Heaven's Firmament*).

Something happened on October 25 that was to have important consequences for the music life of the city. A group of men with a love for chamber music—led by Svendsen's friend, Alexius Ræder—took the initiative in establishing a Quartet Society in order "to give the various amateur quartets an opportunity for joint performances and cooperation" (18:56). Svendsen was not present at the meeting creating the society, but he quickly got involved in it and became one of its driving forces. Each Sunday morning he coached the so-called *Mediciner* quartet, and in a short time he functioned as leader at meetings of the society. During the first season there were eight meetings, with music-making followed by socializing around a large punch bowl.

In the autumn of 1876 it became evident that it would not be possible for the Music Society to give any concerts, but Svendsen once again began making arrangements for a concert of his own where he could premiere his latest works: the second symphony, *Romeo and Juliet*, and the arrangements of two Swedish folk melodies. This concert was given on October 14, 1876.

Bergljot Svendsen performed at this concert—it was the first and only time she appeared at a public concert in Norway—singing a serenade by Gounod and two Scottish folk ballads. Her accompanist was Martin Ursin. Svendsen had been reluctant to present his wife as a singer but acceded to the strong urging of her friends.

The critics tried to be kind. To be sure, mention was made of the fact that her voice was too weak for the concert hall, but *Aftenposten* wrote that she "made it clear in a very beautiful way that she is a fine artist."

The general public must have been relatively disinterested in the premiere performances of Svendsen's three latest works, for the attendance was pitifully low. The receipts were not even sufficient to cover expenses, so Svendsen himself had to make up the difference of some 125 *spesiedalers*. *Aftenbladet* stated that "such a result must be more than enough to paralyze the most idealistic man's energy and spirit."

But although the concert was not a financial success, it was in any case an artistic triumph for Svendsen. Both the audience and the critics realized immediately that he had now entered a very important phase in his artistic development.

The arrangement for string orchestra of *The Mourner* is no longer extant, but in 1878 Svendsen published *Everything Under Heaven's Firmament* together with *Thou Ancient, Thou Free* as *Two Swedish Folk Melodies,* op. 27.

The critics were somewhat guarded in their estimate of *Romeo and Juliet. Aftenbladet* (October 17) identified it as the least significant work on the program, and *Morgenbladet* (October 19) asserted that it "did not strike us as exhibiting the stamp of his artistic individuality as did the symphony." *Ny illustreret Tidende* (October 29) wrote: "We missed the bounteous eroticism that the mere mention of the Shakespearean love story causes one to expect."

Svendsen was not the first composer who had been charmed by Shakespeare's immortal play. Berlioz's dramatic symphony bearing that same title was premiered in Paris in 1839, and Gounod's opera had had its premiere there in 1867. Better known than either of these by the concert-going public is Tchaikovsky's great concert overture. The original version of this piece was performed for the first time in 1870, but it did not reach its final form until 1879. It is unknown whether Svendsen was familiar with any of these works at the time he wrote his "Fantasia for Orchestra."

Romeo and Juliet was for the most part designed in much the same way as *Sigurd Slembe.* The programmatic element appears, however, to be less direct in *Romeo and Juliet* than in the earlier composition.

There is some question as to how closely Svendsen has tried to follow Shakespeare's tragedy, even with respect to its central significance as the symbol of unhappy love. To be sure, one can identify passages that seem to touch on certain aspects of the play: the slow introduction that provides the background, the strife between the rival Capulet and Montague families, the intense emotion of the young lovers where the music reaches great dramatic heights, and the quiet conclusion as the lovers are united in death. The composer has not attempted, however, to relate the details of the love story. He has attempted only to create a lyrical prelude that heightens expectations before the curtain goes up and the play begins.

On May 11, 1879, Svendsen proposed to the Breitkopf & Härtel firm in Leipzig that they publish *Romeo and Juliet.* He requested an honorarium of 500 *riksmarks* and also specified that arrangements be made for a piano four-hands version of the piece to be published at the same time as the orchestral score. The firm accepted this proposal.

On May 5, 1880, a very positive review of the piece appeared in *Allgemeine musikalische Zeitung.* Svendsen's orchestral fantasia has not succeeded in winning a place in the international repertoire, however. The reason for this undoubtedly is to be found first and foremost in the weak thematic material, which lacks the driving appeal that characterizes Tchaikovsky's scintillating composition based on the same literary material.

No apologies are necessary, however, in the case of Svendsen's finest work, the *Symphony No. 2* in B-flat major.

THE SECOND SYMPHONY

Musical insiders in Oslo looked forward with great anticipation to the premiere of Svendsen's second symphony, op. 15, on October 14, 1876. There were rumors that it was a masterpiece of major proportions. It soon became apparent that Svendsen had created music that appealed to everyone, even those who customarily reacted to a symphony like a bull to a red flag. The excitement in the concert hall was enormous. There was loud applause after each movement; indeed, the third movement had to be repeated.

The critics were unanimous in their positive judgment. Aimar Grøn-vold, whose extensive review appeared in *Aftenbladet* on October 17, began by saying that the three first movements had a formal elegance reminiscent of Mendelssohn. He then continued as follows:

> The first *Allegro* is distinguished by its powerful, bouncy motive (3/4 time) and its vibrant rhythm—something one nearly always finds in Svendsen's music, the quality that gives his works this character of fresh youthfulness. There then followed by way of sharp contrast a deep, somber, darkly colored *Andante* that in our opinion is the most beautiful and noblest movement in the whole symphony. In place of a *scherzo* there is an *Intermezzo*, which with its reel-like motive and its unrestrained merriment was nonetheless a genuine Svendsenian *scherzo* on a par with the famous one in his D-major symphony. The middle section with the energetic motive in the lower register was particularly effective.
>
> In these three movements Svendsen is at his very best, partly because here everything seems to be tied together. In the *Finale*, however, which struck us as being qualitatively different from the three preceding movements, the overall effect—despite many brilliant passages—was more episodic.
>
> In any case Svendsen has produced a splendid work, one that is significant for his development. In our opinion it demonstrates that his musical power is richer than ever and his work is as exacting and serious

as always. The imaginative motives, the bold harmonization, and the
brilliant colors of the instrumentation cover the whole symphony with
an enchanting power and a ripe clarity that are manifestations of genius.
These qualities elevate the symphony as a work of art even as they appeal
to every musical temperament.

The judgment of his professional colleagues was more important to
Svendsen than that of the local press, however, and after he had conducted
the German premiere of his symphony with the Gewandhaus Orchestra in
Leipzig on November 8, 1877, he did in fact receive predominantly en-
couraging reviews. E. Kipke had a long article in the November 16 issue of
Musikalisches Wochenblatt in which he described the symphony as a resounding success and had kind words for the pleasing way in which the ideas were
presented. Each movement, he said, had its own individuality, yet the work
as a whole had a beautifully crafted unity. With a clear understanding of the
limits of his own talent, the composer had consciously avoided "strutting
about in the garb of tragedy," but had "confidently given expression to
what was on his heart, and that was the right thing to do, for in that way he
could elicit the healthy, natural and free character that is far removed from
pretentious artificiality." Kipke's principal criticism of the work had to do
with Svendsen's development technique, which he found somewhat too
rhapsodic.

The November number of *Signale*, however, carried a deadly review by
Eduard Bernsdorf, who always wrote in a similar vein when discussing contemporary Norwegian music. He admitted that he had an *a priori* bias against
any "nationality principle" in music, particularly with respect to such genres
as the symphony and the sonata. Therefore, he said, he was not at all impressed when Svendsen made use of explicitly Norwegian motives: "We
are not at all interested in being reminded every moment that a composer
was born and bred in a country that he is now striving to reflect in music."

This symphony, in our view, is Svendsen's most mature and distinguished work. It has a probity and an originality of expression that place it
among the very best symphonies written by Nordic composers. The musical structure is exceptionally well conceived, and as always in Svendsen's
compositions the instrumental garb is sonorous, at times dazzling in its richness of color.

A striking example of his innovative instrumentation occurs in the first
movement where the solo flute introduces the principal theme in the reca-

pitulation. The flute is undergirded by a gossamer web of strings: the violas carry the bass line and the violins are divided into eight parts. The first violins play *sul ponticello* while the seconds play *pizzicato*. Obviously inspired by Berlioz, Svendsen in this way achieves an accompaniment for the delicate flute melody that is both ample and light.

Svendsen has not ventured out into the fathomless depths in this composition, but neither was it his intention to do so. The music does not communicate a drama of fate or of turbulent passions but is, rather, a resounding expression of happiness and *joie de vivre*.

How does the B-flat major symphony differ from its predecessor, which was written ten years earlier? Does it provide evidence of a demonstrable artistic development?

The answer is both "yes" and "no". Svendsen's technical mastery was already evident in the D-major symphony, and his style had not changed perceptibly during the intervening years. The difference between the two symphonies is most evident in the character of the themes. In the first symphony, as also in the chamber-music works written during Svendsen's student days, the themes exhibited a certain glib rhythmic symmetry that sometimes created the impression of short-windedness; their youthful freshness gave them a driving, almost aggressive character. That is no longer the case in the second symphony. The difference is evident from the very first measure as the symphony begins with a well-balanced, restrained, singable main theme, monumental in character despite the allegro tempo:

Example 12   *Symphony No. 2, op. 15, 1st movement*

The theme, which starts in the lower-voiced instruments in *p*, traces a long, 16-measure melodic arc, with an octave leap at the beginning followed by a broken triad and then another octave leap before continuing in a more stepwise fashion.

Strangely enough, this motive (a) plays a relatively minor role in the subsequent development, while the b-motive is given unusual prominence. This circumstance is related to the fact that a slightly altered version of the b-motive constitutes an important part of the subsidiary theme. In this way Svendsen has built a bridge between the two themes.

The subsidiary theme, which begins in F minor, has a somewhat capricious character. Once again Svendsen smiles in a minor key. The theme contrasts nicely with the broad opening theme. Interestingly, Svendsen has departed from tradition and from his own earlier practice by audaciously reversing the customary characters of the principal and the subsidiary themes.

Formally, the first movement exhibits a completely conventional sonata form with no major surprises. The themes appear in their expected places, the various sections fit naturally together to constitute larger divisions, and the latter come together convincingly to yield a unified whole.

Consistent with his usual practice, Svendsen has made extensive use of the sequence technique both in the formulation of the themes and in their development, with the b-motive serving as the movement's most important source of building material. His customary employment of chromatic voice-leading is not particularly prominent in the various iterations of the motives but is all the more pronounced in the accompaniment.

The second movement, *Andante sostenuto*, is one of Svendsen's most beautiful creations, permeated from beginning to end with a sublime lyricism. Formally, it is unique—a blend of elements drawn from sonata form, rondo, and theme with variations. The truth is that it cannot be classified in terms of any of the traditional abstract forms. It is an expression of Svendsen's playful, unfettered experimentation with form, and the result goes beyond the time-honored classical patterns. No doubt it was this free form that the German critic Bernsdorf found so hard to stomach and that led him to characterize the movement as "unusually boring."

The material, the various elements of which exhibit a certain similarity, is presented in a series of different keys, but Svendsen keeps it under firm control at all times. His procedure is somewhat reminiscent of Brahms, who also maintained a firm anchor in the classical tradition while creating a natural sense of wholeness in a movement within the context of an intricate and advanced harmonic style.

The movement, the principal key of which is E-flat major, has a four-measure introduction followed by an exposition with a broadly conceived A-theme and a short B-theme. In a relatively long middle section the motives are presented in various keys. After an abbreviated recapitulation the movement concludes with a 7-measure coda. Especially effective is a passage in which three distinctive countermelodies bring the themes together contrapuntally. The result is a significant heightening of intensity.

In the third movement, *Intermezzo – Allegro giusto*, the national element comes prominently into view in the form of a stylized *halling*. The most important thematic material in the movement is this little A-theme in F major:

Example 13   *Symphony no. 2*, op. 15, 3rd movement

The 2-measure a-motive is repeated immediately with a tiny alteration. Thereafter it is constantly repeated in several keys and with varying instrumentation. From time to time some development occurs, but for the most part the motive retains its original form and functions as a kind of *ritornello*. In measure 21, B flat is replaced by B natural, thereby creating a hint of the Lydian mode.

Next appears a contrasting element in the form of a singable B-theme in A minor. The contrast is owing not only to the fact that it is in a minor key but also to its modulating, modally tinged character and not least to the rhythmic change: from feather-light sixteenth notes to more robust dotted notes and triplets.

Thereafter the A-theme returns, but this time in G major—not, as in a traditional sonata rondo, in the principal key (F major in this case).

The most important contrasting section of the movement occurs not in the form of a development of the material previously introduced but rather in a presentation of the principal theme with doubled note values in C major, for the most part tightly harmonized in the typical Svendsen fashion with gliding chromatic lines. Grieg frequently employed a similar augmentation technique—for example, in *Norwegian Dances*, op. 35, nos. 1 and 3.

The recapitulation starts out in a totally nontraditional way: the A-theme appears in A minor, the B-theme follows in D minor, and only then is the A-theme given in the home key of F major. A coda in F major based on material derived from the augmented form of the principal theme brings the movement to a close. Especially noteworthy is a contrapuntal passage in which no less than six motives are used in some highly fascinating ways.

One can analyze this movement as a more or less standard "additive" form: $A - B - A^1 - A^2 - A^3 - B^1 - A^4 - A^5$, but one can with equal justification regard it as a free sonata rondo in which the break with tradition in relation to the classical models consists first and foremost in the sequence of keys employed. If one analyzes it in the latter way, $A-B-A^1$ constitutes the exposition, A^2 the contrast section (that takes the place of development section in sonata form), and $A^3-B^1-A^4$ serves as a recapitulation. A^5 then becomes a coda in which the "i" is dotted by a solo bassoon playing a metrically dislocated a–motive.

This *intermezzo* is one of Svendsen's most consummate movements. Its appeal to both audience and performers is owing not least to its infectious humor and luxuriant instrumentation.

The fourth movement, *Finale, Andante – Allegro con fuoco*, exhibits clear parallels with the last movement of the D–major symphony. They both begin with a slow introduction in dark colors which leads, by way of a powerful *crescendo*, to the principal theme of the movement in *allegro*.

The thematic material in the introductory section consists of two parts. The unison strings introduce a theme that will later become the basis for the first subsidiary theme of the *allegro*. A new theme establishes a motivic connection with both the second and third movements.

Formally, the *Finale* is a freely constructed movement in sonata form. In the exposition, both the principal theme section and the subsidiary theme section consist of two parts. As previously mentioned, the first subsidiary theme (in F minor) is related to the first theme in the introduction, albeit changed from a slow to a fast tempo. The second subsidiary theme is in F major. In the development section, main attention is given to the initial motive of the first principal theme. The recapitulation contains certain developmental passages, first segments from the second principal theme and then a development of the first subsidiary theme, with modulations all the way to C-sharp major. Motives from the second theme in the introduction then lead to the recapitulation of the first subsidiary theme in B-flat minor and the second in B-flat major. A grandiose coda in which the first subsidiary theme is allocated to the trumpet and trombone in *ff* concludes the movement.

The *Finale* underscores the life-affirming character of the symphony. All the themes have melodic vitality, and as always in Svendsen's works there is an attempt to achieve thematic coherence throughout. We are carried away on a torrent of sound without the slightest hint of anything resembling clichés or abstract models.

The B-flat major symphony marks the high point of Svendsen's achievement as a composer. It proved to be the climax of his work as a symphonist and, as well, of Norwegian orchestral music in the 19th century. Internationally, this inspired work ranks as one of the most brilliant symphonies of its time.

THE FOUR NORWEGIAN RHAPSODIES

As the year 1876 began, Svendsen was heading in a new direction as he undertook the composition of four Norwegian rhapsodies for orchestra. The first of these was ready by February, and before the year was over the second and third had been finished. The last of the four was completed in Rome the following year.

The inspiration for these works undoubtedly was Liszt, whose *Hungarian Rhapsodies* for piano (from 1846 and later) were among the first examples of a rhapsodic treatment of folk melodies. Svendsen had arranged two of these (nos. 2 and 6) for orchestra with great success in 1866 and 1871, and he had approached the genre himself when he had used a Norwegian bridal march and a Neapolitan melody in his *Norwegian Artists' Carnival.*

These experiences strengthened his desire to create substantial orchestral works based on folk tunes, a generous supply of which lay ready to hand in L. M. Lindeman's large collection. The title and pattern for the free treatment was taken from Liszt, but Svendsen became the first composer to write *orchestral* rhapsodies based on folk melodies. In the years that followed a number of other composers in many countries would follow in his footsteps.

A Norwegian model available to Svendsen was Ole Bull's composition *A Visit to the Seter* for violin and orchestra (1849). This composition was well known in Norway, and its interweaving of folk-tune material and the composer's own folk-like pastiches gave it a markedly rhapsodic character.

Svendsen used a beautiful mixture of vocal and instrumental folk tunes in the *Norwegian Rhapsodies*—a total of 17 melodies in all. Dance tunes— *hallings* and *springars*—were employed especially in the more animated parts, folk ballads primarily in the contrasting and more lyrical sections. Fifteen of the melodies were taken from Lindeman's *Older and Newer Norwegian Mountain Melodies* (1853–67), two from other sources. Several of the Lindeman melodies used by Svendsen had previously been arranged for piano by

Kjerulf (6) and Grieg (4). Grieg later used three of the same tunes in *Norwegian Dances* (1880), *Old Norwegian Melody with Variations* (1890), and *Symphonic Dances* (1896–98). Indeed, there was a certain degree of friendly competition between Grieg and Svendsen in this area.

Like Kjerulf and Grieg, Svendsen did not feel bound in any way by his source material. He occasionally made small melodic changes, especially with respect to ornamentations. He shortened melodies in a couple of cases, but in other instances he added notes to the original melody. He took considerable liberties with respect to rhythm, clearly in order to create greater vitality and to introduce variation into a rhythmic pattern that might otherwise appear too static. Now and then he introduced accents, especially on the second or third beat in the *springars*. In a few places he altered the note values—in the case of dotted notes, for example, and syncopations involving ties across bar lines. The most radical example of rhythmic change occurs in his handling of *Den siste laurdags kvelden* (*Last Saturday Evening*) in Rhapsody no. 4. In Lindeman it is notated in 6/8 time, but Svendsen—by making significant rhythmic alterations—adapts it to a 2/4 pattern.

Like Lindeman, Kjerulf, and Grieg, Svendsen adds to the melodies by supplying preludes, interludes and postludes derived from the folk-tune material. Because Svendsen's arrangements occur in the context of compositions of much broader scope than those of his predecessors, however, the newly composed sections often play a more important role. The postlude that concludes each of the rhapsodies, for example, functions much like a symphonic coda.

Svendsen once again demonstrates his prowess as a master of form, creating interesting solutions to structural problems in several of the rhapsodies. This is especially true of *Rhapsody no. 2*, which is a combination in miniature of elements of a four-movement symphony and sonata-form structure.

All of the rhapsodies except the second have an introductory section. Thereafter the folk melodies are presented one by one, with *Fortspinnung* and motivic work of various kinds and with repetitions in which the material is varied melodically, rhythmically, and harmonically. Such contrapuntal and rhythmic subtleties as *strettos*, motivic combinations, augmentations and diminutions never appear artificial, but fit naturally into the whole.

The harmonies exhibit Svendsen's usual gliding chromaticism and characteristic preference for abrupt shifts between mediant-related chords and keys. The folk character is emphasized through pedal notes (usually on the tonic or fifth), open fifths, and certain harmonic devices derived from the church modes. The national coloring is also underscored rhythmically by means of pronounced accents and dance rhythms in the *springar* and *halling* sections.

The rhapsodies call for an orchestra of moderate size, and the demands on the performers are not especially heavy, so they are appropriate fare for amateur as well as professional players. Even so, the orchestration is sophisticated and meticulously worked out, often in exciting and colorful instrumental combinations. Constantly changing contrasts in sonority are typical. The principal burden is assigned to the strings, with a mellow and yet distinct sonority also in the *divisi* passages. In one section of the second rhapsody, marked *tremolo sul ponticello*, the strings are divided into ten groups.

As Steinar Stolpe has pointed out, Svendsen achieves amusing effects in the last two rhapsodies when he employs muted strings in passages with a jocular, dance-like character (111). The woodwinds, often in a high register, play a larger role than the brass—though the latter, too, from time to time have important parts that are well adapted to their distinctive character and most comfortable register.

Rhapsody no. 1 (B minor) is dedicated to L. M. Lindeman, but oddly enough the first folk tune Svendsen uses is one of the two melodies *not* taken from Lindeman's collection. It is a folk ballad that had appeared in Henrik Wergeland's musical comedy *Fjeldstuen* (*Mountain Chalet*, 1845) under the title *Air norvégien*. It serves as a slow introduction to the main section, marked *Allegro* (D major), where a *halling*—no. 8 in Lindeman's collection (L 8)—constitutes the building material. This is followed by a contrasting section based on the third and last folk tune used in this rhapsody: *Astri, my Astri* (L 77) in E major. The *halling* is taken up again in the concluding section, this time in B major. *Astri my Astri* returns in the coda with augmented note values and in *ff*, giving the conclusion an almost triumphal effect.

The well-designed *Rhapsody no. 2* (A major) is dedicated to Ole Bull. Its four distinct sections make it possible to regard it as a kind of one-movement symphony, but in its inner structure it is closely related to sonata form. The first section constitutes the "exposition," where the principal theme, in A major, is the last half of the folk ballad *Elland and the Fairy Maiden* (L 71), the character of which is typical of a *halling*. The subsidiary theme is the same melody with augmented note values, but in the key of C-sharp major. The second and third sections comprise the "development." The second section presents two contrasting passages. Section two, *Andantino*, is based on the folk ballad *Sjugur and the Troll Bride* (L 22), with a harmonization on a par with that later created by Grieg on the same melody in *Old Norwegian Melody with Variations*, op. 51. Section three is in ABA form and is a kind of *scherzo*. The A section makes use of a *springar* in E major (L 328). As a "trio" Svendsen gives us yet another *springar* (L 386), in G-sharp minor. Section four, which features a return of the *halling* with which this rhapsody began, has the character of a "recapitulation." The subsidiary theme, as one would expect, in a sonata form, is in the home key. The first motive of the principal theme eventually becomes the cornerstone of a highly concentrated "coda."

The first section of *Rhapsody no. 3* (C major), which is dedicated to Edvard Grieg, is based on a *springar* (L 464). The next melody, which has the character of a subsidiary theme, is a *springar* in E minor (L 194). The first *springar* then returns in a somewhat altered form. The calm middle section (G minor) begins with some chromatic progressions that anticipate in a striking way the opening measures of Svendsen's *Violin Romance*, op. 26, written five years later. Then follows the folk ballad *Aasmund Fregdegjævar* (L 42). A fast section (notated without an explicit key signature!) concludes the work. Two lively folk ballads are employed: *Ho Guro* (L 250) in G major and *The Sheriff Had a Dapple-gray Mare* (L 516) in A major. The latter melody is taken back to C major near the end of the section. A long *stretto* part, based on motives derived from this folk tune and played *ff*, forms a rousing coda with an almost symphonic drive. Traces of symphonic structure and sonata form can also be found in the third rhapsody, albeit less markedly than in the second.

Rhapsody no. 4 (D minor), which is dedicated to Karl Hals, opens with an extended "symphonic" introduction that is related to melodic material that will be introduced in the third section of the piece. Then *Hildalshalling*, a folk dance in D major with a Lydian tinge, is introduced. It does not come from Lindeman; rather, it is a slightly abbreviated version of the fourth of Halfdan Kjerulf's *XXV udvalgte norske Folkedandse* (*Twenty-five Selected Norwegian Folk Dances*). It is the only example we have of Svendsen arranging a Hardanger-fiddle dance for orchestra. The subsidiary theme (F-sharp minor) consists of the folk tune *Last Saturday Evening* (L 303). A bridge passage is followed by a return of both melodies, but transposed a fifth downward. The second main part of the rhapsody is *scherzo*-like in character and is built around two folk tunes: a *springar* (L 463) and *The Woman with the Stick* (L 25), both in E major. Toward the end, motives from *Last Saturday Evening* are also drawn in. In the third main part, *Andante* (A minor),

Svendsen employs the folk tune *The Backward Song* (L 587), which he colors with a wide brush. As in *Rhapsody no. 2*, the concluding part has something of the character of a recapitulation, but in contrast to the two preceding rhapsodies the coda builds not on the material that had just been employed but on the *springar* from the *scherzo* section. The result is to strengthen the impression that the conclusion is a summing-up of the entire rhapsody.

Svendsen expressed his admiration for Lindeman in words as well as in his compositions. We have a document that he drafted during the 1870s— an appeal for funds to support a projected new and expanded edition of Lindeman's folk-tune arrangements. This presumably occurred with Lindeman's encouragement. The exact date of the appeal is not known inasmuch as the manuscript, which is in the library of Oslo University, is undated. We also do not know if it was ever printed. It reads as follows:

> The publication of *Older and Newer Norwegian Mountain Melodies, Collected and Arranged by Ludvig Lindeman* was interrupted several years ago because no publisher thought the undertaking would be profitable. Meanwhile Ludvig Lindeman, with admirable diligence and intelligence, has continued his collecting with the result that, in addition to the two volumes already published, he now has about a thousand folk melodies in manuscript form. The rapid development of music in our country has contributed mightily to awakening an awareness of the national aspect also in this area, and interest in our unique folk music, especially, has increased considerably. These national melodies with their joy and sorrow, their power and beauty, constitute what is perhaps the noblest expression of the spiritual life of our people and have, therefore, great cultural-historical significance. They also constitute invaluable material for the further development of Norwegian music in a national direction. It is my deepest wish, therefore, that Lindeman's rich collection may soon become accessible to everyone. Thus the publication of Ludvig Lindeman's new collection is of great significance for our national artistic life, and I therefore take the liberty of encouraging to the utmost every friend of art and of our homeland to support this truly patriotic endeavor.

SVENDSEN GETS AN "OSCAR"

1877 proved to be a happy year for Svendsen. In January his D-major symphony was performed in Strasbourg, and on February 7 *Morgenbladet* quoted from a number of effusively positive reviews. The string quintet was performed on March 9 and the string octet on April 25 at chamber-music concerts in Oslo. The composer played viola on both occasions.

Although Svendsen had by now developed a considerable reputation in both Norway and Sweden, in Denmark he was still more or less unknown. This situation was about to change, however. On July 9 the D-major symphony was played in the Tivoli concert hall in Copenhagen under the baton of the well-known conductor Balduin Dahl. The Copenhagen newspaper *Nær og Fjern* wrote a week later that this symphony "established acquaintance with an undoubtedly very gifted artist, who on the basis of his eclectic artistic outlook composes with great originality and with an intelligence in his treatment and a shrewdness in his inventiveness that are quite unusual."

The biggest event in Svendsen's life at this time was a concert for King Oscar II on February 12. The monarch, who had heard of the success of the B-flat major symphony, invited the composer to give a matinee for invited guests at the royal palace in Oslo. Only compositions by Svendsen himself were to be played, with the symphony as the centerpiece of the program. The orchestra consisted of both professional and amateur players. One of the amateurs, F. G. Gade, later described the event:

> It was an unpleasant, bitterly cold forenoon when we assembled. White tie and tails in the forenoon, the empty dining room where the orchestra was placed on the floor without a podium, and then farther off in the room a row of fine chairs placed in a half-circle—it was not stimulating. I also think the professional musicians and the veterans among them were not in very good spirits. Obviously Svendsen noted this poor morale among the troops, and it was almost time for the king to come in. But then Svendsen jumped up on the cloth-bedecked conductor's platform and said in an authoritative voice: "Gentlemen, when the royal entourage comes into this room, there is just one king—and that is—*me*." There were sparks in his eyes, and that created sparks in our minds as well. And a moment later, when the king and his companions had come in and taken their places, the *Coronation March* resounded through the hall more festively and brightly than I think I have ever heard it since (47).

In addition to the *Coronation March*, the program included the second symphony and *Last Year I Was Tending the Goats*. The king was so enthusiastic that he requested that two of the numbers be repeated. A correspondent from Oslo reported in the March 7 issue of the New York newspaper *The*

Johan Svendsen in the late 1870s.
(Universitetsbiblioteket, Oslo)

World that during parts of the symphony the king walked around the room talking with his guests, who were drinking chocolate and eating cakes. After the concert, however, he went up to the composer, greeted him warmly, and said: "Maestro, I regard you as one of the greatest composers in the world. I had thought of giving you the Royal Vasa Order, but everyone who has a medal has that one. You deserve a more distinguished medal, and I hereby confer upon you Oscar II's Medal of Honor in gold." This Oscar medal had been awarded for the first time at the coronation in 1873 "as a reward for services to the royal house, to art, science, and literature." The Norwegian authors Henrik Ibsen and Jonas Lie were among those who had previously received it, but Svendsen was the first musician to get such an "Oscar."

After five consecutive years in Oslo, Svendsen was burning with longing to go south again—something that had been financially impossible until now. After the concert at the royal palace, however, the financial picture improved. King Oscar granted him the sum of 1,600 crowns for a trip abroad and Alexius Ræder took the lead in gathering additional funds for him. Thorvald Meyer, a businessman in Oslo, contributed 1,500 crowns and a "women's auxiliary" gathered 2,400 crowns. The total, as Ræder wrote on April 28, was "in truth a respectable sum"—not least in comparison with the annual state grant of just 1,600 crowns.

On September 25, shortly before he was to leave, Svendsen gave a farewell concert that included both the second symphony and the premiere of first Norwegian rhapsody. The applause lasted for a full ten minutes! Two days after the concert, a lavish party was given in his honor at the Grand Hotel. *Aftenposten* reported that those in attendance included "most of the artists currently in Oslo, including musicians, painters, sculptors, actors, writers, businessmen, and many others who in one way or another have had much or little to do with Mr. Svendsen and his art." The principal speaker was J. G. Conradi, who thanked Svendsen warmly for everything he had created in Oslo. Everyone hoped that he might be given opportunities to continue his work when he came back. The Craftsmen's Chorus and the Students' Male Chorus added further zest to the party by singing several numbers saluting the guest of honor.

According to *Aftenposten*, Svendsen thanked those assembled "in a few moving words for the attention shown him, which he chose to view not as something he deserved personally but as a sign of the high degree to which artistic efforts are appreciated, a sign that art in Norway must have awakened interest, since it can claim so many good and noble friends."

There was "the most animated mood at the punch table, where a long series of toasts were given," and the party lasted until the wee hours of the morning.

5

THREE YEARS ABROAD

1877–80

IN AUTUMN OF 1877, thanks to the generous gifts he had received in Oslo, Svendsen's financial situation was for the first time fairly secure. Thus he could confidently make plans for an extended trip abroad.

The laborious years in Oslo that required much from him both as a conductor and as a composer had taken their toll on his inner resources. He looked forward to getting away and renewing his creative powers in stimulating contact with the throbbing music life on the continent. He also harbored dreams of conducting Europe's renowned orchestras in performances of his own symphonic works.

With his winning personality, he had no trouble during his journey abroad making friends with leading performers and composers, and he acquired first-hand knowledge of the latest music. His hope for artistic triumphs as a conductor in such music metropolises as Rome, London, and Paris was not realized at this time, however. An even more troubling omen was the stagnation he experienced as a composer. All that he managed to produce during these three years was ten short songs and a few brief orchestral works.

TO GERMANY, ITALY, AND ENGLAND

On September 29, 1877, Svendsen and his family went by boat to Copenhagen. After two days there they continued on to Lübeck, where Johan greeted "old man Leche and many other friends." On October 5 they reached Leipzig, where they visited other friends. One Sunday Johan and

Bergljot attended a party given by Heinrich Brockhaus, who had been Johan's travel companion on the trip to Iceland ten years earlier.

In Leipzig, Johan fed his virtually insatiable appetite for good music. During his first three weeks there he attended four operas, four symphony concerts, and two chamber-music evenings featuring "the famous Florentine Quartet." He wrote to his father on October 26:

> With such hectic activity, life down here is in the long run getting somewhat exhausting. I rarely have an evening to myself. One invitation after another, no rest, and consequently no composing. . . . Sigurd, poor fellow, wishes he were back in Oslo. Recently he asked me in all seriousness if we couldn't soon go home again.

But although he couldn't find time to compose, he at least took the time to read the proofs of *Carnival in Paris* and the second symphony, both of which were being published by E. W. Fritzsch. Fritzsch had paid him 750 German marks for these two works plus *Two Icelandic Melodies* and *Last Year I Was Tending the Goats*. That Svendsen was pleased about his collaboration with Fritzsch is evident from a letter to Iver Holter dated April 6, 1878: "Still, he has quite a different sort of interest in our art than most other publishers, who may be better businessmen but who seldom subordinate their own interests to those of art."

Svendsen began to realize that in Germany he was regarded as a composer of significance. He wrote to his father: "It is most regrettable that I don't have any unpublished compositions, for now I could have sold them for a good price. I have been contacted by several publishers (yesterday, for example, by none other than the director of Breitkopf & Härtel), all of whom want something from me."

He had originally planned to stay in Leipzig for two weeks, but he received an unexpected and flattering invitation to conduct his new symphony at the fifth subscription concert in the Gewandhaus on November 8, and of course he could not turn it down. This was the first performance of the second symphony outside Norway. With the predictable exception of Bernsdorf, the critics were for the most part enthusiastic about the work.

Svendsen's music also scored a success in New York at about this time when Walter Damrosch included *Two Icelandic Melodies* and *Last Year I Was Tending the Goats* in a matinee concert at Steinway Hall. The *New York Herald* wrote on November 18, "The musical jewels on this occasion—the things that moved one's heart most deeply—were, however, the Icelandic and Norwegian melodies of Svendsen, especially the latter. It was musical poetry with an aura all its own, a world of nuances, a perfect balance."

On November 9 the Svendsen family left Leipzig for Bavaria. The painter Eilif Peterssen, who had been passing through Leipzig, had surprised Svendsen by inviting him to sit for a portrait in Munich. Thus he had to remain in Munich for about a week, and, as he told his father, he "made the acquaintance of many splendid people and heard a lot of good music." Unfortunately, he did not visit Ibsen. In a thank-you letter to Peterssen from Rome dated December 4 he wrote, "I greatly regret that I neglected so many things in Munich. I didn't get to talk with Dr. Ibsen. Do you think Ibsen would be willing to write an opera?" In Munich he had been so immodest as to borrow 150 marks from Peterssen.

After crossing the Alps, Svendsen stopped for two days in Verona. As composer of the orchestral work *Romeo and Juliet* he was especially interested in seeing the house of the Capulets, "the very place where Juliet lived." He also saw a new opera, which, however, "wasn't worth a pipeful of tobacco; but the military music we heard was excellent." The Svendsens continued on to Florence via Mantua, Modena, and Bologna, but their stay there at this time was pitifully short: after only an hour they had to leave the city "owing to a shortage of funds."

On November 20 they arrived in Rome, where they were to remain for four months. With his enthusiasm for history and art, Svendsen—like Grieg in 1865–66 and 1869–70—had many beautiful experiences "in this city that is so rich in great memories, magnificent works of art, and interesting people." On his visits to the various sights he was often accompanied by Ludvig Josephson, a Swede, who was director of the Christiania Theater in Oslo. The two of them spent many happy evenings together in the wine cellars of Rome. He also met Grieg's Danish friend Niels Ravnkilde and became better acquainted with Professor O. P. Monrad.

For the year 1878 there is an almanac in which Svendsen made almost daily entries. These entries contain little in the way of personal information and make no mention of financial matters. A number of letters from this time period are much more informative. On March 18 he wrote to Eilif Peterssen:

> I went to the opera to hear *Traviata*, with none less than Patti in the title role. Now one would think that a work by their most significant contemporary composer—for Verdi is that—performed as well as it was in this case would be able to command their attention. But no! They

chatted, laughed, and visited with each other so that the few who had
come to enjoy the opera were constantly being distracted. They have
absolutely no sense for what we call classical music.

On March 24 he wrote to his father, "As far as music is concerned I have not
gained much from my visit." Rome was obviously a center for church music, but Svendsen never had much interest in this area. Nonetheless, it was a
religious work that provided the only important musical experience he had
this winter, namely a magnificent performance of Cherubini's *Requiem* at a
solemn ceremony in the Pantheon following the death of King Vittorio
Emanuele.

There was little time for composition, but Svendsen did manage to
complete his fourth and last Norwegian rhapsody, which he had begun in
the autumn, and he made an arrangement for strings of the Swedish folk
melody *Du gamla, du fria* (*Thou ancient, thou free*) which is dated Rome,
March 1878. He also read the proofs of *Romeo and Juliet*, which he dedicated
to Giovanni Sgambati, a leading figure in Italian music who was helpful to
him during his stay in Italy. Svendsen considered him "an excellent composer, strongly influenced by the new German school, but not in such a way
as to lose his originality. . . . His piano-playing is some of the most masterful
I have heard."

Sgambati arranged for a performance of Svendsen's string quintet at a
private concert for invited guests at Salla Dante on March 21. Johan wrote
to his father: "I am glad to be able to report that it was well performed and
scored a considerable success. It was a happy coincidence that Wilhelmy
played my string quartet the very same evening, also with decided success."
The latter performance was at the Chamber Music Society in Milan.

Perhaps the most prominent guest at the concert in Rome was Liszt's
lady friend, Polish Princess Caroline Sayn Wittgenstein, whom Svendsen
had visited as early as January 6. They had gotten to know each other well as
they discussed Nordic literature and music, in which she had a lively interest. Svendsen had hoped to meet Liszt in Rome, just as Grieg had done
eight years earlier, but the great man was in Budapest at the time. Liszt,
however, was instrumental in getting two of Svendsen's orchestral works
performed in the Hungarian capital during the winter. Giula Cáldi conducted *Last Year I Was Tending the Goats* at a concert given by the Budapest
Friends of Music Association on January 28, 1878, and on March 6 the two
Icelandic melodies were played.

Liszt wrote about the first concert in a letter to music publisher Carl

Warmuth in Oslo dated January 25. He also had words of praise for Svendsen's first three *Norwegian Rhapsodies*, which Warmuth had sent to Liszt at the suggestion of the composer. He wrote that the rhapsodies were "excellent, well-conceived and well-crafted compositions" which he would recommend to his colleagues.

The Svendsens left Rome on March 23, going first to Florence for a four-day visit. They then made a brief stop at Turin before continuing on to Paris, where they remained for four days. Once again, as in Rome, it was a requiem that provided the most memorable musical experience, namely Berlioz's monumental work (with no less than 16 timpani) conducted by Édouard Colonne.

The family arrived in London on April 3. They remained there for nearly five months, living with Bergljot's American parents, who had given them "a very cordial reception."

On April 25 Svendsen wrote to Grieg for the first time since his departure from Norway. He complained about not having heard a single word from him and asked if the reason was that Grieg "in a fit of delicacy perhaps has decided not to write to me in order to avoid the appearance of reminding me that up in Bergen or thereabouts there is someone whom I owe a lousy 30 *speciedalers*. To hell with such delicacy!"

He soon made the acquaintance of several prominent musicians: Sir George Grove, Jules Massenet, Pablo de Sarasate, and Max Bruch. On May 28 his string quartet was played at the Royal Academy of Music and five days later the string octet was performed at a private concert, with Sarasate playing first chair.

As a composer, Svendsen had now been unproductive for an extended period of time, and things did not improve in London. On May 5 he noted in his diary, "many (perhaps too many) visits," and three days later he wrote to Iver Holter: "Things are really hopping here. Every day concerts, dinners, or excursions. If I am going to get any work done I will have to lock my door. . . ." But Svendsen was not the kind of person who could shut himself off from the world. The social whirl was far too attractive to him for that.

Grieg was able to report that in Hardanger he had just successfully completed his string quartet in G minor. On Grieg's 35th birthday—June 15—Svendsen wrote:

> Regarding rural life and enjoying the beauties of nature, I have long
> shared your view: in the long run one cannot stand it. You lucky fellow,

who have finished a quartet. I've started on one, but I find the task more difficult every day. If this keeps up I have little hope of finishing it in this century.

Not until mid-summer did he get going on a couple of short compositions. On July 13 he wrote the song *The Violet*, op. 25, no. 1, which later became very popular. He also wrote the text. In a letter to Grieg dated February 15, 1879, he characterized this composition as "a most insignificant song." A week after writing the song he completed *Norwegian Springar* for orchestra (Work 123). Unfortunately, another year was to pass before he again took up his composer's pen.

But other dark clouds were also on the horizon. He wrote to Grieg on June 15:

> What I am going to do this autumn is to date a mystery to me. You certainly understand that I have little desire to return to Oslo so soon, all the more so inasmuch as the music conditions there are worse than ever. Since a stay in Paris is *very* costly I have decided to stay here at least two, perhaps three months more and only go to Paris for a few days in the autumn—if, indeed, I get there at all.

It was Sarasate who came to his rescue. The famous violinist offered his Paris apartment at 33 Rue St. Petersburg to the Svendsens when they left London on August 28, 1878. This generous act enabled Svendsen to remain in Paris much longer than he had considered possible.

BACK TO PARIS—"THE MOST WONDERFUL PLACE IN THE WORLD"

At the end of August 1878, then, Svendsen arrived for the third time in his favorite city, and he was to remain there for more than a year and a half. As had been the case a decade earlier, this stay proved to be one filled with rich experiences. Despite the international renown he had achieved as a composer and conductor, however, he found it impossible to make a living as an artist.

It all started out in a very promising way. At the end of July his string octet had been played at a concert of Scandinavian music held in connection with the world exhibition, and it was greeted with unanimous praise in the Parisian press. Adolphe Julien wrote on August 12 in *Le Français* that this was "a first-class work, filled with remarkable ideas and with a highly unusual wealth and variation of texture."

Svendsen was received by Léonard and Wieniawski and other old friends and acquaintances with open arms. On September 1 he visited Saint-Saëns, three days later Édouard Colonne, and on November 7 another well-known conductor, Jules Pasdeloup. He "had a delightful breakfast with Duparc and Chabrier" and visited Édouard Lalo for the first time.

The city abounded with musical events. At the world exposition Svendsen heard Greek, Arabian, and Hungarian folk music. He wrote to his father on September 19, "Naturally the big concerts given in the magnificent hall of the Trocadero palace, with an orchestra consisting of 160 selected instrumentalists, are the most interesting."

He had it in mind to settle down for an extended period, since "for the moment there is nothing for me to do [back in Norway]." So he asked his father to send him "all the bedclothes, pillowslips, tablecloths, towels, curtains, tablecloths, rugs . . . and as many pillows as there is room for."

Three days later he told his father about a concert where Nikolai Rubinstein conducted a huge orchestra in a program of Russian music. The concert hall was filled with celebrities, including some from Russia, and Svendsen was introduced to the most prominent one among them:

> I have made many acquaintances here, and especially today I made one that I am more than a little proud of. Just listen! This morning Wieniawski dashed into my room and said, "Grand Duke Constantin (the tsar's brother), who has heard that you are in Paris, wishes to make your personal acquaintance! Come with me immediately!" I threw my clothes on and rode with Wieniawski over to the Russian embassy hotel, where his imperial highness stays when he is in Paris. We were received in the most friendly manner. The Grand Duke began by expressing his pleasure *at being able to shake the hand of the man whose works he so admired*, and he ended by assuring me that "he would always be happy for each new work from my hand" and I had to promise him that I would send him the next new chamber-music work I compose.
>
> Don't think for a moment that it is just the man's high rank that makes me so happy about this acquaintance. No, it is far more the conviction that he has understood my artistic endeavors even better than many of the musicians I know, and that he has embraced my work with an interest seldom accorded any artist.

On October 4 he wrote to his sister that he had received "the most brilliant offers" to become a conductor in the United States, but he had no desire to go to America so he had turned down all the flattering invitations.

On October 24 the family moved to new quarters at 31 Rue Mosnier. They shared the apartment with Bergljot's parents and brother, who had now come to Paris from London. Svendsen wrote to Grieg in Leipzig on January 30, 1879:

> Sarasate's is a ground-floor apartment where one is absolutely deafened by the racket from the street, and it is also cold and impossible to warm properly. Besides, Sarasate, with true Spanish hospitality, invites everyone in the world to stay with him, so one is never sure of being able to be there alone. I tell you this in case you also should find yourself among those who are invited. Learn a little French and come here! You should have seen Paris, which is not only the world's most beautiful city but the most interesting one as well.

One of Svendsen's benefactors at this time was Baron d'Erlanger, who frequently invited him to big parties followed by music-making. The baron, who was a competent amateur violinist himself, participated during November and December in a number of such private performances of Svendsen's chamber music: the string quartet and string quintet (each twice) as well as the string octet.

Svendsen also spent a lot of time with such Norwegian artists as Frits Thaulow and Hans Heyerdahl, both of whom were painters. Heyerdahl painted his portrait, and in December the sculptor Mathias Skeibrok did a bust of him. In a Christmas letter to Grieg dated December 15, 1878, Svendsen talked about his plans for the future:

> You ask if I am thinking of staying permanently in Paris. It is quite true that I have sold my household goods [in Oslo], but that was done to make possible a temporary stay here, not to make this my permanent home. It is now perfectly clear to me that my place is home in Norway, and if it is possible to arrange circumstances at home in such a way that I can make a fairly reasonable living, I would like to go home again. You understand from what I have said that I consider my visit to Paris to be temporary. On the other hand I will not deny that if one can manage to get a position here—which, for that matter, is associated with almost insurmountable obstacles—then Paris is the most wonderful place in the world.

Svendsen had the pleasure of seeing four of his works performed in the great metropolis in the space of a month. Pasdeloup had *Norwegian Rhapsody*

Mathias Skeibrok's bust of Johan
Svendsen. (Universitetsbiblioteket,
Oslo)

No. 3 on his program at the beginning of January 1879, and on February 1
Norwegian Rhapsody No. 4. Regarding the former, Svendsen wrote to Grieg
on January 6 that it "was only partially successful and consequently did not
create the effect it might have. The reaction of the audience was positive but
not wildly enthusiastic."

January 21 was a day to remember. On the same evening that his string
octet was played at a chamber-music soirée he had an opportunity to conduct his second symphony at a rehearsal of the renowned Pasdeloup Orchestra. Three days later he wrote to Grieg:

> It went brilliantly and ended with the entire orchestra standing and ap-
> plauding. I have never experienced a greater triumph. After this I natu-
> rally have a confident hope of getting something performed here.

But discouragement was not far away. A week later he poured out his feelings to Grieg:

> You ask about the quartet that I began last summer. I have given up on it
> for the present. I don't really know what is wrong with me just now, but

nothing that I try works out. On the one hand self-criticism that is destructive of everything, on the other hand a hard and burdensome
struggle to make a living. The only thing that I think could get me back
in the groove is a peaceful, fairly secure existence. Would that we—that
is to say, you and I—could get something substantial going in Christiania
[Oslo].

Grieg fully shared Svendsen's thoughts to the effect that their rightful place
was back in Norway, and in a letter dated February 15 Svendsen spelled out
his visions for the future:

You wouldn't believe what a joy it was for me that you are in agreement
with me on so many points, and above all on the main thing: *that we
should settle down in Norway.* It would be very strange if you and I through
our united efforts couldn't manage not only to earn a secure living but
also to improve the musical conditions to such a point that artistically,
too, we could be happy to be there. I take it for granted that we—once
the situation has improved—would have to take the initiative to establish
a proper music academy with the help of a *significant annual subsidy from
the government.* This operation should then immediately incorporate the
mission of the Music Society and continue it on a broader scale. That is
to say, private instruction of students in all directions, public performance
of masterworks from all schools and all periods. In this way the cultiva-
tion of music life in Norway will at last be in the right hands.

Grieg was undoubtedly more realistic. In view of the bad experience he had
had with his own music academy in 1867–68, he thought his friend was in
the process of building castles in the air. He also was not at all attracted to the
idea of continuing his work in the Music Society in Oslo. Svendsen commented on his friend's reaction in a letter dated February 23: "That you will
not go along with the idea of a possible academy—not a conservatory, if
you please—I cannot understand and prefer to think that when the time
comes you will yield to my arguments."
    In a February 15 letter he again touched on his stagnation as a composer:

Since leaving Norway I haven't composed a thing except for an extremely insignificant song [*The Violet*], the conclusion of the fourth Norwegian rhapsody and beginnings of a couple of things that probably
will never be finished. These are the results of the last 18 months! Terrible! . . . What it's leading to I do not understand. Maybe I am like that

fellow Bjørnson wrote about who cut the three top strings of the violin.
If only I were sure that the lowest string of *my* violin has enough sound, I
would immediately try the experiment.

In order to avoid falling into total indolence he had reworked *Zorahayda*,
but he was still not completely satisfied with it. Regarding the performance
of *Norwegian Rhapsody No. 4* on February 1, he was able to report that it
went well and that Pasdeloup had been most obliging:

> You ask if I conducted myself and, if so, why not rather the symphony. It
> is unfortunately not the custom here to let composers conduct the per-
> formances of their works, nor are the composers allowed to decide for
> themselves which work they want to have performed. Otherwise I
> would have chosen the symphony. The Norwegianness of the rhapsody
> made it too far removed from the Parisians' musical understanding, but as
> I said, I had no choice.

In a letter to Grieg dated February 23, Svendsen expanded on his opinion of
Pasdeloup: "Just between you and me, I have not gotten a very high opinion either of Pasdeloup's insight or of his talent as a conductor. He didn't
understand the rhapsody at all." On the other hand, Pasdeloup had been
very gracious and did as well as he could. Svendsen continued: "Perhaps I
have no right to reproach him. It's a lamentable custom here that the regular
conductor never gives up the baton—not even to the composer himself."
     On March 2, however, Svendsen was given the opportunity to conduct
his second symphony at the twentieth and last *Concert Populaire* of the
Pasdeloup Orchestra in Salle du Cirque. The program also included *Last
Year I Was Tending the Goats* and *Norwegian Rhapsody No. 3* as well as
Mendelssohn's *Melusine* overture.
     Svendsen's music was making considerable headway in London at this
time. On February 22, the third rhapsody was played at a Crystal Palace
concert. Three days later *The Times* reported, "After the first few bars of the
rhapsody, it became apparent that a born master of the orchestra was speaking." On May 29 the first symphony was performed in St. James Hall. *The
Daily Telegraph* wrote, "The symphony played yesterday is beyond doubt
the fullest revelation yet made in our country of the composer's genius. It
pleases us much to say that it is also a remarkable and, in several respects,
a masterly work." Several of his compositions were also performed in
England the following year. *Carnival in Paris* was played in London on

February 14 and *Romeo and Juliet* on May 29. Charles Hallé also had the third rhapsody on the program in Manchester and Liverpool.

Although Svendsen did not manage to establish a firm foothold in Paris, he had some major triumphs in Angers, where he was invited to conduct a concert of his own works in late March of 1879. The press was outspoken in its praise. The Nantes paper *Phare de Loire* stated in its issue of March 28 that these works revealed "an intense and deep poetry; the melodies, the harmonies and the rhythms continuously spoke the most beautiful language." On May 22, Svendsen sent his father a detailed report:

> It was a little strange to read my own name in huge letters at every corner as I was riding to my lodgings. . . . I was lucky enough to find complete understanding on the part of the orchestra. You wouldn't believe how splendidly they played. The concert itself was the greatest triumph I have ever experienced. Five wildly enthusiastic curtain calls, several encores— including the *scherzo* in the symphony (no. 1) and *Last Year I Was Tending the Goats*—but the piece that made the biggest hit of all was *Norwegian Rhapsody No. 3*. When it was finished they just wouldn't stop clapping. The men clapped and stamped their feet and shouted, the women waved their handkerchiefs, and the whole orchestra stood up and pounded on their instruments while the trumpets blew fanfares. The triumph was all the more impressive because of the fact that I was totally unknown there. As a matter of fact, I learned later that before the concert many in the audience had been annoyed that I had been given so much space on the program.

At the end of April the family had moved to 63 Rue Monsieur le Prince, near the home of Saint-Saëns—in "the merry old Latin Quarter, where I have rediscovered many friends from my first stay," Svendsen wrote to his father on May 22. Living with Bergljot's family had gotten on his nerves: "I couldn't get along with them, so I had to decide to move. This change was not exactly convenient, as I had planned to stay where I was until autumn, but I couldn't stand it any longer."

The summer, he reported to his father on September 22, was rather uneventful:

> It has been very quiet in the musical world during the last four months, but the new season is about to begin and things will soon be hopping again. Last week I was pleasantly surprised by a friendly greeting from Richard Wagner. This evening Bergljot and I are going to Saint-Saëns's, where I hope to meet Sarasate and others.

During these weeks Svendsen was busy giving lessons in composition. One of his students was the young Finn, Robert Kajanus. He also finally got down to doing some composing himself, the result being a number of songs.

On November 16 he wrote to Carl Warmuth regarding the new concert season: "Unfortunately, my resources do not permit me to participate in it very much. Money! Money! Oh, money!" He offered Warmuth the Scandinavian publishing rights for the two volumes of songs, opp. 23 and 24, which he had recently composed. The songs had already been accepted for publication in Paris by J. Hamelle, "who made me such an attractive offer that I abandoned Breitkopf & Härtel. Of course, since they are going to be translated into French it will be some time before they come out."

The first time Svendsen went to see Hamelle he was received with effusive congeniality. When Svendsen cautiously raised the question of money, however, the publisher said that now they should just be happy and not talk about anything so mundane. He then invited Svendsen to take a drive with him through the Boulogne forest.

The Bergen poet John Paulsen reported in his memoirs (95) that one day as he was walking along the Seine he ran into Svendsen, whom he had recently met at a party at the home of world-famous singer Madame Pauline Viardot-Garcia. Svendsen asked if Paulsen didn't have some poems that he could set, saying that at just that time he was in the mood to write songs. So Paulsen sent him several poems, and some time thereafter he was invited to dinner at Svendsen's to hear *Venetian Serenade*, which had just been completed:

> After dinner Svendsen's wife, a very musical American woman, sang the melody for me while Svendsen himself played the accompaniment. I predicted a huge success, and I was not mistaken. Few songs are now as popular in Scandinavia as this one.

The song, a somewhat banal serenade with a folk-like melody, also became such a hit in southern Europe that it was often sung by the gondoliers in Venice!

Of the nine songs Svendsen composed in Paris, *Venetian Serenade* (op. 24, no. 3) was the only one that employed a text by Paulsen. Two of the other texts in this opus—*O show some mercy, howling wind* (no. 1) and *The Birch Tree* (no. 2)—are by O. P. Monrad and one—*Longing* (no. 4)—is by Bjørnstjerne Bjørnson.

The five songs comprising op. 23 are all settings of German texts taken from F. M. von Bodenstedt's *Mirza Schaffy*. They are: *Zuleikha* (no. 1), *Was ist der Wuchs der Pinie* (no. 2), *Seh' ich deine zarten Füßchen an* (no. 3), *O, wie mir schweren Dranges* (no. 4), and *Schlag' die Tschadra zurück!* (no. 5).

All of the texts in opp. 23 and 24 were translated into French by Svendsen's friend, the poet Victor Wilder. Op. 25, the last song opus from Svendsen's hand, contains just two songs. No. 1, *The Violet*, was written in London in 1878. The text is by the composer. No. 2, *Spring Jubilation*, was composed at Larkollen, Norway in 1880. The text was a Norwegian translation—in all probability by Svendsen himself–of a poem in Bodenstedt's *Mirza Schaffy*.

Several of the songs in opp. 23 and 24 were sung in France from time to time during the ensuing years. The seductive melodies obviously appealed to the taste of the time. They are extremely simple, mainly strophic, and totally lacking in subtlety of any kind. The accompaniments are characterized by rhythmic simplicity and uninterrupted chains of eighth notes. There are some unmistakable hints of salon music in these songs, and they are not entirely free of hackneyed harmonic clichés. All things considered, they lack the fresh inventiveness that could have elevated them artistically.

In contrast to the pearls in Grieg's works in this genre, Svendsen's songs have not withstood the test of time. Three of them, however—*Venetian Serenade*, *The Violet*, and *The Birch Tree*—still enjoy a certain popularity in Norway.

In 1879 a book was published in Leipzig under the title *Aus dem Tagebuch eines Gesanglehrers* (*From the Diary of a Voice Teacher*). The author used the pseudonym Joh. Venzoni, and there has been some speculation that the real author was Svendsen—a quite plausible supposition in view of his lack of funds at the time. The mystery has now been solved, however. In the Musikhistorisk Museum in Copenhagen there is an extensive collection of source material assembled by the Danish scholar S. A. E. Hagen, and in this collection there is a note regarding a conversation Hagen had with Svendsen in about 1900. Svendsen was amused by the speculation that he was the real Venzoni. He informed Hagen that the pseudonym was not his but, rather, that of an older Danish singer by the name of Johannes Svendsen.

Svendsen did get an opportunity to try his hand at writing about music during the winter of 1879–80, however. Warmuth had asked him to find someone who could write reports about Parisian music life for *Nordisk Musik-Tidende*, a new monthly journal that Warmuth planned to publish in Oslo. Svendsen replied on November 22:

> Regarding the article you wanted for your journal, I approached Johan Selmer, but he will not write anything without an honorarium. Since you had not authorized me to promise him any such thing, and since on the other hand I think it would be a pity to ask a non-musician to do this sort of thing, I have decided to give it a try myself. Early in December, then, I will send you an article, and you can then see if it is something you can use.

On December 6 Svendsen sent the article to Warmuth and asked him to correct "any possible errors in style and spelling." It appeared in the first number of *Nordisk Musik-Tidende* in January 1880 under the pseudonym "Quintus Octavus" (113). The first part of the article dealt with the difficulties the big Paris opera had to contend with, including "the absurdly exorbitant demands being made by the singers." Despite large governmental subsidies, the singers' demands made it impossible to stage new French works. "Saint-Saëns had the nerve to express his irritation in one of the local newspapers in an article that was as vehement as it was imprudent." Svendsen's article concluded with words of praise for the city's principal orchestras.

In Paris there was keen competition among both performers and composers, but the successes Svendsen had enjoyed in the early spring unfortunately did not lead to any public engagements. As the year 1879 was drawing to a close his financial circumstances were absolutely miserable. In the letter to Warmuth he mentioned that he was completely destitute and didn't know how he was going to get through the winter unless he got help from home:

> I have never been in a worse pinch than this. I can't come home now in the middle of winter because I don't have the money for the trip. Dear Carl! Do not fail me. It is just a matter of enabling me to stay here another six or seven months.

The following weeks were difficult ones for the Svendsens. In a Christmas letter to his father dated December 20, Johan reported that the temperature was -20° Centigrade: "I have never experienced such a miserable winter.

We don't have a regular heater in any of our rooms, so it is impossible to make it warm. We sit in front of the fireplace . . . and burn our knees while our backs freeze."

There is no diary from Svendsen's hand for 1879, but the University of Oslo Library has a French almanac for 1880 belonging to Svendsen that contains brief memoranda that are more complete than the diary entries from 1878. Thus it is easier to follow his life and work in this particular year. The almanac does not touch on his financial situation, but we know that in January Svendsen sent a letter of thanks to King Oscar II and that at about the same time he received a "nice letter" from Dr. Julius Nicolaysen in Oslo. Thus it is evident that Warmuth had managed to gather some funds as Svendsen had begged him to do. He could, therefore, resume a more active life. He attended a dozen public concerts, went to the theater four times, and heard Delibes' opera *Jean de Neville* at Opéra Comique.

It was in private concerts at the homes of friends and acquaintances that he heard the most music, however, and he also participated in the performance of numerous chamber-music works by Bach, Haydn, Beethoven, Schubert, Schumann, Sgambati, Saint-Saëns, César Franck, and many less famous composers. During the first four months he was a guest at no less than thirty such parties where the principal activity after dinner was music-making—sometimes for as long as "three solid hours." Among the prominent party-givers were Madame Viardot-Garcia, Baron d'Erlanger and Saint-Saëns, but most often he was a guest of his violinist friends Lascoux and Reynier. He was regularly in the company of Gounod, Franck, Chabrier, d'Indy, Duparc, Lamoreux, Sarasate and Ysaye.

The almanac diary has little to say about the compositions he heard. Svendsen did, however, describe a piano quartet by Fauré as "most interesting" (February 14). On April 9 he wrote that a concert of chamber-music works by contemporary French composers "consisted of nothing but trifles except for a couple of short piano pieces and two songs with piano by the young Miss Cécile Chaminade."

Several of his own compositions were played at these private concerts. The string quintet was played five times and the string quartet and string octet once each. The violin concerto (with piano accompaniment) was played three times by the young violinist Herwegh. On April 20 Svendsen wrote that he had been "to dinner at Lascoux's along with many distinguished friends. After dinner . . . Sally sang some of my songs and received loud applause."

The only one of his compositions to be performed publicly in Paris in 1880 was the string octet, which was played on January 6 at a soirée given by the chamber-music society *La Trompette*. On January 30 the same piece was given "an excellent performance" as the concluding number at a soirée in Salle Pleyel, and on February 7 it was again on the program at *La Trompette*. "This was the sixth public performance of this work here in Paris," he wrote to Warmuth the following day. The February 8 issue of *Revue Gazette Musicale de Paris* stated regarding the octet that "few chamber-music works offer such a richness of new instrumental combinations and such a piquant freshness and natural originality in the motives."

On March 1, 1880, Svendsen dispatched another report from Paris to *Nordisk Musik-Tidende*. In the cover letter to Warmuth he wrote:

> It was written in haste and probably needs to be edited before you send it to the printer. . . . You must feel free to make changes, but *nothing must be omitted*. Write soon and let me know if you want me to continue as a correspondent so that I can gather and organize the mass of material in some kind of comprehensible way.

The article dealt with the poor performances by both Colonne and Pasdeloup of the first part of Berlioz's opera *The Trojans*. Both of these orchestras also played "a new orchestral suite by Massenet, a composer who is much overrated here . . . with the remarkable result that while Colonne's performance was applauded, Pasdeloup's was met with indifference." Tchaikovsky's fourth symphony as played by Colonne "didn't please many, although the performance was excellent." Svendsen regarded the Paris Conservatory orchestra as the best of the lot. It was "incomparable . . . , and it is no exaggeration to describe this orchestra as the finest in the world."

In conclusion he mentioned that "Master Verdi has arrived and is in the process of preparing for a performance of *Aida* that is soon to be given at the Grand Opéra." Svendsen did not attend the opera, however, nor did any further articles by Quintus Octavus appear in *Nordisk Musik-Tidende*.

Svendsen mentioned in the letter to Warmuth that he was planning to return to Norway in April, and he asked in all candor:

> Do you think it might be possible to get free passage for me and my family on *Kong Magnus* from the steamship company? First class, of course. Furthermore, do you think I can count on being able to earn something when I come home? If you have any ideas along that line, let me hear

them. I have received Alexius Ræder's letter, and like you I am very pleased that the first step toward the establishment of a music school has been taken.

Four days later he and Bergljot went to Angers, where preparations had been made for a new concert. On March 7 he conducted *Carnival in Paris* and *Symphony No. 2*. The local newspaper *L'Abeille* wrote:

> There is a surprising enthusiasm in this music, a brilliant originality, a continuous inspiration. The listeners were deeply moved, dazzled by an admirable orchestration, warm and colorful. We will also remember him as the splendid conductor who knew how to communicate to the musicians the same fire that had inspired him. . . . I need only add that he was given an ovation worthy of his enormous talent.

The result of this triumph was that the orchestra in Angers wanted to engage him as its permanent conductor. A March 20 entry in the almanac states, "Received offer to take over leadership of the concerts in Angers for next season," and five days later a second offer was made. Though the offer was tempting, however, his desire to return to Norway was too strong to be denied.

At the end of April he sent "most of our baggage via mail car to Le Havre" and began a series of farewell visits to such friends as Saint-Saëns, Baron d'Erlanger and Hamelle. On May 4 César Franck came to visit, and early the following morning several friends came to the station to say *au revoir*.

In Le Havre they "immediately boarded *Kong Magnus*. Captain Becker was so kind as to give us the best quarters on the whole ship." They got under way the following evening, and after a voyage in "clear, nice weather but strong wind" they came within sight of the coast of Norway on May 10. The next day Svendsen wrote in his diary: "Arrival in Oslo 5 A.M. Got a room at Hotel Victoria. Immediately visited the family and several friends and were heartily received. Talked with the king."

6

THE LAST OSLO PERIOD

1880–83

SVENDSEN HAD STATED several times during his years abroad—to Grieg and others—that his rightful place was in Oslo. There he would resume with renewed vigor the task of elevating the quality of music life, and he also had a fond hope that his ability to compose larger works might return once he got established in his homeland.

A YEAR OF HARD WORK

Immediately after returning home on May 11, 1880, Svendsen began to make preparations for an evening program featuring his own compositions. An unusually large orchestra of professional and amateur players was assembled, and after three intense rehearsals the concert was given on May 29. The program included *Norwegian Rhapsody No. 3, Zorahayda, Romeo and Juliet, Carnival in Paris, Last Year I Was Tending the Goats*, and a work still in manuscript, *Norwegian Springar*. Four of the new songs were also premiered by soprano Amanda Kolderup with piano accompaniment by Martin Ursin.

Svendsen received a warm welcome by the hometown audience. The packed auditorium gave him many ovations and the orchestra sounded a flourish even as he mounted the podium. The critical reviews of the concert were highly positive. *Nordisk Musik-Tidende* wrote:

> The execution, which was exceptionally precise and attractive, showed how much power there is in the conductor's personality. It was as if every player in the orchestra was striving to do his very best to help place

the compositions in the most favorable light, as if the players themselves
were inspired by the beauty of those compositions.

The only new orchestral work on the program was *Norwegian Springar*
(Work 123), an unpretentious composition that soon thereafter was forgotten. Unlike the Norwegian rhapsodies, it is built not on authentic folk tunes
but on material presumably invented by Svendsen himself.

Svendsen was so popular in Oslo that Warmuth was able to advertise for
sale a 10-inch bust "fashioned by Mathias Skeibrok in the finest porcelain,
price six crowns."

For the first eleven days after arriving in Oslo the family stayed at Hotel
Victoria. They then lived for a time at No. 11 Rosenkrantz street, then at
No. 47 Pilestrædet, where they remained until the summer of 1883.

The social whirl that had been such a large part of their life in Paris continued in Oslo. The city's upper crust welcomed Johan and Sally with open
arms. Svendsen's diary for May contains many references to such social engagements: "Dinner at Joh. Magelsen's. . . . Warmuth's birthday celebrated
at his home with a very animated and elegant evening meal . . . spent the afternoon and evening with Prof. Nicolaysen at his lovely home on Sjursøen
along with Dr. Storm and Grønvold . . . evening at Schirmer's together
with his father and Sinding, the sculptor . . . enjoyable sailboat ride and
open-air dinner at Hovedøen with the Gulowsen and Gunnestad families—
supper at Egebergs."

Among prosperous families living in Oslo it was the custom to spend
the summer months in the country, and Svendsen chose to do the same. On
June 5 he and his family took the steamboat *Stærkod* to Larkollen, a resort
community near the south end of the Oslofjord, "where we were met by
the maid, who had arranged everything perfectly . . ." A correspondent for
the Oslo newspaper *Dagen* reported on August 7: "The only one of the six-
teen families of resort guests . . . being borne on the wings of inspiration
seems to be the composer Svendsen. . . . His latest work, which came to life
amidst Larkollen's natural beauty, is an exceptionally beautiful song,
Frühling." The reference was to the song *Spring Jubilation*, which had already been accepted for publication by Warmuth.

Svendsen enjoyed Larkollen so much that except for a few quick trips to
Oslo he remained there for almost three months—until August 26. His diary gives a picture of partying in the grand style: "horrible toddy . . . went to

Johan Svendsen during the
early 1880s. (Universitetsbiblioteket, Oslo)

Gulowsen's at 11 P.M., where we found a rollicking party that lasted until
1 A.M. and that then continued at my place until 3 in the morning." He
wrote to Grieg on September 24:

> I haven't composed a thing this summer. Instead I have fished, swum,
> sailed, and walked a lot. If I am going to be able to write anything in the
> near future I must try to get away from my many "tribulations". It is
> especially my financial circumstances that make my life unpleasant.

Was Svendsen's financial situation really so difficult? Naturally enough,
upon returning from his long stay abroad his funds were exhausted. Nonetheless, with the profit from the concert in May plus his monthly state grant
of 133 crowns in his pocket he had lived like a king and set out on a costly
summer vacation! And then, when the funds ran out, reality once again
stared him in the face.

From September and on he advertised regularly in *Nordisk Musik-
Tidende:* "Johan Svendsen takes students in harmony, violin, and ensemble

playing." No doubt he earned something from such teaching, but he none-theless found it necessary to take out a loan to maintain the standard of living to which he had become accustomed.

His diary makes it clear that throughout the autumn he frequently went to parties and occasionally gave them as well. He also attended many concerts and plays. The latter included Holberg's *Jeppe of the Hill* ("masterfully played by Johannes Brun"), Bjørnson's *Leonarda*, and Ibsen's *The League of Youth* and *The Pretenders* (twice). He also attended Verdi's *La Traviata* as well as a number of light operas.

Late in the autumn he got started on what he regarded as his principal task, namely the work with the orchestra of the Music Society. During his absence the composer Ole Olsen had conducted the orchestra, but during those three years only ten concerts had been given, and that included some chamber-music programs as well. Ole Olsen was a fine musician, to be sure, but he lacked Svendsen's stature and leadership qualities. Thus the Music Society looked forward to getting the baton back into the proper hands.

Six concerts were planned for the 1880–81 season, but to begin with the preparations went slowly. Svendsen wrote to Grieg on October 27:

> I still haven't gotten anything done other than to run around to theater directors, directors of military bands, amateurs, and to the current manager of Tivoli to get the orchestra organized. Damn it, I think it's getting more difficult every year to get together a concert here in Oslo. I've finally gotten to the point that I could schedule the first concert for November 6.

This concert offered three pieces being performed for the first time in Oslo: Schubert's *Symphony No. 8* ("Unfinished"), Berlioz's *Roman Carnival*, and Tchaikovsky's *Andante Cantabile* (for strings).

The Music Society's concerts were popular. The number of regular subscribers was around six hundred and ticket prices were two crowns per concert. The orchestra consisted of some 40 musicians, each of whom received eight crowns per concert. Soloists usually got a hundred crowns for their contribution; Svendsen, as artistic director, received two hundred crowns for orchestral concerts and one hundred for chamber-music concerts. Thus during the 1880–81 season he must have earned eleven hundred crowns for his work in the Music Society.

The second concert of the season (November 20) was devoted to chamber music. The principal offerings were Grieg's string quartet in G minor and Mozart's string quintet in G minor (with Svendsen playing one of the viola parts).

Svendsen, by virtue of his special interest in chamber music, again became the chief promoter of the Quartet Society, in which he and Grieg and Sarasate were honorary members. He participated enthusiastically in performances, sometimes as first violinist, sometimes as violist. From time to time he also rehearsed and conducted larger ensembles—for example, two of Beethoven's quartets were performed with four instruments on each part. The Society's meetings were held each Tuesday at the home of Halvard Emil Heyerdahl, an engineer, who lived at 9 Rosenborg Street. Large quantities of Munich beer were consumed and special parties were thrown at every opportunity. The high points of the year were Haydn's, Mozart's and Beethoven's birthdays.

The Music Society's third concert on December 4 featured Svendsen's second symphony and Grieg's piano concerto, the latter with Erika Lie Nissen as soloist. Svendsen wrote to Grieg on December 23, "You will be glad to hear that Mrs. Nissen's performance was marvelous. The orchestra was also excellent. Impressive, powerful and sonorous."

Six days later he wrote to Iver Holter that it had been a joy to work with the orchestra, for "it has shown both will and ability in full measure, and the result of our common labor has been excellent."

Svendsen also received reports of a number of performances of his works abroad: *Symphony No. 1* in Leipzig, *Symphony No. 2* in Edinburgh and Rotterdam, the *Violin Concerto* in Sondershausen and Dordrecht, *Norwegian Rhapsody* No. 1 in Baltimore, Nos. 2 and 3 in Munich and Moscow, No. 4 in London and Madrid, *Carnival in Paris* in Brussels, London and Karlsruhe, *Sigurd Slembe* in London, *Romeo and Juliet* in Brno and Boston, the *String Quartet* in Bremen and Baltimore, and the *String Octet* in Kassel and Naples.

After a December 4 performance of *Zorahayda* in Copenhagen under the baton of Balduin Dahl, several critics wrote laudatory articles about their "new discovery." Charles Kjerulf, in particular, became a strong advocate of Svendsen's music. On December 6 he wrote in *Dags-Avisen*: "Svendsen is not merely the Nordic composer who for the moment undoubtedly enjoys the greatest esteem abroad; he is in general one of the most brilliant musical figures of our time in the realm of orchestral music."

Four months later (April 4, 1881), after Niels W. Gade had presented *Sigurd Slembe* in Copenhagen, Charles Kjerulf wrote:

> At last! At last Johan Svendsen achieved a place on a program of the Copenhagen Music Society. It was almost an oddity that our first musical society, our musical "supreme court," still had not found Svendsen worthy of being introduced via one of his compositions that are played all over the world and are universally acclaimed. It is quite true that Svendsen belongs to the Progressive party—but that, one would think, should not be a hindrance to his admission to the ranks of the chosen!

In January 1881 Svendsen was made a Knight of the Order of St. Olav, and he celebrated the occasion by giving a concert of his own works on January 29. A "female amateur" sang four of his songs, but the principal numbers on the program were *Symphony No. 2, Zorahayda,* and *Two Swedish Folk Melodies for String Orchestra.* This was the first performance of No. 2 of the Swedish melodies.

The Oslo Music Society's fourth concert (February 12) presented Iver Holter's *Norwegian Midsummer Eve,* Bach's concerto for three harpsichords and strings—and a curiosity: Svendsen's string octet played by the whole string orchestra including double basses! The fifth concert (March 19) consisted entirely of chamber music.

The season was brought to a grand and glorious climax on April 2 when Beethoven's ninth symphony was performed for the first time ever in Norway. The orchestra was enlarged to 54 instruments for the occasion. The 85-voice Lammers Choral Society sang in the last movement as did also four of Norway's leading soloists: Sofie Bonnevie, Hildur Schirmer, Hans Brun and Thorvald Lammers. It was an unparalleled event in Norwegian musical life. According to *Aftenbladet,* the listeners were gripped by an irresistible power: "Without a conductor like Mr. Svendsen it could hardly have been accomplished. It is certainly the most dazzling testimony he has given of his knowledge as a musician and his skill as a conductor."

The concert was so successful that it had to be repeated a week later, this time in a larger auditorium. Svendsen wrote to Iver Holter on April 6 that the Beethoven symphony had been a ray of light amidst everything he had to contend with, plagued as he was by "students, creditors, committee meetings" and countless other things:

> Everything went well; indeed, many things went very well. All the "dangerous" places (for example, the horn solos in the first and third move-

ments, the violin passages in the *Adagio* and the bass and cello recitatives in the *Finale*) went splendidly. The chorus, too, was very good. The whole thing gave the impression of confidence and precision. I hadn't dared to hope for this when we first began, but it was remarkable how with each rehearsal it got lighter and clearer—and as I said, the final result was excellent. Yes, I daresay that many things went so well that they could hardly have been better. How I have labored to bring this about is indescribable. Just think that for three solid weeks I was busy almost constantly drilling the various sections of the orchestra. In so doing I went through the score innumerable times in great detail, as a result of which I was able to conduct the performance from memory.

A big event took place on Constitution Day—May 17—when Brynjulf Bergslien's statue of Henrik Wergeland was to be unveiled in Student-erlunden Park. Bjørnson was the principal speaker and Svendsen, who as a five-year-old had attended Wergeland's funeral, had agreed to compose a cantata using a text written by Jonas Lie (*Wergeland Cantata*, Work 124).

The performance of this well-written piece of occasional music for baritone solo, male chorus and janissary orchestra was most impressive. Several choral groups were combined for the occasion to provide a huge chorus of four hundred male voices. J. G. Conradi, O. A. Grøndahl, O. Koppang and Thorvald Lammers all assisted in preparing the chorus, and Lammers also served as soloist.

The effect on the enormous audience attending the event was overwhelming. They were especially moved at one point where the chorus, in the middle of a passage in A-flat major, suddenly shouted out Henrik Wergeland's name in a bright, resounding C-major chord. One reviewer described it as follows: "This shout was so powerful that it sounded like a mighty storm even in the open air where all sounds usually are drowned out."

In September Svendsen was at work on a cantata to be sung on October 18 at a festive University event honoring the newly married crown prince Oscar Gustav Adolph (later King Gustav V) and Sofia Maria Viktoria (later queen Viktoria). The text for the cantata was written by Professor Lorentz Dietrichson. The *Wedding Cantata* (op. 29) for mixed chorus, baritone solo and orchestra was completed on September 26.

Among those attending the event were Oscar II, prime ministers Posse, Kierulf and Selmer, Norwegian and Swedish cabinet members, all the members of the supreme court, and a number of bishops and generals. Professor O. P. Monrad gave a flowery keynote address in the course of which, according to *Dagen*, he "spoke at length about the ethical as well as the social significance of marriage and emphasized especially the influence the recently concluded marriage contract in our royal family would have on the future of all our people."

Svendsen himself conducted the performance. Thorvald Lammers was the soloist and his own chorus—the Lammers Choral Society—of more than a hundred voices handled the choral parts. The performance was a great triumph and was repeated the next day "for all those who have been admitted to the university." On October 23 it was repeated once more, this time for a sold-out audience of ordinary concert-goers who packed a large gymnasium to hear the performance. Writing festival music was a task dear to Svendsen's heart, and as in the Wergeland cantata he managed once again to express himself in melodious tunes that fit the taste of the time. The critics were effusive in their praise. *Aftenposten* described the event as "a totality that had a quite wonderful effect." The climax of the cantata—the concluding hymn, which to our modern ears sounds almost stereotypical—was characterized by the critics as magnificent.

The composer got more than praise for his efforts, however: he received in hard cash an amount almost equal to his annual state grant. On November 4 he received a letter of thanks from the Academic Council of the University together with a commission fee and honorarium totalling six hundred crowns. In addition to that he received income from the above-mentioned public performance in the amount of seven hundred crowns.

Compared to these amounts, it is sad to learn how little he received at about the same time for his *Violin Romance* (op. 26). This composition proved to be an enormous success and earned huge sums of money for its publishers. For writing it, however, Svendsen received a one-time honorarium of a mere two hundred crowns!

THE VIOLIN ROMANCE

The *Violin Romance*, op. 26, is the only Svendsen composition that is frequently played outside Norway today. The story of how it came to be written is rather amusing.

In autumn of 1881, Svendsen was very busy with his students. The teaching was done in a room that Warmuth had placed at his disposal in the building occupied by his publishing company. Warmuth, who was a capable amateur violinist, had once asked Svendsen to write a piece for violin and orchestra but Svendsen just never got around to doing it. One day, because of a misunderstanding, several students failed to show up for their lessons, and this gave Svendsen an opportunity to surprise his friend. His creative juices were running that day, and in the space of a few hours he sketched out the entire work. That evening he wrote out a fair copy and the next day he marched into Warmuth's office with the completed score.

Warmuth played through the solo part and realized immediately that what Svendsen had written was a real gem. Elatedly he declared that the piece would be published by his firm without delay. Svendsen was so delighted about Warmuth's enthusiasm that when the matter of an honorarium was brought up he told the publisher that he would take whatever he wanted to give him. "He gave me 200 crowns," Svendsen later told an interviewer (133), "and I, who didn't have much confidence in my work, was very happy. After all, it was 200 crowns in pay for a mere two days' work!" Thus for all time to come he had sold the birthright to what was to become his most famous work.

That autumn Stanislaus Barcewicz, a well-known Polish violin virtuoso, visited Oslo and Svendsen showed him his new composition. The result was that Barcewicz had the honor of premiering the work before a full house in Oslo's Akershus Fortress gymnasium on October 30, 1881, with Svendsen himself conducting. *Aftenposten* wrote that the composition "made an unusually favorable impression; the audience demanded that it be repeated, and after much loud applause it was."

The following week Barcewicz was called upon to substitute for the ailing Edmund Neupert as soloist at the Music Society's first subscription concert of the season. He played Mendelssohn's *Violin Concerto* and Svendsen's *Violin Romance*. In September 1882 he introduced the new work in Dresden and a short time later it was performed in Leipzig by Heinrich Schradieck, concertmaster of the Gewandhaus Orchestra.

What is it about the *Violin Romance* that has made it so popular? By the time of Svendsen's death in 1911 it had appeared in 68 editions and it continues to be played frequently to the present day. It appeals to concert violinists, who can let their instrument sing brilliantly in the lyrical cantilenas of the outer sections and show off their technical skill in the passionate figurations of the middle section. Its versatility and fairly modest technical demands also make it accessible to advanced amateurs. The main reason for the enduring success of the work, however, is the glorious, soaring melodic lines that are supported and further ennobled by the distinctive harmony. The piece as a whole is filled with intense feeling, yet it never succumbs to sentimentality.

Only a few romances for violin have been written. The best-known of these, in addition to Svendsen's, are Beethoven's romances in F major and G major. But Svendsen's composition is less similar to them than, for example, to Wieniawski's *Legend* (1860), a work in a related style with which he undoubtedly was familiar.

In the *Violin Romance*, Svendsen once again demonstrated his skill as a master of form. Despite great contrasts in dynamics and tempo, the composition is highly unified. A four-measure phrase at the beginning of the A section undergoes a series of transformations. Unity also is created by the use of a motive from the Introduction in the climax of the middle part of the B section.

After a 20-measure Introduction, which begins with descending chromatic lines, we hear the principal melodic idea of the A section. This theme constitutes the material from which the rest of the composition evolves. While the slow A section is given a simple harmonic garb and precise tonality, the agitated middle section tends toward tonal vagueness—an effect achieved through the use of modal harmonies and sudden shifts in the modulations. The melody of the first four-measure phrase, for example, which is clearly derived from the A theme, is in D Phrygian but is harmonized in G Aeolian:

Example 14   *Violin Romance,* op. 26

The middle part of the B section breaks the pattern of motivic variation that has governed the structure up to this point and restates the motive taken from the Introduction, first *molto animato e appassionato,* then very slowly in *pianissimo.*

The violin part, which at the beginning of the somewhat modified recapitulation of the A section is transposed down an octave, ascends step by step all the way to b^3 in a mighty climax in *fortissimo*.

In the Coda, marked *Lento*, the principal motive from the A section is given a decidedly Phrygian twist above a typical Svendsenian chromatic chordal basis. The music then dies away, *morendo*, in luminous brightness.

FURTHER ARTISTIC TRIUMPHS

In January 1882 Svendsen composed a new orchestral polonaise, this time in D major. The score bears the inscription, "Dance on Attila's Fortress." The title is thought to have resulted from the use of the polonaise as incidental music for *Attila*, a play by C. M. von Scholten presented at the Royal Theater in Copenhagen in ca. 1908. Svendsen's student Joachim Bruun de Neergaard also provided music for this production.

Polonaise (op. 28) is a fresh and engaging composition with catchy melodies, but despite these qualities it has not achieved the popularity of *Festival Polonaise* (op. 12). Strangely enough, the score has never been printed. *Festival Polonaise*, on the other hand, was published by Warmuth in 1886. The composer's honorarium was four hundred crowns.

Svendsen also received four hundred crowns from Christiania Theater for incidental music for the celebrated festival presentation *From Mountain and Fjord*, which took place on February 13, 1882 in connection with a visit by the royal family. The event was grandly conceived. The first part was built around three enormous tableaus created by the painter Knut Bergslien. The tableaus were framed by a prologue and an epilogue written by Lorentz Dietrichson, and four orchestral pieces by Svendsen were played: *Prelude*, *Allegro* (*Tempest*) for the tableau *From the Winter Fisheries*, *Andantino* (*Calm*) for the tableau *A Hunt in the Mountains*, and *Springar* for the tableau *A Peasant Wedding*. We have no further information about the first two numbers, but the third may have been *Andantino quasi Allegretto* (Work 403). The fourth undoubtedly was *Norwegian Springar* (Work 123).

The second part of the presentation was preceded by an orchestral piece by Grieg entitled *Intermezzo* (probably *Borghild's Dream* from the incidental music for Bjørnson's *Sigurd Jorsalfar*). This was followed by a performance of Act 2 of Ibsen's *The Vikings at Helgeland* by the theater's leading actors and actresses.

In 1882 Svendsen conducted seven concerts in Oslo. On March 25 he demonstrated his support of two young Norwegian composers by premiering Catharinus Elling's *Serenade* for string orchestra and Christian Sinding's *Piano Quintet*, op. 5. The latter work was performed in an unusual version: piano and string orchestra, including double basses!

The next concert of the Music Society, on April 15, featured first performances in Oslo of several works including Grieg's *The Wounded Heart* and *Last Spring* for string orchestra, Mendelssohn's *Die erste Walpurgisnacht* and Saint-Saëns's *Omphale's Spinning Wheel*.

A short time thereafter Oslo enjoyed visits by four world-renowned artists: the pianists Hans von Bülow and Anton Rubinstein, the violinist Eugène Ysaye, and the cellist David Popper. Svendsen had close contact with all of them, and shortly after his visit von Bülow wrote a long article, "Skandinavische Concertreiseskizzen" (21), in which he expressed regret that he had not met Grieg during his visit to Norway. He continued:

> But on the other hand, in Svendsen I got to know a Nordic musician with an unusual, special talent and fecundity. Moreover, he had a wide-ranging cosmopolitan education that is seldom found among his countrymen! He is surprisingly well versed in the contemporary literature of the culturally advanced countries and he has learned to speak their languages with perfect fluency.

David Popper, who participated in a performance of Svendsen's string quintet at a public concert by the Quartet Society on April 19, remained in Norway until that summer. On June 19 Svendsen noted in his almanac: "Enjoyable evening at Prof. Nicolaysen's (Popper, Warmuth, Eilif Peterssen, Grønvold and others)." Popper was so enthralled with Svendsen's *Violin Romance* that he arranged it for cello and piano. This version was published by Warmuth in December.

Both Ysaye's and Rubinstein's visits occurred as part of long concert tours that ended in Russia. Svendsen persuaded the Belgian virtuoso violinist to participate in a benefit concert in Oslo on April 21 to raise money for the Ole Bull monument in Bergen. One of the items on the program was Bull's *A Mother's Prayer*. In May, Ysaye played four solo concerts, and at two of them he played Svendsen's *Violin Romance*, once with the Christiania Theater Orchestra.

In 1882 Svendsen's compositions continued their triumphant march into concert halls all over the world. The first symphony was performed in Cologne, the second symphony in Königsberg and Stockholm, *Zorahayda* in Karlsbad, *Carnival in Paris* twice in New York, the cello concerto in Würzburg, the third Norwegian rhapsody in Stockholm, Chicago and London, the string octet in London, and the string quintet in New York and Baltimore. Audiences and critics were equally enthusiastic. Svendsen was at this time the most widely played Nordic composer in the world. During the years 1872–82, the Chamber Music Society of St. Petersburg presented fourteen performances of Svendsen, eight of Grieg, and twelve of Niels W. Gade.

On September 30, Svendsen celebrated his 42nd birthday with a festive concert in the Freemasons' large auditorium. Thorvald Lammers sang three of Grieg's Vinje songs (op. 33). On June 22, Svendsen had written to Grieg that he had studied his new opus with steadily growing interest: "I have been especially gripped by *The Youth*. Here music and poetry are intimately united in such a way as to create such extraordinary pathos that I know of nothing in song literature that is its equal, perhaps with the exception of Schumann's *Die alten, bösen Lieder.*"

Of Svendsen's own works the program included the *Wedding Cantata*, *Zorahayda*, and *Norwegian Artists' Carnival*. The last-mentioned work, which here received its premiere performance in a concert hall, was now given the following subtitles: 1. *Festival in the Castle of the Mountain King*. 2. *Parade of Elves, Fairies, Dwarfs and Trolls*. 3. *Arrival of Prince Carnival and his Entourage*. 4. *Dance and Jubilation*. These titles were not included in the printed score, however.

One week later Svendsen left for Copenhagen on a visit that was to have unexpected consequences.

INTERLUDE IN COPENHAGEN

During the summer and fall of 1882 there was a movement afoot in Copenhagen to get Svendsen appointed as musical director at the Royal Theater. It was widely felt in the Danish capital that the musical standard at the theater had been slipping for several years. 72-year-old Holger S. Paulli, who had been musical director for 18 years, was well-liked for his amiability and competence, but discipline in the orchestra was steadily declining and Paulli was no longer very inspiring as an orchestral conductor. His interest in contemporary music was also waning. To be sure, he had staged three Wagner operas, but one can question how well he understood Wagner's works—as is evident from a story told by violinist Fini Henriques: " 'It sounds awful,' he often said during rehearsals. 'Stop! It must be wrong.' And then when it really *was* played incorrectly, it sometimes happened that he thought it was right"(41).

A number of opera enthusiasts got impatient with the way things were going. They wanted Czech-Danish violinist Frantz Neruda to be appointed musical director, and in the spring of 1882 they launched a campaign against Paulli in the local press. When court chamberlain Morten Edvard Fallesen, who had been theater director for six years, made absolutely no effort to defend his musical director, Paulli indignantly submitted his resignation. Meanwhile, several of the musicians expressed the opinion that Neruda was totally unacceptable as an opera conductor, and in July when he was asked to apply for the position he firmly refused.

In this critical situation, friends of Paulli persuaded the ministry to intervene and extend the old man's appointment. In the meantime, Svendsen had been mentioned in the press as the right man for the job but he paid little attention to it.

That autumn, however, some leading figures in Copenhagen's musical circles put out some tempting bait. Leading the effort were two Svendsen enthusiasts: Henrik Hennings, a leading impresario and music dealer, and the distinguished music critic Charles Kjerulf. Their first move was to invite Svendsen to present himself as a conductor and composer in the Danish capital at two concerts (October 14 and 21). Both programs were to consist exclusively of his own works. On October 5 Kjerulf published a long article in *Dagsavisen* that concluded with these words: "For myself, I can proclaim Svendsen as one of the brightest stars in the realm of music, and among contemporary musicians absolutely the greatest. I am inclined to think that I will have quite a few people sharing this view when he lays down the baton after his first concert here . . ."

For these two concerts, Hennings had engaged the orchestra of the Copenhagen Music Society augmented with a number of string players from the cabaret orchestras. Carl Gottschalksen, who was one of the musicians, later described Svendsen's first rehearsal with the orchestra:

> As we all sat in our places, Mr. Hennings came in with Johan Svendsen and introduced him to us. Young, slender, elegant, he stood on the podium. His way of rehearsing was quite new to all of us. He took indi-

vidual sections one at a time—first the violins or the cellos and double basses—and slowly worked up to the full orchestra. But what a result! What a *pianissimo*, and what dynamic power in the big *fortissimo*! One can confidently say without exaggeration that he was the first conductor who taught Danish musicians to play a *pianissimo* and a gradual *crescendo* leading to the loudest possible *fortissimo*. Always the most exquisite amiability during rehearsals. Smiling his winning smile, he could take an instrument from one of the violinists and play the passage himself, and then explain that such and such a stroke in all the string sections would produce the best result for the whole ensemble (44:81).

The concerts were given in the large Casino auditorium in Tivoli. The first program consisted of *Symphony No. 1, Romeo and Juliet, Norwegian Rhapsody No. 3, Two Icelandic Melodies,* and the *Violin Romance.* Even though ticket prices were held to a minimum, however, the turnout on the first evening was small. A program devoted entirely to new music by a Norwegian composer who was virtually unknown in Copenhagen obviously had little public appeal.

Karl Larsen, a writer who was at the first concert, reported that at the end of the program the famous Danish composer Niels W. Gade walked quickly up to the front of the auditorium and motioned toward Svendsen with a strangely regal, jovial wave of his hand: "Johan Svendsen had been accepted—his name inscribed in the book of the gods, as Oehlenschlæger puts it—and there was a bit of the young god about him at that time too. We clapped fanatically (79)."

The newspapers reported that the audience had responded with great enthusiasm. All the critics emphasized that Svendsen had conducted without a score—something that obviously was unusual in their experience. Angul Hammerich wrote in *Nationaltidende* about Svendsen's baton's "calm, commanding path through the air, with the magical capacity to, as it were, verbally convey the rapid-fire orders to the orchestra."

Charles Kjerulf later reported an amusing little episode that transpired between Svendsen and one of the musicians during the first rehearsal for the second concert:

It had to do with the fast passages for the woodwinds in the *scherzo* of his B-flat major symphony. The oboist couldn't keep up—kept getting stuck—just couldn't get it. Svendsen cut them off. The oboist was offended. "This can't be played—in that tempo," he blurted out. "My dear sir," Svendsen replied with extreme calmness and politeness, "you cannot say that, for this passage *can* be played in *that* tempo! What you can say is that *you* cannot play it—in *that* tempo" (71).

Svendsen's visit revived talk of his possible candidacy for the conductorship of the Royal Theater Orchestra. *Dansk Dagblad* wrote on October 15:

> All in all the concert was so successful that it appears to constitute a request for the Theater leadership to make an attempt—by means of a permanent appointment—to secure for our capital city an outstanding musician whose Nordic birth, German professional training, and earlier activity as conductor at several important concert institutions constitute the most promising conditions for the solution of the difficulty that during the past season appeared insurmountable.

Five days later *Dagsavisen* carried an anonymous article (undoubtedly written by Charles Kjerulf) under the title, "Who shall be musical director?" This article stated:

> A musical director will be chosen. Whether it will occur tomorrow or the day after tomorrow, in a month or a year—that is known only to the Lord and the court chamberlain [Fallesen]. But it will occur. Paulli cannot go on being both sacked and not sacked. . . . Svendsen's name has been in our paper again and again of late, but I have not with a word—not with a single letter—referred to him as a candidate for the conductorship. That was deliberate. I knew what an unlikely prospect it was at that time (126).

But *now* the time had come, and the following day Kjerulf had more to say—and this time he signed his name to it:

> The setting for the first rehearsal was not exactly propitious for Svendsen, for quite a few members of the orchestra were inclined to look down their noses at "the foreigner." But when the rehearsal was over, everyone was of the same opinion: that was a man we could use. Next to him all the others were but midgets. People told him so. He laughed and treated it as a joke. He took it for what it *had* been earlier: idle talk, gossip. But *now* it was something different: an unusual, unanimous opinion in our musical world. Virtually none of our musicians have talked with

Svendsen during these days without asking him or advising him to "apply" for or—what shall I call it— do "something" regarding the conducting position. Thus far his only answer has been a smile, a shrug. He still doesn't know for sure whether it is serious talk or nonsense. It's high time for him to learn that we are in dead earnest.

These days in Copenhagen were like a grand party. On October 20 Svendsen sent Warmuth several newspaper clippings—both pre-concert announcements and critical reviews—and asked him to make arrangements to get them published in the Oslo press. His cover letter included an account of the splendid reception he had received:

> All the leading local music people, led by Gade and Hartmann, vie with one another to be nice to me. As you can see from the clippings, my first concert was a true triumph. The financial outcome wasn't bad either, as the income proved to be sufficient to cover the *very big* expenses. Sally came here on Wednesday and both of us are now staying with the Robert Henriques family, where we are taken care of in grand style. Hennings is particularly pleasant to work with; he is bright and quick and always has time. . . . My presence here has contributed—much against my will—to a revival of the conductorship question in several of the local newspapers.

It is obvious, however, that his attitude toward Kjerulf's article published the same day was anything but negative, for in a new letter to Warmuth dated October 21 he wrote: "See to it that one of the papers—preferably *Aftenposten*—prints Kjerulf's article about the conducting position *in its entirety*."

The presence of the Danish crown prince and princess lent added luster to Svendsen's second concert. This time the program consisted of *Symphony No. 2*, *Carnival in Paris*, and three songs: *Venetian Serenade*, *The Birch Tree*, and *Spring Jubilation*. Again the critics tried to outdo one another in their choice of superlatives to describe Svendsen both as a conductor and as a composer—though Angul Hammerich averred in the October 25 issue of *Nationaltidende* that "Svendsen is not by nature a vocal composer, not yet in any case."

A big banquet was given in Svendsen's honor at Hotel d'Angleterre, and it was reported in detail in the press. To the right of the honored guest was "the amiable and youthfully vital old man" J. P. E. Hartmann. To his left sat his wife, who was accompanied to the table by Niels W. Gade. Among the 70 guests were many of the leading people in Danish music life including the composers Ludvig Schytte, Christian Barnekow, and Robert Henriques. Also present were the two rivals, Holger Paulli and Franz Neruda. Theater director Fallesen was not there, however. Guests from Norway included the poet Andreas Munch and the wife of the prominent writer Alexander Kielland. The writer himself was not there, however: "Of course he had signed up, but he didn't come, since as a matter of principle he never goes to banquets."

Hartmann opened the festivities with a toast to his Norwegian colleague, stressing "how rare, but for that very reason all the more deserving of approbation it was" that a creative artist had come to Denmark to present his works. "We have been living in the time of the virtuosos, but Svendsen didn't come to us as a performing artist except in the sense that he abundantly demonstrated what supreme mastery he had in conducting the orchestra." Hartmann "dwelt partly on his brilliance as a composer, partly on his eminent ability as a conductor," and emphasized that both ordinary and professional friends of music had to rejoice in "the elegance and grace with which he gets the instruments to produce an orchestral sound—now in the course of interesting movements containing counterpoint's secrets, now in singularly beautiful tonal colors. His concerts have been inspiring, and we can only hope that he may have felt so welcome that this first big visit will be followed by many more."

In his thank-you speech, Svendsen assured those present that he had received so warm a welcome in Copenhagen that the weeks he had spent there had given him some of the richest experiences of his life. He then returned the tribute that he had received with a toast to Hartmann, Gade, and Paulli, the three deans of Danish music.

Holger Drachmann had written a poem for the occasion which he read aloud:

You come to us, a bracing mountain breeze
Wherein the breath of life and youth is stirring,
Wherein the scent of verdant mountain trees
Our sluggish Danish hearts to life is spurring.

The pantheon of Danish men of art
Is good enough—their works must be applauded;
But new is new, though every Danish heart
Extol the works of Hartmann and of Gade.

I thank you from the bottom of my heart
And that of every music-loving Dane.
Be well assured: you've won us with your art.
Goodbye—and come to see us soon again!

The artistic triumphs and the effusive praise made an impression on Svendsen. He no doubt realized that a metropolis such as Copenhagen offered opportunities for him to realize his potential as a conductor in more exciting, varied and important ways—both in the theater and in the concert hall—than did Oslo. He had not yet received an official offer of the position at the Royal Theater, but it was not long in coming—and then he would have to make an agonizing decision.

FAREWELL TO A SYMPHONY—AND TO NORWAY

Immediately after returning to Oslo from Copenhagen, Svendsen began rehearsing Beethoven's *Eroica* symphony for an October 30 concert by the Music Society orchestra, the first concert of the season. The next two subscription concerts were given on November 11 and December 2, and Svendsen took the opportunity to thank his Danish friends by presenting Oslo premieres of Gade's *Symphony No. 5* and Robert Henriques's *Aquarelles* for orchestra. It is quite possible that he also had an ulterior motive, i.e., to increase his chances of getting the Theater Orchestra position in Copenhagen.

Grieg, who had received reports from Denmark about Svendsen's success there, wrote on December 20 to his friend Gottfred Matthison-Hansen:

> This could be a suitable occasion to say something about my great countryman, who has everything that I lack. He is in my opinion the greatest *artist* (in contrast to *poet*) in all Scandinavia—and one of the few great spirits in Europe. That is why I am surprised that you say so little about something so significant. Was Svendsen really lauded most as a conductor? If so, one can only say that the Danish musicians have let themselves be fooled by the brilliance of his conductorial skills. For he is just as brilliant a composer (inventer, master of form and instrumentation) as he is a conductor—indeed, even more so. But to be sure, to see this requires a somewhat broader vision. Besides, there is something that makes this Danish opinion understandable, and that is that Denmark has had such a frightful lack of capable conductors. This has always seemed strange to

me, but it has been one of the main factors in keeping new currents out of Denmark. Promise me that next time you write you will tell me about *your own* impressions of Svendsen.

In the middle of December Svendsen gave a concert in the Drammen Theater. Early in the new year he completed a short orchestral composition, *Persian Dance* (Work 125), which may have been written for a theatrical performance in Oslo.

He was also at work at this time on a new symphony that unfortunately was to experience a tragic fate. After the success of his second symphony in Germany he had come into contact with Max Abraham, director of the C. F. Peters music publishing firm in Leipzig. Abraham saw in Svendsen another potential Norwegian gold mine and proposed that he write a third symphony—an idea that was not new to the composer. Several years passed without result, however, and in autumn of 1882 Abraham sent Svendsen a reminder. Svendsen replied on November 21 that it would be an honor to have his new symphony published by Peters and stated that "hopefully it will not be long before I can devote myself to the task with all my strength."

The symphony presumably was completed during the winter of 1882–83. What happened thereafter has been reported by Svendsen's friend John Paulsen:

> Svendsen, who was as handsome and charming as he was brilliant, was always being pursued by the women. They sent him letters and flowers, and occasionally they tried to establish a more intimate relationship with him. But this was painful to Sally. She, understandably enough, wanted to keep her husband for herself.
>
> It happened that after one of his concerts, one of Oslo's most celebrated beauties, Miss E., sent him a big bouquet of roses, and hidden among the pale red blossoms was a love letter. Unfortunately, both the flowers and the letter fell into the hands of the suspicious Sally.
>
> So what did that demonic woman do—she who had more than a few similarities to [Ibsen's infamous heroine] Hedda Gabler? She took the manuscript of Svendsen's new symphony, which he had been working on for a long time and had just finished—took it out of his desk drawer and threw it in the fire . . .
>
> One evening when I was visiting Svendsen at his home on Classens Street in Copenhagen, he himself told me about this dreadful experience. I became very indignant and finally asked my old friend:

"But what did you do to her then? She deserved to be killed on the spot."

Svendsen became absorbed in thought. He adopted a serious expression, and stroking his dark moustache he replied:

"Believe me, I was firm."

I didn't expect much, for I knew all about Svendsen's "firmness". He was one of the most charitable and indulgent people I have ever known.

"So what did you do? Did you immediately divorce her?"

"No, not that! But I said to her in an imperious tone of voice: 'On your knees!'"

I could only smile and I wanted very much to embrace my dear Svendsen (9).

The tragic story of the fate of Svendsen's third symphony got around in artistic circles in Oslo. Ibsen also heard about it and made use of it in *Hedda Gabler* as the point of departure for one of the most dramatic episodes in any of his plays. Paulsen got confirmation of this connection in conversations with Susannah Ibsen, the wife of the playwright. Paulsen recounts it as follows:

> How attentive Ibsen was, how adept he was at picking up the little things that add color to life, is most evident in that famous scene in *Hedda Gabler* where Hedda stands by the fireplace and burns up Eilert Løvborg's manuscript [of his doctoral dissertation]—their "spiritual child." In reality it was a tragic episode in the life of a great Norwegian artist, and it came to Ibsen's attention at just the right moment and gave him the idea.

The destruction of the manuscript of Svendsen's third symphony must have occurred in the spring of 1883, and it is possible that this fateful blow was one of the reasons for the sudden interruption of his productivity as a composer. Be that as it may, in the remaining 28 years of his life he composed nothing except a few pieces of occasional music.

During the Copenhagen visit it became clear that Svendsen was the obvious choice to lead the Royal Theater Orchestra. Henrik Hennings, especially, got deeply involved in the process. On December 22, 1882 he sent the following telegram to Svendsen in Oslo:

> Decision on conducting position imminent. May I apply on your behalf? Trust me completely. Will be mindful of everything affecting you and your position. September starting date. Will you leave everything to me?

We do not know the details of Svendsen's reply, but it was not until a couple of months later that things began to move rather quickly. The board of the Royal Theater then decided by a large majority to make a definite offer. On March 1, theater director Fallesen sent the following telegram:

> By the authority of the Minister of Culture, I hereby offer you the position of Conductor beginning July 1 next. Salary: 6,000 crowns annually. With a simple "yes," which would make me very happy, the matter is decided.

Hennings, as an impresario who presumably had a prospective financial interest in the outcome of the negotiations, sent a separate telegram the same day:

> Am aware of the offer. If this is not accepted, for God's sake don't give a negative reply before I have an opportunity to talk with you and inform you regarding several conditions that could not be discussed in the offer but that nonetheless are very significant elements in the total picture. If you say yes immediately it will all work out. If you can't bring yourself to do this right away, let me know immediately by telegram that you want to see me. In that case I will leave for Oslo early tomorrow morning. That you have been offered the position is still an absolute secret down here.

The theater director sent a second telegram the following day with further details regarding the responsibilities of the position:

> The choral director rehearses the choruses. Rehearsals with the soloists are handled by the musical director. The opera rehearsal pianist serves as accompanist at these rehearsals. Rehearsals with the orchestra are the responsibility of the musical director, who has final authority on all musical matters. Recommendations regarding opera repertoire and casting are made by the musical director, whose duties, in brief, are the customary ones. Operas as a rule are performed only two times a week.

Svendsen did not reply at once, for an effort was under way in Oslo to raise a substantial sum of money in the hope of keeping him in Norway. On March 3, 36 prominent citizens published an "invitation to the public" to pledge an annual contribution, initially for five years. The aggregate sum was to be presented to Svendsen as a gesture of thanks for what he had done

for his native city and "if possible, to retain his artistic skills for Norway"—
i.e., to make sure that he was not compelled for financial reasons to seek a
position abroad. The initiative did not, however, generate the response that
had been hoped for.

In responding to the Danish offer, Svendsen asked especially for clarifi-
cation regarding his eligibility for a pension in Denmark. He also made it a
condition that he have the right to give his own symphony concerts with
the Royal Theater Orchestra.

Fallesen then sent a new telegram in which he promised Svendsen a salary of 7,000 crowns after the first year if it should be decided that he was ineligible for a Danish pension. He would also receive travel expenses plus a
per diem allowance during a short initial period. Further, he would have a
contractual right to give four symphony concerts annually with the theater
orchestra.

It is possible that this last provision was the deciding factor in Svendsen's
decision. During the preceding two years he had had substantial income,
but even so he had not managed to get his finances in order. He was perpetually in debt. The prospect of receiving the net profit from four concerts
each year in Copenhagen—in addition to a salary that was quite substantial
for that time—was undoubtedly very attractive. Even more alluring, however, were the purely artistic aspects: having a fully professional orchestra at
his disposal would give him vastly greater opportunities than he had in Oslo.
The constant struggle to maintain an acceptable standard had undoubtedly
been a challenge, but in time it proved too burdensome. Moreover, in
Copenhagen he could engage world-renowned artists to perform at his
concerts and could use his position as a springboard to win guest appearances on the continent, thereby furthering his international reputation both
as a conductor and as a composer.

Nonetheless, he waited several days before making his decision. Only
after Fallesen had sent a final telegram—"Dear Svendsen! I continue to
await your answer, which has to do only with that little *yes!*"—did he accept
the offer. His telegram consisted of just this one word. On March 12 the
Danish Minister of Culture confirmed the appointment:

> The Ministry approves the appointment of Johan Svendsen effective
> July 1 with an annual salary [of 6,000 crowns] and with the further
> promise that, in the event that he is ineligible for the [Danish] pension
> program, his salary will be increased by 1,000 crowns per year beginning
> July 1, 1884.

Svendsen's decision made a deep impression in Oslo. *Dagbladet* wrote on March 19:

> Norway's capital city with its well over a hundred thousand inhabitants still has no proper use for such a significant musical figure as Mr. Svendsen. Prominent scientists are recruited by the university and their activity is preserved for the homeland, but artists and especially musicians are still, if not exactly superfluous, at least not as absolutely indispensable as those who work in other areas of our cultural life. This is said not as a reproach but as an expression of regret.

Two days earlier Svendsen had bid farewell to the Music Society with a concert that included Wagner's *Tannhäuser* overture as well as his own second symphony. *Nordisk Musik-Tidende* reported that there was an extraordinary atmosphere in the concert hall. When Svendsen mounted the podium the audience began to applaud and would not stop. The musicians were inspired to do their very best; indeed, Oslo had never before heard such a sublime orchestral sound.

On April 7 he gave a valedictory concert on his own initiative, and both King Oscar II and Prince Oscar were present. As he entered the green room before the concert, he was met by a delegation of ladies from the community led by fellow composer Agathe Backer Grøndahl and the distinguished concert pianist Erika Lie Nissen. Mrs. Nissen presented him with a splendid gift and said, "We remember all these hours of beauty and noble joy and thank you for everything you have given us. On behalf of hundreds of the women of this city I have the honor and pleasure of presenting to you this ebony baton inlaid with gold and diamonds."

The concert included the Oslo premiere of Grieg's *The Mountain Thrall* as well as Svendsen's second Norwegian rhapsody and his first symphony. There were innumerable curtain calls, and Svendsen was presented with a laurel wreath. After the concert Svendsen invited the musicians and a number of other friends to a reception, where he expressed sincere thanks for everything the city had given him.

During the last week of April he made his first visit to Stockholm. He had been engaged to conduct the Royal Theater Orchestra in two concerts of his own works. The compositions he selected were the two symphonies, *Zorahayda*, the *Coronation March*, and the second and third Norwegian rhapsodies.

He took a room at the Grand Hotel on April 24, and on that same day *Stockholms Dagblad* carried a highly complimentary article about him: "Ar-

Johan Svendsen at about the time of
his departure from Oslo in 1883.
(Det kgl. Bibliotek, Copenhagen)

riving in our national capital today is one of Scandinavia's—not to say one
of the world's—most distinguished living composers in the realm of purely
instrumental music." On May 1, *Svensk musiktidning* carried a three-page
biographical article about him (127).

Rather soon after his arrival he was granted an audience with King Oscar II, who received him warmly. Svendsen wrote to his father on May 2
that the king had been most friendly and had "talked about my art and my
future with so much interest that my heart was warmed."

He went to the opera, where he heard two new works: Verdi's *Aida* and
Arrigo Boito's *Mefistofele*. He was especially attracted to the latter work,
which was "full of brilliance and beauty."

He made the most of his stay in the Swedish capital. He wrote to
Warmuth on May 6 that he had been very busy with "visits, dinners, rehearsals, and suppers." The royal family attended both concerts, which took
place on May 3 and 8 in the Royal Theater.

The Stockholm press also took notice of the fact that Svendsen conducted without a score, and the reviewers praised him lavishly. The May 10

issue of *Figaro* averred that these concerts were "the most distinguished events in Swedish musical life" in recent years:

> Svendsen's great reputation preceded his arrival here, and he has ex-
> ceeded even that. He is a maestro blessed by God. . . . The man that we
> need just now to gather together our very great but splintered musical
> forces—who through his superior talents as composer and conductor
> could give our musical life a boost worthy of the old traditions—that
> man is named Johan Svendsen. He is a Norwegian, our brother and
> orchestral conductor—in Copenhagen.

Svendsen returned to Oslo on May 10 and immediately began making preparations for the move to Copenhagen. The same day, *Aftenposten* reported that an attorney in Paris by the name of Sebbelow had sent him "a large sum of money as an expression of his appreciation for Mr. Svendsen's good work in his native land."

The Quartet Society gave a farewell banquet on May 16 and the president of the Society, Professor Nicolaysen, presented their "celebrated guest" with "a big drinking horn made of silver as a gift." A few days later he was honored with a rather strange farewell poem by John Paulsen that appeared in *Nyt Tidsskrift* in June 1883. It began as follows:

> In the door of the hut stands the mother old,
> Scarce knowing what she should say;
> She wipes a tear with her calloused hand:
> Her boy is going away.
>
> The dashing young man with a song in his heart
> Will go forth and extend his fame;
> But mother feels only loss and tears:
> Home, without him, will not be the same.
>
> "Farewell, dear Johan, my darling son!
> There is much here that should be corrected;
> Where bread must be earned by the sweat of one's brow
> Art and beauty are often neglected.
>
> I, your old mother, am poor, so poor,
> Our house is so simple and small;
> The big, bustling world now calls you, my son:
> Go forth and answer its call!"

At the end of May Svendsen took a trip to Copenhagen to assess the situation. In a letter to Warmuth he reported that he had been obliged to conduct one of his symphonies (the B-flat major) at a benefit concert at the Royal Theater on June 1 to raise money for the ballet's pension fund. The program also included Hartmann's ballet *The Valkyrie*, conducted by Paulli.

Even at this first performance with the Royal Theater orchestra, Svendsen demonstrated that he was not afraid to depart from the beaten path. Not only were the musicians placed up on the stage, but except for the cellos they stood as they played—an old practice that had recently been revived in Germany. It was used, for example, by Hans von Bülow in his performances of Beethoven symphonies.

Nationaltidende wrote that when Svendsen heard the deafening applause that greeted him as he mounted the flower-bedecked podium, he must have gotten the impression "that he did not come as a stranger, but that to his energetic and intelligent leadership the audience added expectations of considerable breadth."

The day after the concert he was present when Paulli, who had been associated with the theater for 55 years, bid an emotional farewell to "his" orchestra. The much-loved old man was thanked and praised at a huge banquet, where a brotherly spirit reigned between him and his Norwegian successor.

The same spirit was not present, however, in the hearts of a highly nationalistic group who could not accept the appointment of a Norwegian to such an important position, particularly a Norwegian who had no experience at all in conducting operas. During the years that followed this clique resisted Svendsen's efforts and in various ways made his life difficult.

The final departure from Norway occurred on July 17. On that date he wrote to his father, who was vacationing in Sandefjord: "I feel so bad about leaving my native land. You can't imagine how sad I am! Hopefully I will find so much diversion in my new surroundings that I will not die from homesickness."

The next day he was in Copenhagen. He probably did not intend at that time to stay in Denmark permanently; he would just give it a try for a few years before making a final decision.

But that is not what happened. The temporary stay became permanent, even though he never took the step of becoming a Danish citizen. During the next 28 years he was in Norway only for short periods of time as a visitor. Norway had lost forever one of her most gifted sons.

7

NEW CHALLENGES IN COPENHAGEN

1883–90

FROM THE SUMMER of 1883 until his death on June 14, 1911, Svendsen lived in Copenhagen. Thus for an entire generation Denmark reaped the benefit of his unique talents, especially as an orchestra leader but also to some extent as a male-chorus conductor, administrator and teacher.

The newly appointed musical director of the Royal Theater Orchestra had no experience as an opera conductor, but it quickly became apparent that he was more than equal to the task. In the years that followed, Europe was abuzz with accounts of his exemplary performances and of the high standard he achieved with the orchestra in Copenhagen. One result of this reputation was that the most renowned artists of the day practically vied with one another for the opportunity to make a guest appearance in Copenhagen under his baton. Another was that he was frequently invited to conduct several of Europe's leading orchestras.

But his success had a negative consequence as well. As the perfectionist that he was, he made great demands not only on his musicians but also on himself. The intense and demanding character of his work at the Royal Theater combined with some purely personal problems made it impossible for him to do what he had formerly considered his highest calling: to compose music. The creative juices that had once flowed so richly through his veins simply dried up, and he felt that he had no more to give. All that he wrote during his years in Copenhagen was a small number of relatively unimportant occasional works. This was unquestionably a tragedy for him personally and for Norwegian—and Nordic—music.

A NEW BEGINNING

Svendsen's living quarters in Copenhagen when he first arrived there were not especially comfortable. He moved into a small apartment at Havnegade 43, and a few days after his arrival he described the situation in a letter (dated July 27, 1883) to Carl Warmuth in Oslo:

> After a lot of work I finally have things sufficiently organized in my house that I can think of writing letters. Unfortunately my apartment is altogether too small, and even its location—which at first I found so charming—is now proving to have major disadvantages. Just think! Each day, right under my window hundreds of big, fat pigs are shipped out to various locations. The racket that these charming creatures make is indescribable. If I ever get around to writing a musical illustration of my first impressions during my stay here, it probably will be in the form of a symphonic poem with the title *Pigsty*.
>
> Just a moment ago I had a visit from Gade. He was, as always, amiable and jovial and looked surprisingly young and healthy. In general it is notable how well all these older musical fellows get on down here: nothing but youthfulness in Gade, Hartmann, and Paulli. My little work room will soon be full of huge opera scores from the Royal Theater. You can just bet I'm reading like crazy. I wish I could soon get down to work so that in the demands of the job I might find something to counterbalance the longing I feel for home and for my dear friends there.

Svendsen also found time for relaxation, however, spending some of his summer evenings at Tivoli amusement park. Here he experienced success in a new genre—as a composer of popular music—with two pieces dating from his earliest years. *Nordisk Musik-Tidende* reported in its August issue:

> Two of these youthful works—*At the Seter* and *Anna Polka*—have now, after a lapse of nearly thirty years, been unearthed and are being played daily by the Tivoli orchestra. Since there have been many inquiries about these two dances in the music stores, Warmuth has obtained Mr. J. Svendsen's permission to let them be published.

They were printed in November, not for orchestra but in arrangements for three different ensembles (Works 101 and 102). The composer's honorarium of two hundred crowns was used to pay down the debt he owed his Norwegian publisher.

In a letter to Warmuth dated August 9, 1883, Svendsen wrote, "Sometimes I don't see how in the long run I am going to tolerate living so far from everything that I now feel so strongly I have grown up with. Still, one thing may help: work and more work. I am surrounded by a disagreeable mob of people of all kinds, all of whom have something or other to do with the theater: legions of male and female singers, composers, and orchestral players.

Svendsen had overall responsibility for the music at the theater; his principal duties were to hold rehearsals and to conduct opera performances. Prior to Svendsen's arrival the theater had also employed two assistant conductors, one for ballets and another to conduct incidental music for ordinary plays. Just at this time, however, these two positions were combined into one, and on July 1, 1883, Frederik Rung was appointed "Music Conductor." In 1895 both Svendsen and Rung were given new titles, namely Musical director and Associate Musical director.

Svendsen wasted no time in reacting to the theater's long-standing practice of having the orchestra play during intermissions at theatrical performances and demanded that it be done away with. When the theater management expressed its misgivings, he roared "Damn it all, it's an outrageous misuse of the orchestra!" He got his way in the very first season, "despite the obligatory outcry intoned by public and press" (40:263).

On September 15 he held his first orchestra rehearsal for an upcoming production of Wagner's *Lohengrin*. Victor Gandrup, in an article in *Dansk Musiker-Tidende*, told the story of how theater director Fallesen—a small and very cultivated man, the consummate royal official—accompanied Svendsen to the rehearsal and introduced him to the musicians:

> Ladies and gentlemen! May I present to you the renowned composer and conductor, Mr. Johan Svendsen. I also wish to inform you that from this day forward the musical director has full authority to reorganize the theater's musical affairs and to manage and discharge personnel in whatever way he deems necessary (39:276).

One would not think that such an introduction would set the stage for harmonious cooperation between musical director and musicians, but it was quite in character for the autocratic theater director. However, the new musical director exercised his authority so adroitly that the important period when he and the orchestra were getting to know each other went better than anyone had anticipated.

The Royal Theater in Copenhagen at the end of the last century. (Det kgl. Bibliotek, Copenhagen)

Svendsen demonstrated at the very first rehearsal that he knew how to combine a demand for quality with a compassionate understanding of human problems. He had noticed that an elderly double-bass player was not playing his part correctly and went over to him to see what might be the cause of the problem. He discovered to his surprise that the man was almost blind: his music was upside down! He helped him apply for a sick leave, and the following year arranged for him to receive early retirement with full pension. Three other members of the orchestra were also replaced owing to "old age and infirmity."

As an experienced orchestral player himself, Svendsen demonstrated throughout his life a genuine concern for his colleagues' welfare. He considered it disgraceful that musicians' salaries were so low that several of them sometimes found substitutes to take their place because they could earn more playing occasional jobs elsewhere (137). Musicians at the entry level earned 1,200 crowns per year and the top salary was 2,400 crowns. Svendsen regarded such salaries as indefensible, and at Christmas time he wholeheartedly supported an appeal from the musicians for a raise. They requested, among other things, that the top salary be raised to 2,800 crowns per year. The Ministry was not able immediately to accommodate their request, but it recommended that the matter be taken up again as part of the budget debate for the coming year.

On August 24 Svendsen held the first combined rehearsal for *Lohengrin*, but the very same day he wrote to Warmuth that he still was not comfortable with the situation: "Unfortunately, I am having a hard time learning to feel at home down here, and the worst part of it is that I absolutely do not enjoy working in a theater setting."

Nonetheless, his debut as an opera conductor was a smashing success. The reviewer for *Dagens Nyheder* wrote on September 9 that "the many friends that our opera house has kept during its lamentable decadence have real reason to look to the future with greater confidence." The orchestra played "with a perfect elegance and purity, a precision, an animation and festiveness that the listeners could not fail to note."

The critics were less pleased with the singers, for the opera company had only a few top-flight voices—a problem that was to persist for several years to come. Reading between the lines, one can tell from a letter to his father on September 11 that Svendsen, too, was unhappy with the soloists: "Believe me, it required a lot of effort to whip this difficult work into reasonably satisfactory shape. The performances by the orchestra and the choir made me very happy."

On September 12 he conducted Ambroise Thomas's *Mignon* for the first time. He wrote to his father on September 24: "This evening the tsar of Russia and the kings of Denmark and Greece are coming to the theater with their consorts and children, and for that reason all the tickets have been sold at doubled prices."

A Danish work was premiered on October 21: P. E. Lange-Müller's comic opera *Spanish Students*. The audience liked it but it was panned by the critics.

Svendsen rarely took time to attend concerts, but he did hear two performances of Beethoven's ninth symphony presented by the Copenhagen Music Association under the baton of Niels W. Gade. "It really was very good," he wrote to his father on November 26. This letter also provides an interesting glimpse of the working conditions at this time:

Believe me, there is a lot to do here. As soon as one opera is ready, re-hearsals begin immediately on a new one. For me, a beginner in this area, there is double work, for of course I have to study the score ahead of time to familiarize myself with the music that I am going to rehearse and con-duct. To begin with I spent 8 to 10 hours a day studying the music. The orchestra . . . is very good; indeed, the first violins and all the woodwinds are excellent. I have almost absolute authority over the orchestra as well as the soloists. Nobody dares to appoint or discharge anyone without my concurrence. . . . The chorus is outstanding. Unfortunately, the same thing cannot be said about the soloists, for at the moment we have only two excellent singers and a couple of others who may develop into something; the rest of them aren't worth a thing. It's obvious that with such substandard soloists it is difficult to produce results that will win and hold the audience's interest, and if this lack cannot be remedied the situa-tion as far as I am concerned will become intolerable. . . . Despite all the friendliness and consideration I regularly encounter here, I constantly think with longing about old Norway. How I miss my home, my family, and the many wonderful friends there! Sometimes I feel as if I can't hold out down here in the long run. Still I console myself with the thought that here, too, I can serve my art.

On December 8, in Casino's large concert hall, Svendsen conducted the first of the four annual "philharmonic concerts" by the Royal Theater Or-chestra specified in his contract. The orchestra, which normally consisted of 49 musicians, was expanded to 69 for this concert. The hall was packed; the queen was among those in attendance. The program consisted of Beethoven's seventh symphony, Wagner's *Tannhäuser* overture, and Cho-pin's second piano concerto. The soloist in the concerto was Vera Timanoff, a Russian pupil of Franz Liszt.

The Copenhagen musicians had demonstrated during his guest appear-ances in 1882 what they could do under his baton. This time the audience was especially impressed over the wealth of delicate shadings that he was able to coax out of them. *Berlingske Tidende* wrote, "One had the feeling that Svendsen was playing the orchestra as if it were a single instrument . . . and he achieved an absolutely beautiful tonal color." Charles Kjerulf used even stronger words in *Dagsavisen*: "The musical heavens were opened." Angul Hammerich wrote in *Nationaltidende*:

That an orchestra exceeds a *mezzopiano* and a *mezzoforte* as the outward extremities of the dynamic range of the performance is for us the exception. Johan Svendsen, to his great credit, has inspired his subordinates to the mental and physical effort that is required to produce an inaudible *pianissimo* or a deafening *fortissimo*.

Even Niels W. Gade, "the lion of Danish music," took note of the finer points of Svendsen's conducting. Concertmaster Johannes Schiørring reported in *Berlingske Tidende* (January 27, 1942) that once when Gade was going to conduct the Concert Society orchestra "he called facetiously for 'a *pianissimo* that not even a devil can hear.' It was with reference to Svendsen's subtle nuances that he said it."

As conductor of the tradition-rich Concert Society orchestra, Gade was Svendsen's principal rival for the favor of those who wished to hear high-quality orchestral music. While the Concert Society was firmly grounded in the Classical-Romantic tradition, Svendsen's programs gave more and more emphasis to the performance of contemporary music.

In a Christmas letter to his sister, Albertine, Svendsen wrote, "The day after the concert I was summoned to an audience with the queen—an amiable lady who is knowledgeable about music—who told me the most gracious things both about the concert and about my work at the theater. . . . I'm afraid it's going to be a hectic Christmas. We've already received a ton of invitations." The active social life was in full swing.

1884: TRIUMPH AND TURMOIL

Svendsen, by virtue of his conscientiousness and thoroughness, quickly established a solid reputation as an opera conductor. On January 20, 1884, the royal family added luster to the premiere of François Auber's *Fra Diavolo*, and *Dagens Nyheder* wrote that the excellent result was owing above all to "the beneficial life and the precision that gives abundant proof of a superior competence on the part of the musical director that is unmatched in the history of Danish opera."

The Norwegian-Italian fraternization of the *Norwegian Artists' Carnival* had a curious transcontinental sequel on January 26. On that date, as a result of efforts by Svendsen's friend Giovanni Sgambati, Svendsen's second symphony was performed at a concert by Società Orchestrale in Salla Dante in Rome. The concert was conducted by Ettore Pinelli. At the same time, Svendsen was presenting his second philharmonic concert in Copenhagen, and his program included Sgambati's symphony in D minor. Svendsen's symphony was well received in Rome. The reviewer in *Libertà* wrote, "The original style and form, the uniquely Scandinavian sounds, might cause a few difficulties for the hearer, but it was nonetheless evident that one was in the presence of a master of the highest order." The Copenhagen critics, on the other hand, denounced Sgambati's symphony, which today is considered one of his best works. An angered Svendsen wrote on February 1 to Niels Ravnkilde in Rome that in his opinion the local critics' harsh judgment was owing to the fact that a certain Anton Rée had arranged for a strongly negative discussion of the symphony—a review by the renowned Viennese music critic Eduard Hanslick—to be published in one of Copenhagen's leading newspapers.

The philharmonic concert on March 1 consisted of a number of newer works, including Tchaikovsky's *Capriccio Italien* and the prelude to Wagner's *Tristan and Isolde*. The soloist in Isolde's *Liebestod* was the famous soprano Lilli Lehmann, who also sang excerpts from *Tannhäuser*. On March 3 Svendsen wrote to Warmuth that the concert had drawn a huge audience: "Just think! Both at the dress rehearsal and at the concert I had a full house. The queen was present for the whole dress rehearsal."

The concert also included the overture *Olaf Trygvason* by Svendsen's friend Robert Henriques. It proved to be an unfortunate choice, however, as both the critics and the musicians were strongly displeased with it. The orchestra had not been consulted on the matter, and this became one of their complaints the following autumn when they got into a row with Svendsen regarding the philharmonic concerts.

The great Russian piano virtuoso Anton Rubinstein gave two concerts in Copenhagen during the spring. "He is in a class by himself," Svendsen wrote to Warmuth on April 9. "To come in personal contact with him is extremely pleasant, for he is the very picture of amiability." Later that month Rubinstein left for Oslo, where he was to give four concerts. On April 27 Svendsen wrote to Warmuth, "Be sure that he gets a good impression of the public and of conditions up there. Don't pester him to play any *unnecessary* music, and don't forget to *surround* him with the *prettiest women* possible if you arrange any parties for him."

When Rubinstein returned to Copenhagen, he was engaged as soloist in Beethoven's *Emperor Concerto* for the philharmonic concert on May 10. Svendsen had no objection to turning the baton over to composers conducting their own works at his concerts, and on this occasion Rubinstein was on the podium for the performance of his fifth symphony. He was so

delighted with both Svendsen and the orchestra that he declined the honorarium of 1,500 crowns to which he was entitled for the dress rehearsal.

On May 11 a long article in *Nationaltidende* stirred up a bit of excitement in Copenhagen's music life. The writer of the article (identified only
as "R") sharply attacked theater director Fallesen, particularly for his failure
to engage good singers and for his unwillingness to revitalize the repertoire.
The writer thought it was a pity that operas of universal importance—such
works as *Carmen, Aida,* and the latest operas of Wagner—still had not been
granted "rights of citizenship" at the Royal Theater. It was absolutely impossible, "even for a bundle of energy like Johan Svendsen," to force the
new operas onto the stage when the theater director lacked interest in musical drama: "We really would not be served by losing a man like Johan
Svendsen, who has assumed the unenviable position of musical director
where there is nothing to direct—because court chamberlain Fallesen
would rather have a poor opera than a good one."

This view of the matter presumably was fairly representative. People
wanted Svendsen to play a bigger role in determining the repertoire, but he
felt that during these first years he had more than enough to do taking care
of his primary tasks as musical director. Also, he did not want to get drawn
into conflicts with Fallesen, with whom he always got along well. Nonetheless, it was Fallesen who infuriated him just a few weeks later. On June 6,
Svendsen wrote to his father that he had just received an offer to conduct his
own compositions at a series of five Saturday concerts at Tivoli for 3,000
crowns:

> But then came the theater director and the minister [of culture] and
> raised objections. I have to decline the offer, thereby losing 3,000
> crowns. Isn't that a damn shame? Just now, when I could use every
> penny I can scrape together, I have to suffer such a painful loss.

How could Svendsen be in such a financial bind once again, now that he
was receiving such a good income? One reason was that the family had recently moved from Havnegade to a much more fashionable apartment at
Peder Skramsgade 24, and the furnishings for the new residence had been
very costly. On March 28 he had written to Warmuth asking for an extra act
of friendship because he had "incurred a number of unanticipated expenses
and am compelled to try in every way possible to gather at least part of the
sum I need." He asked, therefore, that Warmuth arrange for the April in-

stallment of his state grant to be sent to him. This request sounds strange, but the fact is that ever since he had moved to Copenhagen the grant had been used each month to reduce his debt to several creditors in Oslo. According to Warmuth's records, as of August 1, 1884, Svendsen owed him 1,250 crowns. If some of the other creditors—especially wine merchant Glørsen and Mr. Siewers—were willing to wait for their money, Svendsen thought there would be "nothing to prevent this arrangement; I take it for granted that you will forgo your share for this month."

During the summer he spent two weeks with a Danish friend—a gentleman farmer named Rolf Viggo Neergaard—at Fuglsang estate on the island of Lolland. There, he wrote to his father on September 24, he enjoyed splendid company: "These were the most beautiful days I have had for many, many years." But nothing came of the plans he had made to write music: "This summer, for which I had such big and happy hopes, . . . is now past and I have achieved nothing of all that I had proposed to do."

The opera season got off to a successful beginning. It was said that the Royal Theater had never presented anything as good as this production of *The Flying Dutchman*. The high quality was owing not least to the fact that Svendsen had worked very hard to improve the quality of the singing. The chorus had been reorganized, one result of which was that choirmaster Carl Helsted was replaced by Carl Gerlach. Before the premiere on September 7 there had been no less than 27 rehearsals. The Copenhagen *Morgenbladet* wrote two days later, "It is no accident that Svendsen has chosen to conduct the first performance of the *Dutchman* in Copenhagen. When the score is really complicated, that's just when Svendsen is in his element. With the glance of a genuine expert he dissects the various groups of instruments."

The opera chosen to succeed the stormy sounds of the Wagnerian work was drawn from the older repertoire: Étienne Méhul's *Joseph and His Brethren*. But as early as November the performers were busy rehearsing a new and exceedingly demanding work: Arrigo Boito's *Mefistofele*, which had so charmed Svendsen in Stockholm the year before.

At this time Svendsen, who had composed nothing since coming to Denmark, once again picked up his composer's pen, but only to write a piece of occasional music. In honor of the bicentennial of the birth in Norway of the great playwright Ludvig Holberg, the Royal Theater had commissioned Holger Drachmann and Svendsen to create a cantata for a performance on December 3. The work was finished in November, but like Grieg, who wrote a Holberg cantata for the commemoration festivities in

Bergen, Svendsen judged his composition to be so insignificant that he did not wish to include it in his opus list. On November 24 he wrote to Grieg, "Just between you and me, I'm afraid it's not exactly a masterwork."

A standing-room-only audience, led by the royal family, filled the hall for the presentation of the cantata, and thanks to a brilliant performance it proved to be a greater success than the composer had anticipated. To be sure, a critic in *Politiken* suggested that Drachmann's text did not lend itself very well to a musical treatment, but he allowed nonetheless "that there is much in Svendsen's music that is first-rate. The solo parts are least successful."

The *Holberg Cantata* (Work 126) is scored for baritone solo, mixed chorus and orchestra. An orchestral introduction is followed by two choral and one solo movements. Orchestra, chorus and soloist all participate in the concluding movement.

Another Holberg cantata was performed at a festival held at the university on the forenoon of the same day. The text of this one was written by Chr. Richardt, the music by J. P. E. Hartmann and Otto Malling.

Although things were going well for Svendsen artistically, this autumn proved to be one of the most difficult periods of his life. Bergljot and he had been drifting farther and farther apart during the preceding years, and the tragedy of the burnt symphony had obviously not improved the situation. One of his friends, the violinist and composer Fini Henriques, has said that Svendsen sometimes even came to rehearsals with scratches on his face (53). It is quite possible that his temperamental wife suspected—perhaps with good reason—that he was spending altogether too much time in the company of other adoring women. In December, in any case, they separated. Bergljot left home, thereby giving Svendsen—as he himself expressed it— "peace in his own house" (53). Six months later she left Denmark for good and returned to Paris.

Svendsen's financial problems continued to oppress him. He wrote to Warmuth on September 22 that "a couple of people in Oslo to whom I owe money have recently bombarded me with dunning letters accompanied by threats to send a lawyer after me." Equally frustrating was a crisis in September-October between Svendsen and the musicians of the orchestra regarding the philharmonic concerts authorized in his contract. The Museum of Music History in Copenhagen contains two letters from the orchestra members regarding these concerts. The agreement that had been signed the year before specified that Svendsen was to receive 25 percent of the net income, the musicians the remaining 75 percent. On September 8, however,

33 of the 49 members of the orchestra led by Valdemar Tofte signed a letter addressed to Svendsen. The tone of the letter was very courteous, but it was nonetheless obvious that the musicians were unhappy about the fact that they were not being consulted either regarding programming or with respect to administrative and financial arrangements. They therefore requested an opportunity to talk with the musical director with a view to establishing a committee to deal with these matters. Two auditors, one appointed by Svendsen and the other by the orchestra, would have responsibility for the account. They also recommended that in the future the conductor's share of the proceeds would be 17 percent. In return, the members would assume responsibility for any deficit that might be incurred.

The musicians' initiative in this matter must be seen against the background of the fact that the four philharmonic concerts together with public dress rehearsals for each had produced total revenues of more than 15,000 crowns. The net income, however, was only 7,000 crowns. Of this amount, Svendsen, as provided in his contract, received 1,700 crowns while each musician received a mere 106. The members protested that they could not understand why the expenses for administration were so high.

Svendsen perceived the letter as a veiled attack on his artistic integrity and an insinuation that he had somehow conspired to manipulate the finances. The impresario who had arranged the concerts was Svendsen's friend Henrik Hennings, a music dealer.

The musicians did not intend for their letter to be made public, but it was anonymously leaked to the press. The result was a heated newspaper debate, with both friends and foes of Svendsen speaking their minds. The emotionally charged situation that ensued gave rise to rumors of serious financial irregularities.

On October 21, the Oslo paper *Aftenposten* reported on a decisive meeting between Svendsen and the musicians in a long article entitled "The musical director war in Copenhagen." At this meeting, Svendsen asked directly if some of the musicians would not protest against what he called the "insult" against him personally. But the musicians stood firm: not one of them responded to his plea. The inevitable result was that he angrily broke off negotiations.

A lengthy editorial on the controversy was published in the Copenhagen paper *Avisen* on October 18. Here Svendsen was characterized as "the foreign musical director" whose perception of the Danish artists' significance and authority "is owing to a misconception that can be cleared up only through bitter experience. Within the theater he can and should exercise firm discipline; outside the theater the musicians are his equals, and in any case independent men who can refuse to work for pay that is scarcely equal to that of an ordinary craftsman."

On November 4 the musicians—35 this time—sent another long letter to Svendsen. It, too, was written in an urbane manner that underscored the musical director's artistic achievements. But its tone was more acrimonious than that of the first letter. It stated, for example: "*Thus what we desired was first and foremost a discussion*, and it was only your absolute unwillingness to enter into discussions of any kind on the basis of our proposal that gave rise to the dissent that has now developed." Their desire that in the future the orchestra should have a "very essential influence on the artistic leadership of the concerts," they pointed to the cooperative arrangements for similar philharmonic concerts in Berlin under Joseph Joachim and in Vienna under Hans Richter.

This time the musicians themselves published their letter. The situation was at an impasse, for Svendsen was unwilling to compromise. The result was that for the time being Svendsen's series of philharmonic concerts with the Royal Theater Orchestra ceased. Nonetheless, in the years that followed he led the orchestra at several public concerts—special festive occasions, benefit concerts, and the like.

Though the Royal Theater Orchestra thus became unavailable to him for the purpose, Svendsen was determined to give the four annual philharmonic concerts he had planned. Within a short time he put together a completely new orchestra of first-rate musicians. Most of them came from the Concert Society and Tivoli orchestras, but some members of the Royal Theater Orchestra were also willing to participate.

The first concert by the new orchestra, which included Beethoven's *Eroica* symphony as well as Svendsen's *Zorahayda*, set a high standard. On November 24 Svendsen wrote triumphantly to Grieg:

> Have you heard rumors about my quarrel with the Royal Theater orchestra? For a long time those fine gentlemen have been making me madder than hell; they've done everything they can think of to present me with an ultimatum. Now the battle is over and I have won a total victory. On the fifteenth I had my first concert, which thanks to my newly organized orchestra achieved an artistically brilliant result. And the financial result left nothing to be desired either, for both the dress rehearsal and the concert played to a full house.

He also mentioned that he now was hoping for a little peace so he could resume work on his third symphony.

Svendsen continued to give philharmonic concerts with this orchestra for ten years. With the help of a series of world-renowned soloists, it made a splendid contribution to the music life of Copenhagen.

On Christmas Day he summed up the events of the year in a letter to Warmuth. 1884, he wrote, had been a year of great triumphs, but he had been on the verge of despair many times. As for the future he foresaw "hard struggles and big changes," but he knew the struggle was worth the effort, "and this will give me strength and perseverance."

ARTISTIC SUCCESSES AND PERSONAL PROBLEMS

The first philharmonic concert of the new year on January 17, 1885, included Gade's *Symphony No. 4*, Saint-Saëns's *Omphale's Spinning Wheel*, and three of Dvořák's *Slavonic Dances*. Svendsen had always thought well of Gade's compositions and performed a number of them through the years. There was, of course, a certain rivalry between the two of them, not as composers but as conductors, since Gade wielded the baton at symphonic concerts given by the Concert Society orchestra, which he had conducted ever since 1850.

On January 20 Svendsen conducted the successful premiere of Boito's *Mefistofele*. Of all the 52 operas produced by the Royal Theater during the years 1877–89, this work, strangely enough, was the most popular of the lot. A total of 39 performances were given, including 22 during the first season.

At the end of the month, Svendsen asked for a two-week leave to conduct several of his own works in St. Petersburg. The request was granted, and on February 19 he started out. It was his acquaintance with Anton Rubinstein and his contact with the tsar's brother in Paris in 1878 that had opened the door for him in Russia, where his music already was highly regarded. Enroute to St. Petersburg by train he made a short visit to Berlin, where he again met Anton Rubinstein. They made a great fuss over him in St. Petersburg, where he spent much time in the company of such leading Russian composers as Rimsky-Korsakov, Lyadov and Glazunov, with whom he stayed in friendly contact thereafter.

The orchestra for the concert at the Royal Russian Music Academy consisted of 100 musicians, including 72 strings. The program comprised *Symphony No. 1, Carnival in Paris*, and *Last Year I Was Tending the Goats* as well as a piano concerto by Henry Litolff. The concert was a great success and the critics singled out the symphony as the concert's undisputed high point. *Carnival in Paris*, however, did not seem to appeal to the Russians' taste. Both the string octet and the string quintet were performed at a chamber-music concert.

Svendsen had an audience with the tsarina in the course of which he delivered a letter from her mother, the queen of Denmark. Grieg, ever the radical, made a caustic remark about Svendsen's association with royalty and the upper crust in a letter to his Danish friend Gottfred Matthison-Hansen dated March 27, 1885:

> Do you ever see Svendsen or does he spend all his time with the royal court and people with silk gloves? It's a good thing that there are various tastes in the world. I think it is healthier to do as you do: to associate with Bach and Handel!

It appears that it annoyed Grieg that his friend, who in the past had been politically engaged and radically inclined, was spending more and more time in the company of the bourgeoisie.

Returning to Copenhagen, Svendsen had the good fortune to engage a promising new international star, Eugène d'Albert, to play Liszt's first piano concerto at his next philharmonic concert on April 11. Another renowned musician, pianist Vladimir de Pachmann, was the soloist in Chopin's second piano concerto on May 2.

Svendsen's financial problems resulting in part from his wife's move to Paris and his regular contributions to her support led him in April–May to send several desperate letters to Warmuth begging for immediate assistance. May 6: "Every day that I wait is a prolongation of an indescribably painful situation." June 24: "If you knew what a pinch I am in and how greatly I am in need of help without delay, I'm sure you would hurry up. . . . There has been a change in my personal circumstances in that my wife, who two weeks ago left the hospital, is now in Paris. I hope she stays there a long time so that I can find time to recover the tranquility that I need in order to work properly." Sigurd, his step-son, was to stay with him until the end of the school year; thereafter he would go to live with an uncle in Paris.

At a time when he needed to "scrape together" everything he could, on May 24 he asked Warmuth to send a copy of the conductor's score and instrumental parts for the four Norwegian rhapsodies to the conductor

Balduin Dahl, who "definitely will present them at his truly fine Saturday concerts at Tivoli." Two of them received their Danish premieres during the summer of 1885; they were described by one reviewer as "beautiful thoughts in a beautiful form."

In June Svendsen was a guest for two weeks at Petershøi, the Henriques family's imposing country home on the Øresund, but he took a trip into the city every day. On July 2 he wrote to Warmuth that all his closest friends had left the city, so he was very lonely:

> It's hard to say how long I can hold out. Who knows? Maybe one fine day I'll get aboard one of the many steamboats that go from here to Oslo. At the moment, though, there's not much hope of that.

Two weeks later the loneliness got the best of him and he crossed the Øresund to visit a friend in Helsingborg, Sweden. His financial circumstances had now worsened to such an extent that he had to ask Warmuth for a three-month advance on his state grant. "Finally," he wrote, "you must be so kind as to wait awhile before I resume payments on my debt to you."

At the end of July it was reported in the Copenhagen press that Svendsen had gone to Norway for his summer holiday, but this was not the case. On August 4 he wrote to Warmuth that he had indeed packed his bags a few days earlier and was all ready to board a ship, but suddenly he was stricken with such severe rheumatic pain that he had to cancel the trip and go right to bed.

In the same letter he discussed another matter that was dear to his heart. He was concerned that his countrymen—even the readers of *Nordisk Musik-Tidende*—were so poorly informed about the music life of Copenhagen:

> It is so very regrettable since Copenhagen is the one of the three Scandinavian capitals that has the richest public music life. Since through your own letters I have long known where the shoe pinches, I have been unceasingly on the lookout for a *bright* and *reliable* correspondent for you. I can now report that I have found such a person. This person writes excellently and is also one of the most musically knowledgeable and gifted people I know. Since this individual has *very important* reasons to desire to remain absolutely anonymous, you must agree that his person, name and occupation shall remain a secret that even you will not know. You must also promise not to let *any* unauthorized person see such manuscripts as may be sent to you, and they must be sent back to me as

soon as you are finished with them. I also think he expects a definite honorarium. Consider this! I think you should accept, even if the conditions seem harsh.

Warmuth accepted the recommendation, and on September 14 the first report was sent to Oslo:

> The author asks that you be charitable in judging this article as he has had to write it on what he considers too short a time. . . . Don't forget now, dear friend, that you are to send the manuscript back to me as soon as it has been used. The honorarium should also be sent to me.

During the next eight months, each issue of *Nordisk Musik-Tidende* contained an article by the anonymous correspondent in Copenhagen, who used the pseudonym "Adrean."

Against the background of the cryptic letter to Warmuth it is tempting to think that Svendsen himself was the mysterious "Adrean" and that he had concocted the whole scheme in order to scrape up a little extra money. Reading "Adrean's" well-written articles today, however, it soon becomes clear that Svendsen could not have written them. They reveal such a well-rounded coverage of various matters and contain so many details about the music life of Copenhagen as to leave no doubt that they were written by a well-informed Dane. But who? To this day the answer remains unknown. Perhaps the solution is hidden in Svendsen's almanac for 1885, which on a single page has the following entries: "Adrean" and, to the right of this, "A'Drêan," both in pencil. Beneath this, in pen, is written "Thorvald Hamann, Tordenskjoldsgade 25."

The summer of 1885 was not a good time for Svendsen because of illness, and nothing came of his plans to spend some time composing. The June issue of *Nordisk Musik-Tidende* had reported that he was about to release a volume of program music on a Polish theme based on a text by Herman Bang, also that he had started work on an opera, *The Vikings in Constantinople*. Neither of these projects came to fruition. The only artifact dating from this summer is a small notebook that has been preserved in the library of the University of Oslo. It includes a dozen miscellaneous themes, some with underlying chords. Only one of them is dated: July 25.

On September 26 Svendsen sent his father a moving birthday letter that contained expressions such as one rarely finds in his correspondence:

How wonderful it would be to be able to press you to my bosom and tell you how infinitely much I love you. Yes, dear father, the older I get the clearer it becomes to me that you are not only my dear papa: you are also my best friend. Would that you might always have a little joy on account of your son, for whom you have done so much.

The first philharmonic concert of the autumn season was held on October 24. Eugène Ysaÿe was the soloist in Wieniawski's *Violin Concerto* in D minor, Saint-Saëns's *Introduction and Rondo Capriccioso*, and Svendsen's *Violin Romance*. The program also included *Two Icelandic Melodies* and Schumann's *Symphony No. 1*.

The big news at the Royal Theater this autumn was the production of *Aida*, which was launched with great success on October 4. On November 18 Svendsen was named a Knight of Dannebrog by King Christian IX in recognition of his great contribution to Danish music life.

On December 1 the curtain went up on a new production of Heinrich Marschner's opera *Hans Heiling*. A few days later Grieg came to Copenhagen for a six-month visit. In a Christmas letter to his father, Svendsen expressed his great joy over the fact that his friend was in town: "He is as splendid as a human being as he is great as a composer. He has given two sold-out concerts here to wild applause. It was wonderful. Yes, we can be proud of a countryman like that."

Once again there had been some things in the newspapers about problems at the theater, but this time the focus was on Svendsen. He commented on the matter in a letter to his father:

> Of course you have read a little about my latest feud, which ended with the entire press taking my side. Even the king, in awarding me the Dannebrog, revealed his sympathy for me. Now I have been left in peace for some time, but it won't last long. In any case I know that a few incompetent people at the theater who think they have been snubbed hate me like the plague, and they are just waiting for an opportunity to attack me. Well, let them come. I have a hunch that next time, too, I will come out of the fight unscathed.

In late autumn of 1885 Svendsen conducted rehearsals for Gounod's *Faust*, but according to *Nordisk Musik-Tidende* he suddenly fell ill and had to yield the baton for the December 29 premiere to Frederik Rung, who acquitted himself well. In February 1886 Svendsen was again on the podium in productions of two light operas: Halévy's *The Lightning* and Cherubini's *Two Days*.

January 30, 1886, was a kind of "Norway day" in Copenhagen. At a philharmonic concert on that date, Grieg was the piano soloist in a performance of his piano concerto and also conducted *Åse's Death* and *Anitra's Dance* from *Peer Gynt*. Svendsen wielded the baton for his first symphony and in a Danish contribution to intra-Scandinavian brotherhood, viz., J. P. E. Hartmann's concert overture, *Hakon Jarl*. Grieg discussed the event in a letter to Frants Beyer dated February 8:

> And now a few words about the fine philharmonic concert. Yes, "fine" is the word, for Svendsen showed up with his knight's ribbon, the queen attended the dress rehearsal, and the whole royal family was at the concert. Everything went well and made everyone deliriously happy. Believe me, *Åse's Death* sounded great with that huge string orchestra. And it wasn't so bad to sit there and play with Svendsen as conductor—despite the fact that conducting a piano concerto isn't exactly his long suit. Yes sir, we Norwegians are something to be reckoned with just now. *Peer Gynt* continues to play to sold-out audiences at the Dagmar Theater, Bjørnson's *Geography and Love* is steadily attracting people to the Royal Theater, and concerts are being given consisting of practically nothing but Norwegian music! A veritable annexation!

In connection with Grieg's visit, the Copenhagen Chamber Music Society gave a party for the two Norwegian artists. *Nordisk Musik-Tidende* wrote: "After the punch a number of speeches were given, and if Grieg had been the hero in the past, now it was Johan Svendsen's turn." Holger Paulli emphasized that in just a little over three years Svendsen had accomplished more than he himself had in a much longer time. Grieg sounded the same theme and averred that "as long as he had known the Royal Theater Orchestra it compared favorably with the best orchestras in the quality of its personnel, but he couldn't deny that with respect to precision, finesse and musical discipline it seemed to him to have made significant strides since he was last in Copenhagen."

Svendsen received a flattering invitation from Finland to conduct his own works in Helsinki, but his finances were in such bad shape that on February 15 he had to ask Warmuth for a loan of five hundred crowns. The reason was that before leaving for Finland—"in order to avoid unpleasantries"—he had to pay off a couple of important debts. Making the trip to Finland, however, was "almost a question of life and death," and he promised to pay back the loan as soon as he received the Finnish honorarium.

Warmuth was not particularly pleased with this request, so Svendsen had to send several begging letters. Finally on March 24 word came to Copenhagen that the loan was forthcoming. On April 4, having duly sought and received permission from the theater, Svendsen set out for Finland via Berlin and St. Petersburg.

The Finnish hospitality was overwhelming, and at various festive gatherings Svendsen had an opportunity to meet the leading figures in Finnish music life: Fredrik Pacius, Martin Wegelius and Robert Kajanus. He was also a frequent guest of Edvard Neovius, a friend who was Professor of Geometry at the University of Helsinki and one of the people who had initiated the invitation to Finland.

The first concert was given on April 10, the second a few days later. The programs included both symphonies, the *Violin Romance, Last Year I Was Tending the Goats,* and several of the songs. Both concerts drew a full house. Svendsen was honored with a flourish by the orchestra and was presented with a laurel wreath by his former student, Robert Kajanus. *Nya Pressen* wrote that the composer's brilliant inspiration was transmitted to the musicians and resulted in a dazzling ensemble. He had shown what a conductor's real task was and what an orchestra could achieve under the baton of a master. An evening program of chamber music by Svendsen was also presented during his stay in Helsinki.

In May *Nordisk Musik-Tidende* carried an enthusiastic full-page article entitled "How Svendsen Conducts a Rehearsal." It was written by one of the Finnish musicians under the pseudonym "Bis" (129). It stated in part:

> If the gentlemen in the first and second violin sections would just be nice and play the *pizzicato* more delicately, take the *pianissimo* as an almost inaudible echo and at such and such a place use just the tip of the bow, and then again at the energetic *crescendo* use the frog end [of the bow], I would be grateful," says Svendsen. And one must agree with the esteemed composer that all of this is absolutely necessary, for when one heard a *crescendo* or a *pianissimo* of the sort Svendsen can get out of an orchestra, you never forget it but wish it could always be done like that. . . .
>
> At one place I am having trouble with my part, but to prevent the sharply observant leader from noticing the mistake I am playing the

passage so *pianissimo* that I can't hear it myself. But it doesn't work: he has heard it, and when the movement is finished he asks me if I won't do him the kindness of playing the measures in question *somewhat more clearly*. Nothing escapes him. That is the kind of care with which he rehearses everything, and one really becomes convinced that in order for anything to be performed excellently, *each player* must play his part to perfection.

Another story about Svendsen's prowess as a conductor also came out of the visit to Finland. The bassoonist, an elderly German musician, was having great difficulty with a demanding solo part. Even at the dress rehearsal it went badly, but at the concert he played the part brilliantly and without a mistake. His colleagues could hardly believe their ears and asked him afterward what had happened. He just shook his gray locks and said, "Was weiß ich? Der Mann hat mich angesehen, und es ging." ("How should I know? The man just looked at me and I was able to do it.")

On April 20 Svendsen returned to Copenhagen. Awaiting him was a letter from Bjørnstjerne Bjørnson which he answered a few days later:

> Just home from a trip to Russia and Finland I find your letter with a poem that you want me to set. At the moment I have an awful lot to do and must, when I am free of theater duties, get seriously to work on a composition that I started on a long time ago, so I cannot accept the commission. Please forgive your devoted admirer.

The concluding events of the theater's spring season as well as two philharmonic concerts were about to take place. The May 1 concert program included Beethoven's *Pastoral Symphony* and Tchaikovsky's *Andante Cantabile*, and on May 8 Svendsen conducted Schubert's *Unfinished Symphony*, Borodin's *Caravan March*, and Saint-Saëns's *Suite Algérienne*.

But the many triumphs of the years 1885–86 were darkened by more mundane problems. The work at the theater was no bed of roses, and when Svendsen found himself at odds with some of the opera people during this period it was because he refused to compromise with respect to artistic standards. He was, as he wrote to Johan Selmer on January 6, 1886, accustomed to seeing his best efforts "opposed by some wretched, scheming scoundrels who, because they themselves never accomplish anything, can't stand to see anyone else do anything either." In Svendsen's opinion there was only one way out of such a morass: "One works tirelessly on and lets these ugly mongrels howl and bark until they get hoarse and tired."

Sometimes he felt almost as if he was hated. On February 22 he concluded a letter to Selmer with these words: "The many lazy and undisciplined theater people at the Danish Royal Theater torment, abhor and curse musical director Johan Svendsen."

Grieg understood what Svendsen had to contend with. He realized that for a Norwegian it could be very difficult to hold such an exposed position in Copenhagen. In a February 8 letter to Frants Beyer he wrote:

> For *everything* that is Norwegian is not viewed negatively by the Danes, but don't come and displace them from their prominent positions. Then they get furious. That's what Svendsen is experiencing, for he holds a position that many a Dane goes around looking at with covetous and jaundiced glances. Today one reads in the Danish papers Svendsen's statement to our Ministry of Church and Culture that he doesn't think he will be here very long. God knows that this will certainly cause some uproar. I have a feeling that Svendsen will end up in Oslo again, because he wants to go there. And he would like to have me there too.

Svendsen also had a serious misunderstanding at this time with his impresario, Henrik Hennings, with whom he had previously had such a good relationship. On January 10, 1886, he reported to Warmuth that he had just barely gotten back on his feet after a bout with illness when new problems arose: "This time it's Hennings who in a quite condescending way reminds me that I am his debtor." The result of the controversy was that he had to sign a letter promising to pay Hennings 117 crowns monthly out of his annual state grant, so on May 13 he asked Warmuth to send this amount each month to Hennings's attorney. The words that follow are absolutely pathetic: "The remaining 16 crowns, together with 5 crowns that I will send you each month," should be sent to his sister, Albertine: "That is the help I have promised to give my poor old mother."

He also encountered problems of another kind, namely in his relations with women. Grieg wrote to Beyer on December 11 that his friend was "such a complex person that he will surely always be an enigma to me. He is on the outs with virtually all the musicians here, so we don't see anything of him at our post-concert gatherings. But we often have dinner together at

Johan Svendsen and ballet dancer Juliette Haase, whom he married in 1901. The picture dates from the 1890s. (Universitetsbiblioteket, Oslo)

the hotel, and many times he comes to our quarters and tells Nina about his heartaches when I am in my workroom."

The heartaches to which Grieg refers had a factual background. At the time when Svendsen's marriage was falling apart he had become infatuated with Juliette Haase, a 19-year-old ballet dancer at the Royal Theater. On New Year's Eve 1885 he wrote a love poem to her:

My heart once beat with youthful aspiration,
With longing and with dreams too sweet to tell.
Then came the bitter time when all the beauty
Departed and bequeathed an empty shell.

Still I was lonely, feeling loss and yearning,
I doubted everything, not least myself,
Until that day when first I knew you loved me,
Your trusting face to mine sweetly upturning.

My precious jailer, hold me fast forever!
In your embrace I am secure, at peace,
And I would not exchange that resting place
Though every other earthly bond be severed.

Each day that goes, each hour that you are gone,
Enlivens our desire and our need.
In life and death we share a priceless treasure,
Blest memories that yet are sweet indeed.

The relationship with Juliette at this time was probably nothing more than a brief episode in Svendsen's unstable life, for soon thereafter another woman came into the picture. In May of 1886 this development led to a personal crisis that affected him so deeply that he felt it necessary to get away from Copenhagen for awhile. May 24 he wrote to Warmuth, "Hopefully a few weeks in my dear homeland will have a beneficial effect, for I won't conceal from you the fact that I am coming home miserable, sick and depressed. A terrible period of my life is now over, but I'll tell you about it in person." Later (October 8) he used equally strong words in describing his situation to Grieg:

> Since you left Copenhagen I have experienced a lot of that which takes its toll on one's life, and I could easily fill page after page were it not that there are things I am reluctant to put down on paper. When we finally get together again I will pour out my heart to you, but today I will limit myself to saying that I came to Norway in such a wretched state that it was impossible to think of either visiting you or writing.

What was it that he was unwilling to put down on paper at this time of crisis? Presumably it had something to do with the fact that at this time he was romantically involved with the 32-year-old Danish pianist Golla Hammerich. This relationship, which until now has not been a matter of public knowledge, is reported in a note by Victor Gandrup entitled "Johan Svendsen and Golla Hammerich's Love Affair" (41). Gandrup's account is based on information from librarian-author Julius Clausen. This information was later confirmed by Dr. Albert Øigaard, Svendsen's physician and friend for many years, and also by Mrs. Anna Enna, wife of the composer August Enna. The event is dated "last half of the 80s." Gandrup writes:

> As is well known, *numerous* stories have been told about Johan Svend-
> sen's charming personality and irresistible charm vis-a-vis the fair sex, but
> notwithstanding the apocryphal character of the gossips' loudly pro-
> claimed tale of the "list of 1,003" . . . there was in fact an intimate rela-
> tionship [between Mrs. Hammerich and Svendsen]. . . . Apparently the
> feelings of both parties were extremely strong, for after having known
> each other for only a relatively short time they decided to move abroad
> and live together somewhere or other, and the first place they got to
> without obstacles was Aarhus.

The couple evidently set out without considering the consequences, but after a few hectic days they encountered a serious problem that was not entirely new for Svendsen: he suddenly found himself out of cash! They had
no choice, therefore, but to hang their heads and slink back to Copenhagen.
Love's poetry had to yield to the harsh prose of reality.

Svendsen's infatuation with Golla Hammerich found expression in a
small piano piece, *Album Leaf* (Work 130), which he dedicated to her. According to Gandrup, his passionate feelings for her were not just a passing
fancy and he felt the loss deeply when she died suddenly on May 2, 1903. He
secretly kept a letter from her, and the night before he himself died he asked
his friends Fini Henriques and Alfred Tofft to "see to it that after his death the
letter was discreetly and secretly placed with him in the casket" (41).

After the agonizing experiences of the spring of 1886 Svendsen found a
remedy in a nine-week stay in his homeland, which he had not seen for
three years. He stayed for the most part in Oslo but took one trip to
Lillehammer. He also visited Henrik Hennings, who was vacationing at
Lake Randsfjorden. The two of them presumably patched up their earlier
misunderstandings and renewed their friendship, for in the years that followed Hennings continued as business manager for the philharmonic
concerts.

Nordisk Musik-Tidende mentioned in its July issue that Svendsen was
making "rapid progress" on his third symphony and that it "probably will be
finished by autumn." Whether this reference had to do with an effort to re-
construct the symphony that had been consigned to the flames in the spring
of 1883 or with an entirely new symphony we do not know. What we do
know is that the report was excessively optimistic. Even if Svendsen had
hoped to do some composing, all that remains from that summer is seven
short theme fragments that he wrote down in his almanac. On October 8 he
wrote to Grieg about what this summer had meant to him:

Association with the dear, lovable people and the constant enjoyment of
the magnificent scenery up there had a remarkable influence on me.
Little by little my courage and love of life returned. I began to realize that
I still had something to live for, that it was my duty to make a serious
attempt in this direction, and thus I came back to Copenhagen more or
less as a human being once again.

Grieg understood clearly the seriousness of the problems his friend had to
deal with both as a composer and as a person. In a letter to Frants Beyer
dated February 8, 1886 he described the matter as follows:

> We are together daily, and although I never really feel that I know him
> completely, I must say that he is more amiable toward me than ever. He
> often nearly reveals his inner self, but then one suddenly bumps into a
> brick wall. Just between you and me, there is one thing that worries
> me—and I have said this in all candor to Svendsen himself: I am worried
> about *his art*, for his future as an artist. He has peculiarities of character
> which hinder the unfolding of his rich creative gifts. This hurts me so
> much that I could weep, for there is no one from whom I have expected
> greater things. I will not give up hope yet, but I must say that his outward
> circumstances seem to me to be getting into greater and greater disarray.

Grieg appears to be touching on some persistent traits in Svendsen's character: his hopeless naiveté regarding finances, his attractiveness to and weakness for women, and probably also his overuse of alcohol. Svendsen had
entered a vicious circle that was to have devastating consequences for his
productivity as a composer.

Fortunately, however, the problems that he had to contend with did
not have a negative influence on his work as a musical director, in which capacity he continued to serve until after the turn of the century.

THE STATE GRANT CONTROVERSY

Ever since 1874 Svendsen's annual state grant had provided a financial foun-
dation for him, but in 1885—two years after he had taken the position in
Copenhagen—the Norwegian government proposed to the National
Assembly that the annual grant of 1,600 crowns not be awarded "as long
as he holds the position of musical director at the Royal Theater in
Copenhagen."

This proposal must be looked at against the background of the presuppositions that were asserted for the awarding of the grants to Grieg and Svendsen in 1874, namely that they "dedicate their talents to the furtherance of music in their homeland." To be sure, during the debate in 1885 it was not this paragraph that was cited most frequently, but it is evident that it lay behind the vote of many representatives.

That the Norwegian government proposed to take away an honorary grant from one of the country's most distinguished composers because he, having found it impossible to make a living at home, accepted an important position in a neighboring country aroused strong reactions in artistic circles. The first person to express his displeasure was Grieg, who sent a strong letter of protest to H. A. Bentsen, president of the lower house:

> I will only add that Svendsen certainly has not given up hope that in a not too distant future the circumstances will become more favorable for an end to his enforced exile. I think, in other words, that he, like the rest of us who speak for our national art, waits with longing for the moment when the National Assembly, through an academy of art and other measures, will take the initiative to bring Norwegian artists home again. You will understand, Mr. President, that a discontinuation of his grant at this point in time without doubt will embitter him and contribute to the result that Norway will lose forever one of her most brilliant sons. And it cannot be said loud enough: *such* a luxury we cannot afford.

The next one to speak up was the composer Johan Selmer, who on May 30 wrote to President Bentsen arguing that it was unreasonable to take the grant away from Svendsen. The governing boards of the Music Society and the Quartet Society joined in sending a stern letter dated June 13: "We are afraid that robbing him of the honorary grant awarded by the National Assembly could be perceived, especially abroad, as a belittling of his significance as an artist, and for him personally it could decrease the desire to return to his homeland, which needs very much to retain so gifted a man." The letter went on to say that Svendsen was not a Danish civil servant but held an appointment that could be terminated by either party at any time (112h).

The issue came up in the National Assembly on June 17, 1885. It was evident that the protests had had an effect, for during the debate the only representative who spoke in favor of the committee's recommendation was J. M. O. Ueland. All the other speakers favored postponing the decision pending the receipt of more information about the details of Svendsen's appointment. It was pointed out that Danish composer Niels W. Gade, who received an annual grant of no less than three thousand crowns in Denmark, also held an appointment as an organist and engaged in other important activities for which he was paid.

The proposal to postpone was approved by a large majority (112i). Thus the immediate crisis was briefly averted.

On October 16 Prime Minister Johan Sverdrup wrote to Svendsen requesting further information. Svendsen's reply, dated November 25 and printed in the Copenhagen press on February 8, 1886, included the following paragraphs:

> I serve at the pleasure of the ministry and can be discharged or quit at any time. Thus I am not a member of the Royal Danish civil service with a permanent appointment and pension rights, nor can I become so unless I will give up my nationality and become a naturalized Danish citizen— something I have thus far not desired to do.
>
> My salary is 7,000 (seven thousand) crowns per year. I should like very much to retain the composer's grant once awarded to me by the National Assembly because I have a strong feeling that in the not too distant future I will be giving up my present position, and then I will have no income whatsoever. As musical director [of the Royal Theater Orchestra] I have the best possible opportunity to continue in a practical way my studies in the area of musical drama and, at the same time, to learn many other things as well. That, in addition to the fact that I do not want to leave my position until I have carried out the reforms that I have initiated in the institution whose overall musical leadership has been entrusted to me, is why I consider an extended stay here both useful and desirable—all the more in that conditions in Norway at the moment are anything but favorable for music and its devotees.

Svendsen's visit to Oslo in the summer of 1886 happened to occur just as the National Assembly was about to vote on his case. The information he had sent had made an impression, for when the matter came up before the National Assembly on June 22 the government proposed that he continue to receive his annual grant. However, a majority of the members of the Pension and Grant Committee continued to support the committee's earlier recommendation that the grant be discontinued as long as Svendsen continued to hold the position in Copenhagen.

S. P. Jaabæk made a motion from the floor that the grant be withdrawn unconditionally, based on the following reasoning: "Where he is now he naturally has a wage of such magnitude that he doesn't need the money from Norway, and when he comes here again he can ask for a new grant." This motion was voted on separately and received only ten votes.

The chairman of the Budget Committee, W. Konow, who had dissented from the recommendation that the grant be terminated, spoke warmly on Svendsen's behalf but declined to offer an alternative course of action. During the discussion in the National Assembly there was only one representative other than Jaabæk who spoke against the government's recommendation that Svendsen continue to receive the grant. That was Ole G. Ueland, who said, "When a man has 7,000 crowns a year, I think he must be so well situated that he can get along. I wish there were many in this country who had an income of 7,000 crowns."

The issue was decided by a roll-call vote with the result that the government's proposal was rejected and the committee's approved by a vote of 73 to 24. Svendsen's annual grant was to be terminated so long as he remained musical director of the Royal Theater Orchestra in Copenhagen (112j).

Thus ended a sorry chapter in Norwegian cultural life. Narrow-mindedness had won the day.

YEARS OF HARD WORK

In early August of 1886, when Svendsen was about to leave Oslo at the end of his holiday, a party was held in his honor and he was presented with a handsome gold chain and medallion. *Nordisk Musik-Tidende* reported on the event: "The enthusiastic speeches that were made about him all bore witness to how much he was missed and how great was the desire to eventually get him back. Upon his departure Mr. Svendsen received a large landscape painting by [Ludvig] Skramstad and an ornately bound copy of *La Captive*, a composition by Joh. Selmer dedicated to him."

The very day after returning to Copenhagen he held two strenuous rehearsals. He wrote to his father on August 15: "That is how we work every day, to the great irritation of the many lazy ones among the personnel." He continued: "I am also in the process of planning the program for my concerts this winter and am thinking of doing many new things by Liszt, Wagner, Berlioz and others."

This autumn there would be new productions of *Tannhäuser* and *Lohengrin*. The title roles were to be sung by the renowned German Wagnerian tenor Anton Schott, who also participated in Svendsen's first philharmonic concert of the season.

Nordisk Musik-Tidende carried reviews of the opera performances. They were written by Svendsen's friend and supporter Charles Kjerulf, who had succeeded "Adrean" and during the next eight months delivered a series of witty vignettes of Copenhagen's music life. He reported that Jacob F. Scavenius, the Danish Minister of Culture—in a nationalistic outburst occasioned by the Danish-Prussian war of 1864—had decreed that Schott could not sing his parts in the original language: *Never German on the Danish stage!* Schott, therefore, was compelled to sing in English, "which largely ruined his performance. . . . That language, which is so ill suited to singing, sounded both ugly and incomprehensible."

Queen Louise had to intervene with the minister, telling him that one should not mix art and politics! Scavenius had to eat crow, and at the performance on September 26 Schott was permitted to sing in his native tongue.

Svendsen wrote to his father on September 24 that the Wagner operas had gone very well. "The orchestra, especially, has done its job excellently, but some of the singers, too, were almost equal to their parts." He mentioned further that he had gotten a letter from Professor Neovius in Helsinki about another visit to Finland during the coming winter: "But I don't think I will go so far north this season. Moreover, it's dangerous to go again so soon to a place where one has been treated so well. One is very easily disappointed when one appears the second time."

At the theater there were intense rehearsals on a series of operas: Auber's *The Black Domino*, Hérold's *Zampa*, Rossini's *The Barber of Seville*, and Donizetti's *The Daughter of the Regiment*. On November 4 Svendsen wrote to his sister, Albertine: "I'm in work up over my ears. Today, for example, I am conducting no less than three long rehearsals, and that's the way I've had it more or less ever since the beginning of the season. I go to my room in the evening totally beat and wiped out. I have now learned that the Norwegian peasant boy was right when he said that sleeping is the most enjoyable thing in the world."

Things didn't get any easier during the weeks that followed, for in connection with the celebration of the centennial of Weber's birth (November 18) the theater was going to present a new production of *Preciosa* and a Danish premiere of *Oberon*. (*Der Freischütz* was presented in February 1887.)

Svendsen thought the leaders were exploiting the personnel, and as Christmas approached he got them to agree that both singers and instrumentalists should have a whole week without rehearsals.

In a Christmas letter to Mrs. Neovius in Helsinki, Svendsen told a bit about music life in Copenhagen: "The numerous concerts given here are always well attended despite the difficult times. The support for my philharmonic concerts has been tremendous: a full house for both the dress rehearsal and the concert."

The December issue of *Nordisk Musik-Tidende* reported that Svendsen was working on "a new symphony in C major that he hopes to perform in Copenhagen and in Oslo during the current season." The symphony was also mentioned in the issue of August 1889: "Svendsen has recently been hard at work on several new compositions, including his symphony." That he really was engaged in such a task was confirmed by Fini Henriques in 1939 in a conversation with Professor Olav Gurvin of the University of Oslo. Henriques had studied composition with Svendsen during the latter part of the 1880s, and he said his teacher had finished the entire first movement and was well along with the second movement of a symphony in E major. But Henriques had never seen anything more of the composition (53).

Svendsen was always vitally interested in what was going on in Oslo. When Christian Krohg's book *Albertine* was seized by the police on the day it was published—December 20, 1886—he was outraged. Such an act looked like a "low, contemptible concession to 'the Christian left.' If this is the case, and there is much to indicate that it is," he wrote to Johan Selmer on December 28, "then things undeniably look very bad for old Norway. What is the meaning of that freedom that at any moment can be silenced by an intolerant party, and what shall one think of a people who let themselves be governed by such elements? Ish!"

Svendsen also received clear proof that he had not been forgotten elsewhere in Europe when, toward the end of the year, he received an invitation from Colonne in Paris to conduct his orchestra. He had to turn down the tempting offer, however.

In January of 1887 Copenhagen enjoyed a visit by Joseph Hofmann, a ten-year-old musical prodigy—a pianist—from Poland, who made four appearances in the course of a week. Svendsen engaged him as soloist at the philharmonic concerts, where he played, among other things, Beethoven's third piano concerto and Liszt's arrangement of Weber's *Polacca Brillante*. In a letter to Grieg dated February 9, Svendsen reported that the concerts had gone exceptionally well: *"Completely sold out*, but then we don't fail to do everything possible to make them attractive." He also revived memories of the happy times with Edvard and Nina a year earlier, but added:

> Now everything is changed. Then enjoyable togetherness, now sad loneliness; then bright hopes, now dark resignation. But I am struggling for all I am worth to get back on track again and am beginning to think I will succeed. As for work, I have started to work even though the results are meager—but I have already experienced the practical result, for I feel a possibility of regaining my peace of mind.

Gade's seventieth birthday on February 22 was observed with a festival concert at the Royal Theater. According to one press report, Svendsen conducted the honoree's *Symphony No. 4* in B-flat major "in such an inspired and stirring manner that a festive mood spread throughout the theater." Carl Gottschalksen reports in *Diary of a Happy Musician*: "Gade sat in the first row beside J. P. E. Hartmann. As the king of music in our country, Gade normally didn't tolerate having anyone above him, but after the performance he rushed up onto the stage behind the orchestra and called out for Svendsen, and when he came he embraced the brilliant conductor and musician" (44:81).

It was an historic moment for these two masters, who were generally regarded, if not as opponents, at least as opposites and rivals. In April, at the last philharmonic concert of the season, Svendsen again honored Gade by performing the latter's first symphony.

On April 1 Svendsen's annual salary was raised from 7,000 to 8,000 crowns. A new effort to increase the compensation of the musicians was also successful.

The theater offered two major productions during this winter-spring season. In January it was the premiere of Holger Drachmann and P. E. Lange-Müller's comic opera *Der var engang (Once Upon a Time)*, and in April Bizet's *Carmen* was produced for the first time in Denmark. As the theater's music consultant, Svendsen considered it practically a formality to recommend the music by native son Lange-Müller. *Der var engang* has since become one of Danish theater's biggest hits.

Carmen, which had been performed in Copenhagen by a touring Swedish ensemble a few years earlier, was received with jubilation. Svendsen emphasized the dramatic and emotional elements in Bizet's music and succeeded in getting both the singers and the orchestra musicians to do their very best.

In a letter to Grieg dated May 21, Svendsen wrote about the exhausting work in the theater. He was annoyed with his "present colleagues' wretched, mean tricks." It is also sad to read what he wrote about his new symphony: "Several times this winter I have tried to get back to it, but it just never worked out. It is as if I have lost interest in the ideas already written down, and it's possible that some fine day I'll decide to turn to something else."

The philharmonic concerts were for the most part successful, but according to Svendsen that did not prevent some journalists from censuring them:

> Some of the aforementioned colleagues inspired some hack writers to come out with the most foolish and unreasonable criticisms. If I play new music they complain because I am neglecting the classics. If I play older things they mutter about having to listen to the same things that they have already heard at Tivoli. (They always forget to mention the Music Society in this connection.) Yes, even the fact that at each concert I present a famous soloist is sometimes used as an excuse for vilification: they write that the concerts are degenerating into a showcase for stars. Yesterday I saw it maintained in all seriousness that it's destructive of art when the performance is excellent because then one easily forgets the composition itself. What else can you expect when idiots try their hand at being Jesuits?

Svendsen greatly appreciated an invitation from Grieg to visit him at Troldhaugen, his new home outside Bergen. The holiday that he so much desired would make it possible for him to "get away from all this nonsense in a few weeks, because I'm so tired, worn out and dispirited that it is vitally necessary to get some rest soon."

As he had done the year before, he went in June to Oslo. He did not go to Troldhaugen to see Grieg, however, but instead visited his father in Sandefjord as well as friends in Tønsberg and Åsgårdstrand and on the island of Hankø.

Svendsen was displeased to learn that a false and damaging rumor about him had been making the rounds in Oslo during the preceding year. He wrote to his father on August 4 that according to this rumor he was leading a life of debauchery in Copenhagen: "I am supposed to have been such a lush that I spent a good deal of my time sleeping off my drunkenness." There was little he could do about such rumors, but he was especially irritated by the fact that they were started by a former friend who should have known that there was nothing to them.

By the middle of July he was back in Denmark. "Just think," he wrote in the August 4 letter to his father, "in the space of three weeks I have conducted rehearsals for six big operas . . . in addition to the necessary work at home reading scores and consultations with the director and producer."

On October 22 he conducted the premiere of *Loreley*, a new Danish opera by Johan Bartholdy. It was very nearly a fiasco, however, and lasted for only three performances. On November 29 he conducted the Danish premiere of Verdi's *La Traviata*, which proved to be very popular with the public: "Nearly every opera performance during the past two months has been a sell-out," he wrote to his father on December 28.

An important part of Svendsen's work at the theater was the preparation of evaluations as music consultant. These have been preserved in the Royal Archives among the documents dealing with "theater appraisals". Each year a substantial number of works were submitted for appraisal; during the 1887–88 season, for example, 105 works—mainly plays—were submitted. All had to be "appraised" regardless of their quality. As the music expert on the staff, Svendsen wrote about fifty evaluations during the years 1887–1907. Most of these concerned Danish operas and comic operas, and his discussions of these works—which run the gamut from pure trivialities to Carl Nielsen's *Saul and David* and *Masquerade*—make highly interesting reading.

In 1887 Svendsen produced two such evaluations. On January 23 he characterized P. E. Lange-Müller's *Fru Jeanna (Mrs. Jeanna)* as "pretty, interesting and effective" and gave it his warmest endorsement. Jørgen Malling's *Lisinka* struck him as not very original but nonetheless "free of banalities and well orchestrated" (December 13).

In mid-January of 1888 Svendsen had to make a quick trip to Paris. His wife Bergljot, who had been living there for two and a half years, was seriously ill. He wrote to Grieg on February 22:

> I went there with a feeling of terrible anxiety. The telegram asking me to
> come indicated that my poor wife was on the verge of death and that I
> had better hurry. When I approached her bed, where she lay in a feverish

sleep after a painful attack, it was as if she was fighting for consciousness. Finally she recognized me. She tried to reach out her hand toward me and stammered some affectionate words of welcome. I have never had such a strange feeling. Now I understood what she has been going through these past years and with what admirable pride she has been concealing her sorrow and misery. It struck me as an inescapable duty to do everything for her, and it was decided that she should come home to me again. I think something good will now come out of it.

Bergljot's convalescence took a long time. In a later letter to Grieg (April 17), Svendsen wrote that he presumably would be going to Paris to get her sometime during the summer. "I hope to be able to spend a couple of weeks there, and I look forward to that more than I can tell you." He never made the trip to Paris, though, and at the end of August Bergljot returned to Copenhagen alone. But despite the best intentions of both parties, the Svendsens were unable to resolve their differences. Johan wrote to his sister on February 4, 1889: "She was not happy here and no doubt felt also that the old relationship between the two of us could never be restored. But we parted as good friends."

How happy had this marriage really been? After the harmony of the first years it probably was not so surprising that a couple with such dissimilar backgrounds and incompatible temperaments encountered problems. They had no children together. Johan's work was his top priority; Bergljot was constantly forced to play a secondary role, and this was hard for her to accept. But although the marriage went through many crises, there is no record of Johan ever having said an unkind word about her. But neither can one deny that his often irresponsible relations with other women had much to do with the breakup of their marriage. After the brief time together in autumn of 1888 they never saw each other again.

So they parted as friends, and according to Olav Gurvin, Svendsen, as the gentleman he was, continued to send her half of his annual salary until he left his job at the Royal Theater in 1908—an arrangement that seriously undermined his financial situation. Moreover, there is evidence that Bergljot, who after a few years in Paris moved to London, continued to incur debts. For example, a letter from S. Forsell in Stockholm dated May 21, 1895, demands on behalf of attorney Bernard Abrahams, London, that Johan pay a delinquent bill of £12, "which sum your wife borrowed from Mr. Abrahams some time ago."

At the first philharmonic concert of the new year on February 4, 1888, Svendsen renewed his acquaintance with Pablo de Sarasate, who was soloist in Max Bruch's *Violin Concerto* in G minor and in Svendsen's *Violin Romance*. He wrote to Grieg on February 22 that Sarasate had not changed in the least during the preceding ten years: "He was just as amiable and pleasant as before. Yes! Believe me, we had a good time together, especially one evening when he came to my house and played some quartets along with Neruda and a couple of other fellows."

Grieg was in Leipzig at this time and frequently saw Tchaikovsky, who asked him to greet Svendsen. On February 23 Svendsen again wrote to Grieg:

> I was glad to receive the greeting from Tchaikovsky. Thank him for me. Tell him that I have been studying his compositions for several years and that I have expressed the respect and admiration I feel for him by performing some of his things both in Oslo and here and that I would be pleased if next year he would favor one of the philharmonic concerts with his presence and participation [as a conductor].

The same letter contains a strongly ironic comment about his and Grieg's common enemy, the Leipzig music critic Eduard Bernsdorf, as well as a sharp reaction against the anti-Semites:

> So Bernsdorf is still as charming as ever, works eagerly to help people understand the significance of Wagner's *Das Judenthum in der Musik* (*Judaism in Music*). Unfortunately there are scoundrels like that everywhere and not least here in Denmark's capital city, which is in other respects so nice. Fortunately all of their efforts are ineffective against that which is really good. Nobody should pay any attention to these fellows' grimaces or scribblings. Ish!

On March 20 Svendsen conducted the Danish premiere of Gounod's *Romeo and Juliet* and four days later a philharmonic concert. This spring he also had several operas to evaluate. He characterized C. F. E. Horneman's *Aladdin* as "a very talented work which I highly recommend for performance at the Royal Theater." He counseled strongly against performing C. C. Møller's *Kunstnerliv (Artists' Life)*: "I think the work is unperformable, at least at the Royal Theater." He also rejected a work by his old teacher Carl

Reinecke entitled *Auf hohem Befehl* (*By Royal Command*). The music was listenable enough, but the many spoken lines made the opera unsuitable for performance in Denmark.

Svendsen also made two trips to London in late spring of 1888. Grieg had visited the English capital on a concert tour in April, and while there had been invited to conduct the Royal Philharmonic orchestra at two concerts in May–June. He had been obliged to decline for reasons of health but had recommended Svendsen in his place. The recommendation had been accepted, for Svendsen was not unknown in London. Just a few weeks earlier (March 22), for example, the Royal Philharmonic orchestra under its permanent director, Frederic Cowen, had played Svendsen's second Norwegian rhapsody.

Svendsen at first declined the invitation. He was swamped with work at the theater and was also busy with preparations for the big Nordic music festival that was to be held in Copenhagen at the beginning of June. Furthermore, as he wrote to Grieg on May 6, he considered the proposed honorarium too small.

Then he received a new and more tempting offer from London, and this time he accepted. On May 25 he left by boat for the British Isles and the first concert took place on June 4. On June 24 he wrote to his father that he quickly got on the same wave-length with the 80-piece orchestra and that when he mounted the podium "the audience and the orchestra greeted me with a long, wild burst of applause that was repeated after each movement of the symphony. (It was my first, in D major.)" *The Standard* wrote: "His stage presence is highly engaging, and as a composer he makes an excellent impression with his colorful, animated and often strikingly original symphony. The *scherzo*, especially, generated enthusiastic applause."

Svendsen hurried home to participate in the music festival in Copenhagen, but by June 16 he was back in London for his second concert: Beethoven's *Pastoral Symphony*, Rubinstein's piano concerto in G major, and Brahms's violin concerto.

Svendsen's visits to London had also been noted in Vienna. The July issue of *Nordisk Musik-Tidende* quoted from an article by the renowned critic Eduard Hanslick in *Neue Freie Presse*: "Ever since the time of Weber, Spohr and Mendelssohn, Germany's most famous composers have received invitations to London, and during the past couple of years the same has been the case with Gounod, Saint-Saëns and Dvořák, and now with Svendsen. That's a good thing and a good example for other major cities."

Further triumphs awaited Svendsen in England. On August 28 Anton

Seidl conducted the *Coronation March* at a festival concert in Brighton, and that autumn Svendsen was made an honorary member of the Royal Philharmonic Society.

The Nordic Music Festival held in Copenhagen June 4–9 was the realization of an idea first proposed by Danish composer Leopold Rosenfeld. A big Nordic trade exposition was scheduled to be held in Copenhagen during the summer, and plans were under way to present a display of Nordic art works as well. A year or so before this event was to take place, Rosenfeld had urged that the occasion be used to showcase some of the best music of the three Scandinavian countries. A committee was appointed to plan the event, with Otto Malling as the leading figure. Svendsen's special responsibility was to make sure that Norway was appropriately represented.

The music festival presented a number of outstanding concerts and was extremely well received. It included three evening programs of chamber music as well as three concerts by an orchestra of 106 musicians, of which the nucleus consisted of 46 players drawn from the Royal Theater Orchestra. Svendsen had substantial conducting responsibilities. The programs were centered around four major figures in Nordic music: two Danes, Hartmann and Gade, and two Norwegians, Svendsen and Grieg.

At the opening concert, Grieg conducted his piano concerto with Erika Lie Nissen as soloist. During the following days Svendsen was represented as a composer by his second symphony, *Two Icelandic Melodies*, and the string octet, but he was not able to offer any new composition. Several writers criticized him for this. William Behrend, for example, wrote in *Tilskueren* that he was "genuinely saddened at the thought that this composer, at a time when he is still in full possession of his powers, has laid down his lyre and will probably never take it up again" (5). Charles Kjerulf voiced similar thoughts in the June issue of *Nordisk Musik-Tidende*: "Does *that* man really feel that he is *so* old and *so* finished that he will never write another note? That cannot be true. There have long been rumors to the effect that Svendsen was writing a new symphony. Before we know it—we'll certainly have it."

According to a letter from Christian Sinding to Frederick Delius (May 20, 1889), Grieg had big plans to take Feruccio Busoni, Delius, Sinding and Svendsen along on a trip to the Jotunheimen mountains this summer. After the hectic season, however, Svendsen felt a greater need for a completely restful vacation so he chose instead to spend a few quiet weeks in the little fishing town of Skovshoved on Øresund.

On August 12 and 13 he was back on the podium, this time as principal conductor at a male-chorus festival held on the grounds of Christiansborg castle—an event arranged by the Union of Danish Singing Societies that drew over a thousand singers. Svendsen had responsibility for five hundred singers from Copenhagen, and he also had the honor of conducting the massed chorus.

In the years that followed, Svendsen often participated in song festivals of this kind in his capacity as principal conductor of the Association of Singing Societies of Copenhagen—a position that carried no salary. According to Victor Gandrup, he "entered into this activity with the greatest interest and energy, and it was a real joy for the singers to sing under him" (41). One result of his work in this area was that in the 1890s he was chosen to edit three volumes of compositions, including a number of Norwegian ones, for Denmark's Male Chorus Singing Society.

In September of 1888 Svendsen received a telegram from the conductor of the Berlin Philharmonic reporting that the audience had greeted his first symphony with enthusiastic cries of "bravo" and had been absolutely electrified by the *Finale*. It had been a success without equal, according to the September issue of *Nordisk Musik-Tidende*, and it was stated further that Svendsen's other orchestral works "will now in rapid succession be rehearsed and performed at the Berlin concerts. He has recently received invitations from Hamburg, Dresden and Vienna to conduct concerts in these cities this winter." The Berlin orchestra performed *Carnival in Paris* at a guest appearance in Holland on September 14 and in Berlin on October 30.

In autumn of 1888 Svendsen introduced a future international star from Norway to the Danish public: soprano Gina Oselio. Theater Director Fallesen had heard her in Paris and immediately engaged her to appear in Copenhagen. She first sang the title role in *Carmen*, then the part of Margrethe in Boito's *Mefistofele*—a part she had rehearsed with the composer himself.

On November 15 a special event was planned at the Royal Theater to mark the 25th anniversary of Christian IX's accession to the throne. The featured work was the world premiere of C. F. E. Horneman's *Aladdin*, which the composer had been working on for more than twenty years. As Carl Behrens related in his memoirs, the overwrought composer created quite a stir during the rehearsals:

> The rehearsal was rendered exceedingly difficult by Horneman's personal presence. He flitted around the auditorium, both the gallery and the main floor, to hear how the music sounded, complained on the stage

about Svendsen's tempos, and refused to leave, so Fallesen had to be called. Only when he gave Horneman an "apology" did he leave.

For a variety of reasons, the premiere of *Aladdin* was not a great success. The decision to perform it had been made so late that there was not enough time for rehearsals. Also, a number of cuts were made at the last minute, as a result of which the production was somewhat disjointed. Only Svendsen's skillful leadership prevented it from falling apart altogether.

An overview of the 1888–89 season provides a clear picture of the schedule of activities at the Royal Theater in a typical year. There was a total of 73 performances of 14 different operas. Of these, one (*Aladdin*) was a world premiere and another (Adolphe Adam's *King for a Day*) a Danish premiere. The other operas presented that year were *The Barber of Seville, Carmen, Don Juan, Faust, Hans Heiling, La Traviata, Mefistofele, Romeo and Juliet, The Daughter of the Regiment, The Treasure, Il Trovatore,* and *William Tell.*

In January of 1889 Svendsen posed for a bust by sculptor N. W. Holm. *Nordisk Musik-Tidende* reported with a touch of unintended humor that as soon as he was finished with the bust it was the sculptor's intention "to start working on a half-size statue of Svendsen in the hope that the Norwegians would some day have use for such a monument to their famous countryman." But 22 years were to pass before there could be any talk of a monument.

On January 15, 1889, Svendsen was strongly criticized by H. V. Schytte, a major government official, in the Copenhagen newspaper *Dagbladet.* The burden of the complaint was that Svendsen used inappropriate tempos and that he was altogether too strict in his treatment of "young performers." The criticism was repeated in *Avisen* on February 27. The writer insinuated that Svendsen had done little to earn all the money that had been spent on him and he was compared unfavorably with Gade and Paulli.

Twice during the first half of 1889 Svendsen felt compelled to write to the editors of the local newspapers to defend his name and reputation. On February 23 he found it necessary to counter charges of bigamy, writing to *Dagbladet*: "Regarding a report in *Gazetten* today to the effect that I was married in a civil ceremony to Miss Haase, a dancer at the Royal Theater, permit me to inform you that this rumor is false. I trust that in the future the honorable editor will refrain from repeating this rumor in his paper."

Svendsen had in fact entered into a romantic relationship with Juliette

Haase some three years earlier, but there could of course be no talk of marriage so long as he was not officially divorced from Bergljot.

The slander sometimes took other forms. On April 1 he felt obliged to threaten *Morgenbladet* and *Politiken* with a civil suit:

> Inasmuch as a man has told me that he intends to send your esteemed paper an article stating that I am implicated in a case that at the moment is pending trial, permit me to inform you that I have nothing at all to do with the unlawful acts in question. Therefore I will be obliged to immediately initiate legal action if this article, the falsity of which I have reported to the writer, nonetheless is published.

These were the sorts of calumnies he had in mind when he wrote to his sister on September 24: "Illness, shameless schemes, slander and lies have during these last months made my life so miserable that it makes me nauseous just to think about it."

Complaints about financial problems run like a red thread through Svendsen's correspondence throughout his first years in Denmark. There's no denying that it seems strange that a man with such substantial income should have been constantly in financial difficulty. With the concert honoraria in addition to his regular salary, he earned over ten thousand crowns a year—a very large sum in those days. But he was bogged down in a financial quagmire from which he was never able to extricate himself.

A considerable part of his income went for support payments to his free-spending wife. In addition, he was constantly juggling debts both old and new; indeed, his finances seemed always to be in complete chaos. He touched on the matter in the September 24 letter to his sister: "And now this permanent lack of money. I am so constantly pestered by creditors and attorneys that sometimes I don't know which way to turn."

But there were also some bright spots in his life. From abroad came a steady stream of reports regarding successful performances of his compositions. Madrid's philharmonic orchestra under Thomas Breton performed *Zorahayda* as well as the second and third Norwegian rhapsodies. No. 2, which had to be repeated at the concert in Madrid, was also played by the Boston Philharmonic under Arthur Nikisch. *Carnival in Paris* was on the program for the first subscription concert of the Budapest Philharmonic in autumn of 1889, and a few weeks later it was also played in Amsterdam and Bremen.

In September of 1889 Svendsen was granted a two-week leave by the

Minister of Culture "to take an art-related trip to Berlin." Nothing further is known about the details of this trip. That autumn, however, he was busy with rehearsals for three new operas: Gluck's *Iphigenia in Aulis*, Offenbach's *Tales of Hoffman*, and Hermann Götz's *Taming of the Shrew*. But many bouts with illness made it difficult for him to maintain his planned schedule. In order to avoid too many cancellations it became necessary to insert ordinary concert numbers into some of the productions: vocal selections, even violin and piano concertos. During a period of a year and a half this was done no less than nine times—an odd footnote to the history of opera in Denmark.

In early November a vicious attack on theater director Fallesen appeared in *Politiken*. Fallesen defended himself in a half-page article in *Berlingske Tidende* on November 8 in which he described the conditions at the theater. Svendsen, as a rule, did not get in involved in newspaper polemics. This time, however, fearing that his silence might be misunderstood, he endorsed Fallesen's views in an article published on November 22.

On November 16, the newly restored *Koncertpalæet* (*The Concert Palace*)—a concert hall on Bredgade formerly known as the *Schimmelmannske Palæe*—had a grand opening that was attended by Hartmann, Gade, Grieg and others. Svendsen conducted the orchestra. This auditorium (which in 1902 was renamed *Odd Fellows-Palæet*) became a major music center in Copenhagen, and Svendsen immediately began to use it for his philharmonic concerts. The first such concert of the autumn season was given there just two weeks after the grand opening. Agathe Backer Grøndahl, a new world-class Norwegian pianist, appeared as soloist in Schumann's piano concerto at this concert.

On December 3 Svendsen received a query from Grieg regarding the opera fragment *Olav Trygvason*, which was about to be published by C. F. Peters in Leipzig. Max Abraham, the Director of the Peters firm, had asked Grieg to get Svendsen's opinion regarding the advisability of making some cuts in the last part. Svendsen, who had been in the audience when Grieg conducted the work in Copenhagen on November 16, emphasized in his reply on December 6 that the composer himself had to be the sole authority on such a question. Nothing should be cut, but a couple of repeats could be omitted without injury to the work: "Dear friend! Don't let anyone mislead you into making any other cuts in your splendid work, which in every respect has just exactly the right proportions of length and breadth. Listen!"

Grieg decided to insert parenthetical notes in two places indicating that in concert performances the repeats could be omitted.

On November 18 Svendsen, for the second time in his life, became the father of an illegitimate son. The boy was given the name Johan. The mother was Juliette Haase, with whom he had been romantically involved for some time, though they did not live together. Two more children were born to them in the years that followed: Sigrid, born February 23, 1894, and Eyvind Severin, born January 5, 1896. They did not marry until December 23, 1901, one week after his divorce from Bergljot was finalized.

As one looks back over Svendsen's first six years in Copenhagen it is clear that his artistic impact on the city was substantial. This fact was clearly expressed by Charles Kjerulf in an article in the July–December 1889 issue of the semiannual journal *Af Dagens Krønike* (72): "Svendsen obviously was a man of discipline, and not least for that reason one viewed him as the saving Messiah that some expected and everyone knew we needed." He had in a short time succeeded in elevating the orchestra from mediocrity to excellence: "The conductor swept the orchestra along, egged it on, inspired the players to do better than their best." During the controversy regarding the philharmonic concerts, Svendsen had shown the musicians of the Royal Theater that he could get along without them at these concerts and that discipline in the orchestra was not affected in the least by their assault on his authority: "The result, then, is this, that discipline in the orchestra now is as it should be and the musical director by and large is as well-liked as he is respected." But Kjerulf criticized Svendsen for his lack of independence in relation to the leadership of the theater. With his artistic superiority he should have seized the reins and given leadership to the whole organization, not just the orchestra: "*He* should always be the driver because he knows, and if it becomes necessary he can change direction. . . . He has a right to say: I am responsible, I have my duties—but then I also want to have the rights. And he should."

Kjerulf also discussed the opposition Svendsen had encountered during those first years from the anti-Svendsen clique in the Danish musical world, "the very same people who, when the conductorship was vacant, constituted 'the national guard,' but later were reduced to silence by the new musical director's rapidly growing popularity and only in recent years have resurfaced with more or less undisguised attacks." This gang now stood "ready to carry out the death penalty against Svendsen; his deeds, the six seasons, have condemned him. But this jury is not impartial, and a study of the facts of the case will show that in this matter Johan Svendsen should be acquitted of the charge, even if one might at the same time express a desire that the coming years will show even richer results." Svendsen was no reac-

tionary: "His heart beats warmly for that which is new and great, he possesses a superior intelligence and a well-informed admiration for the old as
well as enthusiasm for the new."

Svendsen's reaction to the attacks from "the national guard" is expressed in a letter to Grieg dated December 6, 1889: "I am so annoyed by
inane criticism that it makes me sick. You will soon be the only person in
the world whom I can think about with unmitigated joy."

It is also sad to read his summing-up of recent events in his New Year's
Eve letter to Johan Selmer:

> The past year has for me been anything but pleasant. Untoward circum-
> stances, both personal and financial, together with the artistically demor-
> alizing and physically exhausting work at the theater—thank your God
> that you are not a theater musical director—has sometimes so over-
> whelmed me with sorrows, irritations and all sorts of hardships that the
> very thought of them gives me a chill.

8

The Conductor in His Prime

1890–1900

THE GRUELING TOIL and countless problems that made life so difficult for Svendsen during his first six years in Copenhagen were followed by a decade of relative calm during which he played a dominant role in the music life of the city. He was still criticized from time to time, especially for not standing up strongly enough to the theater leadership, but he did not let it bother him. The 1890s were to be the best years of his life as a conductor. Secure in his position, he dared to be bolder than he had before. His Danish premiere of Wagner's *The Valkyrie* in 1891, for example, created a furor. He also lent his support to younger Danish composers, premiering a number of their operas at the Royal Theater. Several of Carl Nielsen's compositions, including his first symphony, were premiered at Svendsen's philharmonic concerts.

His relationship with the musicians in the theater orchestra also improved steadily. He made a point of this in an interview held in connection with his seventieth birthday (*Politiken*, 71): "Nothing has made me happier than the fact that, after those first stormy years, the orchestra and I became such very good friends."

Calmness, control, and unquestioned authority characterized his style of leadership. He radiated a unique, irresistible charisma that inspired the musicians to do their very best. Many of them have told of how they practically idolized him. His work both in Copenhagen and abroad came to be so well regarded that a number of leading artists, including Grieg and Carl Nielsen, considered him one of the foremost conductors of that time.

FRIENDS AND FOES AMONG DANISH COMPOSERS

Svendsen experienced several triumphs during the spring season of 1890. The philharmonic concerts went exceptionally well, and the Royal Theater scored great successes with *Fidelio*, *Aida*, and *Mignon*. The season concluded with a big song festival in Århus at the end of May in which Svendsen was principal conductor of a huge massed chorus of Danish male singers.

In August he conducted the combined male choruses of Copenhagen—a 700-voice ensemble—in two concerts given to raise money for the victims of a terrible fire that had ravaged the Norwegian town of Hammerfest on July 22. The program consisted of pieces by several Nordic composers and concluded with a rousing rendition of the Norwegian national anthem.

Four years earlier, it will be recalled, the theater leadership and the minister of culture had prevented him from conducting concerts at Tivoli. By now, however, his position had become such that they could not deny him this opportunity. At three concerts—July 26 and August 2 and 9—the table was set for a veritable Svendsen festival. At the invitation of music director Balduin Dahl, Svendsen conducted programs consisting exclusively of his own music—nine pieces in all.

When the autumn season opened at the Royal Theater, the stage area had a new look: the orchestra pit had been lowered by about five feet and extended under the floor of the stage. Svendsen hoped that these alterations would produce a better blend from the instruments and a better balance with the singing voices. This arrangement, which was copied from Bayreuth, proved, however, to be unpopular with both singers and orchestra members. The singers didn't like the big chasm between the stage and the audience, and the orchestra musicians' spokesman, Anton Svendsen, wrote in *Berlingske Tidende* on September 11 about the "underground orchestra" where the musicians didn't have the slightest idea what was transpiring on stage. The strings sounded too faint, the brilliance was gone: "Under such conditions, how is it possible, even with the best of intentions, to maintain interest in one's work?"

The criticism was so intense that in October Svendsen had to agree to place the strings on a raised platform while the winds continued their "subterranean" existence. The podium was also moved farther back so the conductor would have the whole orchestra in front of him.

The opera repertoire during the autumn season was not especially exciting, however. The "old favorites" were dusted off and presented once again—for example, *The Marriage of Figaro* was performed for the 195th time. The press was angered over the lack of anything new and attacked the theater director. *Politiken* wrote on September 22, "Because Mr. Fallesen is one of the aged wise men for whom nothing under the sun is new, no doubt he should realize that other people are more impatient due to lack of experience." This avoidance of new works was not due to Svendsen, however, for he was always open to new music and new talents.

The freshness and immediacy of Svendsen's own works often made them strongly appealing to younger people—a fact that is reflected in the fine relationship that developed between him and Carl Nielsen. The young Danish musician was appointed as a member of the second violin section of the Royal Theater orchestra on September 1, 1889, thereupon coming under Svendsen's influence as a person, a conductor and a composer. In autumn of 1890 Nielsen made a study trip to Berlin, and on November 13 and December 30 he made some entries in his diary concerning Svendsen:

> People here don't understand Svendsen, who is so wonderfully clear. How, then, will it go for me? The Germans are not open to the music of the future; they don't want anything new any more. Could it be that the Messiah will be born in Eastern Europe? . . . At a philharmonic concert this evening I heard Johan Svendsen's *Carnival in Paris*, which seems to me to be the most daring thing Svendsen has written. He is a great master of orchestration.

Nielsen's high estimate of Svendsen was expressed again in *Politiken* as late as 1931: "My admiration for him was boundless; when Johan Svendsen approached, my legs began to shake, because from the first time he waved his baton over the orchestra in which I was playing, I felt that I was standing face to face with a genius" (91).

Svendsen quickly took note of Nielsen's talents and did much to advance his career. He premiered three of his compositions, used him as a substitute conductor, and turned the baton over to him when his opera *Saul and David* had its premiere in 1902.

Two deaths in the space of a couple of months cast a shadow over Svendsen's life in autumn of 1890. At the end of October he learned that his 75-year-old mother had died on October 28. There had been some sporadic correspondence between them, but so far as we know he had visited her in Rendalen only once or twice since she had left home nearly fifty years earlier. He had received a forewarning that she was seriously ill in a moving letter from her dated May 6, 1890—the last letter he was to receive from her:

> I hear only rarely from the family in Oslo and even more rarely from you. Except for what I see now and then in the newspapers about your triumphs, I really know very little about you.
>
> I am glad to see that you are doing so well as an artist, may luck continue to smile on you in that respect. Warm thanks for the money you have sent me on many occasions, it is so nice to see that you remember me. Yes, of course I know you always do. If you would be so kind as to send me a little money again now I'd appreciate it. I have been ailing a lot this winter, so I have had to and still have to see the doctor now and then, and as you know that costs money. I really can't expect it, but if you could send me a little each quarter I would be very grateful. . . . So best wishes, my son. God bless you always. Accept the warmest greetings from Mama.

It was a sad day for Danish music life when Niels W. Gade died unexpectedly on December 21. On January 7, 1891, the Royal Theater Orchestra held a "memorial festival" at which Svendsen conducted several of the Danish master's compositions. Three days later, at the first philharmonic concert of the new year, the program included several compositions by Gade including the *Ossian Overture*.

Two new operas were scheduled for the spring season of 1891. The first of these was P. E. Lange-Müller's *Mrs. Jeanna* on February 4, with Elisabeth Dons in the title role. Svendsen, who four years earlier had written an evaluation strongly recommending this work, now gave his wholehearted support to the production. The critics, however, turned thumbs down. The success of Lange-Müller's fairytale opera *Once Upon a Time* had created expectations that the new work was totally incapable of fulfilling.

In his position as consultant regarding the musical quality of new works and as musical director of the orchestra, Svendsen sometimes got into skirmishes with Danish composers. That is exactly what happened in this case. He had gotten along well with Lange-Müller for many years, especially after the premieres of *Spanish Students* and *Once Upon a Time*. He had gone so far as to let Lange-Müller conduct the premiere of his D-minor symphony at one of the philharmonic concerts. After the unsuccessful premiere of *Mrs. Jeanna*, however, the Danish composer turned against Svendsen with a vengeance. Helge Bonnén wrote about this in his biography of Lange-Müller:

The result caused Lange-Müller to launch an attack on Maestro Johan Svendsen, whose [allegedly] slovenly preparation of the opera he blamed for reducing its chances of success. It is surprising that this man, who as a composer is very pampered, didn't consider himself above taking such a cheap shot to defend an (to put it bluntly) ill-conceived opera. Not surprisingly, Johan Svendsen became furious and thereafter refused ever again to evaluate or to conduct any of Lange-Müller's compositions. He later described Lange-Müller's harmonic progressions in words that are unprintable (14).

THE VALKYRIE IN DENMARK

The most important event of the season, however, was the March 7 Danish premiere of *The Valkyrie*. Svendsen had long been urging the theater to present one or more of the four *Ring* operas, but the leadership had been resisting the idea on grounds that it was altogether too big and costly an undertaking. Svendsen finally had to threaten to resign to get his way. According to Peter Gradmann, "the combatants crossed swords many times. Fallesen clenched his teeth in exasperation, Svendsen tore his hair—but finally got his way with a trump" (45).

Once the decision was made, however, they immediately went to work to make it a success. The orchestra was increased to 70, and Karl Gjellerup, who was later to win a Nobel prize in literature, was commissioned to prepare the translation. Since there were few Wagnerian singers in Denmark, two artists were imported from the Stockholm opera: Ellen Nordgren Gulbranson as Brünnhilde and Gustaf Holm as Hunding. The other principal roles were sung by Danes: Sieglinde by Sophie Rung Keller, Siegmund by Frederik Brun, and Wotan by Algot Lange.

Svendsen had actually started rehearsals thirteen months earlier. In an undated letter to his father written in September of 1891 he reported, "We really had worked hard. In addition to innumerable piano rehearsals with the singers I held about 30 rehearsals with the orchestra alone and ten with singers and orchestra. . . . This stunningly beautiful work indeed received an unusually attractive performance and had a great success." Peter Gradmann wrote:

> Our music-loving public greeted the fulfillment of their long-held wish with demonstrations the likes of which we have never seen. People shouted for Johan Svendsen, wanted to have him up on the stage beside

the celebrated guest [Ellen Nordgren Gulbranson] to overwhelm him with thanks and praise. But strict regulations forbade such extravagances, and the cold iron curtain separated the maestro from his army of admirers. Nobody who was present on that rare evening will ever forget the experience.

Grieg, who was in Copenhagen at this time, was also enthralled. He wrote to Frants Beyer on March 26, "I have attended seven of the eight performances and would like to attend seven more. It was an event of the highest order, the likes of which one rarely sees in Scandinavia. Svendsen and his orchestra deserve the greatest admiration."

There were only eight performances in March because Ellen Nordgren Gulbranson had to return to the Stockholm Opera, but in April she came back for four additional performances. Svendsen was so impressed with her that he sent a warm letter of recommendation on her behalf to Cosima Wagner in Bayreuth. For a variety of reasons she did not appear at the Wagner festivals until 1897, but she quickly won such acclaim that from then until the beginning of World War I she was regarded as the world's leading Wagnerian soprano.

The success of *The Valkyrie* created pressure from various quarters to mount productions of the other operas in the *Ring* series as well, but nothing came of the idea at this time. *The Valkyrie* was performed for the last time in October of 1892, and a new production was not undertaken until ten years later. *Siegfried* was performed in 1903, *Twilight of the Gods* in 1905. In 1908 the *Ring* was finally completed with *The Rhine Gold*, which is, of course, the point of departure for the whole cycle. *The Rhine Gold*, however, which came at the very end of Svendsen's career, was conducted by Frederik Rung. Svendsen had hoped to be able to perform the complete cycle as a unified whole, but illness prevented him from doing so. His great dream was, however, fulfilled by Rung in 1909.

TOWARD A NEW COMPOSITIONAL SPRING?

Svendsen spent the summer of 1891 in rest and relaxation in Denmark in the hope of finally getting back to doing some composing. Once again, however, he failed to complete anything. On December 22 he wrote to his father, "About my work there is little to say. A large composition that I started a long time ago—a symphony—is still waiting to be completed. I have also begun a group of Norwegian dances for large orchestra that I think will be very nice, if only I could find enough time and inclination to finish them." This is the last time Svendsen makes mention of this symphony. It is also the first and only time we hear about the Norwegian dances, no trace of which has ever been found.

The first two orchestra concerts of the autumn season took place on October 24 and November 28 with Franz Neruda on the podium. The autumn season at the theater offered performances of *The Flying Dutchman* and *William Tell*, the latter for the 103rd time. The main attraction was the Danish premiere of Mascagni's *Cavalleria Rusticana*, which had taken the opera houses of Europe by storm since winning a competition among seventy-five operas in Rome the year before. The Copenhagen production was not a great success, however. The press criticized the staging for being too stiff and for the lack of typical *bel canto* singers in the principal roles. It closed after just fourteen performances, and a successful production of this opera was not launched in Denmark until seven years later.

A much greater furor was created by the premiere on January 22, 1892, of *The Sorceress*, a new opera by Danish composer August Enna. The composer had submitted it for consideration in May of 1890, and Svendsen's written evaluation of the music had been extravagantly positive:

> During the entire time I have been employed by the Royal Theater, no
> Danish musical work has been submitted that gives evidence of a more
> outstanding talent than Mr. August Enna's *The Sorceress*. His music,
> which is rich in distinctive and beautiful things, is remarkably well
> adapted to the text, the vocal parts for both solo voices and chorus are
> first-rate, and the handling of the orchestra is absolutely masterful. I am
> therefore happy to give this work my very warmest recommendation.

The Sorceress was the first of ten operas that Enna was to write. Thanks not least to Svendsen's "brilliant leadership," it was a smashing success. *Nordisk Musik Tidende* reported: "The audience clapped wildly for the composer to come out and take a bow, but he did not appear. He had fainted backstage from joy over the great success."

According to Robert Neiiendam (85/VI:117–19), Enna's somewhat Wagnerian musical style—the opera contains no less than thirty-eight instances of *leitmotifs*—created something of a stir and the composer became famous almost overnight. In June of the same year the opera was performed in Prague and six months later in Berlin. Thereafter it continued its triumphal march in the opera houses of Germany, Austria, Holland, Belgium, Russia and Sweden. In Copenhagen there were 18 performances during 1892, the last one taking place on December 3.

Svendsen did get involved in small controversies with the musicians from time to time. On February 6, 1892, the principal double-bass player sent him a letter of complaint, and four days later forwarded a similar letter to the theater director. Svendsen later told about the incident:

> I have never complained about or "reported" anybody, everything got settled at the time, amicably. On the other hand, a member of the orchestra did once complain about me—to the director—on many pages of paper. And what had I done? Well, the man, who was a double-bass player, at a rehearsal started playing *fortissimo* one measure too early and was about to get others to do the same, so the whole thing was on the verge of being ruined. . . . So naturally I turned around and gave him a look. . . . Just looked at him—that was all! But how *he* complained (133).

The claim that he never wrote a complaint about musicians to the theater director, however, is not quite true. Orchestra records indicate, for example, that on one occasion two of the musicians—tubaist August Petersen and his son, trombonist C. A. Petersen—in 1898 requested a lengthy leave to tour the provinces and play the bronze *lurs* that had recently been discovered in Denmark. They were granted a leave, but only for a short period, and when they extended their absence by ten days without permission, Svendsen blew the whistle. He recommended a big fine for each of them— 400 and 200 crowns respectively. It was only for "humanitarian reasons" that he did not ask for their immediate dismissal. The musicians found the fines so humiliating, however, that they immediately submitted their resignations from the orchestra.

On August 1, 1891, Svendsen asked the theater director for permission to increase the number of philharmonic concerts from four to ten. The series would include programs of chamber music as well as concerts by the Philharmonic Choral Society, the leadership of which he had assumed in January. Neruda would conduct three of the orchestral concerts and would assist in the chamber-music concerts. Permission was given, and the concert season proved to be a hectic one.

At Svendsen's first philharmonic concert of the new year on February 20, 1892, Vassily Sapelnikoff was soloist in Anton Rubinstein's piano concerto in D minor. The program also included Beethoven's seventh symphony and Bizet's symphonic suite *Roma*. In a letter to his sister dated April 5, Svendsen characterized the concert as "extremely successful." Charles Kjerulf, however, thought otherwise, writing acidly in *Politiken*: "The whole concert took three hours. That doesn't make any sense at all."

On March 10 the scene was set for Svendsen's first appearance with the Philharmonic Choral Society. In the letter to his sister he reported that the chorus consisted of "200 ladies and gentlemen with whom I worked for a whole year before I presented them to the public—but the result was brilliant. The sound was so big and beautiful, it was a joy to hear." The program included Haydn's *Der Sturm* and Beethoven's *Fantasia* for piano, chorus and orchestra. The program was brought to an impressive conclusion with Handel's *Halleluia* chorus.

Svendsen conducted only two concerts during the 1891–92 season. His absence from the podium for the remaining concerts may be one of the reasons why the attendance fell far short of what had been expected. After a particularly sparse turnout for a concert on March 24, *Politiken* wrote: "Our concert-going public has gone on strike." Svendsen got the point and made less ambitious plans in the years that followed.

That Svendsen reduced his involvement in concert activities was due not only to the press of duties at the theater but also to other tasks in which he was engaged in the spring of 1892. Preparations were under way for some big celebrations in connection with the golden wedding of King Christian IX and Queen Louise on May 26, and Svendsen had been commissioned to write three major works for the occasion. He had to put everything else aside, so he moved to Hotel Constantia in Charlottenlund in order to work without interruption. In the April 5 letter to his sister he wrote:

> As you can see from the return address above, at the moment I am living away from Copenhagen. The reason is that I have agreed—after numerous urgent requests—to compose no less than three pieces for the upcoming royal golden wedding, and if I was to have any chance of getting this done in time I had to get away from the theater and all the fuss there in the city in order to get the required solitude and to have all my time available for the task. I am now at work writing the music for the new ballet *The Arrival of Spring*, which will be the concluding number of the festival performance at the Royal Theater. It's going to be a pretty large

opus. As soon as it is finished I will start work immediately on the hymn for chorus and orchestra that will open the same performance. [Vilhelm] Bergsøe has written the text for this. Then I must write the cantata with which Copenhagen's combined choral societies will greet the royal couple the morning of the festival. It is a little strange and unfamiliar to me after such a long hiatus in composing to suddenly be thrown into such feverish activity, but I hope I will be able to accomplish the task. For the moment, in any case, I am living under the most favorable possible circumstances, i.e., I am living in complete solitude. . . . I am naturally very glad for the vacation which I am benefitting from as a result of the theater director's friendly courtesy. I only hope that my artistic efforts will also be somewhat successful.

The next day he sent a letter to his future wife, Juliette Haase, the earliest such letter that remains from his correspondence with her. (The letters are preserved in the Musikhistorisk Museum, Copenhagen.) He wrote: "I have been working very hard today and have accomplished something, but I almost despair when I think about how much remains to be done. Now I hope I will get a cheery letter from you tomorrow, because otherwise I'm afraid my work will not go well."

Svendsen just barely got finished in time. The *Festival Cantata* (*The Singers' Morning Greeting*, Work 127) is dated April, 1892. The final double bar of the 149-page orchestral score for the ballet *The Arrival of Spring* was not put in place until "May 7 at 4:15 A.M."—less than three weeks before the date of the performance!

Early on the morning of the royal couple's wedding day, May 26, Svendsen, followed by the male chorus and a military band, marched into Amalienborg Square and conducted a performance of *The Singers' Morning Greeting*. It is a relatively short but sonorous festival cantata in a typical "homage" style. Toward the end, the music employs broad strokes to illumine the text, "Our good king, receive our greeting! Our good queen, receive our greeting!" *Politiken* reported that when the piece was over "the king bowed toward the square and expressed thanks for the beautiful song." Svendsen wrote to his father on July 15:

The chorus of over seven hundred men in combination with a huge military orchestra did an excellent job. The sound was both big and beautiful. When I got back to the hotel after this first expedition my room was filled with flowers and with women and men expressing congratulations. That is when I learned that I had been made a Commander of Dannebrog; in fact, the case containing the new decoration was lying on my table.

The gala event at the Royal Theater was resplendent with diadems as well as medallions signifying membership in various royal orders. Among those present were the tsar of Russia and his family, the Greek royal family, the Prince of Wales, and members of several other European royal houses. The tsarina and Queen Louise wore diamond-studded crowns. To quote again from *Politiken*:

> Svendsen, sporting his new Commander cross, presided. . . . The first number on the program was an homage cantata [*Hymn*, op. 32] sung by all the theater singers, with interspersed spoken text by Mr. Emil Poulsen and a concluding verse [the Danish national anthem, but with a new text by Vilhelm Bergsøe] which the audience was asked to join in singing. The cantata was a newly written text by Professor Bergsøe with pompous music by the suddenly productive Johan Svendsen.

"Pompous" is exactly the right word for this music. *Hymn* is scored for mixed chorus and symphony orchestra and is somewhat longer than *The Singers' Morning Greeting*, but stylistically it is in fact simpler. It has a solemn melody, and powerful chords—mostly simple triads with no Svendsenian characteristics of any kind—give the piece a majestic character.

In order that the foreign guests might also hear a sample of the latest Danish music, Svendsen's *Hymn* was followed by a performance of Act I of August Enna's popular opera *The Sorceress*.

The main event of the evening was a performance of Svendsen's new ballet *The Arrival of Spring*. The ballet was based on an idea proposed by the Royal Theater's financial director, the painter Pietro Krohn, who had been responsible for the staging of many important theater productions including *The Valkyrie*. He also prepared the staging of *The Arrival of Spring*. The choreography was by Carl Price.

In the Musikhistorisk Museum in Copenhagen there is a synopsis in Svendsen's handwriting of the progress of the action on stage, with notes in the margin about where the several musical selections were to be played. This synopsis was printed in a somewhat abbreviated form in the program booklet for the performance:

The scene represents a clear winter day in a forest, with Kronborg Castle in the background. People glide by on skates. . . . Boys frolic around the big snowman. . . . The sky darkens, the winter storm begins to blow. . . . The snowman comes to life and becomes the personification of winter. . . . The snowflakes hop out and swirl around him. . . . Fishermen appear in despair: ice has crushed their boat.

A little poor girl hands out snowdrops to the mourners. The winter storm that has angrily begun crashes down upon his victim, but each time he thinks he has her in his power she avoids him with a leap into the air. . . . The sky darkens and the storm aims all its fury at the little girl. Then suddenly there is a break in the darkness. A ray of sunshine beams down upon her and she stands forth as the young, light-giving spring. She gathers the sun's rays in her hand and flings them out against winter and his entourage. They give way before the sun's mighty power.

Spring flowers in the form of slumbering young girls spring up from the earth. Spring drives through the land with a team of insects. Work and life begin anew. Happy sounds can be heard in the distance. They are announcing the arrival of the special holiday that coincides with the most beautiful season of spring. In old-fashioned, festive national costumes people stream in from every part of Denmark, and from the Danish colonies come people from Greenland, Iceland, the Faroe Islands, the West Indies. Then we hear the strains of the Danish national anthem, and Denmark, personified in the form of a woman, strides proudly forward. Boats with English sailors, Scottish guardsmen, Greeks and Russians sail in. They are received by Denmark and greeted with jubilant shouts by the people. Denmark and her guests celebrate the golden wedding in the spring.

Svendsen composed original music for the most important parts of the ballet including *Winter, The Snowflakes' Dance, Spring, The Flowers' Dance* and *The Insects' Dance.* The last part of the ballet music, on the other hand, consists of arrangements of Danish and other folk songs directly related to the action. The whole score gives evidence of having been worked out with great skill and is highly effective.

The Arrival of Spring created considerable interest in Copenhagen and was performed ten times during that year. Svendsen made no attempt to get the score printed, however. After the composer's death, Fini Henriques made piano arrangements of the five pieces of original music mentioned above and had them published by Wilhelm Hansen. Later they were also published in an arrangement for small orchestra. On the rare occasions when these pieces have been played by a symphony orchestra, copies of the original material dating from 1892 have been used.

When Svendsen—after a hiatus of eight full years—finally managed to complete three new works, one cannot help but ask: was there also a "spring" in his creative activity? Is there any evidence of a renewal?

The answer, unfortunately, is: no. There are some lovely passages in *The Arrival of Spring*, and the master of instrumentation sometimes comes into his own, especially in the stormy winter scenes. Listening to the work today, however, it does not give the impression of rising very far above what is often called *Kapellmeistermusik*—a functional, easy-flowing and somewhat glib type of music that is competent but uninspired. In nearly all of his earlier mature compositions Svendsen had put his own distinctive stamp on the music, but in these three golden-wedding works there is virtually no sign of individuality. One can only conclude that by 1892 he was burnt out as a composer. Thereafter he would write only two short orchestral pieces before laying down his pen for good in 1898.

CONCERT TRIUMPHS IN DENMARK AND ABROAD

In March of 1892 Svendsen accepted an invitation to conduct a program of his own works at a summer concert in Vienna. On July 26 he left for Austria; the concert was scheduled to take place nine days later. He wrote to his father on July 31: "Here it is so pretty and grand, people are so full of life, and life is so pleasant that I wish I could stay here a month instead of a week." He had already visited Beethoven's grave, St. Stephen's Cathedral "and many other magnificent things, but tomorrow the rehearsals begin— two a day, 9–12 and 3–5—so that's the end of all the wonderful times. Yesterday I had an opportunity to hear the orchestra that I will be conducting. It's absolutely first-rate."

The program included *Symphony No. 1, Zorahayda, Carnival in Paris, Last Year I Was Tending the Goats,* and the *Violin Romance.* On August 18 he wrote to his father:

> The concert was successful in every way. During the four rehearsals the
> remarkably multi-faceted orchestra's performance reached higher and
> higher levels, and on the evening of the performance when I strode into
> the well-filled auditorium it was with the full and happy knowledge that
> everything would go well.

And it did in fact go well:

> There was an animation, a fire and sense of motion in the performance
> that charmed everyone, and as soon as the first part of the symphony had
> been played the audience was already in such a keyed-up mood that the
> success of the entire concert was assured. Two huge laurel wreaths, sev-
> eral demands that pieces be repeated, and God knows how many curtain
> calls. All the press reviews that have come to my attention are extremely
> flattering. Oddly enough, my serenity as a conductor seems to have im-
> pressed them beyond description. One reviewer compares me in this
> respect with the mountain peak that stands firm and immovable while
> the troubled waves—i.e., the orchestra—rage at its feet.

On the trip home he stopped for three days in Leipzig. Vienna had been
beautiful, but it was even better to return to the city in which he had spent
his student days and renew acquaintances with old friends and familiar
places:

> There, where I had lived my happiest and perhaps most productive years,
> I became so strangely moved that I think I almost got tears in my eyes.
> That I visited the new concert hall and the new conservatory goes with-
> out saying. There those clever and intelligent Leipzigers have created two
> splendid and exemplary institutions. I also met some wonderful old
> friends.

He got back to Copenhagen on August 11, and at the beginning of September he received another invitation from abroad, this time from America.
The Chicago Symphony orchestra wanted him for some concerts, but he
found it necessary to decline the flattering offer.

The autumn season at the theater focussed primarily on works from the
standard repertoire, including *Tannhäuser* and *The Valkyrie*. In December,
Meyerbeer's *Dinorah* was offered in Copenhagen for the first time, with
Frederik Rung as conductor. It was not well received, however, and lasted
for only six performances.

On November 23 the Private Chamber Music Society gave a subscription concert in *Koncertpalæet*'s small auditorium. Svendsen, as the Society's
honored guest, was invited to attend the performance of his string quintet,
and thereafter a party at Hotel Phoenix, together with the performers and

the governing board. The president of the Society, Julius Borup, who was also a member of the Royal Theater Orchestra, told Victor Gandrup what happened:

> After they were finished eating and it was time for cognac, whisky, liqueurs etc., Svendsen chose cognac. As president, Borup naturally considered it his duty to keep the Society's renowned member functioning at his best and took it upon himself to prepare the requested drink using all the cunning of a skilled bartender: calibrated jigger, soda water, etc. But when Svendsen saw what he was doing he exclaimed with a gesture of revulsion, "No, damn it. Shame on you! You can drink that yourself. These days I drink only the pure stuff!" Thereupon Svendsen took the cognac bottle, filled Borup's empty whisky glass to the brim, hoisted it with zest and drank it down. Then, smiling, he went around greeting everyone and, absolutely unaffected by the speed and quantity of his drinking, he put the glass down.

During the next hour everyone anxiously anticipated that in one way or another Svendsen would react to the large quantity of cognac he had consumed, "but as the maestro seemed to go on feeling just fine—indeed, he continued to be sociable, steady on his feet and unaffected the rest of the evening—people eventually stopped expecting to see any peculiar reaction in the rugged guest" (42).

On December 14 Svendsen gave a special all-Beethoven benefit concert to raise money for the widow of Balduin Dahl. Dahl (1837–91), conductor at Tivoli, had long championed Svendsen's music, and Svendsen wanted in this way to honor his memory. He wrote to his father on Christmas Eve:

> I assembled an excellent orchestra of almost 100 men. The entire Royal Theater Orchestra cooperated. Everything went very well. There was life and precision in the performance the likes of which I have not heard even in Vienna, Paris, or St. Petersburg. And now this great sound throughout the concert! It was wonderful, and it seemed as if the audience's jubilation would never end. It was also wonderful a couple days later to be able to hand the widow 6,600—six thousand six hundred—crowns that the concert had brought in.

Nonetheless, he was feeling "tired and nervous from all this music-making" and hoped to be able to spend a couple of days during his Christmas holiday at the estate of one of his friends, count Schulin-Zeuthen, from whom he had a standing invitation.

At the beginning of January, 1893, Svendsen received something of a shock when his long-time supporter, music critic Charles Kjerulf, published a long, front-page article in *Politiken* in which he unleashed a stinging attack on him personally (73). In this article, entitled "Music in 1892," Kjerulf expressed disappointment that Svendsen had not fulfilled the expectations that people had held for "his energy, his independence, his capacity for work and his devotion to his calling." At the theater he had bowed his neck under the yoke of the civil authorities:

> It's a crying shame the way Johan Svendsen has acted with the treasure entrusted to him. It is worse than inexcusable in that he has left Danish music life in the lurch. The only thing we can do for him now is to say this right to his face.

Svendsen was understandably furious over this vicious attack. Carl Nielsen touched on this in his diary entry for January 9: "He was very upset by Kjerulf's article in *Politiken* this morning. . . . Svendsen is decent and nice; he has been and is his own worst enemy. He reminded me for a moment of [Carl Nielsen's sculptress wife] Marie's lovely, dying Assyrian lion." Kjerulf continued to be critical of Svendsen from time to time, especially in connection with his programming, but he always spoke positively of his skills as a conductor.

On June 23 Svendsen asked for permission to spend his summer vacation in Norway, and on July 4 permission was granted by the Minister of Culture. It had been six years since he had made a summer visit to his homeland. He wrote to his father on July 5:

> Thanks for the friendly invitation to stay at your place; I accept with joy and gratitude. . . . I get almost "wild" at the thought that I will soon see all the dear people there at home. . . . About the same time that I got your welcome letter I received an offer from [Oslo] Tivoli's board to conduct three concerts, and since the honorarium they were offering was considerable, albeit not huge, I accepted.

The first concert took place July 13 at Christiania Circus in Tivoli Park. Warmuth's concert bureau announced it as "the only Johan Svendsen concert in Oslo," with 52 musicians, including many from the Christiania

Johan Svendsen in 1893 on the
day that his second symphony was
played at the Tivoli concert hall in
Copenhagen. (Universitetsbiblioteket, Oslo)

Theater and Tivoli orchestras. Svendsen had the joy of having his 76-year-
old father, who was still going strong, as a member of the viola section. The
program consisted entirely of his own works including the *Violin Romance*,
with Arve Arvesen as soloist.

The following week he conducted the next concert at the same location. The program included his second symphony and third Norwegian
rhapsody as well as Johan Selmer's *Scène funèbre*. Martin Knutzen appeared as
soloist in Grieg's piano concerto. In an unsigned article in *Morgenbladet* it
was stated that this concert was "even richer and more beautiful than the
first one."

The last concert, on July 27, was advertised via countless handbills as a
"big folk concert in the open air." Following the concert there was to be a
large-scale variety show, which was included in the price of the ticket. The
orchestral program included Beethoven's sixth symphony, overtures by
Weber and Gade, and Grieg's *Elegiac Melodies*. The concluding number was
Svendsen's own *Festival Polonaise*.

The opportunity to spend some time in Oslo this summer with old friends, including his boyhood friend Theodor Løvstad, was very enjoyable for Svendsen. On September 2, after returning to Copenhagen, he sent the following jovial greeting to Løvstad (53): "Senza morendo, sempre crescendo, molto grasati, tempo Sperati."

Svendsen's friend, Judge Theodor Hindenburg, wrote to August Enna on August 16: "Svendsen enjoyed tremendously his concerts in Oslo and has paid off the entire debt that his wife had incurred for him in Norway."

Svendsen's second symphony also scored a success in Copenhagen this summer when it was performed at Tivoli on August 12 by Georg Lumbye (son of H. C. Lumbye), who had succeeded Balduin Dahl as conductor. Robert Henriques wrote in *Dannebrog* that the symphony is "one of the finest works in Nordic music literature."

Just eight days later, however, the same newspaper carried another article by Henriques sharply attacking Svendsen regarding his work as conductor of the Royal Theater Orchestra:

> Never within memory has the opera had a more dismal season. There was an aimlessness in the method of work, an error of judgment in the assigning of parts, a wasting of time, and the outcome can be seen not only in the paucity of positive results but also in the mediocre performance of the few operas they were able to produce. . . . And it is greatly to be desired that the talented man will pull himself together before it is too late. The first condition, if the work is to produce greater results, is that he must come to the rehearsals completely familiar with the scores he is going to conduct, and he must carefully go through the orchestral parts before the first rehearsal.

This sharp attack is, to say the least, somewhat surprising, and one cannot help but ask what might lie behind the use of such strong language. It is true, of course, that at this time the opera was struggling with a chronic lack of qualified singers and that both the public and the critics were unhappy about this. But behind-the-scenes matters of a personal sort seem also to have played a role. Henriques, who for several years had been a regular substitute in the Royal Theater Orchestra, had auditioned in late 1892 for a vacant position in the cello section. He had expected to get the appointment; indeed, according to a newspaper account Svendsen had promised him the position. But he did not win the audition. According to Niels Friis, Henriques's disappointment was so great that he gave up performing altogether and became instead a music critic, "an activity that unfortunately bore the stamp of his bitterness in ways that were not always commendable and that for many years took the form of a kind of aimless persecution of Johan Svendsen" (36:200).

Despite all the criticism, there was no improvement in the opera situation in the autumn season of 1893. Just one new production was launched: Tchaikovsky's *Iolanthe*, which premiered on September 29. In his evaluation of this opera on October 17 of the preceding year, Svendsen had written: "The way in which the renowned Russian composer has handled this text musically seems to me to be so lyrical and distinctive that I confidently believe it will be of interest to produce this work at our theater."

On September 10 *Dannebrog* reported that Svendsen was at work on a new symphony in E major. On October 28 Charles Kjerulf wrote in *Politiken*: "This year the philharmonic concerts will be given without Johan Svendsen, who desires peace and quiet in order to resume composing."

The *Dannebrog* and *Politiken* reports were, however, a misreporting of the facts. In a letter to his father dated March 30, 1894, Svendsen gave a totally different account of the matter: "I have not wanted to get involved with the philharmonic concerts this winter, mainly because I wanted to devote all my strength to my work at the theater." It appears almost as if the attacks in the press had had their effect.

The real reason that Svendsen declined to lead the philharmonic concerts this season, however, was that serious disagreements had developed once again between him and Henrik Hennings, who administered the series. After purely commercial aspects of the undertaking came increasingly into the foreground for Hennings, Svendsen became more and more indignant. Finally, when Hennings made some financial demands on him personally, he pulled out completely.

Thus the philharmonic concerts during the 1893–94 season went on without Svendsen's involvement. Three world-famous artists were engaged as guest conductors: Grieg, Tchaikovsky, and Karl Muck. Grieg conducted the first concert on October 28. The program consisted entirely of his own compositions and it was an enormous success—indeed, even the dress rehearsal was sold out weeks in advance.

Richard Hildebrand later reported in the journal *Musik* (1920, No. 1, p. 4) that in late autumn of 1893 he received a letter from Tchaikovsky telling him that he would soon be visiting Copenhagen. According to Hildebrand, the last letter that Tchaikovsky wrote in his life was to Svendsen. He thanked his Norwegian colleague for the fine success he had achieved with *Iolanthe*, a success that had pleased him all the more because the opera had previously aroused little interest.

It had been planned that Tchaikovsky would conduct a program of his own compositions in January, 1894. Early in November, 1893, however, while still in St. Petersburg, he fell ill and on November 6 he died. "It was with a very strange feeling" that Svendsen opened Tchaikovsky's letter, Hildebrand wrote, for the letter "reached him after the telegram had already brought news of the master's death."

Tchaikovsky's replacement was Polish composer Moritz Moszkowsky, who on January 27, 1894, conducted a program of his own compositions. The concert was not at all successful. The critics were charitable in their evaluation of his conducting but had little or nothing good to say about his music.

Presumably it was Svendsen's connection with Tchaikovsky that led to his receiving an invitation on February 22 to visit Moscow as guest conductor at the conservatory. His next trip to Russia did not take place, however, until two years later.

Since the break with Hennings was irreparable, the idea of resuming collaboration with the musicians of the Royal Theater Orchestra—a collaboration that had been terminated in 1884—once again came to the fore. The two parties opened negotiations with a view to launching public concerts, and the musicians enthusiastically agreed to start the new venture in association with their esteemed conductor. The Wilhelm Hansen music firm was selected to serve as impresario.

The first concrete result of the happy reconciliation was a benefit concert for the orchestra's Widows' Pension Fund. The concert was given with considerable fanfare in *Koncertpalæet* on March 14, 1894. The royal family was in the audience. The concert was billed as a "symphony concert by the Royal Theater orchestra under the direction of Mr. Johan Svendsen" and the orchestra was enlarged for the occasion.

The critics emphasized what a happy occasion it was that the maestro and his musicians were again making music together in the concert hall. Angul Hammerich, writing in *Nationaltidende*, averred that it had been abnormal that for many years the musicians had been giving chamber-music recitals while their conductor had been cooperating with a different orchestra. Finally this state of affairs was at an end. Everything seemed, therefore, to be in place for a still richer music life in Copenhagen.

The program consisted of Brahms's violin concerto with Fredrik Hilmer as soloist, the Prelude to Wagner's *The Mastersingers*, and two recent Danish works: Otto Malling's orchestral suite *Oriental Scenes* and Carl Nielsen's *Symphony No. 1*. While the critics turned thumbs down on Malling's piece, Carl Nielsen's symphony created quite a stir. Svendsen had pulled out all the stops to present his young friend's symphony in all its glory, and the critics were almost unanimous in their praise. The only dissenting voice was Angul Hammerich: "Chief impression: noise, . . . many peculiarities, and no significant motives." Charles Kjerulf's review in *Politiken* was, however, more representative of the general consensus:

> The symphony is a work from which there radiates a bright flash of talent and that seems to hold promise of a forthcoming storm of genius. The harmony and modulation are restless and reckless, yet everything is as remarkably innocent and subliminal as if one were watching a child playing with dynamite. . . . Three times the youthful composer had to come forward from his humble position in the second violin section to stand beside the beaming Johan Svendsen to acknowledge the enthusiastic applause. One experiences a moving moment like that at a concert only once in many years.

When the symphony was published later that year, Svendsen was sent a copy. In his September 30 letter of thanks to the publisher he wrote, "With the performance still fresh in my mind I have now read through this work, and again I felt myself strongly attracted by the fine inventiveness and by the genuine symphonic power that permeates it."

PLEASANTRIES AND UNPLEASANTRIES AT THE ROYAL THEATER

During the spring season of 1894 the Royal Theater presented premieres of two Danish operas: August Enna's *Cleopatra* and Axel Grandjean's *Oluf*. Enna's work was received just as well as his *The Sorceress* had been and was performed 20 times during the years 1894–97. Grandjean's *Oluf*, however, was denounced in no uncertain terms. Charles Kjerulf wrote in *Politiken*: "If one wishes to be very charitable one can certainly say that Mr. Grandjean has talent. But then one must add, like a popular old theater tailor used to do: it's just that his talent isn't good enough."

Svendsen's Wagnerian triumphs led to increasing pressure to present other operas of the great master. It was 22 years since *The Mastersingers* had been staged in Copenhagen, and after Svendsen performed the Prelude at the philharmonic concert on March 14 Kjerulf published the following lament: "That Johan Svendsen, after an evening like *that*, early in the morning on this very day does not immediately go off and start rehearsing *The Mastersingers* in spite of the theater director, sick leaves, chatter and nonsense and humbug . . . it defies understanding." But the opera was not produced in Copenhagen again until three years later.

These ironic comments on conditions at the theater were justified. Svendsen wrote quite candidly about this in a letter to his father dated March 30, 1894. He said he was pleased with the outstanding orchestra, but added:

> The unfortunate fact is that the very thing that should make the opera interesting to the audience, namely the presence of outstanding singers, is seriously lacking. Only a couple of our opera personnel can be said to be capable of somewhat more demanding roles. And all or nearly all of them are very slow to learn their parts.

The situation was further complicated by "the great amount of illness among the personnel, with frequent ensuing sick leaves." During the 1892 season, for example, more than fifty—20%—of the planned performances at the Royal Theater were canceled due to illness! Svendsen was especially annoyed that some of the newspaper people "appear to want to lay the blame for the present deplorable situation on me. For I do have a few enemies here who try to get at me any way they can, and God knows they are not picky in their choice of means."

Svendsen experienced a telling example of such venom during the summer, when Robert Henriques once again launched an attack on him. The July 18 issue of *Dannebrog* carried a long article entitled "The New Opera Leadership," written a couple of weeks after the sudden death of theater director Fallesen. This time Henriques vented his spleen in a manner that made no pretense of civility:

> He never has been the leader of the opera. He just went meekly along with the decisions made by the more principled but less musical theater director. . . . And the result was a product so pitiful, so poor, that nothing like it can be found in the annals of Danish theater history. Had Fallesen remained for just one more season it is likely that public opinion would have insistently demanded Johan Svendsen's dismissal. After all, it never did make sense that a foreigner should occupy the country's most impor-

tant musical position without even coming close to filling it as well as one of our own could have done. It would please us if Mr. Svendsen this time would finally demonstrate that he has the energy and will without which he might just as well without further ado give up his position as musical director of our national opera.

Svendsen had made it a rule never to defend himself publicly against attacks, and he remained silent this time as well. Against the background of Henriques's cruel salvo one can well understand his words on New Year's Eve to his friend Iver Holter, conductor of the Music Society orchestra in Oslo, who had failed in his bid to become conductor of the Christiania Theater Orchestra: "To speak frankly, I am not sorry for you. There is no other position that is so unpleasant, so artistically ruinous and destructive, as that of musical director of a theater orchestra."

But illness was not the only thing that led to cancellations and changes in performance and rehearsal plans. Fallesen's diary entries from autumn 1887 provide some amusing glimpses of some of the trivial personnel problems the theater director had to deal with:

> August 2: Mr. E. Poulsen declares that he cannot play Leander in [Ludvig Holberg's] *Masquerade* because it is too hard for him to go around for a whole evening in shoes and silk stockings. In a role where the excitement gives him some support he might be able to do it, but not in *Masquerade*, where the role is less active. Answered that since he firmly maintained that his health didn't allow him to play the role, he could give it up.

> August 17: Simonsen asks to be released from rehearsal because he is going on a bird hunt. "Fine, if Mr. [Svendsen] has no objection to rescheduling the rehearsal." Simonsen doesn't want to be indebted to that man. "Yes, it is necessary for you to make your request to your superior." "I won't do it, I'll just miss the rehearsal without permission." "You'll be sorry if you do." "Well, then I'll go to the rehearsal and tell the king that you have refused to let me go to the hunt." "Fine. Do that." He went away angry. But an hour later he asked [Svendsen] to reschedule the rehearsal. It happened.

> August 19: Miss Regina Nielsen expressed thanks for the engagement. Gave her a little course on "contacts on the stage."

> August 24: Miss [Emma] Lange can't wear the blue velvet "child's outfit" she's supposed to wear in [the play] *Nuances*. It makes her feel improper. She wants to have a red bodice. "It has to remain the way it was de-

cided." The color was chosen in relation to the other costumes. If the costume designer says that the "bodice" is not appropriate then she'll have another, but he probably won't. The theater won't give anyone a costume that is not appropriate in every respect. She starts to cry. I ask what is the problem. She mumbles something and finally leaves.

August 26: Miss [Emanuela] Schrøder asks for a top salary since she hasn't received a bonus. "You can't expect one every year. You get a salary of 2,000 crowns, and I think that's what it should be. I don't think you are entitled to a top salary." But she was older than Miss [Elisabeth] Dons, and *she* has top salary. "Yes, Miss Dons can carry an entire opera— and you can't."

September 13: Mr. [Peter] Schram finds it deplorable that he is going to be fined because he didn't come to rehearsal yesterday. He swore "by God in heaven above" that he is living at Bellevue [six miles from Copenhagen] for the sake of his health. It's shameful that theater secretary Jensen didn't telephone him—he should be fined and not Schram. "Let's be reasonable. You are to live inside city limits, not at Bellevue. You have to pay the fine; we'll make it as small as possible. Then will you play the doctor's tiny little role in *La Traviata*?" Yes, if he can either sing one of the lower parts in the ensembles or have someone else sing them." "Fine, I'll see to it; so, then, that matter is settled." (85/V: 84–88)

Fallesen was a superb administrator with a singular ability to tackle all kinds of difficulties. Svendsen, on the other hand, found the bureaucratic treadmill stifling. The archives of the Royal Theater record numerous examples of how even the smallest matters had to be sent up the chain of command all the way to the "Minister of Culture." As leader of Danish music life, Svendsen had to formally request permission on behalf of the opera singers any time it was desired that they should participate in orchestra concerts. We also note as a curiosity that in 1884, in response to a request, Svendsen was informed that "The Ministry will not object if once or twice a week Svendsen is given a free ticket to the box seats for use by his wife."

Like Fallesen, Svendsen was swamped by performers requesting to be excused from rehearsals, but he usually gave them the cold shoulder. Victor Gandrup has reported some typical episodes (41):

Trombonist Adolph Levin knew that Svendsen couldn't stand to be detained on his way to and from the podium. Nonetheless, one time he ventured to stop him as he walked by at the end of an act.

"Dear maestro!" Levin began. "Surely you won't get angry, but I should like very much to have the day after tomorrow off."

"Is it a matter of life and death?" Svendsen asked sternly.

"Uh, no, but . . ." said Levin hesitantly.

Svendsen cut him off: "No. Well, I won't get angry at all—but you can't have the day off!" And with that he walked away. But the theater director got him to calm down and arranged for Levin—despite his blunder—to get the day off.

Svendsen got along much better with another trombonist, Carl Christensen. It was common knowledge, according to Gandrup, that Christensen never turned down a drink even in the middle of the forenoon. Svendsen, who in his later years was also not averse to a glass or two in the morning to slake his thirst, bumped into Christensen one day before a rehearsal and said jovially:

"Well, good morning my dear Mr. Christensen! Say, right now a cognac sure would be good for the human body!"

"But maestro," the trombonist answered with obvious embarrassment, "I think it's, well, a little too early in the day."

"God damn it!" Svendsen shouted, "can something that is good for the human body be too early in the day?"

Christensen was completely disarmed. They parted, and with the same goal in mind went their separate ways.

The frequent requests for days off were a constant source of concern, but on one occasion Svendsen untied the Gordian knot in an elegant way. Violinist Vilhelm Bartholdy and cellist Emil Bruun had been invited to join a female pianist for several concert engagements in Jutland. Unfortunately, a new opera was to be launched at the Royal Theater just at the time they were proposing to be gone, and "the anxious musical director, with the premiere staring him in the face, was understandably enough not amenable to such requests." In a final attempt to get Svendsen to change his mind, Bartholdy assured the maestro that the two substitutes they had identified were much better artists than they were. "But my dear Mr. Bartholdy!" a relieved Svendsen replied, "in that case I recommend that you send those two so much better artists on tour and you and Mr. Bruun stay here!" And that was the end of the matter.

FROM MOSCOW TO OSLO

In June of 1894 Svendsen's creative juices flowed once again, this time in the form of an orchestral work, *Andante funèbre*. The occasion for the work was a sad one. Two of Svendsen's friends, Judge Theodor Hindenburg and his Norwegian-born wife Anna Margrethe, had lost their only child, Georg. The 23-year-old young man had died of tuberculosis on June 15 during a visit to Lofthus, Norway. Georg had been a musically gifted man for whom Svendsen had held great expectations, and his death affected him deeply. At the urging of his friends, he wrote *Andante funèbre* for the funeral in Our Lady Church in Copenhagen on June 30. The piece made a deep impression on those who heard it and was published by the Wilhelm Hansen firm later that year. It has since been often used in Denmark on ceremonial occasions.

There are some parallels between Svendsen's composition and Grieg's *Funeral March for Rikard Nordraak*. Both were written in memory of a 23-year-old musical talent. The structure is also similar, with somber sections in A minor flanking a brighter section in A major. Svendsen's piece, with a performance time of eight and a half minutes, is slightly longer than Grieg's. The music is sincere and distinctive and demonstrates that Svendsen still had something to give as a composer. After *Andante funèbre*, however, he was to compose only one more piece of music.

Svendsen went to Norway again in the summer of 1894. This time, however, he went first to western Norway, where he had never been before. He traveled by boat from Copenhagen and on July 31 wrote to his father from Stavanger: "I am enroute to Bergen primarily to visit Grieg, whom I have been promising to visit for ten years, but also to see a bit of this part of the country."

After a brief but festive visit to Troldhaugen he went by way of Lofthus, Voss, Stalheim, Lærdal and Valdres to Oslo, where he had planned to visit his father. But he fell ill in Oslo and decided to hurry home to Copenhagen "to continue in peace and quiet the cure begun in Christiania [Oslo]. . . . My diet consists essentially of milk, bread, a green tonic, quinine and pills," he wrote to his sister on August 10. A little later he received some better-tasting food from Norway: a piece of goat cheese and a jar of cloudberries sent to him by his father on the occasion of his 54th birthday. In a letter of congratulation dated September 29—one of the few extant letters in his father's hand—the elder Svendsen wrote that he had just had a visit from Judge Hindenburg, who had informed him of Johan's latest controversies in Copenhagen: "He told me who are your 'biggest *supporters*' down there— Hennings, Lange-Müller and others—and he has written a long letter to *Morgenbladet* that tells something about Henning's conduct down there and a refutation of the stuff these gentlemen have chosen to write about you."

In August 1894 an authoritative new appointee, Count Chr. C. S. Danneskjold-Samsøe, took the helm as theater director at the Royal Theater. The offerings during the autumn season, however, consisted mainly of old war-horses that sauntered along at a leisurely pace. The main attraction of the season was supposed to have been *Falstaff*, Verdi's last opera, but the premiere had to be postponed. In an October 20 letter to Iver Holter, Svendsen wrote that he had been forced to cancel rehearsals due to the illness of several of the singers, "which will of course be cited as further proof of [my] incompetence and idleness."

The benefit concert in the spring of 1894 that led to a resumption of philharmonic concerts by the Royal Theater Orchestra under Svendsen's leadership has already been mentioned. The resumption of "symphony concerts by Johan Svendsen and the Royal Theater orchestra" was announced that autumn, and the series continued to play an important role in the music life of the city until 1908. The musicians themselves undertook the administration of the series in collaboration with the Wilhelm Hansen music publishing firm. Two concerts were given each year during the period 1894–99 (except for 1897, when there was only one.) Thereafter the number was increased to three or four concerts per year.

The first such concert took place on November 21, 1894. The program included Beethoven's fifth symphony and Chopin's second piano concerto, with Fanny Bloomfield Zeisler as soloist. Launching the new series of concerts with such thoroughly standard fare provided fuel for the fire of reviewers who were prone to be critical of Svendsen in any case: the maestro, they said, seems to be abdicating his role as a champion of exciting new music. But Svendsen was clear about what he planned to do. On New Year's Eve he wrote to Iver Holter that he had spent his Christmas holiday studying several new Russian orchestral scores. The most important morsel was undoubtedly Tchaikovsky's last work, the *Pathètique* symphony, which he planned to perform as soon as he could find an opportunity.

A New Year's Day letter to his sister, Albertine, provides a glimpse of his family life at this time. He had spent Christmas Eve with Juliette, and their son Johan Jr. had been "in seventh heaven." The proud daddy reported that the four-year-old boy, who had just started nursery school, "seems to be especially gifted in certain directions, has an almost unbelievable perceptive ability, a superb memory for music and verse, and physically he is a real champion." He also wrote: "Yesterday I had dinner at Grieg's and it was enjoyable beyond description. It's great to be with him and his wife, amiable and interesting as they are."

The next orchestra concert, given on February 16, 1895, was also not especially exciting. The Tchaikovsky symphony was for some reason or other not performed. The program was devoted to works by Gluck, Mozart, Schubert and Schumann with Niels Juel Simonsen, the opera company's best-known singer, as soloist.

The 1895 spring season at the Royal Theater finally brought an important new offering, not from Russia but from Italy. On January 16, Verdi's *Falstaff* finally received its Danish—indeed, its Scandinavian—premiere. On May 3, *verismo*—the new, naturalistic direction in musical drama which Svendsen had introduced in Copenhagen with Mascagni's *Cavalleria rusticana* in 1891—once again was the order of the day when the theater premiered *Bajazzo*, the sensational new opera by Ruggiero Leoncavallo. Svendsen had recommended the opera in a written evaluation two years earlier:

> This music reminds one in every way of the music in *Cavalleria rusticana*.
> Here as there the same sharply delineated passion, the almost reckless
> drive of the dramatic action, but also the lack of finesse in musical inven-
> tiveness that seems to be characteristic of the operatic art of the young
> Italians.

In autumn of 1894 Bjørnstjerne Bjørnson had been commissioned by the University of Oslo to write a text for a large work that was to be used at the annual festivities in September marking the beginning of the new academic year. The result was the cantata *The Light*. Svendsen received the manuscript at the beginning of March, 1895, and on April 3 he sent a letter of thanks to Bjørnson:

> At Christmas time, when Johan Halvorsen brought me your greeting and
> told me that you intended to entrust to me the composition of the music
> for your cantata, I was too happy for words. I had long cherished the
> deep wish to be able one day to work with you, and with this expression
> of confidence by you that wish is now fulfilled. For that I say: many,
> many thanks!. . . . Your poem, the content of which is so grand and

all-inclusive and which is carried forward in noble, sonorous rhythms, creates a marvelous task for the composer and no one would be happier than I if I were to succeed in doing it. But I must have time—a lot of time—to consult my inner self, to see to what extent my imagination is able to follow you, to find motives, to organize and form these in such a way that the music can at least to some extent measure up to your sublime poetry.

Svendsen made it clear that he had time for composition only during his summer vacation. In the coming months he would be fully occupied at the theater and would also be rehearsing a comprehensive program for a big song festival to be held in Odense at the end of June. "If the cantata *must* be finished in a short time, it's doubtful that I could accomplish it."

Dannebrog reported on May 23 that at the end of the season Svendsen would be going to Tyrol to meet Bjørnson and work with him on the cantata. As it turned out, however, the time available was not sufficient, for Bjørnson had planned to have it performed at the university's next annual matriculation ceremony on September 2, 1895. Svendsen, therefore, felt obliged to decline the assignment, and the trip to Tyrol was called off. Christian Sinding was then approached, but he also was unable to accept the task. *The Light* was finally set by Otto Winter-Hjelm in 1897.

Bjørnson's text nonetheless continued to haunt Svendsen for several years to come. On September 4, 1900, after Bjørnson had requested that Svendsen return the manuscript, the composer wrote: "I do so unwillingly, because the advice and suggestions you have written in at various points would be very important for me when I finally get seriously to work on the composition."

Instead of going south for the summer, then, Svendsen conducted the song festival in Odense. The program, performed by a chorus of 700 singers and a 70-piece orchestra, included J. P. E. Hartmann's *Vølvens Spaadom* (*The Priestess's Prophecy*). A few weeks later he went to Norway to take part in the funeral of his friend, Carl Warmuth, who died on July 19. With the passing of Warmuth he lost one of his strongest supporters in his homeland.

The autumn season at the opera house was hectic but contained no new productions. On September 24 Svendsen shared some of the sorrows and joys of his life with his sister, Albertine:

Each day goes by with the monotonous, enervating toil that drains the joy and interest from everything in the world. I dread the coming winter.

> Fortunately I see one bright spot: I hope to take a concert tour to Moscow, presumably in February, and that will be refreshing. I really need to get away and breathe some fresh air. My little boy is healthy and strong as a bear, but terribly naughty. The women there at home spoil him terribly, and I am very concerned about how this situation can be rectified.

There was just one orchestra concert this autumn; the date was November 30, 1895. It was at this concert that the people of Copenhagen got to hear Tchaikovsky's *Pathètique* symphony for the first time. The program also included Liszt's second piano concerto, with Ferruccio Busoni—one of the big names in the music world at that time—as soloist. In the concert Busoni also played pieces by Chopin and Liszt as well as his own grandiose arrangement of one of Bach's organ works, the *Prelude and Fugue in D Major*. A week later Svendsen wrote to Grieg: "The symphony went excellently and seemed to make a deep impression on the listeners, and Busoni played like a god." He continued in a somewhat ironic tone: "Here everything is as of old. Theater gossip and colossal newspaper controversies about trifles, now as usual, occupy a prominent place in the official consciousness of the Athens of the North."

Grieg, who at this time was staying in Leipzig, had recommended to his friend that he come down for a couple of days to hear Arthur Nikisch perform Svendsen's second symphony and Grieg's *Peer Gynt Suite No. 1* at the Gewandhaus concert on December 19. The aged Carl Reinecke had been asked to step down after 36 years at the helm of the Gewandhaus Orchestra, and 40-year-old Arthur Nikisch had succeeded him. Grieg had tried unsuccessfully to get Svendsen appointed to this important position.

To Grieg's dismay, Nikisch had a serious attack of pneumonia just before the concert and was not able to perform. Grieg wrote to Frants Beyer on December 17:

> Just think what a dirty trick this is for me—yes, I dare say, for Norway.... And under Nikisch's baton I know this would have been a triumph for Norway. He electrifies. (He told me recently that with the *Peer Gynt Suite* he had "conquered America").... Hans Sitt, a competent musician but lacking in genius, will substitute.

In a December 20 letter to Svendsen, who was not able to go to Leipzig, Grieg reported what had happened. "Thank your lucky stars that let you stay where you are," he wrote. "Sitt is a fine technician, but where he ends is the very place where Nikisch begins. Sitt has an incredible ability to lower the level, to make even the greatest into the ordinary."

One evening before the concert Sitt had showed up at Grieg's favorite cafe with the scores for the *Peer Gynt Suite* and Svendsen's second symphony. They had paged through the symphony together and Grieg had indicated the correct tempos. Grieg wrote:

> In the middle of the *scherzo*, where you so beautifully let the motive sing out in augmentation, he said, "But I would take that significantly faster and then *ritardando* before the entrance of the main theme." I said, "For God's sake, it is just the opposite: the composer intends that this passage should be rather tranquil." He didn't like this, but fortunately he gave up his plan, so the movement was rescued to some extent.

In mid-February Svendsen went to Moscow to appear as guest conductor at concerts on February 20, 24 and 28. The venue was the city's largest concert hall, the Noblemen's Club, which could accommodate several thousand people. The programs included, in addition to his own works, Beethoven's sixth symphony, Wagner's *Tannhäuser Overture*, Saint-Saëns's piano concerto in C major and Tchaikovsky's *Andante cantabile*. In a May 1 letter to his sister, Svendsen wrote that his visit to Moscow had been successful in every way:

> The concerts, which were attended by an audience that was as large as it was attentive, were, with the help of a well-manned and excellent orchestra, enormously successful and won me many new friends. With respect to the Russian hospitality I can report that *every single day* I was invited to something or other, usually a big party given in my honor. When I finally was sitting in the compartment to go home again I was almost dazed from all this merry-making.

Svendsen was in poor health in the spring of 1896; he was on sick leave from the theater for the entire month of May due to influenza and associated complications. He hoped to regain his health in Norway during the summer, and he was given two extra weeks of vacation so that he might spend some time in rest and relaxation at the Holmenkollen sanatorium. Grieg commented on Svendsen's illness in a letter to Bjørnson dated July 15:

> If you haven't heard from Svendsen, the reason presumably is that he is not up to writing. I was told recently that he has been very close to dy-

ing, is extremely worn out and is trying to regain his health at Holmenkollen. He is by nature strong as a horse. Otherwise he would have collapsed long ago with that dissolute life-style of his. I weep inwardly when
I think of what he is and what he should have been with his beautiful
talent—one of the greatest of our time. One can say about the Norwegian national character what Peer Gynt says about God: "He may be a
fine enough fellow, but he's no economist!" It's terrible what Norway
loses because so many of its best people treat themselves like berserkers. It
is that which is uncontrollable that misses the mark.

The autumn season of 1896 reflected to some extent the fact that Svendsen
was not well. The Danish premiere of Gluck's *Orpheus and Euridice* on September 30 had to be conducted by Frederik Rung. On December 27, however, Svendsen was able to conduct the premiere of *Ragnhild*, a new Danish
opera by Emil Hartmann. The remainder of the repertoire during this autumn season consisted of such standard works as *Carmen*, *Faust*, and *The
Magic Flute*.

It seems strange today to note that as recently as 1896 oil lamps were still
being used for lighting in the orchestra pit at the Royal Theater. Only in
that year did they install electric lighting, and even then it was not primarily
to help the orchestra but to save money: electricity provided cheaper lighting. The reform, which according to the orchestra's account ledger cost 963
crowns, was welcomed by both conductor and musicians.

In September there was again some public speculation in the press about
why Svendsen had been so unproductive as a composer since coming to
Copenhagen. Niels Friis mentions in his book about the Royal Theater Orchestra (36:212) that it was Robert Henriques who initiated the discussion.
On September 11 an article defending Svendsen appeared in *Berlingske
Tidende*. The author, music critic H. V. Schytte, pointed out that composing was not an explicit duty of the musical director of the theater orchestra
and, moreover, that it was desirable that Svendsen, "after he has just gone
through a serious illness this past summer—an illness from which he has not
yet fully recovered—should be spared criticisms of this kind."

Whether it was to answer such criticisms or not is impossible to say, but
the program for Svendsen's concert on November 21 included not only
Symphony No. 1, Carnival in Paris, and *Sigurd Slembe*, but also two works that
were unknown to the audience: orchestral arrangements by Svendsen of
Andante funèbre and of Edmund Neupert's large piano composition, *Before
the Battle*. Charles Kjerulf, writing in *Politiken*, was full of praise:

There was above all a festive mood over the orchestra's playing and over the audience as in the early days of the philharmonic concerts. On such an evening the maestro is irresistible. One forgets his big and small opera sins through the years, forgets that he so deplorably early has abandoned creative work. One surrenders unconditionally.

Svendsen took another trip to Oslo in November. Iver Holter, artistic director of the Music Society, had invited him the previous September to guest conduct his old orchestra, but for a time it was doubtful that he would be able to make the trip. Svendsen wrote to Holter on October 11:

> Professor Peter Hansen [theater director] has misgivings about giving me
> [a leave] *now*—or, more correctly, about recommending the requested
> leave for the approval of the Minister of Culture. Hansen thinks it won't
> look good if I again leave my post after having had a long travel leave
> (Moscow) the previous season, in addition was sick the whole month of
> May, and lastly got my vacation extended by two whole weeks in order to
> be at Holmenkollen.

It all worked out, however. On November 13 he wrote to Holter that he had just "received the long-awaited ministerial permission to take the trip, unfortunately for only six days." On the other hand, he was obliged at this time to decline invitations to conduct concerts of his own works in Vienna, Budapest and London.

The Oslo concert, which took place on November 28, was part of a celebration marking the silver anniversary of the founding of the Music Association. Iver Holter conducted two new Norwegian cantatas, one by Sinding and the other by himself. Svendsen conducted *Last Year I Was Tending the Goats* and the first symphony. *Morgenbladet* wrote that Svendsen's conducting was "so brilliant that breathing a quiet sigh of resignation one could only regret that our best talents have to go into exile."

The main opera event of the spring season in Copenhagen was a new production of Wagner's *The Mastersingers*, which had not been performed in Denmark for 25 years. Svendsen had begun making plans to perform the work as early as 1885, and had even scheduled some rehearsals of the piece at that time, but the first public performance did not take place until January 27, 1897.

The event was celebrated with a gala party at the *Skydebane* (*Shooting Gallery*) restaurant. According to Victor Gandrup (41), who got his information from Svendsen's doctor friend Albert Øigaard, the party featured "unceasing clinking of glasses filled with Bacchus's joy-giving power":

> In the wee hours, when spirits were at their highest and reason had largely been thrown overboard, the singer Niels Juel Simonsen (Hans Sachs) suggested that Chr. Zangenberg (an actor, one of the master-singers), Svendsen and he be the principal actors in a "very over-exposed, physically demanding party game." The idea was that each in turn should empty the restaurant's famous "Figaro" cup, which held three liters of beer, without pausing for breath! Simonsen managed it without difficulty, as did Svendsen. But when it was Zangenberg's turn, after he had consumed a large portion of the beer he suddenly collapsed, appeared to lose consciousness, and slipped under the table. Alarmed, Simonsen asked: "Do you think this is the fault of the Mastersingers?" "No," Svendsen replied, "I just think there's something wrong with Zangenberg's master-kidneys."

The story illustrates Svendsen's wit and, in particular, his skill in repartee, which was legendary.

The Mastersingers was an ambitious undertaking for the theater. No guest singers were brought in for the production, and according to Charles Kjerulf writing in *Politiken* the shortage of typical Wagnerian singers was quite noticeable. Kjerulf's over-all verdict on the premiere was: "not good in every way, but neither was it totally bad." What especially elevated the performance was that "the orchestra and the conductor led the way with splendid enthusiasm and interest."

A symphony concert by the orchestra just five days after the premiere of *The Mastersingers* was devoted entirely to works by Wagner: the overture to *Faust, Karfreitagszauber* from *Parsifal, The Ride of the Valkyrie* from *The Valkyrie,* the *Funeral March* and the concluding scene from *Twilight of the Gods,* and the *Vorspiel und Liebestod* from *Tristan and Isolde.* The soloist was Ellen Nordgren Gulbranson. Kjerulf's review in *Politiken* was effusive: "With a sure hand, inspiring his musicians at every point, the maestro created a series of Wagnerian renderings that left nothing to be desired. There was rhythmic precision, excellence of sound, delicacy and exhilaration in every single piece."

However, he could not resist the opportunity to gently prod the theater leadership:

> If one might dare to hope that our opera company knows how to strike while the iron is hot, then surely they are already planning a production of *Tristan and Isolde*. But one hardly needs to over-exert one's imagination in this matter. After all, they are doing *The Mastersingers*. Obviously they're going to rest on their laurels.

Kjerulf's prediction proved to be correct: Svendsen never did have an opportunity to conduct *Tristan*, which had its Denmark premiere in 1914 under the baton of Georg Høeberg.

In February of 1897 there were performances of Svendsen's music in both Paris and Leipzig. The Paris concert featured a performance of his second symphony and on February 25 Arthur Nikisch and the Gewandhaus orchestra performed *Zorahayda*. So far as is known, however, the performance in 1897 marks the last time that the venerable Gewandhaus orchestra has played a work by Svendsen.

MUSIC FESTIVALS IN STOCKHOLM AND BERGEN

Following the lead of the Danes nine years earlier, in 1897 the Swedes advanced the idea of a pan-Scandinavian music festival, this one to be held in Stockholm. National committees were formed to plan the programs, with the Norwegian committee being headed by Iver Holter. Svendsen, who was not kept well informed about the plans, became irritated about the possibility that he might be represented by only one short orchestral work. He wrote to Johan Selmer on May 14 that his feeling of being excluded from the planning was further strengthened when "the Danish committee also saw to it that I had nothing to do with how Denmark is to be represented on this occasion." He continued: "Tired and worn out after almost ten months of conducting, it won't be any wonder if I stay away and ask either Holter or Nordquist to conduct anything of mine that might end up on the program."

Svendsen did go to Stockholm, however, despite the fact that he was not entirely healthy. He was invited as a guest along with J. P. E. Hartmann, Emil Hartmann, Chr. F. E. Horneman, Frederik Rung, Chr. Barnekow and others.

There were six concerts in all: three big concerts by a 130-piece orchestra (including 92 strings), all in The Music Hall, and three chamber-music concerts given in the Royal Music Academy. At the second orchestral concert (June 8) Svendsen conducted *La Captive* by Johan Selmer, and at the concluding concert (June 10) he conducted his own *Symphony No. 1.* *Svensk Musiktidning* wrote that the symphony "from beginning to end enthralled the listeners by its vivacity, melodic beauty and brilliant orchestration. The composer was applauded enthusiastically." His string quintet, however, which was performed by a Danish ensemble on June 9, was somewhat overshadowed by Grieg's string quartet in G minor.

On August 9 he wrote to both his father and his sister about the Stockholm trip. He had been seriously ill with malaria at the time and had been obliged to stay in bed every other day. Nonetheless, he had had a wonderful time as a "guest of the most amiable people in the world." At one of the grand banquets at the royal palace he had talked with King Oscar II, who had made him a Commander of the Vasa order, an honor that "has caused the cheeks of many to turn pale with envy."

The malaria attack was unfortunately to have disastrous consequences for Svendsen's life and career. There is written evidence that his physician at that time prescribed "liberal use of cognac" to combat the disease. Thus a man who had long demonstrated a weakness for alcohol received added encouragement to indulge his weakness—with the result that, according to a medical record from the Finsen Institute in Copenhagen, in 1908 he was diagnosed as suffering from "chronic alcoholism."

Svendsen had hoped to take a trip to Norway again in the summer of 1897 but was not able to do so because of pressing duties that required his attention. He also had provisionally accepted an invitation to guest conduct at two concerts in Brussels in February-March, but the trip did not materialize.

In July of 1897 a committee that had been established four years earlier to study conditions at the Royal Theater delivered its report. One important question considered by the committee was whether the opera company and the orchestra should be separated from the Royal Theater. The committee completely rejected this proposal and underscored the role of the Royal Theater, not only as a fixed center for the music life of the city but also as a source of inspiration for the rest of the country.

Svendsen gave no philharmonic concerts in autumn of 1897. At the theater he was especially busy with rehearsals for a new production of Mozart's *The Abduction from the Seraglio* and for the premiere of *Vifandaka*, a new Danish opera by his young pupil, Alfred Tofft. The latter work, which was based on an Indian legend, premiered on January 1, 1898. Two years earlier Svendsen had written the following evaluation of it: "The composer has succeeded in giving his music the unique coloration required by his

Johan Svendsen toward the end of the 1890s. (Det kgl. Bibliotek, Copenhagen)

foreign/Indian libretto; the purely lyrical sections are for the most part characterized by warmth and soaring imagination." The opera was well received
and was performed 25 times.

In spring of 1898 Svendsen received a flattering inquiry from the
United States. The famous Austrian conductor Anton Seidl, musical director of both the Metropolitan Opera and the New York Philharmonic Orchestra, had died suddenly at age forty-seven on March 28. He had made an
outstanding contribution at these institutions, and a search was quickly
launched for a successor of similar caliber. Svendsen was immediately mentioned as the most promising candidate. On April 2 the Danish-born music
agent L. M. Ruben of New York wrote to him. Seidl's place, he said, could
be filled only by "one of the few world-class conductors, and I think that if
you have any interest in changing your surroundings—and satisfactory and
advantageous arrangements could be made—the time is now upon us when
it would be possible to meet your requirements." He asked Svendsen to tell
him without delay on what conditions he would consider engagements in
New York.

On April 12 Ruben sent a follow-up letter requesting an answer by telegram. He mentioned that the New York press had already broken the news that discussions were under way with Svendsen as a possible successor to Seidl.

Ruben had a solid position in American music life. He was, among other things, a close friend of Maurice Grau, manager of the Metropolitan Opera, who had made the Met into the leading opera house in the world. Thus he spoke with some authority when he told Svendsen of the high salary and generous honoraria he might expect in New York. He had earlier had direct contact with Svendsen, both personally in Copenhagen and by mail, regarding guest appearances in the United States. Svendsen, however, had always made it a condition that he must be engaged for a period of at least two or three years.

As before, Ruben could once again guarantee engagements for only one year, but he claimed that there were good prospects for an extension of from five to ten years. Seidl had held the position at the Met for thirteen years and at the New York Philharmonic for six. The possibility of taking over these positions, the highest in the music world, was very tempting, but Svendsen felt he had to turn it down. He did not dare to risk his secure position in Copenhagen for an uncertain future in a foreign environment, no matter how attractive the financial arrangements might be. His tangled family situation and declining health probably also played an important role in the decision.

On March 13 the Royal Theater premiered *Vølund Smed* (*Vølund the Blacksmith*), a play by Danish playwright Holger Drachmann with incidental music by Svendsen's pupil Fini Henriques. Svendsen had no obligation to conduct music for plays, but he specifically requested the opportunity to conduct his pupil's composition. The production played 19 performances over a period of three months.

On April 20 Svendsen conducted the Danish premiere of Verdi's *Otello*. Three years earlier Svendsen had introduced Copenhagen operagoers to Verdi's last opera, *Falstaff*, and the excitement attending the forthcoming staging of *Otello* was considerable. Strangely enough, when it finally appeared it aroused little interest and was performed only five times.

Theater problems had long been a favorite theme in the local press. On February 26, 1898, *Berlingske Tidende* presented some statistics on opera performances during Svendsen's tenure at the Royal Theater, concluding that the Norwegian maestro had made a relatively good contribution to Danish musical drama. Four days later, however, William Behrend published a strong attack on Svendsen in *Politiken*. He chided him for having had too few new operas in the repertoire and complained that even those that had been presented had not been good enough!

On July 18 a writer who signed his/her name "L. R." published an almost four-column article in *Berlingske Tidende* comparing the opera repertoires under Paulli and Svendsen. The writer pointed out that Svendsen had performed much more new music than Paulli had and asserted that claims that the work at the Royal Theater was not satisfactory were completely untenable. The debate in the press continued to rage, however, with articles both for and against the opera leadership appearing from time to time.

After both the Danes and the Swedes had hosted Scandinavian music festivals, the Norwegians decided that it was time for them to arrange for a similar event in Norway. Bergen was chosen as the site for the event, and it was decided that it should be held in connection with a fishing and industrial exposition during the period June 26–July 3, 1898. The Danish and Swedish festivals had presented music from all three Scandinavian countries, but this time the decision was to focus exclusively on contemporary Norwegian music. One should not, in this connection, charge Grieg, who was the prime mover behind the festival, with narrow-minded chauvinism. It simply was his opinion that the Bergen festival provided a golden opportunity for people to hear for once the best music Norway had to offer and to hear it performed as well as was humanly possible. His goal, he wrote in *Aftenposten* on April 18, 1898, was "to perform Norwegian music as excellently as can possibly be achieved. These compositions will then be better understood and will enter more deeply into the hearts of the people. Whether this goal requires Norwegians, Germans, Japanese, or Dutchmen makes no difference to me."

Grieg's idea had been to bring in the Concertgebouw Orchestra of Amsterdam as the festival's main attraction. At the end of January, however, according to a letter from Grieg to Svendsen dated February 8, the arrangements committee had gone behind his back and, contrary to their agreement and without his knowledge, had engaged the Music Society Orchestra of Oslo instead. Grieg was furious and withdrew from the committee in protest. "Thereupon," he wrote, "the committee was dissolved and the festival idea was abandoned." The very next day, however, he received a telegram informing him that a new committee had been formed and that this committee agreed with the proposal to invite the Dutch orchestra. "What's happening is unbelievable: the Hollanders are coming, and not only that, but it was arranged with the greatest ease that in support of the cause they will make the trip virtually without compensation."

Now that he could offer Svendsen a first-rate orchestra, he invited him confidently: "Just do one thing for me. *Give me a definite answer.* . . . It will be one of the greatest joys of my life to hear your marvelous music performed up here with an orchestra like that playing under your baton."

Svendsen was enthusiastic and replied on June 10 that he was looking forward enormously to the event. Noting, however, that he had to buy a number of things and was, therefore, badly in need of money, he requested an advance of five hundred crowns. He also stipulated that the "absolutely necessary explanations" regarding the programmatic content of *Zorahayda* were to be printed without alteration in the concert program.

Grieg had also privately invited three other friends from Copenhagen: music publisher Alfred Wilhelm Hansen and two young composers, Alfred Tofft and Hakon Børresen. Both of the latter were also pupils of Svendsen. Tofft, in an article published in *Berlingske Aftenavis* several years later (115), gave a vivid account of the Norway visit:

> Poor old Svendsen was ill when he left Copenhagen, but our good humor had an effect on him and we literally *laughed* him into shape. He himself said as much, and judging from his liveliness and perseverance during the strenuous but splendid music festival, he appeared, at least, to be feeling fine, and during the rest of his time in Norway he didn't give his illness another thought.

Svendsen conducted the Concertgebouw Orchestra, whose regular conductor was twenty-six-year-old Willem Mengelberg, in performances of his own compositions on no less than six occasions. At the opening concert on June 26, which was repeated on June 27, he conducted *Norwegian Rhapsody No. 3*. On June 29 and 30 he conducted *Zorahayda* and *Last Year I Was Tending the Goats* and his arrangement for strings of Ole Bull's *The Shepherd Girl's Sunday*. And at the two last concerts on July 1 and 2 he led sparkling performances of his first symphony. Johan Halvorsen appeared as soloist in the *Violin Romance* at the last two concerts.

According to Alfred Tofft in a July 6 article in *Berlingske Tidende*, at the end of the concluding concert Svendsen invited the audience to join him in applauding Grieg: "We Norwegians can produce good music, but especially when a man like our friend Grieg leads the way. Let's hear a 'hurrah' for him—a 'hurrah' such as has never been heard in Norway before!"

Grieg then presented Svendsen with a laurel wreath, and a group of Norwegian students placed a tasseled cap on his head.

Svendsen had planned to wear his honorary medals during the festival, but since Grieg didn't want to wear his—and when Svendsen learned that his friend had received neither the Dannebrog nor Vasa crosses—he dropped the idea. "He was very pleased," it was reported in the Danish press, "that in that way the festival acquired a more democratic character."

Bergen had pulled out all the stops to honor its foreign visitors, especially the members of the Concertgebouw Orchestra, and invited them to several excursions and banquets. According to Victor Gandrup, on one occasion Svendsen toasted Willem Mengelberg so persistently that the poor fellow almost passed out. One day at an orchestra rehearsal Svendsen also took young Mengelberg to school in a delightful way. Grieg related this priceless story in a letter to his Dutch friend Julius Röntgen dated July 10, 1898:

> Personally I found Mengelberg very amiable. I was not at all unwilling to receive practical advice on orchestral matters. But when he—very cautiously, to be sure—wanted to give Svendsen some instruction about how to conduct one thing or another in his own works—Svendsen, who is a hundred times better conductor than Mengelberg—then we got a truly delightful experience. Svendsen gave him a short glance and said something like, "I must say, you have a nice jacket!"

In a July 2 letter to his father, Svendsen reported that the week-long festival had been a great success, with an excellent orchestra and unprecedented attendance. "But now I am tired and looking forward to a couple days of rest with Grieg at his villa Troldhaugen."

The visit to Troldhaugen turned out to be less restful than Svendsen had anticipated, though, for Grieg had other plans. He insisted that his guests from Copenhagen couldn't visit Norway without taking a trip to the mountains. It was decided, therefore, that the three Danes plus Grieg, Svendsen, and Thorvald Lammers would climb Løvstakken, one of the seven mountains surrounding Bergen.

They had sunny weather for the outing, according to Tofft (115), and the climbers' spirits soared: "Everyone was making jovial comments. 'O, God, what a day' kept resounding like a constant refrain from Thorvald Lammers, and then he laughed until his deep bass voice echoed in the mountains." Grieg, who was used to mountain-climbing, took "slow, mountaineer steps—*andante sostenuto*, as he called it—in contrast to the light *scherzo* steps of the young fellows from Copenhagen, who he predicted would not be able to keep it up."

So they climbed, with the "fabulously tall" Børresen walking beside the diminutive Grieg:

> It was the Midget and the Mountain King taking a morning walk to-
> gether in the sunshine. Johan Svendsen had a very hard time. His short-
> ness of breath bothered him no less than the heat, and he quickly got
> tired. At last he wanted to sit down and rest on every stone he saw. Long
> after the others had reached the top, there came the "maestro" accompa-
> nied by his young pupil, who had faithfully encouraged and helped him.
> "This will be my last trip to the mountains," Svendsen gasped, bathed in
> sweat. And then, speaking with a jovial Copenhagen accent, he said,
> "Yes, what I wouldn't give for a cold beer."

The jolly hikers divided into two groups for the trip down, which proved to be a painful ordeal for Svendsen. Hansen helped him as much as he could, but they missed the train to the Hop station and thus were too late for the dinner at Troldhaugen to which Grieg had invited them.

Tofft concluded his article (115) with a report about Svendsen's pleas-ant memories from the visit to western Norway:

> It was the last trip to the mountains that Johan Svendsen undertook "in
> this life," as he said. Moreover, he had to talk about it, not only because
> the trip had caused him pain but almost because it had given him a me-
> mento and made it clear to him that the powers that once belonged to
> him and to his forefathers, the pride of the Vikings—these powers were
> gone forever. On the other hand, he constantly remembered the trip to
> Norway itself, the glittering music festival, and everything associated
> with it. He had seen much of the world and enjoyed major triumphs
> abroad, but whenever anything was said about the trip to Bergen his wise
> eyes lit up—those eyes that fastened so pleasantly on the person he was
> talking with—and then he pulled his moustache down to his mouth so
> he could chew on it, as he always did when he was thinking about some-
> thing, and declared with great solemnity that of all the trips he had taken,
> the trip to Bergen was the one from which he had the most beautiful
> memories and the one he preferred to think about.

Svendsen had originally planned that after the music festival in Bergen he would visit Molde and Trondheim enroute to Oslo for a brief visit with his father. He changed his mind, however, and traveled by coastal steamer via Stavanger.

Because of the press of duties at the Royal Theater, Svendsen did not get around to writing to Grieg until September 18. He then sent him a long letter thanking him for his hospitality in "the wonder city of Bergen." During his visit to Oslo he had sounded out the mood among the musicians there. Grieg had indeed aroused animosity by his unwillingness to have the Music Society participate in the Bergen festival. Among the people with whom Svendsen spoke was one of his former pupils, "who very quietly but at the same time very firmly stated that the Oslo musicians had reason to feel insulted. The insult, in his opinion, was all the more grave in that the musicians had the feeling that they had already been engaged to participate in the festival and had been looking forward to it." Another musician had said angrily that in the future nobody in Oslo should play under Grieg's baton. But, Svendsen added, "these people will certainly learn in time to distinguish between *serious* artistic efforts and envious intrigues. . . . You can safely disregard these contemptible attacks."

THE FESTIVAL PRELUDE—A SAD SWAN SONG

Svendsen was invited to Stockholm in September, 1898, to participate in the dedicatory festivities for the new opera house, Kungliga Teatern. He was not able to go, however, because of pressing duties in connection with *Hero*, a new Danish one-act opera by Ludvig Schytte, which premiered on September 25.

The critics were skeptical. They acknowledged that there were indeed some lyrical qualities in the music but looked in vain for evidence of originality and dramatic nerve. William Behrend wrote ironically in *Politiken*: "The audience more or less nonchalantly let Hero sink into the wet grave."

The November 4 philharmonic concert, which had been postponed from the spring season, was a rare musical event as 67-year-old Joseph Joachim, arguably the greatest violinist of the time, played Beethoven's violin concerto under Svendsen's baton. It must have been a strange experience for Svendsen to reflect on the fact that in his youth, in Hamburg, he had

demonstrated his violin-playing ability for the great virtuoso—with somewhat modest results. Now, 35 years later, they met on a concert stage as artistic peers.

This autumn Svendsen also undertook what was to be his last composition. Entitled *Festival Prelude*, it was another occasional work and was completed on December 10. It was written to serve as the introductory number
for a celebration at the Royal Theater on December 18 marking the sesquicentennial of the dedication of what in 1748 was called *Komediehuset* (*The
House of Comedy*)—architect N. Eigtvedt's imposing building on Kongens
Nytorv in Copenhagen. The main event of the celebration was a performance of Holberg's *The Political Tinker*, and the festivities concluded with a
cantata by Frederik Rung with a text by Peter Hansen. This way of celebrating an important milestone in the national cultural life did not please
one critic (E. B.), who wrote in *Politiken*: "First there was music by the *Norwegian* musical director—a charming idea at a festival honoring the dedication of the Danish theater. I wonder if the Norwegians will dedicate their
new National Theater with music by a Danish maestro?"

Politiken's music critic, William Behrend, had little to say of a positive
nature regarding either Svendsen's or Rung's compositions. Regarding the
latter he averred that it was written "in the traditional cantata style that has
been used on countless festive occasions ranging all the way from poultry
exhibits to special university events." He also ridiculed Svendsen's piece:
"Meanwhile, when Mr. Svendsen went so far in his *Festival Prelude* as to
sink into a meek, melancholy tone that sounded almost like a hymn and was
reminiscent of *Lohengrin*—well, that kind of music would have been entirely suitable for 'The Funeral of Danish Comedy.'"

Behrend is right in asserting that the character of Svendsen's music is
different from what one would expect in a festival prelude. Its stately tempo
and its light, shimmering sonority make it more similar to the prelude to
Lohengrin than to the sparkling music that Svendsen wrote for other festive
occasions. Indeed, Svendsen himself realized that the title did not fit the
character of the music. That is undoubtedly why, in the hand-written score,
he crossed out the word "Festival" in the title. Since its initial performance
the piece has been known simply as *Prelude*.

The composition is in ABA form. The calm A sections, in bright, trans-
lucent E major, enclose the somewhat more animated B section, which
contains some folk-like and modal elements that have an almost Griegian

sound. The climax of the slightly abbreviated recapitulation presents the principal theme in a grandiose *fortissimo*. A subdued coda in E major that is built on motives from the middle section brings the piece to a quiet, gentle conclusion.

Prelude was not printed during the composer's lifetime but has since come out in several posthumous arrangements. The original score has yet to be published.

In our opinion, *Prelude* is the best composition Svendsen produced during his years in Copenhagen. It is sad that this, his beautiful swan song, has been so sorely neglected. It is even more sad that he, having demonstrated that the creative juices were still flowing in his veins, composed nothing at all during the last thirteen years of his life.

It was now ten years since *Don Giovanni* had been performed at the Royal Theater. The new production that premiered on March 8, 1899, was to have been the main attraction of the spring season, but it did not become the triumph that the theater had hoped it would be. Behrend, writing in *Politiken*, was almost surly in his criticism. About Svendsen he wrote, "His erratic, nervous tempo, that has little in common with the classical style, his metronomic stiffness, that largely lacks the melodic suppleness that Mozart's music requires," and not least the inadequacy of the singers, resulted in a performance that "as a whole lacked festivity and style, luster and grace."

Grieg was in Copenhagen this winter and had been looking forward to the world premiere of his *Symphonic Dances* under Svendsen's baton at the first philharmonic concert of the spring season. The concert had originally been scheduled for February 4, but Svendsen became ill and the event had to be postponed. Grieg wrote to Beyer from Rome on April 1:

> I finally had to leave—and soon thereafter, of course, the concert took place [March 21]. Thanks to Svendsen's masterful conducting, I can be very happy about my composition—judging from letters and newspapers. There are just a few Norwegian-haters in the press (*Politiken* and *Berlingske Tidende*), but let them have their fun. I suppose it must be hard for them to see that we Norwegians exist and, as the Scripture says, are growing in wisdom.

Grieg was referring, among other things, to Charles Kjerulf's sarcastic remarks in *Politiken*:

> It was a good sound, very Griegian music—so Griegian that everyone surely thought they had heard it many times before. Melody and rhythm

and harmony and the manner in which these were combined were familiar in every measure. But it was Grieg that reproduced himself.

The second philharmonic concert took place on May 3. The program was German and French, with Brahms's *Symphony No. 3* as the principal offering. The other orchestral works were Berlioz's *King Lear* overture and d'Indy's *Prelude* to the opera *Fervaal*. Vilhelm Herold appeared as soloist in compositions by Wagner and César Franck. Behrend, writing in *Politiken*, echoed Kjerulf in complaining about the altogether too traditional programming. An expert like Svendsen should consider it his duty to include one major new orchestral work at each philharmonic concert. Behrend's conclusion was that these symphony concerts "could and should have played a more significant and deserving role in our music life."

It appears that Svendsen spent the summer of 1899 resting in an attempt to recover from health problems that had been plaguing him for a long time. A birthday letter to his father dated September 25—the last letter he wrote to the old man—has a uniquely light, optimistic tone. He mentioned that he had returned to his work at the theater with great energy: "If the season continues as it has begun it will be a real triumph for the opera company."

The autumn season featured new productions of *The Flying Dutchman*, *Il Trovatore*, and *The Marriage of Figaro*—operas that had not been performed in Copenhagen for seven, six, and five years respectively. The season also included the world premiere on December 1 of *Skøn Karen (Beautiful Karen)*, a new Danish opera by Tekla Griebel.

The great Swedish baritone John Forsell appeared in the title role in *Don Giovanni* during the autumn season. According to Victor Gandrup, at the first rehearsal he sang the famous "Champagne" aria in such a furious tempo that it left the orchestra breathless. Svendsen, who in deference to the limited skill of the local "seducers" was accustomed to taking the piece much more slowly than he wanted to, was delighted with Forsell's uninhibited interpretation. The concertmaster mumbled something that sounded like a protest against the arrogant, young "Mozart vandal." Svendsen cut him off: "No!" he shouted, "this is the right way. It's *champagne*. What we are accustomed to is just *near beer*!" (41).

Svendsen paid no attention to the critics' complaints that the programs for his symphony concerts were too traditional. The program for the November 4 concert consisted of Mozart's *Symphony No. 40*, Schumann's *Symphony No. 4*, and his own arrangements of *Two Icelandic Melodies*.

Shortly after the concert he took a quick trip to Oslo to guest conduct at concerts by the National Theater Orchestra in November. Norway's new theater had been dedicated at a series of three festive events at the beginning of September. The program for the first two of these evenings had included Svendsen's *Norwegian Rhapsody No. 3* and *Festival Polonaise*. He had also been widely talked about as a candidate for the position of orchestra conductor at the theater, but he did not apply and the prestigious position was filled instead by the dynamic Johan Halvorsen. Following Svendsen's example with the Royal Theater Orchestra, Halvorsen immediately launched a series of symphony concerts with a 44-piece orchestra that soon emerged as the finest such ensemble in the city.

Svendsen's concerts at the National Theater were successful in every way. Lengthy applause as well as a flourish by the orchestra greeted Svendsen as he strode to the podium to conduct a program consisting exclusively of his own compositions: *Symphony No. 2, Zorahayda, Carnival in Paris,* and the *Violin Romance* with Johan Halvorsen as soloist. According to *Morgenbladet,* he wielded the baton "as forcefully, freshly and flexibly as in his youth." The full-house audience would not let him leave until he repeated *Carnival in Paris* and one movement of the symphony.

In the aforementioned birthday letter to his father he wrote about how well he was feeling at this time:

> About myself I have only good things to report. Thanks to the manner of living prescribed by Dr. Egeberg—whose instructions I have conscientiously followed—I am now as healthy and agile as ever. Now, for example, I can work with the same strength and ease as I did 20–25 years ago, and if it continues like this I can truthfully say, like the French, that I have begun my second youth.

Now, at the turn of the century and for several years that followed, his "second youth" manifested itself in a large number of sparkling performances as a conductor. It did not, however, lead to any further composing. Thus *Prelude*, which he had written the year before, became a postlude, the actual conclusion of his creative work.

9

THE FINAL YEARS

1900–1911

THE CONCLUDING PERIOD of Svendsen's life was increasingly marked by problems. Nonetheless, during this period he continued to demonstrate his vitality as an orchestral conductor both in Denmark and abroad. But Johan Svendsen the composer remained totally silent.

His health, which had been seriously weakened in 1897 by the malaria attack, steadily worsened. Although there were periods of temporary improvement, it appears that he never fully recovered. The result was depression, increased dependence on alcohol, and periods of hospitalization. By 1908 he no longer had the strength to continue and he was obliged to resign from the Royal Theater. During the last three years of his life he was a mere shadow of his old self.

TRIUMPH IN PARIS

The Danish premiere of Bizet's *The Pearl Fishers* was given on February 25, 1900, but it was not well received. Two days later Svendsen conducted the orchestra in a benefit concert to raise money for "the suffering fishermen from the West coast of Denmark." The orchestra concert on March 10 gave evidence that Svendsen had taken to heart the advice of the critics to be more daring in his programming: the only classical work on the program was Beethoven's fourth piano concerto. There were three contemporary works, all with a program-music tinge: Glazunov's *Le printemps*, d'Indy's *La forêt enchantée* and Richard Strauss's *Death and Transfiguration*.

305

J. P. E. Hartmann, the dean of Nordic composers, died at the ripe old age of 95 on the very day of the concert, and it was of course a remarkable coincidence that Strauss's work should happen to have been played at just that time. William Behrend, reporting on the concert in *Politiken*, wrote: "It felt like a memorial song about the sufferings of the deceased great man and an apotheosis on the occasion of his release and in honor of his life work." Nonetheless, such a decidedly modern program had aroused discontentment in the audience, and many people had walked out in protest. The Royal Theater also honored Hartmann with a memorial concert on March 28 at which Svendsen conducted excerpts from several of the master's largest works.

On April 29 the theater premiered *Viking Blood*, a new opera by Lange-Müller, but for once the man on the podium was not Johan Svendsen but Frederik Rung. The reason was that after his controversy with Lange-Müller in 1891, Svendsen had declared that he would never again conduct anything by this composer. The opera was savaged in the press. William Behrend wrote in *Politiken*: "It must be condemned in its entirety from the very outset." He also had an ironic hint for Svendsen: "One can well understand that Maestro Johan Svendsen, who has been unbelievably busy during this rich opera season rehearsing one—that's one—new opera (*The Pearl Fishers*), has felt a need for rest and has turned over to his younger colleague the work on this *novelty*."

During the spring Svendsen was busy with preparations for another trip to Paris in July–August. More than a hundred concerts were to be given in connection with the World Exhibition, and the music of many lands was to be presented. The Finns were sending their leading symphony orchestra while the Swedes, the Danes and the Norwegians were each sending a choir. Norway had made arrangements for three concerts of Norwegian music to be given in Trocadéro Palace with the 85-man World Exhibition orchestra under the leadership of Svendsen and Iver Holter. The Norwegian "Parisian Chorus," a 100-voice men's ensemble prepared and conducted by O.A. Grøndahl, was also scheduled to participate.

Svendsen carried on a lively correspondence with Iver Holter, who was chairman of the Norwegian program committee. Svendsen was to receive an honorarium of 1,500 crowns for conducting the three concerts, but he was to pay all of his own expenses. In a confidential letter to Holter dated April 19, 1900, Juliette Haase asked if it wouldn't be possible for the committee to give Svendsen an additional travel allowance of 500 crowns, for "the financial aspect of the matter is very important for him and the rest of us

Johan Svendsen in Copenhagen ca.
1900. (Det kgl. Bibliotek, Copenhagen)

as well." On June 15 Svendsen himself wrote to Holter that he had "expenses up over my ears. The children have to be sent into the country, and I
have to buy all kinds of things for the trip; for that reason I have already had
to take out a loan to cover the most necessary items." On July 3 he asked to
have the travel money sent (so it obviously had been granted) as well as "a
small additional advance—800 crowns in all—*soon*. I need to get various
things for the trip and would also like to have enough money in my pocket
when I get to the French capital."

Before leaving for Paris he enjoyed several fine summer days in
Charlottenlund with Juliette and their three children—Johan, Sigrid and
Eyvind. He wrote to August Enna on July 14: "We are enjoying ourselves
so much here in Jægersborg Allé 53. The children, especially, seem to be
profiting from the stay."

He spent a few days in Copenhagen during this period with Robert Kajanus, his former pupil from Finland. He also met Jean Sibelius for the first time, a man whom he characterized in the letter to Enna as possessing "a rich and violent artistic temperament." Kajanus and Sibelius were enroute to Paris with the Helsinki Philharmonic orchestra, which gave concerts at Tivoli on July 12 and 13.

During this visit, Kajanus demonstrated that he, too, had "a rich and violent artistic temperament"—if not as an artist, at least as a party-goer. Svendsen's friend and physician, Dr. Albert Øigaard (41), is our source for the following amusing story. The evening before the first concert, Kajanus, in his characteristically generous way, invited Svendsen and some other friends to join him as his guests at one of the Tivoli restaurants. Here he emptied his pockets, threw all the money on the table and shouted: "Champagne! Champagne!" The waiters scurried around to locate as many bottles of this noble beverage as they could find, and when they ran out of champagne in the wee hours of the morning the revelers switched to Danish acquavit, which they drank out of beer glasses. At about six o'clock in the morning, however, Kajanus's companions were shocked when he suddenly collapsed and lost consciousness. Dr. Øigaard was called immediately, and after giving the unconscious man a shot he told the anxious friends that if he didn't regain consciousness within a couple of hours he would not survive. Fortunately, after an hour and three quarters Kajanus began to get some color back in his face and thereafter seemed to recover quickly. That forenoon he held a short orchestra rehearsal and in the evening, as if nothing had happened, he conducted a highly successful concert of substantial Finnish music. Kajanus's drinking companions were greatly impressed with their friend's demonstration of Finnish stamina. Even the very experienced Svendsen was forced to admit that he was no match for his old pupil in this department.

On July 17 Svendsen left for France. He wrote to Juliette five days later that the two-day train trip to Paris was "one of the most strenuous I have ever taken." Arriving in Paris, he encountered a heat wave marked by higher temperatures than had been seen there for a hundred years: "People and horses were collapsing from sunstroke."

His notebook from this time is extant, and it contains a long list of composers whom he had thought of visiting: Massenet, Duparc, Ropartz, Widor, Fauré, d'Indy, Saint-Saëns and others. A friendly letter from Saint-Saëns was waiting for him upon his arrival. He does not appear to have had much luck meeting the people on his list, however, for as Sibelius wrote to his wife on July 27, "all the Parisians are currently out at the beach. The foreigners are in charge here now." Svendsen wrote to Juliette on August 6, however, that he had met the director of the Grand Opéra and had "spoken warmly and in detail about August Enna's opera *Cleopatra*."

On July 27 he wrote to Juliette that he had visited the Latin Quarter to see once again the area where he had spent many happy days more than thirty years earlier: "I could detect hardly any changes. I even met some people from those days, including my old violin-playing barber, who let out a howl of joy when he saw me."

The short time preceding the three big concerts was filled with hectic activity as Svendsen drilled the French musicians on the many unfamiliar Norwegian works they were to play. On August 1 he wrote to Juliette:

Yesterday we had the first rehearsal. Things looked desperate at first. Nothing was ready. Neither stands nor chairs had been put in place on the stage, but finally things got somewhat organized, I got the musicians placed, and then we began. The music seemed to please the players, and after the first piece—my third rhapsody—they shouted and applauded like crazy. I think that artistically it will go well, but unfortunately we can't count on much of an audience. There's a lot of competition, and the heat drives the real concert-going public out of the city.

We also have a report from another source about Svendsen's rehearsals with the French orchestra:

The good gentlemen were tired, the heat was intense, and they did not seem to find the Nordic music exhilirating. But then Svendsen mounted the podium and raised his baton for them to begin playing his B-flat major symphony. The musicians yawned and started in. They played— and the farther that excellent orchestra advanced the more enthusiastically they played. The violinists absolutely cuddled up to their instruments to make them sing—the trombonists moved their slides in and out with enthusiasm. In short—the orchestra played wonderfully under the inspiration of Svendsen's baton. And when the last sound died away, those short, high-strung Frenchmen stood up as if on cue and pounded their instruments enthusiastically in honor of the maestro (131).

The concerts took place on August 4, 6 and 7, and to Svendsen's surprise the attendance was very good—"significantly better than for all of our predecessors, and artistically it has all gone exceptionally well," he wrote to Juliette after the second concert. A full house was predicted for the concert on August 7, "which, when one considers the size of the concert hall [the 4,000-seat Trocadéro Palace], is quite a feat. This evening the Norwegians living here are giving a gala dinner in our honor." The reporter covering the event for the Oslo newspaper *Aftenposten* wrote that there were two thousand people in attendance at the first and third concerts and over three thousand at the second.

On August 4, Iver Holter conducted his own *Nordic Festival Parade*, Johan Halvorsen's *Vasantasena* suite, and Christian Sinding's *Piano Concerto* with Martin Knutzen as soloist. The chorus, conducted by O. A. Grøndahl, also sang several selections. Svendsen conducted Catharinus Elling's *Gregorius Dagssøn* for male chorus and orchestra, his own *Norwegian Rhapsody No. 3*, and his arrangement of Ole Bull's *The Shepherd Girl's Sunday*. After the last piece there was an outburst of "shouting and applause that would not stop."

The well-known French critic Alfred Bruneau, writing in *Le Figaro*, was highly complimentary: "The concert I attended yesterday was really interesting, not only because of the quality of the works presented but also in that the orchestra was conducted by Johan Svendsen, a composer who has written many excellent works that are often played here and who, like Edvard Grieg, is one of the masters of the Norwegian school."

At the second concert, Holter wielded the baton for Grieg's *Last Spring*, Eyvind Alnæs's *Symphonic Variations*, and his own orchestral suite *Götz von Berlichingen*. Svendsen conducted Johan Selmer's *The Turks Approach Athens* for solo, male chorus and orchestra. *Aftenposten* reported that the Selmer piece "wavered somewhere between brilliance and unintended comedy and in any case was not suitable for performance in Trocadéro." It was further reported that "the biggest hit was made by Svendsen's *Zorahayda*, which really brought forth ovations from both audience and orchestra."

There was also time for a bit of relaxation between concerts. The "Parisian Chorus" and the other Norwegian visitors were duly feted at a gala dinner at Hotel d'Orsay on August 6 to which the Norwegian colony in Paris had invited three hundred guests. A greeting was read from the French president, Loubet, who wrote of his enthusiasm for Norwegian music and expressed regret that he had been prevented from attending the concerts because of the murder of the Italian King Umberto by anarchists a few days earlier. The sumptuous banquet consisted of twelve courses, and the selection of wines and hard liquor was equally large, so it was not surprising that the chorus was not at its best in the concert the next day, when several strange and regrettable mishaps occurred. *Aftenposten* reported that "the singers were somewhat tired, partly as a result of the festive exertions of the previous evening. . . . As the night wore on—and since they wanted to enjoy the Parisian nightlife to the fullest—the party moved to Maxim, which stayed open until 4 A.M."

At the concluding concert on August 7, Holter conducted Grieg's *Land-Sighting*, Gerhard Schjelderup's orchestral suite *Christmas Eve*, and Sigurd Lie's *Marche symphonique*. Svendsen conducted Johan Selmer's *Scène funèbre*. The highlight of the evening, however, according to *Aftenposten*, was "Svendsen's first symphony, which was wildly applauded by the audience . . . and each movement was a triumph in itself." *Aftenposten* summed up its evaluation of the concert series thus: "Johan Svendsen's confident and dignified demeanor as a conductor as well as his magnificent and richly faceted art have cast the luster of success and ovation over the instrumental part of the representation."

On November 17 of the same year, Svendsen was elected a corresponding member of the prestigious French "L'Académie des Beaux Arts."

During the visit to Paris, Svendsen got better acquainted with Sibelius, who, according to Karl Ekman, reported that Svendsen "became very fond of my music and promised to do his utmost to make it better known in Denmark. He was especially impressed with my first symphony. He strongly encouraged me to make arrangements to send it to the printer" (31:155). Six months later (January 14, 1901) Sibelius wrote to his new friend:

> In the hope that you have not totally forgotten me, and remembering
> our conversation in Paris concerning me, I enclose herewith my *Song of*
> *Spring* [an orchestral work written in 1894]. Due to adverse circum-
> stances it has not been possible to send it sooner. If you, with your well-
> known greatness of spirit, would put in a good word for me with Hansen
> [the music publisher], I would be more than grateful. With pleasant
> memories of the last time we were together, I am, with warm admiration,
> yours sincerely, Jean Sibelius.

On August 16, 1900, Svendsen received a telegram informing him that his 83-year-old father had died. He wrote to Theodor Hindenburg the following day: "I will be going to Oslo on Monday. . . . It is as if I were in a stupor."

I have trouble thinking a complete thought, and I feel that I will achieve some semblance of peace only when the funeral is over."

After a quick trip to Oslo for the funeral he returned to the Royal Theater to conduct the Danish premiere on September 1 of Pergolesi's *La serva padrona*, which, however, had a very short run. The other offerings of the autumn season consisted mainly of popular old stand-bys.

On September 30 Svendsen celebrated his sixtieth birthday and was duly congratulated in both the Danish and Norwegian press. Looking back, it is especially interesting to read Carl Nielsen's article in *Politiken* (89). One can only marvel at the discourteous preamble that the editor thought it fit to append to the article even on so special a day in Svendsen's life: "Our readers are aware that in recent years *Politiken* has had to take a stand in firm opposition to the entire leadership of our opera house, for the stylistic posture of which the musical director is partly to blame—because of his regrettable lack of initiative and frequently his all too deficient attention to the *musical* performance of the works. Today, however, we do not wish to dwell on these things but have chosen instead to give this space to an enthusiastic admirer of the excellent composer." In the article itself, Carl Nielsen shows himself to be a fine writer:

> As a composer, Svendsen occupies a quite unique place among well-known musicians of the last century. His individuality comes through with extraordinary purity, sharpness, and clarity. His enormous talent and his superb mastery of form stand in such a precise and harmonic relationship to one another that one could very well characterize many of his works as modern-classical. In this respect he is almost Gallic.

Svendsen's musical language, he wrote, is firm, terse and pregnant. There is never one note too many, never an expansion invented just to fill the time. Form and content coalesce into a single unity:

> Svendsen, in his music, is like a young, shapely swimmer who dives head-first into the water with a smile, happy for the blazing sun above and for the clean, clear, salt water around him. But why not also look at the fine and rare things he finds on the bottom and with happy wonder holds up above the glittering surface? . . . The rhythmical element in Svendsen's talent is the part that heretofore has had the greatest influence on Danish music; there is, so to speak, not a single living Danish musician, singer, instrumentalist or composer who on this point is not either directly or indirectly indebted to him.

Nielsen uses unusually strong words to characterize Svendsen as a conductor:

> He is so unique that since Hans von Bülow's death he stands unrivalled as
> the most brilliant conductor in Europe. . . . Anyone who has played
> under Svendsen, whether in the theater or in the concert hall for a per-
> formance of a major work that has captured his interest, never forgets it,
> partly because he has become thoroughly inflamed and partly because he
> has seen what remarkable power can flow from the one to the many. In
> such a moment a remarkable, absolutely incomprehensible feeling of
> unity can grip everyone—even the exhausted old singers and instrumen-
> talists—and everything "swings" together in a way that can only be com-
> pared to a flock of birds that happily ascend and descend together
> through the air in giant waves. In such moments Svendsen is at his peak
> as a leader and is of inestimable significance.

The following day *Politiken* reported that well-wishers had streamed into
Svendsen's house from early forenoon until late in the evening and that he
had received many evidences of the "esteem he enjoys as a musician and as a
person. His apartment in Nyhavn was filled in the course of the day with
beautiful flowers from many friends including members of the orchestra and
other personnel from the Royal Theater." Among the gifts was a silver cup
"from a private admirer" on which were engraved the opening measures of
one of the *Norwegian Rhapsodies*.

The high point of the day was the presentation of a document from a
committee consisting of chamber singer Niels Juel Simonsen, music publisher Alfred Wilhelm Hansen, and Judge Theodor Hindenburg. The three
of them had spearheaded an effort to collect a gift of money for the honoree:

> That the gift was not presented to him yesterday is due only to certain
> formalities that still have not been resolved. The gift—in accordance
> with the musical director's own wish—is to be given not to himself but
> to his children. The document says nothing about the size of the gift, but
> we would not be wrong in saying that it is closer to twenty than to ten
> thousand crowns.

The program for the orchestra concert on November 17, 1900, was a mixture of the old and the new—Danish, French and Russian—with Tchaikovsky's fifth symphony as the main number. This work had been played in
Copenhagen once before by the Berlin Philharmonic orchestra under
Arthur Nikisch, but this was the first performance by the Royal Theater

orchestra. The Danish compositions were Gade's *Michelangelo Overture*, two pieces from Carl Nielsen's melodrama *Snefrid* (1893), and the world premiere of the Prelude to Act 2 of Nielsen's *Saul and David*—his first opera, on which he was hard at work at the time.

Charles Kjerulf, writing in *Politiken*, called the concert "unusually grand and festive." He said that the sound of Nielsen's opera prelude "rose majestically and passionately and transformed itself into a tone poem full of beauty and character."

In November the Copenhagen press announced an "invitation to a composition contest sponsored by Johan Svendsen and the Royal Theater orchestra concerts." The goal was to remedy the lack of short Danish orchestral works that might be played at concerts by the orchestra. Only Danish composers were permitted to compete. The prize was three hundred crowns. By the deadline date—May 1, 1901—thirteen compositions had been submitted, but when the selection committee (Svendsen, Frederik Rung, Franz Neruda, Orla Rosenhoff and Vilhelm Svedbom) made its decision six months later, not a single one of the works submitted was found worthy of any distinction. Evidently the quality of the works submitted had been commensurate with the size of the prize that was offered.

DIVORCE AND REMARRIAGE

In mid-January, 1901, Svendsen again went abroad, this time to conduct a 100-piece orchestra in the "Concerts Ysaye" series in Théâtre de L'Alhambre in Brussels. Ysaye's Danish pupil Hakon Schmedes, who was concertmaster in the philharmonic orchestra in Brussels, invited him to stay at his house during the visit to Belgium. On January 13 he sent a letter thanking Schmedes for the invitation, adding playfully: "I regret to say that I have already adopted the habits of an old man. I must sleep in and on wool, and I snore terribly."

At the concert on January 20 he performed a representative sample of his own works: *Symphony No. 1, Carnival in Paris, Zorahayda, Norwegian Rhapsody No. 2*, and *Two Icelandic Melodies*. The following day he wrote to Juliette:

> So! Yesterday was the battle. It was won magnificently, thanks to the big, excellent orchestra and the receptivity of the audience. Just think, Ysaye came from London just to play as an ordinary member of the orchestra,

and after the concert he gave a dinner in my honor that was one of the most wonderful such events I have ever experienced. . . . Although I have it great here together with interesting people who are splendid in every way, still I long for home and for you, my dear ones. I long so deeply that it almost disturbs me, and I will be glad when I again breathe Copenhagen's air.

Two years later Svendsen received a Belgian honor when, on February 5, 1903, he was made a member of Académie Royale des Sciences, des Lettres et des Beaux Arts.

The Royal Theater orchestra gave three concerts during the 1901 spring season. The February 26 event was a benefit concert for the "Association for the Support of Needy Music Teachers in Denmark." The program included a new Danish work: a symphony in C minor by Svendsen's pupil Hakon Børresen.

The program on March 28 was devoted to standard classical works, but on April 20 he demonstrated support for his new Finnish friend, Jean Sibelius, by performing *Song of Spring*. Sibelius was in weighty company: the program also included Beethoven's *Symphony No. 2* and no less than two piano concertos: Beethoven's *Emperor Concerto* and Chopin's *Piano Concerto No. 2*, with Ignaz Paderewsky as soloist.

July 7–9 Svendsen conducted a large male chorus—with singers from Copenhagen, Funen and Jutland—in a big song festival in Copenhagen. The several programs included compositions by Hartmann, Gade, Heise, Kjerulf, Nordraak and Reissiger.

On August 14 he petitioned the Minister of Culture for "permission to begin wearing the decoration as 'Officier de l'Instruction publique' awarded by the French government"—an honor he had received following his contribution to the World Exhibition in Paris the year before.

The autumn concert by the Royal Theater orchestra on October 25 featured a performance by Svendsen's Belgian friend Eugène Ysaye as soloist in two violin concertos: Bach's in E major and Saint-Saëns's in B minor.

A new chapter in Svendsen's life began at the end of 1901 when he was divorced from Bergljot. Soon thereafter he married Juliette Haase, the mother of his three children.

When he had married Sarah (Bergljot) in 1871, it was in the confidence that he had found a companion for life. But that proved not to be the case, not least because his own emotional life was too unstable. Those in the know used to joke about his "list of a thousand and three." Victor Gandrup (41) has told about an amusing incident that relates to Svendsen's reputation as a "Don Giovanni":

> A well-known resident of Copenhagen, Professor E. J. Lehmann, had a very prudish old aunt who once was invited to a party where Svendsen also was a guest. She had earlier declared that she was strongly prejudiced against him because of his many love affairs. During the party, however, she found herself very attracted to the courteous Norwegian. When Lehmann later asked how she had gotten along with Svendsen, she answered in a quiet, almost despondent, sympathetic tone of voice, "Svendsen has not found the right woman." Taken aback, the professor blurted out: "The hell you say! He sure has looked hard enough!"

Svendsen's escapades had led to a growing rift between Bergljot and himself, and in 1885, when he began his relationship with the 19-year-old ballet dancer Juliette Haase, Bergljot left him. An attempt at reconciliation three years later did not succeed. She, however, would not hear of a divorce—not even when, during the 1890s, Juliette and Johan became the parents of three children.

That Svendsen and Juliette did not live together until about 1900 may have been because of the so-called concubinage paragraph, which, according to § 178 of the Danish criminal code, specified imprisonment as the penalty for a violation (though it was rarely enforced).

Indicative of Svendsen's erratic emotional life is the fact that in the course of his relationship with Juliette he also had an affair with a married woman who was said to be the true love of his life.

In time his complicated family situation became more and more untenable, and it was not least Juliette and the children who suffered from it. That the royal court viewed the situation as scandalous is evident from a story that made the rounds in Copenhagen. One day old Queen Louise, who had a keen interest in music, invited Svendsen to forenoon tea at the royal palace. This probably was shortly before her death in 1898. After a pleasant chat, as Svendsen was about to leave the queen made a remark that took him totally by surprise: "Now it surely is time for the musical director to get married, isn't it?"

Such a remark by the queen herself had to be viewed as a royal command, and Svendsen undoubtedly felt compelled to make an attempt to get Bergljot to accede to a divorce. Nonetheless, it took over a year to get the process under way.

A letter from his stepson Sigurd in Paris, dated December 28, 1899, shows that Johan and Bergljot had reached agreement regarding a reduction in the amount of support money that he regularly sent to her. Sigurd wrote:

> I was glad to hear that my mother's decision has made your financial situation somewhat easier. She will no doubt now be forced to deny herself many things, but the moral satisfaction compensates for the material loss. Let us hope that from now on you will have fewer cares and that this will enable you to work much more freely.

Two years were to pass, however, before the divorce became final. In 1900, Svendsen's case was submitted for "clerical and secular binding arbitration" in Copenhagen. An important consideration in the negotiations between the two parties was to make Bergljot's economic situation as favorable as possible. One of Svendsen's well-to-do friends, Judge Theodor Hindenburg, functioned as mediator. It will be recalled that it was he who had taken the initiative in raising a large sum of money as a gift for Svendsen on his sixtieth birthday. With this money—about 8,500 francs—in hand, Hindenburg went to Paris to carry on negotiations on Svendsen's behalf (53). It is possible that this substantial sum of money tipped the scale for Bergljot in favor of the divorce that Svendsen was seeking.

When Svendsen was in Paris in July–August 1900 for the World Exhibition concerts, he had contact with Bergljot's family but did not wish to meet her. In a letter to Juliette dated July 22, 1900, he wrote: "I have also spoken with Sigurd's uncle—her brother—and there are no problems there. If things now go the way they appear to be going, namely that *she* won't come here [from London] at all while I am here, I will have every reason to be pleased."

On June 4, 1900, Svendsen borrowed four thousand crowns from the loan fund of the Royal Theater. A condition for receiving the loan was that half of his net income from concerts given abroad were to be held back by the Wilhelm Hansen publishing company, which functioned both as his music publisher and his impresario. The Hansen firm promised to do this in a letter to the loan fund dated June 3. How Svendsen planned to use this large amount of cash is not known. It may have been a matter of refinancing some debts, or it may have been part of a one-time payment to Bergljot in connection with the divorce proceedings that were under way at the time.

Meanwhile, the Danish legal system moved slowly: according to the "Transcript of the Proceedings of the Copenhagen Directorate on Separa-

Juliette Haase with her and Johan Svendsen's children ca. 1900. The children are Johan (top), Eyvind Severin (middle), and Sigrid. (Universitetsbiblioteket, Oslo)

tion and Divorce Cases" the matter was not taken up for final action until December 10, 1901. The divorce petition stated that Svendsen had "in fact lived apart from his wife since January 5, 1889, and that he sought permission to marry Juliette Vilhelmine Haase, with whom he, after his life with his wife was ended, had fathered three children."

One week later the divorce papers were signed by the Minister of Justice, and on December 23 he was at last able to marry Juliette. The marriage ceremony was conducted in St. Paul's Church in Copenhagen.

RELATIONSHIP WITH CARL NIELSEN

The Royal Theater had several very successful productions during the spring season of 1902. On January 8 it was *The Valkyrie*, which had not been performed in Copenhagen for ten years, with Ellen Nordgren Gulbranson appearing once again as Brünnhilde. Mrs. Gulbranson also was the soloist in selections from *Tannhäuser*, *Tristan and Isolde*, and *Twilight of the Gods* in connection with theater performances on January 14, 16 and 18 at which Svendsen also conducted the Prelude to *The Mastersingers*.

On April 4, C. F. E. Horneman—four years before his death—experienced a major triumph with a revised version of his opera *Aladdin*. Tenor Vilhelm Herold, who was at the beginning of what was to become a successful international career, was widely acclaimed for his performance in the title role. The renowned Wagnerian conductor Hans Richter was present for one of the performances, and when Svendsen mounted the podium, Richter rose demonstratively from his seat in the middle of the first row of the balcony, clapped wildly and shouted "Bravo!"—and the audience soon joined in. When the surprised Svendsen turned around to face the audience, he realized that the man who was causing all the commotion was Richter, an old friend and colleague from his youth. He shyly stepped down from the podium and waited until the applause subsided.

Two orchestra concerts were held during this season. On February 13 Svendsen conducted a Norwegian-Danish-French program that included his own *Romeo and Juliet*, Gerhard Schjelderup's Prelude to the opera *The Abduction of the Bride*, Gade's *Frühlings-Phantasie*, Fini Henriques's *Legend*, and two French symphonic poems: César Franck's *Le chasseur maudit* and Chausson's *Viviane*. The principal work on April 18 was Tchaikovsky's *Pathétique Symphony*, but the program also included Liszt's *Tasso*, Wagner's *Karfreitagszauber* from *Parsifal*, and Grieg's *Piano Concerto* with Johanne Stockmarr as soloist.

Rossini's *The Barber of Seville* was launched in the autumn season, with the first performance on September 18. The big event at the theater that season, however, was the world premiere on November 28 of Carl Nielsen's first opera, *Saul and David*, with Niels Juel Simonsen singing the role of Saul and Vilhelm Herold that of David. On May 31 of the preceding year Svendsen, in his capacity as consultant, had given the work an unqualified recommendation:

> An exceedingly interesting work that bears throughout the stamp of an independently gifted artist. Nothing here is borrowed from anyone else. The composer goes his own way with clarity and confidence. Without looking either to the left or to the right, he pursues his goal: to give the dramatic action a musical characterization in an original way. This work is warmly and earnestly recommended for acceptance and early production.

Even during the first rehearsals, however, there were problems. Carl Nielsen wrote to Orla Rosenhoff on September 22: "Rehearsals of my opera have now begun, naturally with some fussing. Singers are certainly a unique and remarkable breed, and they're as vulnerable as crustaceans without shells. We've already had wrangling and quarreling."

It was not Svendsen who got the task of conducting the premiere of this opera, however. The reason for this has been explained by Carl Nielsen himself, who reported that Svendsen let him have both the honor and the responsibility (91):

> At that point in time Johan Svendsen was a man who was being fiercely attacked. When I asked him about the possibility of conducting the first three performances, he thought that I had gone over to his enemies. But when he understood that I was always his friend, he said to me: "I must think about my own youth. If I had not gotten the opportunity to try out my own works, I would never have succeeded. I agree with you. I will permit you to conduct and I will support you and help you to the best of my ability.

The premiere was anticipated with great excitement and a lot of space was given to the event in the local press. The critics made it clear, however, that it was not going to be easy for a composer of Carl Nielsen's bent to break through with such a unique work. *Middagsposten*'s critic wrote that the opera was a "proof of Carl Nielsen's modest ability." He lacked talent, and there was "not a drop of red clown's blood in his veins. . . . An artistic success was created by the persistent clapping of Carl Ploug's son, Dr. Rudolph Bergh's son, and Orla Lehmann's grandson. His Royal Highness the Crown

Carl Nielsen. (Det kgl. Bibliotek, Copenhagen)

Prince was enormously bored." According to *Børsen*, "the entire first act was a desert of boredom to wander through with few oases and many—musical—camels." *Folkets Avis* wrote on December 9: "The general public will not understand twenty measures. . . . A chaos of sounds, a mass of instruments and some unhappy singers." *Samfundet* wrote on the same date that it was impossible to develop any interest in this music, marked as it was by artificiality and unreasonable and crazy modulations: "Why didn't the theater produce Weber's *Freischütz* instead?"

Against the background of such tirades the composer undoubtedly found solace in the comments of critics who were more positively inclined. Robert Henriques, writing in *Vort Land* on November 29, described the performance as a great success. The music, he said, was effective "by virtue of its architectonic logic. . . . Most beautiful is the Introduction to Act 3—

the gentlest twilight effect." H. Ploug stated in the December 7 issue of *Illustreret Tidende* that all the expectations were fulfilled. There was "a greatness in the lines, a strength in the style, that has the ring of old-testament sublimity—as if it were bringing to us a message from the art of a great antiquity."

Between these two extremes we find reviewers in the largest newspapers—*Politiken, Berlingske Tidende* and *Nationaltidende*—who, though they indeed had some positive things to say, were for the most part fairly reserved. William Behrend, for example, wrote in *Politiken* on November 29 that the music certainly contained many lovely passages, but that "Mr. Carl Nielsen suffers from an exaggerated need to be independent." He also commented on the composer's podium skills: "He conducted with a quite natural enthusiasm and an equally natural nervousness that expressed itself in too many arm movements and finger-pointings."

The plan was that after the first three performances the conducting duties would be taken over not by Svendsen but by Frederik Rung. Rung became ill, however, so the rest of the performances were conducted by the composer as well. There were nine performances in 1902–03 and two in 1904. Nielsen wrote about the final performance in a letter to his wife dated December 9, 1904:

> *Saul and David* played to a full house yesterday . . . and after the last act the audience wouldn't leave until the lights were extinguished and the safety curtain was lowered!! The newspapers are furious and deny that I have talent, heart, or taste. Now I will go on with my work; I know what I can do.

That Carl Nielsen managed to develop such confidence in himself and his abilities was owing in no small measure to Svendsen's strong belief in him as a composer. The violinist Thorvald Nielsen has given an apt summary of the relationship between the two artists:

> But there was one man at the theater who did what he could to make life easier for Carl Nielsen: *Johan Svendsen.* I have been told by an older colleague that not infrequently during the period when Nielsen was working on *Saul and David,* Svendsen would give Nielsen a hand signal before the last act of an opera or ballet to indicate that he could now just as well go home and continue his composing. This outstanding Norwegian musician, composer and conductor recognized Carl Nielsen's creative

talents from the very beginning, and at every opportunity he supported him in a grandiose manner in his struggle to gain a foothold as a composer (92:8).

A couple of weeks before the premiere of *Saul and David*, Svendsen scored some triumphs at the opera house in Stockholm when he conducted the Royal orchestra in two concerts of his own works. November 8 he presented *Symphony No. 1*, *Zorahayda*, *Two Icelandic Melodies*, and *Norwegian Rhapsody No. 3*. Three days later he conducted his second symphony, *Carnival in Paris*, and the last two movements of his violin concerto, with concertmaster Lars Zetterquist as soloist. *Svensk Musiktidning* wrote on November 17: "It is true that there was nothing new, but the high musical worth of the compositions and their performance under the leadership of the composer himself should have been enticing enough. Svendsen's orchestral music really is so classically melodic, brilliant, and beautifully constructed that it stands far above the kind of music being written today."

Toward the end of the year Svendsen received a proposal from the C. F. Peters firm in Leipzig that he orchestrate Grieg's *Bridal Procession* (op. 19, no. 2), since the composer had declined to do so himself. Grieg had had an almost reverential respect for Svendsen's supreme ability as an orchestrator ever since 1867, when he first heard the latter's *Symphony No. 1*. In a letter (dated November 21, 1902) to Henri Hinrichsen, director of C. F. Peters, Grieg stated that Svendsen would be able better than anyone else to preserve the Norwegian flavor in an orchestral arrangement. For some unknown reason, Svendsen never responded to Hinrichsen's inquiry and the orchestration was eventually undertaken by Johan Halvorsen.

In early 1903, Svendsen conducted concerts by the Royal Theater orchestra on February 7 and March 30. The February concert featured as soloist a new comet in the violinists' firmament: the Frenchman Jacques Thibaut.

The major operatic event of the season was the Danish premiere on April 22 of Wagner's *Siegfried*, which follows *The Valkyrie* in the *Ring* cycle. For Svendsen, this was a radical new effort in behalf of Wagner's music. Outside of Germany there was scarcely anyone who had so thorough a grasp of this music as he did. But although Svendsen had the greatest respect for Wagner, he did not regard the master of Bayreuth as a saint whose works were not to be tampered with. According to Victor Gandrup (42) he once said (without being especially prescient) to his friend Dr. Øigaard:

If Wagner's works are to continue to live through the ages, they must
inevitably be taken to the hospital and amputated. A competent musician
who possesses the requisite familiarity with this composer's musical
world must tastefully and carefully make appropriate and adequate cuts,
for as the works are currently performed they will not in the long run be
able to survive the shifting tastes of changing times. The German super-
genius's *leitmotif*-laden complexities simply make excessive demands on
the audience's forbearance, greatly exceeding the listeners' mental and
physical carrying capacity.

Svendsen was known as an instructor who was both flexible and considerate, but when the situation seemed to him to call for it he could forcefully
speak his mind. Orchestra members Johs. Schiørring, Kristian Sandby and
William Andersen told Gandrup about an incident that gives a striking picture of the Maestro's authority. During rehearsals of *Siegfried*, Svendsen re-
peatedly pointed out to singer Elisabeth Dons—speaking always in his usual
calm manner—that she had to watch the baton more carefully as she was
constantly singing too slowly. Suddenly Julius Lehmann, the producer, was
heard to say from his vantage point in the auditorium, "It isn't played that
fast elsewhere in the world." Without a moment's hesitation, Svendsen
turned around and thundered, "That's how we play it here!" Lehmann was
almost paralyzed with shock. The theater director crept down from his
chair and slunk out through a back door.

The *Siegfried* premiere played to a full house and was a smashing success.
Even *Politiken*'s William Behrend was extremely positive:

> Yesterday was a red-letter day in the history of our theater. Indeed, it was
> more than that: it marks a major step forward artistically, one that places
> us in closer and long missed association with what is going on in the
> wide world of art. . . . It was prepared with much diligence, enthusiasm
> and understanding, and [the preparation] had reached such a point that
> everything was precise and ready, nothing fell short or turned out badly.

In June of 1903 it was Grieg's turn to celebrate his sixtieth birthday, and the
celebration at Troldhaugen was at least as big as had been the one for
Svendsen in Copenhagen three years earlier. Svendsen sent his friend his
good wishes, and Grieg replied on June 26:

> Yes, dear Svendsen, in spirit I am sending a telegram to you. Thank you
> for *your* great artistic achievements and for your faithful friendship

through many years! Thank you for what you taught me and thank you
for the innumerable times you entranced me!

The autumn season was ushered in with *The Princess and the Pea*, a new opera by August Enna that premiered on September 2. Jacques Thibaut was
again soloist at an orchestra concert on October 8. He played two violin
concertos: Bach's in E major and Mendelssohn's in E minor. The program
also included Svendsen's second symphony, Frederik Rung's rhapsody
Proud Mettelil, and Carl Nielsen's *Helios* overture. Svendsen thought highly
of the overture and gave it a brilliant performance. The audience was enthusiastic and the press was fairly positive. Robert Henriques wrote in *Vort
Land*: "There hovers over this music a power of light that dazzles and a la-
tent intimacy that warms." Charles Kjerulf, writing in *Politiken*, characterized Carl Nielsen as Danish music's most significant talent, but he
nonetheless used the opportunity to suggest with tongue in cheek that the
composer didn't measure up to the ranking "that a small circle of quite fool-
ish zealots would assign to him. They say without blushing: Beethoven—
Mozart—Carl Nielsen. . . . Yes, there is even one who says: Beethoven—Carl Nielsen—Mozart. And that is too bad . . . not for Beethoven and
Mozart . . . but for Carl Nielsen."

The temperamental young composer, who didn't mince words when
he wrote about others, immediately reacted in anger. On October 10 he demanded in *Politiken* that Kjerulf document his "ludicrous" claims. The next
day, Kjerulf replied in a long article entitled "Carl Nielsen and his Body-
guards":

> I grant that I cannot give a literal proof that precisely these words were
> spoken by the fanatics. . . . Carl Nielsen certainly knows that. When he
> himself one day last winter so tastefully (and quite without provocation)
> here in *Politiken* [in an article published November 6, 1902] called Sven
> Scholander a "Swedish monkey who would gladly sing through his a--
> if it would amuse the audience," he would surely have been very taken
> aback (and it would have been quite unreasonable) if I had demanded
> that he prove the *literal* truth of this rather obscene assertion.

A GIANT ON THE WANE

Svendsen had been physically robust and artistically strong throughout his
life, but in 1904–05 advancing age began to catch up with him. His health

became very unstable, and at times he was on sick leave and had to turn over the baton to others. He eventually was compelled to acknowledge that he was not as strong as he had once been, but it felt like a defeat not to be able always to cope with the situation. At times, however, he was able to pull himself together like the maestro he once had been, and on such occasions he was the undisputed master.

On January 15, 1904, he conducted a successful orchestra concert that included the *Tannhäuser* overture, Beethoven's *Violin Romanze* in F major, and his own *Symphony No. 2* and *Two Icelandic Melodies*. February 5 he led the orchestra in a concert at Our Lady Church given for the benefit of the victims of the fire that had destroyed the city of Ålesund, Norway two weeks earlier.

The orchestra concert on March 16 presented a varied mixture of the old and the new: a concerto grosso by Handel, Kuhlau's *William Shakespeare* overture, Saint-Saëns's *Omphale's Spinning Wheel*, and Taneyev's *Symphony No. 4*. A planned performance of Beethoven's ninth symphony had to be postponed until fall because Svendsen came down with a protracted bronchitis attack.

Svendsen's health problems also created difficulties for the theater. He was able to conduct a few performances, but the only new production he led during the years 1903–04 was Tchaikovsky's *Iolanthe*, which premiered January 24, 1904.

Carl Nielsen also began to appear on the podium on occasion during this period. In a February 2 letter to Henrik Knudsen, Nielsen made some harshly critical remarks about the theater leadership and mentioned that director Einar Christiansen had once again started "with his prattle about making me principal music director. I'm tired of listening to that and I do not want the position under the present circumstances. The count [Theater Director Danneskiold-Samsøe] is a first-class idiot. . . ." Nielsen also had some negative things to say about Svendsen, whose performance, he wrote, was "getting poorer and poorer, and he is now making so many purely technical errors that people are beginning to notice. But still, he *was* at one time a significant artist."

Because of Svendsen's illness, Nielsen was given some important assignments during the spring season of 1904. On May 14 he had responsibility for a new production of Boieldieu's *The White Lady*. In a June 20 letter to Bror Beckman in Stockholm he wrote:

I must tell you that during the past 2½ months of the season I have had an unusually large number of things to take care of. I was the only conductor at the Royal Theater during this time as Rung was abroad and Svendsen was ill. . . . But it went very well and I enjoyed this work a lot. The result is that the theater has offered that for the next season I can retain my position as a member of the orchestra without performance duties on the condition that I be available to conduct if I am needed.

This situation became a source of controversy, however. An indignant Frederik Rung wrote to Svendsen on August 15:

Today as I was talking with the boss, Count Danneskiold, he told me in the course of the conversation that during the forthcoming season Carl Nielsen will be taking *your* place if you become ill. Since my appointment specifies that *I* am *supposed* to substitute for you, you can certainly understand that I will not willingly accept such a violation of my contractual rights at the Royal Theater. He also said that you didn't know anything about this, but when the matter is discussed with you—well, now I've told you where I stand on the matter.

The situation remained delicate for a long time. Nielsen functioned as the *de facto* assistant conductor for several seasons, but he did not get the biggest assignments.

It is possible that Svendsen took a trip to Norway for rest and relaxation during the summer of 1904. *Berlingske Tidende* wrote on June 14 that he was planning a trip to his homeland "to spend the rest of his vacation at a sanatorium in the mountains."

The Royal Theater launched the new season on September 3 with the Danish premiere of Gerhard Schjelderup's *The Sacrificial Fire*, which had scored major successes in Dresden and Dessau the year before. Svendsen had never before presented a Norwegian work on the stage, so this was a bold undertaking on behalf of a composer who was almost totally unknown in Copenhagen. Unfortunately, the production was very nearly a catastrophe and the opera was withdrawn after just two performances. The composer's son, Gerik Schjelderup, states in his biography of his father (103:74) that the fiasco was due to the fact that the librettist, Karl Gjellerup, insisted that major cuts be made in the music. William Behrend, in a September 4 article in *Politiken*, also emphasized the impact of the cuts:

> The music had little effect—because there was not much of it left. . . .
> What remained was beautiful and solemn music, consistent with the
> mood of the poetry, but not marked by any notable individuality. The
> spirit of Wagner hovered over it.

On September 18, Svendsen had responsibility for a new production of
Bellini's *Norma*, which he had never conducted previously. The last time it
had played in Copenhagen was spring 1883. The Danish premiere of Peter
Cornelius's *The Barber in Baghdad* on November 21 was entrusted to Rung.

Beethoven's ninth symphony, which had been postponed from the
spring season owing to Svendsen's illness, was performed by the Royal
Theater orchestra for a full house on October 10. It was so successful that
the concert was repeated five days later. Svendsen had the satisfaction of
knowing that he was still capable of scaling the artistic heights. Charles
Kjerulf wrote in *Politiken*:

> His conducting was self-assured and resilient. One noted from the first
> note to the last at the performance this evening what an elite ensemble
> our Royal Theater orchestra really is, and how seriously—yes, rever-
> ently—it approached the performance of this great work. One noted,
> too, what a talented and inspired conductor it was who was leading these
> musicians. It was one of those evenings when Joh. Svendsen renewed his
> fame once again. Small wonder that he was given big and noisy ovations.

The main opera event of the 1905 spring season was the Danish premiere of
Twilight of the Gods, the last work in the *Ring* cycle. The press made much of
the forthcoming production, with long background articles and extensive
critical analyses. William Behrend began his *Politiken* review of the premiere
thus: "Finally once again an *event* on the opera stage at the Royal Theater!"
But he demonstrated his displeasure with Svendsen's understanding of the
score in that he did not so much as mention his name! The music, he
averred, was indeed played correctly and beautifully, but "nothing struck
home, nothing pulled you along or inspired new joy in and understanding
of the drama. . . . The orchestra was at its best where it had nothing to do
with the action on stage, i.e., in the long interlude preceding the first act."

Behrend was virtually the only critic to voice such negative views,
however. Alfred Tofft wrote in *Berlingske Tidende*:

> People were pleasantly surprised that our theater and our singers consis-
> tently mastered the difficult task very well, and that the performance

Johan Svendsen with medals signifying his membership in various royal orders. (Universitetsbiblioteket, Oslo)

here—provided that one does not regard the size of the voices as the only relevant standard—is not far behind many of the German theaters. . . . The orchestra was brilliant, as it always is when Maestro Johan Svendsen leads the performance.

Grieg, who was in Copenhagen at this time, wrote on March 7 to Frants Beyer:

> *Twilight of the Gods*—or *Ragnarok* as it is called here—is currently playing at the Royal Theater, and in the coming weeks both *The Valkyrie* and *Siegfried* are to be presented as well. It's quite an undertaking. Naturally the orchestra under Svendsen is excellent, and much of what happens on the stage is commendable, though the characters do not achieve heroic dimensions.

Grieg also saw Svendsen at a party at the home of music publisher Alfred W. Hansen, however, and was shocked at how depressed his friend had been:

> Can you imagine Svendsen, in the smoking room after dinner, stretching out in an easy chair and lifting his arms over his head and saying, "O, I wish I were dead!" I was really shaken. Because that isn't at all like Svendsen. *I* might say something stupid like that. But the self-controlled Svendsen? Then you understand that he feels completely cowed by the circumstances under which he is living. Plus constant bronchitis and increasing immobility—lack of exercise + the bottle. Yes, it is sad! This life is a drama.

Svendsen's despondency had many causes. Chronic illness reduced his strength and curtailed his activities. Sometimes he felt that his ability to concentrate was slipping, and it pained him when others noticed this as well. His relationship with Carl Nielsen had worsened, as is evident from a March 11 letter from Nielsen to his wife:

> The people at the theater who envy and oppose me—probably, first and foremost, the two conductors—have worked behind the scenes in such a way that today I got dismissed, or more correctly, was forced to ask to be released. For several months now I have been sitting and working in my room and have not been to the theater, but people have been gnawing and gnawing until now the bottom collapsed under me. They couldn't reconcile themselves with the thorn in the eye that I have been and have demanded that either I should play violin in the orchestra like an ordinary good soldier and be their subordinate or else I should be removed. Now it has happened, so I am once again an unemployed man on the street. That's fine with me. The only thing that vexes me is that I have supported Svendsen. He didn't deserve that.

It is hard to know how much weight to give to these bitter words, but it surely would have been totally out of character for Svendsen to join in such a plot.

Carl Nielsen's skills as a conductor were somewhat debatable. He was later remembered mainly for his performances of Mozart, particularly *Don Giovanni*. He had some definite weaknesses as an orchestra conductor, however. Axel Kjerulf has written (69) that the great Danish composer "was more than uncertain as a conductor. . . . It was unfortunately all too true that he had his head in the score more than he had the score in his head."

It is possible that at this time Svendsen may have expressed limited confidence in his young colleague's ability as an orchestra leader. It is more likely, though, that he felt obliged to show support for his old colleague

Frederik Rung. Three years later, when Svendsen gave up his position at the Royal Theater, he strongly urged that Nielsen again be engaged as a conductor—and, in fact, he was. Rung then moved up to the position of principal conductor and Nielsen was appointed to the position previously held by Rung.

Svendsen had his strong opponents in the press, and they didn't hesitate to make an issue of it when something went awry. That they sometimes made a mountain out of a molehill is evident from an incident that one writer called "the Siegfried catastrophe." The newspaper *Klokken 12* reported on May 1, 1905: "The orchestra fell apart in the middle of *Siegfried* Saturday evening. Johan Svendsen looked as if he wanted to commit suicide." *Adresse-Avisen* had written the day before that the orchestra had had an accident, which fortunately was a rarity: "During the Interlude that precedes the scene on the Valkyrie's rock, the orchestra suddenly fell apart. Maestro Anton [*sic*] Svendsen continued to conduct in the hope that it would come together again, but the various instruments continued to play all over the place so the Interlude finally had to be cut short."

According to Victor Gandrup, however, the so-called catastrophe was in reality a very minor incident. At the tempo change in the second theme of Act 3, Svendsen had absent-mindedly given two beats instead of three. The horns, who had the lead at this point, became confused, and the rest of the orchestra evinced a certain anxiety. To forestall a possibly chaotic situation, Svendsen resolutely stopped them, bowed to the orchestra, and instructed them to take the passage over again. Thus the incident passed over so smoothly that the audience was scarcely aware that anything had happened. Within the orchestra, however, the passions ran high: "The horn players didn't get off too easily. Their colleagues read the riot act to them because not one of them had taken the initiative to possibly correct the error, thereby avoiding the dilemma."

Svendsen was angry with himself over what had happened. As he was leaving the orchestra pit after the performance, some of the musicians quietly applauded him to "make known their appreciation for his good judgement at having cut them off and thereby avoided a direct scandal." He, however, was too dejected to find any comfort in their show of support and was heard to say quietly, "Now I'm really starting to get old."

To get old—and to *show* that he was getting old in the way he had done this evening—that, for a man who had once seemed to have boundless energy, was the worst thing that could happen to him.

THE LAST CONCERT SEASONS

In spring of 1905, feeling a need for change, Svendsen moved from Copenhagen to the more rural surroundings of Hellerup, where he planned to remain for the summer.

On May 24, Grieg sent him an upbeat letter in which he again raised the issue of the unfinished third symphony:

> Your friends tell me that you have become a new man out there in the country. That gives me a good idea: take the third symphony out again, pound the table a couple of times and say, "Damn it all, now you'll see what the new man is inspired to do!" You may answer, "That's no concern of yours." But I protest. Nobody feels more strongly than I that you still have much to say. Moreover, I know from my own experience what music a Danish summer like that conceals in its bosom. If the new man even faintly resembles the old one from the 70s, I know what it would mean. I would be happy for a few lines telling me that you have taken out the folder with the sketches, that one thought gives wings to the next, and that you are composing as if your life depended on it!

At the end of the summer Svendsen moved back to Copenhagen. There, on September 30, he received a telegram from Troldhaugen: "Best wishes on your 65th! Thank you because in your marvelous works you pointed the way to the new Norway! Get well soon. Your friends, Nina and Edvard Grieg."

His principal responsibilities at the theater during the autumn season were the Scandinavian premiere of Bizet's *Djamileh* on September 9 and a new production of *La Traviata* on November 12. On November 17 he conducted an orchestra concert; the program included, among other things, Richard Strauss's *Till Eulenspiegel* and the Danish premiere of Grieg's *Old Norwegian Melody With Variations*. Grieg had asked him his opinion on the advisability of making some cuts in the score, and on December 7 Svendsen replied as follows:

> As you will see, I recommend that you delete just one of the variations. On the other hand, I strongly object to the present conclusion of the work. I think that with the big C-major *fortissimo* followed by the *prestissimo* in F-minor 6/8, which also reaches a climax, no further effect is possible. The ending, therefore, should be as short as possible. I urge

you to think seriously about this. It would be too bad if this flaw were not removed from your wonderful piece. The performance here was close to perfect. Seldom if ever has the orchestra played as it did on this occasion. But we also had five rehearsals. It's a pity you weren't here. I think you would have enjoyed it. Everything here is as usual. Unfortunately, I am anything but agile and really should stay in bed, but instead I have to toil and slave like the theater thrall I have become.

Grieg replied on January 4, 1906:

Well, I did it. The whole ball of wax, from the restatement of the theme *pp* to the final measures where the music dies away in F major, has been ruthlessly removed. You were certainly right. . . . Maybe the operations have helped some, and in any case I thank you for your straightforward advice, for which I am most grateful to you.

At the first orchestra concert of the new year on January 25, 1906, Eugen d'Albert appeared as soloist in Liszt's arrangement for piano and orchestra of Schubert's *Fantasy in C Major* ("Wanderer"). Svendsen conducted Brahms's *Symphony No. 2* and Hugo Wolf's *Penthesilea*.

At the orchestra concert on March 3, Eugène Ysaye was soloist in two violin concertos: Mozart's in G major and Bruch's in G minor. He played Svendsen's *Violin Romance* as an encore. The program also included Beethoven's *Pastoral Symphony*, Hugo Wolf's *Italian Serenade*, and Svendsen's *Sigurd Slembe*. On March 18, Svendsen conducted the Danish premiere of Saint-Saëns's *Samson and Delilah*. The other operas at the Royal Theater were repeat performances of previous offerings, and Frederik Rung was on the podium with increasing frequency.

In June, Grieg visited Copenhagen enroute from England back to Norway. As usual, he looked up his old friend, and on June 7 wrote in his diary:

Svendsen, fat, amiable and mild-mannered. How he has retained what is most important: nobility of thought. He has reconciled himself to life as it—unhappily—has turned out for him. How many manage to do that? Only a profound, true nature. Or let me say—a beautiful nature.

The chief object of interest on the opera scene during the autumn of 1906 was Carl Nielsen's new work, *Masquerade*. Svendsen's very last "opera evaluation" had to do with this composition, and therein lies an amusing story. According to Godske-Nielsen (43), the composer hoped to get the opera performed as soon as possible and for that reason was not quite finished with it when he delivered the manuscript. He assumed that Svendsen, in fulfilling his role as musical consultant, wouldn't notice the abrupt conclusion with the clash of booming chords and all that went along with it. Just to be sure, he had put an extra thick double bar at the end. Nielsen said later that it really was intended as a parody. The trick worked. The opera was accepted without Svendsen discovering the deception. He obviously regarded his "evaluation" as a formality and in his surprisingly brief statement dated December 2, 1905, he recommended the work for performance, saying that he found the music "in its faithfulness to the text both enjoyable and distinctive." Reading between the lines, it seems clear that *Masquerade* had made much less of an impression on him than had *Saul and David*.

The premiere took place on November 11, 1906, and once again Svendsen yielded the baton to the composer. The reviews were for the most part positive. Robert Henriques stated in *Vort Land* that the opera "must be characterized as quite specially outstanding. It is so melodic, so accessible, that it enters the ear without difficulty. . . . The whole thing sounds down-home Danish." Angul Hammerich, writing in *Nationaltidende*, suggested that one had to look to *Falstaff* to find anything comparable to it. *Ekstrabladet's* Julius Magnussen, whose judgment was totally negative, was the only discordant voice in the chorus. "The music," he wrote, "is of a kind that will never become popular. There is not a stanza that could be remembered by an ordinary human being."

There were two orchestra concerts in the autumn of 1906. The program on October 27 included Svendsen's *Symphony No. 1*.

The 1907 spring season at the theater was marked by Svendsen's declining effectiveness. Carl Nielsen noted in his diary on January 5: "Met Rung, who talked about all the work he has to do because of everything Svendsen leaves undone." Rung, among other things, had to take over preparations for two big new productions: *The Mastersingers* and *The Daughter of the Regiment*.

Svendsen was able to pull himself together for a stellar performance at the only orchestra concert of the season on March 2, at which Eugène d'Albert appeared as soloist in Beethoven's fourth piano concerto. Alfred Tofft wrote in *Berlingske Tidende* that Beethoven's seventh symphony

A portrait that Johan Svendsen presented to his German son Johann Richard Rudolph. (Universitetsbiblioteket, Oslo)

was "like a revelation under the brilliant baton of Johan Svendsen." He continued:

> It was as if one could see superhuman beings dancing about to a torrent of seraphic sound. It was as if the much-decorated orchestra leader wanted to demonstrate that the holy fire of art still burned brightly in his soul, and the excitement conveyed by the orchestra gripped the listeners as well, so that one felt oneself being elevated to art's highest peaks. The flourish with which the orchestra honored their conductor at the end was richly deserved.

In general, however, Svendsen's performance was of very uneven quality during this period. Grieg took note of this in a diary entry dated March 17 after a performance of *Lohengrin*:

> It was sad to watch Svendsen conduct. His beat is still concise and elastic, and the orchestra sounds wonderful, but the whole performance is what Rubinstein called "Nicht gut." The totality was not worthy of Svendsen's spirit, much less Wagner's.

It is even sadder to read Grieg's diary entry for June 10, written after the two giants of Norwegian music had bid each other farewell for the last time: "Lunch with Svendsen at Hellerup. He was pleasant and lovable, but—his days are numbered. I thought: will we ever meet again?" Grieg's premonition proved to be accurate, but the one who passed away three months later was not Svendsen but Grieg.

Svendsen made his last trip to the continent at the end of July, when he and Juliette went to Ostende, Belgium. Before an audience numbering in the thousands he conducted a 130-piece orchestra in a program that included Sinding's piano concerto, with Karl Nissen as soloist, and his own first symphony.

The young Australian pianist Percy Grainger, who had a lively interest in Norway, was planning a visit to Scandinavia at this time. He had met Svendsen earlier in Copenhagen, and on May 3, 1907, he wrote: "In February or March I hope to come to dear Denmark again. It would mean *indescribably much* to me if this time I could have an opportunity to play under your leadership at an orchestra concert! If only that were possible!"

On September 4 Grainger again wrote to Svendsen. He reported that he had made some phonograph recordings of folk songs in England and that at Grieg's urging he was planning to undertake a similar project in Norway. That very same day Svendsen received word that Grieg had died.

Because of Grieg's death, Grainger's performance with Svendsen in Copenhagen occurred earlier than had been planned. On October 19 Svendsen, the Royal Theater orchestra, and the Danish Students' Singing Society joined forces in a big memorial concert for Grieg, with Grainger as soloist in Grieg's piano concerto. No less than fifteen royal personages were present for the occasion, including the Russian tsarina and the English and Danish royal couples. *Politiken's* Charles Kjerulf used strong words:

> On the podium stood the Norwegian, Johan Svendsen, Grieg's old friend—fortunately resilient and in full command of his artistic prow-

ess. . . . Grainger played like a young Titan; there was iron and steel in his
fingers and wrists, his brain was clear and discerning—but his heart was
as soft as wax. The concerto came back to life under his hands and flour-
ished anew. It was a stunning performance.

John Bird reports in his Grainger biography (10:122) that after the concert
when the pianist returned to the home of his host, cellist Herman Sandby,
he "ran around around the sitting room shouting, crying, and laughing, so
overjoyed was he by the fact that Svendsen had embraced him at the end of
his performance."

A PAINFUL TERMINATION

On November 16, 1907, Svendsen led the Royal Theater orchestra in a
concert at Koncert-Palæet marking the 25th anniversary of his introductory
concerts in Copenhagen. The program, which consisted entirely of his own
works, included the *Festival Polonaise, Zorahayda, Symphony No. 2,* and the
Cello Concerto with Herman Sandby as soloist. Margarethe Lendrop also
sang four of his songs with S. Levyson as accompanist. Svendsen received
many congratulatory telegrams, including this one from Russia: "Heartiest
congratulations on this 25th anniversary to the creator of *Zorahayda* and
many other masterworks. Rimsky-Korsakov, Lyadov, Isokolov, Wihtol."

After the concert the Danish Composers' Association honored him
with a grand banquet in Lille Palæsal to which three hundred guests were
invited. At one point Anton Svendsen, the concertmaster, talked about how
the relationship between the musical director and the musicians had developed through the years. He likened the process to one of Svendsen's own
famous *crescendi*. The beginning of their collaboration was perhaps somewhat *pianissimo* for both parties, but now the relationship had reached such
an extraordinarily strong *fortissimo* that a more powerful one could not be
imagined. No orchestra in the world could have warmer feelings or greater
admiration for its conductor than the Royal Theater orchestra. The concertmaster described Svendsen's authority as a conductor, his ability to
chisel out the rhythm, to coax forth the most subtle phrasings, and (as reported in *Berlingske Tidende*) emphasized further his mastery of orchestral
colors and "the brilliance with which he harmonized and balanced the
various elements of the orchestra and brought forth an absolutely Rem-
brandtian effect."

A high point of the evening was a magnificent speech by Carl Nielsen,

who was president of the Danish Composers' Association. He spoke in
beautiful terms of his mentor as composer, conductor and human being:

> His fresh, unsnobbish naturalness both in his art and in his person has had
> an enormous effect in all aspects of our music life. Well, here sits our
> honored guest in our midst, as big as life. This is not a memorial celebra-
> tion: it's a celebration of gratitude. I know that he—the other one
> [Grieg]—who now belongs to history, would have been happy to be
> present and to celebrate Johan Svendsen here this evening. The names
> Grieg and Svendsen—like Bjørnson and Ibsen—have always been con-
> nected and will continue to be so, even if those bearing those names are
> separated by death. But—dear Johan Svendsen, esteemed Maestro! For
> you we can still express our gratitude. We thank you above all for your
> compositions. You strode forth—no, you didn't stride, you *sprang* forth
> with rhythmically supple flexibility and brightly polished weapons. And
> you triumphed, because your compositions were not only inspired and
> full of life but were also so formally impeccable and so well crafted tech-
> nically that they stand as models. We thank you because as a conductor
> and leader you inflamed us, and with a steady hand and firm will taught
> us to sense the basic element in all music, i.e., rhythm, and with a calm
> and gentle hand and mind you taught us to sense also the beautiful sound
> and the naturally flowing phrasing. And then we thank you for your
> humanity, for your warm heart, for all the things that you yourself are
> unaware of, but for which the rest of us love, respect, and honor you.
> Ladies and gentlemen! Let us ignite all these expressions of thanks and let
> them blaze toward him in a great fire of admiration. So: let us now give
> him three big, Danish *hurrahs!* But they must be on the beat—he himself
> taught us that (90).

Svendsen, in a moving thank-you speech, said that he was completely overwhelmed by all the words of praise. He compared his work at the Royal
Theater to a voyage: "Ladies and gentlemen, I hope that you also think that
we have sailed well, that you also feel that we can soon with a good con-
science cast anchor as I leave the helm." Alluding to "the mystery of music,
humankind's most intimate art" that has the power to unite people with the
most diverse interests, he thanked all of those with whom he had worked in
the artistic vineyard. He concluded with the words, "Long live music in
Denmark!"

　　The joyous celebration was tinged with sadness, however. Charles
Kjerulf said out loud something that was known to everyone: it was time to

face up to the fact that Svendsen's declining strength would soon make it impossible for him to continue to conduct the orchestra (70:35).

Shortly after the twenty-fifth anniversary concert, Svendsen and his wife Juliette traveled by train to Oslo. It had been three years since he had seen his homeland and this was to be his last visit. At Kornsjø, the small border community where the train enters Norway from Sweden, they were met by a journalist, Sven Elvestad, who wanted an interview for *Aftenposten* (32). They had a lively conversation on the train. Elvestad wanted to know, among other things, whether Svendsen was thinking of spending the evening of his life in Norway. His answer had a somewhat ironic twist: there they could certainly offer him, as it says in Norwegian fairy tales, "gold and green forests." At that moment the train was passing through tree-covered Tistedalen, and Svendsen added with a smile: "At least there's no lack of the latter!"

In addition to talking about various aspects of his years in Denmark, Svendsen reported that he had felt worn out after the November 16 concert and mainly wanted to rest. But Johan Halvorsen's invitation to conduct the National Theater orchestra and the prospect of visiting Oslo again had been too tempting. He confided that after getting on the train he had felt so rotten that his wife had recommended that they turn around and go home—but he had told her that he would just as soon die on a train as in a bed.

The Oslo newspapers carried long articles about the visiting native son during the days preceding the concert. Svendsen appeared to be in fine fettle at the concerts on November 23 and 24. A large laurel wreath graced the podium, and when he strode onstage he was greeted with an orchestral flourish. The audience rose respectfully—"as for a king," Otto Winter-Hjelm wrote in *Aftenposten*. The program included many of the same works that had been played at the 25th-anniversary concert in Copenhagen, and the evening ended with a series of wildly enthusiastic curtain calls.

After the second concert, a group of friends and admirers threw a party for him at the Theater Cafe. The party had to be cut short so that he could catch the train back to Copenhagen, but there were nonetheless many speeches and the tributes were extremely warm. *Aftenposten* wrote that the guest of honor had been "in a great mood and kept the revellers going. He has an electrifying ability that does not make itself known only when he is swinging the baton. The excitement that fills the auditorium when he stands on the podium surrounds him at a party as well."

Despite all the festivity, however, the visit to his home city was tinged with melancholy. Juliette Svendsen reported that after her husband received the laurel wreath and many bouquets of flowers, he had turned to her with tears in his eyes and said, "I felt as if I was attending my own funeral" (136).

Grieg's death had deeply affected Svendsen, and he felt that his own strength was ebbing as well. Constant difficulties at the theater led him to think seriously about laying down his baton for good a couple of years before reaching retirement age. But this was a difficult decision to make, for as a Norwegian citizen he had no right to a Danish pension. He had touched on this difficulty in an interview that he gave to a correspondent from *Verdens Gang* (who had come to Copenhagen in connection with the memorial concert for Grieg) on October 22, 1907:

> Svendsen has been very ill, and although he fortunately has gotten the upper hand over his illness he nonetheless, for the sake of his health, has found it most advisable to withdraw now. . . . "To tell the truth, I would like most of all to stay at home all the time," Johan Svendsen said to me when I visited him. "All this public performing is not to my liking. To constantly have to put on my waiter's uniform and appear in front of a bourgeois audience has never appealed to me—yet that has been my fate down here these past 25 years!. . . . Anyway, twenty-five years is a long time out of one's life, and a long time to live abroad. But it hasn't been long enough to make a Dane out of me. I've kept on being a Norwegian, also a Norwegian citizen; and that's a luxury for which I will have to pay a price now when I leave the theater: since I'm not a Danish civil servant I'm really not eligible for a pension, and even if I do get something it certainly won't be as much as I would have gotten if I had been a Dane. But so be it; I'm a Norwegian and I will continue to be a Norwegian citizen."

We have not been able to locate in the archival records of the Royal Theater dating from autumn 1907 anything to indicate that Svendsen was involved in the discussions by the administration regarding the date and conditions of his forthcoming termination. Early in January, 1908, when he had again experienced serious health problems, an action was taken in the matter—and that in a manner that does not appear to have been particularly considerate of Svendsen.

There is no record of Svendsen having submitted a resignation. It appears that Theater director Danneskjold-Samsøe took the matter out of his hands by writing directly to the Ministry of Church and Education. His letter of January 11, 1908, reads as follows:

Since Maestro Svendsen's health in recent years has been very uncertain, as a result of which his work at the theater has suffered greatly, I consider it necessary that at the end of the current theater season he be removed from his position.

Maestro Svendsen, who has held this appointment since July 1, 1883, has demonstrated a quite extraordinary ability during the many years of his association with the theater and has had great influence on Danish music life. He receives an annual salary of 8,000 crowns, and since he will not be receiving any pension I take the liberty of most heartily recommending him for an annual support payment from the state treasury.

Regarding the foregoing, I take the liberty of proposing: that Royal Theater Musical Director Johan Severin Svendsen be terminated from his position at the Royal Theater effective June 30 of this year, and that the Ministry seek to arrange an annual support payment from the state treasury.

The Ministry immediately took the matter up for consideration, and on January 22 the theater director received the answer he was seeking: "In regard to the management's written proposal of January 11 the Ministry hereby concurs that Royal Theater Musical Director Johan Severin Svendsen shall be terminated from his position at the Royal Theater effective June 30 of this year. Which decision is hereby conveyed for your information and communication to others."

The next day Svendsen received the following letter from the theater director: "The Ministry for Church and Education, on the 22nd of this month, has in accordance with my proposal agreed that you will be terminated from your position at the Royal Theater effective June 30 of this year."

The rough draft of this letter contains a short addition which Danneskjold-Samsøe crossed out: ". . . which I regret that I must report to you." Evidently he did not consider it necessary to express regret in any way.

Thus Svendsen's quarter century of self-sacrificing work on behalf of Danish music life came to an abrupt conclusion. Looking at the extant documents today one is obliged to say that it seems almost as if the musical director was summarily fired. At the very least, it is difficult to understand why they could not have worked out a more amicable solution—for example, granting the aging and fatigued old man sick leave for two years, i.e., until 1910, when he would have been obliged to retire.

The newspapers, which were not informed about the matter at the time, reported only that Svendsen himself had sought to be released owing to declining health.

Johan Svendsen surrounded by his valkyries at a farewell celebration held at the Royal Theater, Copenhagen, on May 31, 1908. Johanne Bruun has her hand on Svendsen's shoulder. The other seated valkyrie is Johanne Krarup Hansen. (Det kgl. Bibliotek, Copenhagen)

Despite his fragile health, however, Svendsen was on the podium for a big farewell concert with the Royal Theater orchestra on March 14, 1908. The program was dedicated to his favorite composers, Beethoven and Wagner. The review in *Berlingske Tidende* two days later stated:

At the end of the concert, Mr. Johan Svendsen was once again the object of wild applause by the audience and the orchestra. One ventures to see therein a sure sign that this hopefully will not be the last time that we will find his popular figure at the helm of our first and biggest orchestra at these concerts.

Two and a half months later—May 31, 1908—the Royal Theater sponsored a big "farewell performance for the benefit of Johan Svendsen." When Svendsen came to the green room he was met by a colorful mélange of flowers decorated with a big Danish flag. There were also some gifts for him: from the theater personnel, a handsome bookcase containing selected works in Danish and Norwegian literature, also a card giving him free use of a landau during his summer vacation; from the musicians, a silver cup with roses; and from the choir, a silver cigar case.

The program did not include a full-length opera, for Svendsen's health was too precarious for that. He did, however—after a flourish from the orchestra—lead off with his life-affirming *Festival Polonaise*, "this beautiful hymn to youth and joy, and the Maestro conducted it with all the enthusiasm and power of his glory days," as *Politiken* put it. Then Carl Nielsen took over the baton for the overture and second act of *The Barber of Seville*.

During the intermission, Svendsen was called up to the king's box, where His Majesty thanked him sincerely for the many enjoyable artistic experiences the musical director had given him through many years.

Then Svendsen mounted the podium once again and the mighty sounds of the *Tannhäuser* overture engulfed the rapt audience. At first he conducted from a stool, but as they approached the conclusion he stood up, supporting himself against the guardrail with one hand and swinging the baton with the other. The last item on the program—the actual farewell number—was Act 3 of *The Valkyrie*, which had perhaps been his greatest achievement as an opera conductor.

The musicians had invited him to join them for a glass of champagne in the foyer after the performance. Concertmaster Anton Svendsen expressed the orchestra's sorrow over losing their esteemed leader and suggested that the productions that Svendsen had conducted through the years should be emblazoned in gold on the walls of the theater.

Svendsen wanted to talk to the musicians, but he was so moved that he just stood there, speechless. They heard him say weakly, "I can't do it," and he left the foyer.

A little later Svendsen and the theater personnel gathered in the actors' foyer and Einar Christiansen, financial director of the theater, expressed thanks not only from the theater but from the entire nation: "It is Danish men who thank the Norwegian because he offered Denmark the best years of his life, and because he let his great name and his unique skill redound to our benefit, so that the Danish opera received renown and honor through his art." He emphasized also Svendsen's human qualities, his insightful understanding, his ability to give advice and help, and the confidence that everyone had in him. "All good wishes will follow you when you now leave this place, and your name will be among those that will shine clearly and long in the history of the Danish theater" (38).

An artistically unique era in Danish music life was at an end. Victor Gandrup (39) characterized Svendsen's contribution in strong words: "Only Arthur Nikisch's leadership of the opera house in Leipzig (1878–95) and the Gewandhaus orchestra (1895–1922) and Gustav Mahler's leadership of the opera houses in Budapest (1891–97) and Vienna (1897–1907) and the Vienna Philharmonic (1907–09) deserve comparison with Johan Svendsen's 'Golden Age' (1883–1908) in Copenhagen."

The reviewer (H. S.) in *Politiken*, in his beautiful description of the farewell concert, also emphasized the enormous contribution that Svendsen had made to Danish music life:

> Johan Svendsen conducted this evening for the last time. A poignant, moving evening. A celebration in which tears could be glimpsed behind the smile, and in which everyone in that large auditorium, from the orchestra pit to the last row in the gallery, had the same melancholy thought: the thought of that which was gone forever. . . . Johan Svendsen dedicated his art to Norway and Denmark. He brought his homeland a springtime of art through the compositions of his youth, he offered to us Danes his prime years as a conductor. May he now receive strength and time to give himself and the rest of us the autumn in music, which is still lacking to complete the picture of one of the rarest, most harmonious and noblest artistic figures of our time.

THE ANNUAL STATE GRANT IS RENEWED

As a Norwegian—for he wouldn't even discuss the possibility of becoming a Danish citizen—Svendsen had no right to a pension from the Danish government. Some people in Norway who knew the situation realized that the termination of his appointment at the Royal Theater would, therefore, create serious financial difficulties for him. As early as in the spring of 1907 there had been informal discussions about the problem among members of the Norwegian government, but they didn't want to seriously address the matter until the issue of a possible Danish pension had been decided by the Danish government.

On November 29, 1907, one of Svendsen's old friends—Lieutenant Colonel Alexius Ræder—sent a proposal to Mr. Bødtker, department head in the (Norwegian) Ministry of Church and Education. Ræder underscored the fact that Svendsen had declined for patriotic reasons to become a Danish citizen: "He wanted to live and die as a Norwegian," and it had cost him his right to a Danish pension.

To expedite the matter, on December 17 Ræder sent a formal request to the Norwegian government asking if Svendsen might not again be awarded the annual state grant that the National Assembly had taken away from him in 1886. He called attention to a statement in the 1886 resolution that the grant should not be paid "as long as he holds the position of musical director at the Royal Theater in Copenhagen."

The Ministry recommended that payment of the annual grant should be resumed, and it was widely expected that the issue would be resolved in Svendsen's favor without difficulty. But the unthinkable happened once again. At a preliminary hearing on the matter in the National Assembly's budget committee in 1908, this item was summarily deleted. Even though a majority on the committee acknowledged that they could not defend their decision on juridical grounds—that the Ministry was right in asserting that "the reason stated in the National Assembly's decision of 1886 for the discontinuance now becomes moot"—they insisted that the matter ought now to be viewed in an entirely new light. Their interpretation resulted in a totally different conclusion: the presupposition in 1886 for the possible renewal of the annual grant, they said, surely was that he would return to Norway "while he was still in possession of his ability to work." The majority decision (112 k) further stated:

> The idea can hardly have been that the suspended grant should be reserved for him as an old-age pension when he, after having sacrificed his powers in the service of art in a foreign land, returned to seek rest in his old age. Art is indeed international, and Mr. Svendsen has indeed con-

tributed to the honor of Norway's name out in the world; but Denmark surely has enjoyed the best fruits of his artistic labor, and Denmark will, therefore, certainly also have the decency to grant him the same reward that other men who have served the country receive in their old age. However desirable it might be that Norway were rich enough to show each of its great sons and daughters its appreciation by guaranteeing them financial support in their old age—no matter where in the world they may have done their work, and without regard to their need—unfortunately, circumstances here are such that the scarce resources we are able to dedicate to art and science must be spent in ways that will directly advance these goals in and for the benefit of our own country, and they are sufficient for support only in cases where support can be said to be absolutely imperative. Indeed, there is hardly enough money even for this.

The narrow-mindedness expressed in the committee report was sharply attacked when the matter came before the National Assembly on April 25. Some speakers maintained that they could not now run away from a promise given by the National Assembly and that now, after a 22-year interruption, they should regard it as a "sacred duty" to give Svendsen his annual grant once again. He was, after all, one of those who had contributed the most to the reputation of Norwegian culture abroad. When the issue came to a vote, however, the Ministry's proposal to renew the grant was rejected by a vote of 61 to 57.

The National Assembly's refusal to renew Svendsen's grant created dismay both in Norway and abroad. In Copenhagen, the composer Leopold Rosenfeld published an indignant article in which he wrote: "*We*, who see so much in him, couldn't think of doing such a thing, and still less can we understand that Norway, whose faithful and great son he is, would let him suffer this undeserved insult" (98). The Oslo papers carried a number of articles and letters expressing outrage at the decision. Even Bjørnstjerne Bjørnson had something to say on the matter. The Kristiania Artists' Society wrote a letter to the National Assembly stating that it was "a disgrace to the Norwegian people that the National Assembly has refused to resume paying the annual grant to Johan Svendsen."

On May 1 poet John Paulsen proposed in *Verdens Gang* that money be collected to present as a gift to "Norway's foremost composer and conductor when he, one month from now, tired after lifelong work in the service of art, lays down his inspiring baton for good." Svendsen had emphasized to him that he was and wished to remain Norwegian, "and it is this rare man, who has brought his love for his homeland such a sacrifice, that the National Assembly denies even a modest tip! But should not the whole country—all of us who love and admire Johan Svendsen as an artist and a human being—now try to right the wrong committed by a miserly National Assembly?"

Within a few days, several of the leading men of Oslo made commitments which added up to a sum comparable to the annual state grant. On May 4 the following telegram, signed by Johan Halvorsen, conductor of the National Theater orchestra, and the Oslo newspaper editors Thommesen and Vogt, was sent to Svendsen: "Pleased to be able to report that the 1,600-crown state grant that the National Assembly this year declined to approve, but that certainly will be granted later, will in any case be covered by private contributions. The sum will be remitted annually through us until the state grant is given."

This action by friends in Norway must have felt to Svendsen like a vindication. Somewhat later the Danish government also honored him with an "honorary gift" of three thousand crowns as an extra reward for his work in Denmark. He had no legal claim to a regular pension in Denmark, but it seemed unreasonable that he should spend his old age in Denmark as a pauper.

The prediction by Halvorsen and his friends that the matter would soon be reconsidered by the National Assembly proved to be correct. The letter from the Artists' Society was relayed to the budget committee on January 30, 1909, and was discussed by the committee four days later. The Ministry, in its budget proposal for 1909, again proposed to renew the composer's grant for Svendsen. The records of the National Assembly (112 l) contain the following laconic report from the budget committee: "The committee has been presented with such new information about Mr. Johan Svendsen's health and financial circumstances that it now finds that the composer's grant once taken from him should again be reinstated."

Nothing is said about the source of this information, but it seems clear that the representatives had looked into their own hearts and realized how unreasonable their action of the previous year had been. Therefore, on May 28, 1909, when the new budget was under discussion, the Ministry's proposal to renew Svendsen's grant was unanimously approved, this time without debate. Thus the problem was solved in a way that provided at least a modicum of income for the aging artist and his family to live on.

LAST YEARS, LAST CONCERTS

Svendsen's old age cannot be characterized as his "golden years." No less than two weeks after his farewell concert at the Royal Theater his long-time friend and physician, Dr. Albert Øigaard—a heart specialist—had him admitted to the Finsen Institute in Hellerup. The diagnosis was discouraging: chronic nephritis, degeneration of the heart musculature, chronic alcoholism, cirrhosis of the liver, and fluid build-up, especially in the legs and abdomen.

We learn from an account of his medical history that Svendsen had earlier enjoyed exceptionally good health but had lived carelessly and had been a very heavy smoker. A change in his health had occurred fourteen years earlier when an attack of influenza was followed by malaria. At that time the doctor had instructed him to drink a lot of cognac, and this soon became a habit. Now the slightest exertion led to shortness of breath as well as chest pains. The medical history also states that Svendsen had the appearance of a heavy drinker, i.e., his face was puffy and he was fat. He was in the hospital from June 18 to July 27, 1908. The plan of care consisted of rest and a healthy diet in addition to carbonic acid baths.

Svendsen received several honors at this time. On June 18, theater director Danneskjold-Samsøe wrote to the Minister of Church and Culture calling attention to Svendsen's great importance to the Royal Theater and to Danish music life in general, and this led on June 22 to his being awarded the Danish king's medal of honor in gold. Just a week later he was named a Commander of First Class of the Order of St. Olav by King Haakon of Norway. On December 15 of the same year he became a Knight of the Legion of Honor, and two months thereafter he was made an honorary member of the Danish Composers' Association. On November 19, 1909, he was named Honorary Director of the Malmö Music Conservatory.

In autumn of 1908 he was feeling relatively good. Dr. Øigaard, who checked on him frequently at that time, described for Victor Gandrup what he saw when he visited the Svendsen home:

> When I entered the maestro's drawing room, as a rule he was sitting in a corner in his easy chair, with a lamp behind him, reading a book, or he was sitting at the piano with a candle at either end of the keyboard studying some score or other, now and then trying out instrumental innovations or harmonic constellations on the piano. Otherwise it was dark in the rest of the room, and in both situations the light struck the master's

Dr. Albert Øigaard, Svendsen's
physician and close friend in
Copenhagen. (Det kgl. Bibliotek,
Copenhagen)

thinning pate. The whole mood of the place was in many respects such as
to remind one of an old Dutch painting from about the 1650s. For an
hour or two—all I had time for—Svendsen and I would sit and enjoy
ourselves and converse—that is to say, with only a few interruptions by
me, for most of the time Svendsen constantly talked and told stories, and
how the time flew by during our wonderful time together. Svendsen had
a great ability to talk wittily and amusingly about people, places and
events in his life. He told about his meetings with famous people he had
met on his journeys in various parts of the world—people who, like
himself, meant something to their time. He told about life in the great
metropolises, about the experiences of his youth during various periods
of study, and about his concert tours and triumphs. He was multilingual,
familiar with German, French and English—albeit least with English—so
"he was well-traveled" as his countryman Ludvig Holberg once said. He
enlivened everything, he gave everything a rhythm, everything came to
life under the magic of his impressive story-telling, which was as animated as that of a vivacious 40-year-old. To that must be added his as-
tonishingly convincing argumentative ability (42).

Svendsen at his desk. (Universitetsbiblioteket, Oslo)

On November 27 Svendsen was again admitted to the Finsen Institute. The medical record notes that the edema had been increasing, and he was also bothered by a persistent cough that was very exhausting. This time the doctors decided to make incisions to remove water from his body. The record for November 30 states: "Incisions are made on the right side of the abdomen . . . 7.3 liters of serumal fluid." A week later "6.5 liters of clear, yellowish fluid" was removed.

He remained a patient at the hospital for nearly four months—until March 20, 1909—but by that time his condition had so improved that on March 3 he had been given permission to participate in Fini Henriques's symphony concert at Tivoli, where "with youthful animation" he conducted his first symphony and was honored with an orchestral flourish and a laurel wreath.

He lived at home for a year. He bore his ailments with patience but rarely appeared in public. One consequence of the gross misuse of alcohol was that his hands shook uncontrollably, and for that reason he was hesitant to conduct. Dr. Øigaard has reported that Svendsen's awareness of this malady troubled him greatly. One evening when some concert plans were being discussed, he blurted out, "Yes, by damn, if it weren't for the money I would never take a baton in my hand again!" This frank admission, Øigaard told Gandrup, led him to conclude that Svendsen's merciless self-criticism "was compelled for financial reasons to compromise with his weakened physique."

During the summer of 1909 Svendsen tried to ignore his infirmities, conducting his two symphonies at Tivoli on July 17 and 24. The attendance at these concerts was enormous, but it quickly became evident for all to see that the man who mounted the podium was on his last legs. When he waved the baton, however, the artistic will appeared to be as commanding and electrifying as when he was in his prime. The audience was ecstatic, and the concerts were characterized as musical high points in Tivoli's history. When it was suggested that the success be repeated, however, Dr. Øigaard firmly opposed any further undertakings of this kind.

Despite his physician's advice, Svendsen accepted an invitation from Franz Neruda, permanent conductor of the Music Society, to conduct his second symphony at concerts by the Society orchestra on November 15 and 17. The concerts created something of a stir, for once again Svendsen seemed to be like the Svendsen of old. After the first concert, Charles Kjerulf wrote in Politiken:

The kind of jubilation and emotion that followed is more than rare in our concert halls. And this was in the sober-minded, venerable Music Society? My, how this "foreigner" has won a place in our hearts—yes, in our whole musical culture. This—to use the word in its literal meaning—unique, quite clique-free man whose integrity was always blameless. If only we had many like him!

The November 17 concert was equally successful, and Kjerulf had something to say about it as well: "And afterward there was a lively fanfare from the orchestra while the entire audience stood up, as if to honor a royal person—which Johan Svendsen certainly is within the borders of the world's kingdom of music."

Svendsen's last public performance occurred during the winter of 1910. On February 7 his pupil Joachim Bruun de Neergaard gave a symphony concert in Odd Fellow-Palæets large auditorium, and Svendsen accepted an invitation to conduct *Norwegian Rhapsody No. 3*. The audience greeted him with ovations, and when violinist Marius Hansen played his famous *Violin Romance* as an encore to further honor him it seemed as if the applause would never stop. The composer finally had to be helped up onto the rostrum to accept the applause.

During 1910 the old maestro was hospitalized at the Finsen Institute no less than six times, usually for 3–4 days at a time. The first of these occurred on March 31, and the doctors immediately initiated procedures to drain fluid. The medical records tell about the specific problems the patient had to contend with. He was not a tall man—about 5'-7"—but he weighed over 220 pounds. Large accumulations of fluid in his body made him look more corpulent than he really was. His waistline during periods of illness was about 50 inches, but after the removal of fluid it went down to about 45 inches. This substantial reduction is understandable when one hears that on some occasions they removed more than ten liters of fluid!

Dr. Øigaard told Victor Gandrup something about how Svendsen deported himself as a patient. He was exceptionally forbearing and cooperative, but when he had to take medicine "the ailing artist was absolutely and completely impossible and instantly belligerent." He had to be coaxed like a child to take his medicine.

Svendsen's seventieth birthday was celebrated with appropriate hoopla on September 30. Both Danish and Norwegian flags were waving outside his flat at No. 4 Classensvej at Østerbro. At 9 A.M. a 60-piece wind ensemble consisting of players from the Royal Theater and other orchestras played the Norwegian national anthem. This was followed by the *Festival Polonaise* and the Danish national anthem. Throughout the day, one delegation after another came by to pay their respects. According to the account in *Politiken*, the culmination was reached when a whole parade of carriages drove up to the door and "*all* the members of the Danish Opera Company—sopranos and altos, tenors and basses—jumped out, laughing and chattering, and marched in. The chorus master, the coach, and the prompter were with them too. They also brought a big basket of champagne trimmed with flowers."

Politiken marked the day by publishing a long feature article (71) in which Charles Kjerulf described Svendsen as "the only truly big name that Nordic music has left." The article was in the form of an interview in which Svendsen told about various things but mostly about his meetings with the legendary violinist Ole Bull, whom he had so greatly admired. When the interviewer was ready to leave, Svendsen accompanied him to the door. Kjerulf writes:

> What a fine and proud picture—illuminated by the rays of the evening sun—I took with me of the old musical director, the great artist: so healthy, despite his illness—so young, despite his years—so self-assured and unintimidated, despite many storms. A grand seigneur in art as in life—and what's more, a man without guile or ulterior motives, without underhandedness or pretense. . . . In short: one of the few—the very few nowadays—who is the same in good times and in bad. But it is fortunate and good that *he* was the last one to man the ramparts there where Scandinavia's greatest names stood watch.

There were also many greetings from Oslo, including one from king Haakon and queen Maud. *Aftenposten* carried a long interview (132) in which Svendsen discussed, among other things, his health: "I have been sick for three years now, three long years, but I haven't lost my sense of humor yet. . . . I can't go anywhere. I can't work. But lately I've noticed that I've been getting better."

Asked who in his opinion was the greatest figure in the world of music, he first refused to answer but finally said: "My heart is big and has room for so many. But you know, old papa Beethoven, old papa Beethoven! He is after all the best of the lot!" He also spoke candidly about his relationship to Denmark and the Danish people:

> During the first years I was down here I was dreadfully homesick, but all the work I had to do helped me forget. And then of course I had come to work among a splendid people and got a lot of friends. The Danes are congenial and they are easy to work with. It's part of their national character. They are gentle and good-natured and they have a kind of fear of the unusual. Have you noticed how the press is always trying to bring everything to the same level? That is characteristically Danish. Everyone, in a way, is supposed to be the same size: if there is a protrusion over there, it must be levelled off; if there is a trench here, it must be filled in.

When he was asked if he was homesick for Norway, he stood up abruptly: "Yes, . . . very much." But he realized that it was too late to move back.

DEATH IN COPENHAGEN, BURIAL IN OSLO

During the last year of his life Svendsen lived quietly and almost in seclusion in his modest home on Classensvej. The illness became increasingly serious and he began to experience more and more pain. Dr. Øigaard visited him frequently, but he had trouble getting his patient to take the necessary analgesics. After the last draining of fluid from his swollen body Svendsen got phlebitis, and this slowly developed into gangrene in his left leg. He himself did not realize how serious the condition was, and Øigaard was reluctant to inform his wife or anyone else about what was happening lest it leak to the press.

Svendsen had little appetite during the final weeks because of his fever, and he took little nourishment. Visitors were not permitted into his sickroom, but the little flat was filled with flowers. On May 28, 1911, Mrs. Svendsen wrote to Iver Holter:

> Unfortunately, there is little hope of improvement. His strength is waning day by day and he has no appetite, so the net result will unfortunately be that we will have the infinite, great sorrow of losing him. It will be for us an irreplaceable loss never again to see his beloved face or hear his voice, but that which cannot be avoided we must of course accept, even if the sorrow breaks our heart.

On Tuesday, June 13, Dr. Øigaard realized that the end was near. The patient's pain from the gangrene was almost unbearable, and increasing quantities of fluid in the abdomen made it very difficult for him to breathe. The

The last known picture of Svendsen, taken in May 1911. He died the following month. (Universitetsbiblioteket, Oslo)

doctor wanted to give him a shot of morphine to reduce the agony and calm him down. Svendsen refused, but according to Øigaard's account to Gandrup (41) when the situation became absolutely intolerable he gave the doctor permission to give him the shot:

> Instead of concurring with a "yes" he looked warily up at me with an expression that said, "Yes, yes, I'll take it then, but I know that I won't ever wake up again." In the meantime I calmed the patient by saying that the effect was only temporary. Svendsen got the shot and slowly slipped into a coma. But the look he gave me on that last evening is one I have never forgotten. It expressed such total, inconsolable resignation.

A couple of hours after midnight on June 14 he breathed his last. The next day the Copenhagen paper *Riget* reported as follows:

> Yesterday we visited the room in which he died. At the head of the bed, between two lighted candelabra, was a little Norwegian flag—at half mast. The face, which was unusually handsome in death, was covered with a thin, black veil and the entire body was hidden beneath flowers—mainly bouquets of red carnations, the deceased's favorite flowers. At the foot of the bed lay the laurel wreaths from Johan Svendsen's 70th birthday.

Many years later Mrs. Svendsen reported in an interview (137) that shortly before his death her husband had asked her to gather birch foliage for Midsummer Eve:

> That was a Norwegian custom that we had to take up, that all the vases should then be filled with birch sprigs. Then he died on June 14. I let him have the birch sprigs with him in the casket as a greeting from Norway, for which he always longed. Despite his many years in Denmark he remained a Norwegian in his mind and thoughts to the very end.

The obituary in *Politiken* included one piece of information that caught people's attention in both Copenhagen and Oslo:

> The brilliant maestro's family does not have the means for a funeral. After his body is cremated, the ashes, in accordance with the wishes of the deceased, will be carried to Norway. Perhaps the National Assembly, which did not acknowledge his Norwegianness when he was living, will find the means to honor his remains.

In Oslo, *Morgenbladet* responded as follows:

> Yes, we have both the means and the will. One thing is certain: Johan Svendsen's funeral in Norway will have the dignified character that we owe him—and ourselves. . . . The only thing that Norway has given him is a state grant of 1,600 crowns per year, and then the military band played dance music on the capital city's promenade the day word was received of Johan Svendsen's death. That, then, is how highly he is regarded by the military band and its superior officers. But even his paltry state grant was taken away from him by a National Assembly which, to be sure, later looked into its heart and reversed this act of incredible stinginess. It felt to us like a national humiliation that day when the grant was refused.

The president of the Kristiania Artists' Society now made contact with Prime Minister Konow, who had given a memorial talk at an evening meeting of the National Assembly on June 16. Konow had especially emphasized Svendsen's contribution to his homeland:

> Johan Svendsen was above all a good Norwegian. Although circumstances required him to spend much of his life abroad, still his thoughts

always gravitated toward home. It has touched all of us to hear that in his last moment he expressed the wish that his remains might be laid to rest in Norwegian soil. . . . According to information that has come to me confidentially, and that I wish to have confirmed officially—and this has not yet occurred—I feel constrained to make the following proposal to the National Assembly: The expenses of Johan Svendsen's funeral and the cost of bringing his ashes home shall be paid by the Norwegian state.

The president of the National Assembly recommended that the matter be taken up immediately, and the prime minister's proposal was unanimously approved.

On June 19 a quiet ceremony was held in the home on Classensvej, attended only by the family and a few of Svendsen's old friends. Theodor Hindenburg gave a short talk. Then the casket was lifted up and carried out, and the funeral cortege drove slowly to Our Lady Church. The casket, draped in the Norwegian flag, was carried by friends into the church and into the little whitewashed "Thorvaldsens chapel."

The church was filled for the funeral service, which was held at 2 P.M. the next day. The family sat in the first row together with Johan Halvorsen and Iver Holter, who had come from Oslo to bring the urn home to Norway. The Danish Composers' Association and the Odeon Song Society had placed their banners in the back of the chancel. Countless wreaths covered the floor; they had been sent by the Norwegian and Danish royal couples, the crown prince and princess, the princesses Thyra and Ingeborg, Carl Nielsen (who was in Norway at the time), the officers and musicians and staff of the Royal Theater, and by a host of other institutions.

After a short organ prelude by Professor Otto Malling, the Royal Theater orchestra, under the baton of concertmaster Anton Svendsen, played the *allegretto* movement from Beethoven's seventh symphony, which Svendsen had regarded so highly. The congregation sang a hymn, and then Pastor Hviid-Nielsen talked about the artistic star that now was extinguished, a star that had shone not only over Norway and Denmark but over the wider world.

The congregation rose, the banners were lowered, and against a background of quiet organ music the pastor threw the three shovelfuls of earth over the flower-covered casket. Peter Cornelius sang *Beautiful Savior*, and this was followed by Mozart's *Ave Verum* sung by members of the opera company under the leadership of the choral director Axel Grandjean. The ceremony in the church concluded with the playing of Svendsen's own

Andante funèbre by the strings of the Royal Theater orchestra. Then, to the somber strains of Grieg's *Funeral March for Rikard Nordraak*, the casket was carried out by selected members of the orchestra.

At the head of the procession that made its way to the crematorium at Bispebjærg was a 70-piece ensemble that alternately played Svendsen's, Chopin's and Hartmann's funeral marches. This trip took approximately two hours. Upon arriving at the crematorium the casket was carried in as the ensemble played *Andante funèbre*. The next day, in a ceremony at the railway station, the urn was formally handed over to Halvorsen and Holter, and Mrs. Juliette Svendsen joined them for the trip to Oslo.

The reception at the railway station in Oslo was quiet and simple. Halvorsen and Holter carried the urn, which was wrapped in a Norwegian flag. About fifty of the largest wreaths had been brought along from Copenhagen; the urn, covered with flowers, was placed in an open landau. A large crowd greeted the procession, which made its way to Trinity Church, where the urn was placed on a black catafalque in the choir.

The memorial service took place in Trinity Church on Midsummer Eve. Flags flew at half staff all over Norway, not only on civic and other public buildings but at many private homes as well. The church was beautifully decorated for the occasion. The chancel was shrouded in black, draperies covered the walls, and the chandeliers were wrapped in mourning crepe. Myrtle and laurel branches adorned the chancel. There stood the urn, and on the side that faced the congregation shone the name "Johan Svendsen" in silver. In front of the catafalque lay a large wreath of white lilies and ferns, with black lettering and a royal crown on the white ribbon; it was from king Haakon and queen Maud. The royal couple were in their pews on the right side of sanctuary near the steps leading to the chancel.

The service began with the playing of the *Andante* movement of Svendsen's second symphony by the Norwegian National Theater orchestra conducted by Johan Halvorsen. Pastor Herman Lunde then gave a moving memorial address that must also be regarded as a reproof to Norwegian government officials:

> When he left us, it was not because we did not have the means to keep
> him but because we were woefully lacking in our appreciation of the

value of art. . . . This lack was our poverty. Our Danish friends, on the other hand, understood the importance of offering him a place in which to work—something for which we Norwegians ought to thank them. Johan Svendsen, you came home to ask for a grave. It is painful thus to bid you welcome; we wish we had done so in another way. But when you rest beneath the cypresses in the cemetery, we will go up there and remember you, not only for your symphonies and songs but because you were a good human being, one whom everyone loved when they learned what kind of a man you were.

The orchestra played *Andante funèbre*, and various people came forward to lay a wreath beside the catafalque. Among them was J. M. Halvorsen, president of the National Assembly, who spoke some warm words on behalf of his colleagues. Prime Minister Konow expressed sincere thanks for what Svendsen had given to his country.

The Merchants' Society Chorus under Iver Holter sang Grieg's *The Great White Host* and a new song, the words of which had been written for the occasion, sung to the tune of Svendsen's *Evening Voices*. The urn was then taken to Our Savior cemetery, where the chorus sang Svendsen's *Evening Voices*. Halvard Emil Heyerdahl, an old friend of the composer, spoke a final farewell, after which the chorus sang A. P. Berggreen's *Blessed, Blessed*.

Svendsen's final resting place is right beside that of Bjørnstjerne Bjørnson.

———

Twenty years after Svendsen's death the Royal Theater orchestra gave a memorial concert in Copenhagen, and *Politiken* used the opportunity to interview Carl Nielsen (91). Nielsen stated that he had had boundless admiration for Svendsen, that immediately upon meeting him for the first time he had perceived him as a man of genius. He went on to say:

The language of music is a remarkable one. . . . To the one who understands it, it says everything. Johan Svendsen knew that I composed, and from the first moment we felt like secret foster brothers. I remember one

Niels W. Holm's statuette of Johan
Svendsen. (Det kgl. Bibliotek,
Copenhagen)

time when he was conducting *The Magic Flute*. We were approaching the chorale melody, the place where Pamina and Tamino endure the test by going through fire and water. Then our eyes met, perhaps for only a fraction of a second, but that momentary glance said it all. It said without words, "This is heaven revealing itself. It is greater than both you and me; we will never attain it, but we love it, we two together."

Johan Svendsen loved music, he loved art, he loved his fellow men—and he loved life. And through his life-affirming compositions he has succeeded in communicating these loves to others.

10

SVENDSEN AND GRIEG

An Epilogue

IN OUR ATTEMPT to penetrate as deeply as possible into the life and work of
Johan Svendsen we have followed him from his poverty-stricken upbringing in Oslo, through the decisive years of study in Germany and France, the
period in his home city (1872–83) when his creative powers were at their
peak, and on to the culmination of his artistic career as musical director of
the Royal Theater orchestra in Copenhagen beginning in 1883. In addition
to tracing the story of his life we have also attempted to shed light on his
compositions.

We have frequently had occasion to discuss the relationship between
Svendsen and Grieg. Now, by way of summary, we shall present an overview of this relationship and, at the same time, place Svendsen in a somewhat wider perspective.

PERSONALITIES

Svendsen and Grieg were very different from one another both as human
beings and as artists, but they complemented each other in a fascinating way.
Their basic human idiosyncrasies are in both cases reflected to a considerable degree in their work as performing artists and composers.

Grieg was by nature very sensitive and nervous. Svendsen, on the other
hand, was to all appearances the incarnation of health, a man with a robust
capacity to prevail over life's many difficulties. His journey through life was

characterized for the most part by supreme confidence, straightforwardness, and a happy-go-lucky optimism.

The two men came from totally different socio-economic backgrounds. While the struggle for existence in a broken home in the slum area of Oslo cast shadows over Svendsen's childhood and youth, Grieg grew up in a financially secure and domestically harmonious upper-class family in Bergen. In Grieg's home, the mother was the dominant personality; in Svendsen's, it was the severe father who gave the orders.

Svendsen left his home city on his own initiative at the age of 22. In Grieg's case it was his parents who, on the advice of Ole Bull, sent their 15-year-old son to study in Leipzig. While Svendsen's basic education consisted only of a few years of compulsory attendance at an elementary public school in Oslo, Grieg was more fortunate: at the age of ten he had been enrolled in the well-regarded Tank's School in Bergen. Here he remained for about five years, during which he received a good education that included training in German and other foreign languages.

Both Grieg and Svendsen, however, also learned a lot in "the school of hard knocks." They both tried to expand their horizons through assiduous reading. Grieg was especially interested in drama and poetry, whereas Svendsen preferred novels and political history. Both had a knack for language. Both learned to speak and write excellent German. Svendsen also mastered French and some English—a language that Grieg, for some reason, did not seriously attempt to acquire.

Grieg's intelligence was razor-sharp—a fact that is manifest in many ways, including his letters and articles. It is a sheer pleasure to read his stylistically brilliant prose. Svendsen, who did not share his friend's writing skill, cringed at the thought of putting his innermost thoughts down on paper. Compared to Grieg's letters with their bubbling wealth of original ideas, Svendsen's seem extremely mundane. Only rarely does he allow himself to indulge in passionate outbursts.

In his dealings with others, Svendsen was more open and sociable than Grieg. While Grieg was able to be totally at ease primarily at home or in the company of a few chosen companions, Svendsen was a notorious reveller and, indeed, typically was the life of the party.

Numerous witnesses attest to the fact that Svendsen, like Grieg, made a strong impression on those with whom he came in contact. Hans von Bülow and Carl Nielsen were absolutely effusive in their praise of Svendsen. According to Victor Gandrup, Eugène Ysaye characterized him

as "the greatest artistic personality he had met on his journey through life."
Hugo Seligman's testimonial in *Politiken* on the occasion of the centennial
of Svendsen's birth (109) is both beautiful and pertinent:

> The *human being* was like the artist. The magic that flows from his music
> was in the man, and it captivated everyone with whom he came in con-
> tact. As his art remained young, so also did his mind. The burdens of old
> age pounded in vain on *his* door: he never shrivelled up in narrow-
> mindedness and intolerance, he was above party and clique, artistic arro-
> gance and envy were equally foreign to him. He moved high above the
> hustle and bustle of the crowd. The noble decorum that characterized his
> figure did not lie.

The control and discipline that marked Svendsen's work as composer and
conductor did not, however, characterize some other areas of his life, notably his finances, his use of alcohol, and his relations with women. Throughout his life he experienced crises that resulted from his limited ability to
handle money. He was an extravagant spender, and his perennially optimistic outlook led him to take out loans wherever he could get them without
bothering to calculate how he was going to repay them.

Grieg, who came from a prosperous merchant family in which the measure of a successful life was economic prosperity, had good sense in economic matters. He was by nature frugal and became, in time, a very wealthy man.

Although Grieg had an appreciation of good wine, he was very careful
in his use of alcohol. Svendsen was not. His weakness for hard liquor presumably derived both from the circumstances of his upbringing and, later,
from the temptations of his active social life. During the last decade of his
life this weakness, together with illness, quite destroyed his formerly robust
health.

Svendsen's attraction to the fair sex was legendary: it was not without
some foundation in fact that people in Copenhagen joked about his Don
Giovanni-like list of "a thousand and three" conquests. He entered into a
number of difficult relationships, and his first marriage was notably unhappy. Grieg, on the other hand, early on found in his cousin Nina a life
companion with whom he—with some interruptions, to be sure—remained for the rest of his life. She became the good supporter that he
needed in his often unsettled existence.

In the religious sphere, Grieg plumbed the depths much more resolutely than did Svendsen. Grieg grew up in a traditional Christian home, but

although in the 1870s he rejected the dogmas that he had been taught in childhood, his inquisitive nature was such that he never ceased looking for answers to life's most fundamental questions. Svendsen, on the other hand, came from a milieu where contact with the church appears to have been minimal. He seems to have been largely indifferent to religious values, perhaps with a tinge of negativity.

CAREERS

As performing artists Svendsen and Grieg went different ways, even though for a time they also worked together as conductors. Grieg, trained as a pianist, won international acclaim as an interpreter of his own works and continued to appear as a performer right up to the time of his death. Svendsen was a violinist, but a finger disorder suffered in Leipzig put an end to any hope of a career as a soloist. He didn't put the violin away entirely, however. He played sporadically in several orchestras in Leipzig and Paris, and during the Oslo years he was an enthusiastic promoter of chamber music and participated from time to time as a violist at public chamber concerts.

Both Svendsen and Grieg also did some teaching, but of different kinds. Grieg spent a decade in Oslo primarily as a piano teacher. He also gave lessons in various aspects of music theory, but surprisingly enough he never taught composition.

Svendsen had several composition students—in Oslo (Iver Holter, Per Lasson, and Per Winge), in Paris (Robert Kajanus), and in Copenhagen (Hakon Børresen, Fini Henriques, and others). In Norway it was especially Iver Holter's music that reflected Svendsen's influence. Danish scholars have asserted that Carl Nielsen—though he was never a pupil of Svendsen—was strongly influenced by Svendsen's style, especially in his debut work, *Suite for String Orchestra* in A minor (1888).

The friendship between Svendsen and Grieg, which began in Leipzig in 1865, was further strengthened in 1872–75 when they worked together as co-conductors of the Music Society orchestra in Oslo. As orchestral leaders they were very different from one another. Svendsen was the rock-solid maestro who always had everything under control. He was completely in his element when he had a baton in his hand. Grieg was often tormented by stage fright, but at his best moments he was capable of producing outstanding results. Audiences responded to both of them with tremendous enthusiasm, but while the musicians respected Grieg, they loved Svendsen.

The collaboration in Oslo ended in 1875, and their paths diverged. Grieg, after a period in Hardanger, briefly resumed his work as an orchestra conductor, this time with "Harmonien" in Bergen in 1880–82. Thereafter, however, he appeared on the podium only sporadically as a guest conductor in Norway and abroad. Svendsen, on the other hand, intensified his work in this area. He remained, with some interruptions, sole conductor of the Music Society orchestra in Oslo until 1883 and spent the rest of his professional life as conductor of the Royal Theater orchestra in Copenhagen. After an introductory period marked in some degree by strife and difficulties, he totally won the hearts of the Danes. His enormous contribution over a period of more than twenty-five years can hardly be overestimated—a fact that the Danish theater historian Robert Neiiendam expressed in these words: "After the death of N. W. Gade, he became the soul of Danish music life" (86:180).

The charisma that Svendsen possessed as a conductor has been praised by many. Danish opera singer Vilhelm Herold expressed it thus: "When Johan Svendsen came in and mounted the podium, the ceiling of the auditorium became higher and the walls expanded" (66). Herold had sung under many conductors, but never under anyone whose baton was so alive and so easy to follow as Svendsen's. His beat was simple and clear, and even in the fastest tempos there was a calmness that gave the performers a feeling of total confidence. And his whole face reflected the character of the music.

Eyvind Johan-Svendsen said of his father's conducting, "His expression was calm, the arm movements were small but more expressive and stirring than anyone else's, and then the orchestra resounded and sang with a beauty and fullness such as no one before or since has been able to get it to produce" (66). Victor Gandrup described Svendsen's conducting as follows:

> The hallmark—or rather, the mark of nobility—of Svendsen's conducting was his unique, perfect beat. It was restrained and resilient; nobody who succeeded him has been able to duplicate it. For the orchestra musicians it was more than just a matter of its clarity: they absolutely revelled in this remarkably vibrant revelation of perfection which was at once both bound and free. And down in the auditorium—no matter where— the listener was in a position to follow along precisely and understand the maestro's delicate sign language. By virtue of his powerful, authoritative personality, Johan Svendsen was in fact one of the few unique individuals of whom Georg Brandes has said that it is as if they came into being in a leap of nature. . . . And as the years passed, Svendsen used this natural

ability to nurture and unite the respect and devotion that the theater's various groups of artists felt toward him until it became a well-founded veneration upon which their collaborative efforts could securely stand (40:265).

As a conductor, Svendsen had a singular feeling for rhythmic vivacity, as Carl Nielsen and others have observed. Indeed, Svendsen himself once said as much to a Danish friend:

> One thing I think I have accomplished. I think I have taught Danish musicians and Danish audiences a greater *rhythmic sense*. Gade, for all his musical distinction, was a little too much the product of Zealand's lovely meadows. I came from a land of mountains. In addition, I had been abroad *often* and for long periods (79:14).

While the music critics occasionally described Grieg's conducting—perhaps by way of excusing him to some extent—as *voix de compositeur* (the voice of the composer), they never said this about Svendsen. He was one of the few individuals in music history who, in addition to being a composer of distinction, was also a "superstar" as a conductor.

If Grieg and Svendsen present many contrasts as orchestra conductors, the contrasts are even more pronounced when one compares them as composers. In addition to the fact that they of course began with different natural talents, the contrasts in their output as composers can be explained in part by the very different circumstances under which they undertook their studies at the Leipzig Conservatory. Grieg was only fifteen years old when he went to Leipzig, whereas Svendsen was twenty-three. Unlike Grieg, Svendsen already had a considerable amount of experience as an orchestra musician, violinist and composer. Because of this background, he was naturally much better prepared to benefit from what the conservatory had to offer than was the youthful Grieg.

Svendsen's creative talent manifested itself during his student days in Leipzig in two masterworks: the string octet and the first symphony, both of which contain some national features. In the development of his national consciousness as an artist, Ole Bull played a much more important role than either Kjerulf or Nordraak—which was the case for Grieg as well. There is also reason to believe that Grieg, during his visits to Leipzig in 1865 and 1866, showed Svendsen his newly composed Norwegian-sounding works, i.e., the four *Humoresques*, the *Piano Sonata*, and the *Violin Sonata No. 1*, and that in so doing he ignited a spark that burst into flame in Svendsen's symphony. But then a remarkable thing happened: Svendsen's expertise as a symphonist—and not least his superb mastery of orchestration—made such a strong impression on Grieg (in 1867) that he seems to have acquired an almost lifelong complex about his friend's ability as an orchestrator. One result of this complex was that Grieg withdrew his own symphony, written in 1863–64, from public performance. Nonetheless, whereas Svendsen, in the compositions that followed—the string quintet, the violin concerto, and the cello concerto—was not able to maintain the standard achieved in his earlier works, Grieg, during the same time period, wrote two outstanding large works: the second violin sonata and the immortal piano concerto.

As composers the two men had a deep understanding of each other's art, and there is nothing to indicate that they ever exhibited the slightest hint of jealousy or envy toward each other. They never regarded themselves as rivals. Indeed, they complemented each other in a unique way in that they, consciously or unconsciously, generally chose different musical forms of expression and created their works on the basis of their own respective backgrounds and interests.

Did they influence each other at the purely musical level? In view of the fact that they took such different paths, it is difficult to show any direct influence of one upon the other—except for one single example. Grieg must undoubtedly have studied Svendsen's *String Octet* quite thoroughly, for in his own G-minor quartet there are some obvious motivic-thematic connections with Svendsen's composition (see Examples 4 and 5, p. 00).

Both composers make use of common material from the German Romantic tradition in works where they are not consciously trying to create a national sound. In explicitly Norwegian-sounding compositions it is easier to trace the connections between them—in their melodies (including use of the so-called Grieg formula and modally colored scales), in harmony (e.g., open fifths and sharp dissonances), and in their selection of rhythms (such as those derived from the *halling* and *springar*). These features are especially prominent when they borrow folk-music material from L. M. Lindeman's collections. There are, in fact, three cases in which they have harmonized the same melody. Svendsen, however, uses the Norwegian stylistic features in a far less daring way than does Grieg.

Svendsen's reputation spread rapidly after his international breakthrough in the late 1860s, and from then until 1883, when he moved to Copenhagen, he was riding on a steadily growing wave of fame. Em-

boldened by his early successes, he proceeded to create a long series of mature masterworks including *Carnival in Paris, Festival Polonaise, Zorahayda,
Norwegian Artists' Carnival, Symphony No. 2*, and the *Violin Romance*. These
compositions were well received in concert halls all over the world, and until 1890 or so Svendsen was the Nordic composer who was performed most
frequently outside Scandinavia.

Audiences and critics were unanimous in their judgement: Svendsen's
music was both fresh and buoyant and clearly of high quality. It fit the taste
of the times. It was solidly anchored in the Classical-Romantic tradition,
easily accessible, devoid of revolutionary tendencies, yet free of stale clichés.
Svendsen was a fine melodist, albeit not quite on a par with Grieg. Nor was
his harmonic style as daring as Grieg's. Svendsen employed chromaticism in
such a way as to give his music a distinctly mellower stamp. And listeners
were titillated by something else that was out of the ordinary: pungent, na-
tional-sounding melodies and harmonies and rhythms with roots in Norwegian folk music. To be sure, these features are less prominent in
Svendsen's music than in Grieg's and are integrated with the other elements
of the composition in a completely natural way. Most of all, however,
people were fascinated by Svendsen's inventiveness as a dazzlingly brilliant
orchestrator. His peers also had high regard for his professional expertise,
i.e., for his unsurpassed knowledge of the capabilities of the various instruments and his complete mastery of the forms within which he chose
to work.

In 1883, however—just forty-three years old and at the height of his
powers—Svendsen abruptly stopped composing. He was to live for twenty-
eight more years, but during this time he would write only a few relatively
insignificant occasional works. Looking back, one can only regret this tragic
fact. It is natural to ask whether this early end of his work as a composer was
a conscious choice on his part or an unavoidable result of outward circumstances, notably the exhausting character of his work as musical director of
the Royal Theater orchestra in Copenhagen.

Svendsen, who rarely talked about himself and his achievements, did
address these questions in a letter of April 21, 1905, to Iver Holter, who had
planned to write a biographical work about his friend:

> As you quite rightly suggest, my lack of productivity as a composer dur-
> ing my nearly twenty-two years here in Copenhagen is due to my exten-
> sive activity as a conductor. For nine and a half months each year I have

of course had a lot to do at the theater, and in addition to that I have had a great deal of work as leader of the philharmonic concert series that I established and as principal conductor at several male chorus festivals. This seems to me to be a plausible explanation of my lack of productivity as a composer. The things you say regarding my personal circumstances and their possible influence in this matter don't hold water; it was *only* and *exclusively* the considerable and uninterrupted involvement with all this other music that stifled my *own* thoughts. In my opinion, therefore, it would be appropriate if you in your biography—make that my biography—stress my work as conductor in the three aforementioned capacities. At the theater I got Wagner's *Dutchman, Valkyrie, Siegfried* and *Twilight of the Gods* performed as well as many French, Italian (Verdi: *Otello, Aida*) and Danish works. In the concert hall I have supplemented a main diet of compositions by our old classical masters with a significant number of new works, especially works by French and Russian composers. And finally, through my work as principal choral conductor at the big song festivals in Århus, Odense and Copenhagen, I have, in my opinion, made a major contribution to the increase of interest in this art form. During my long tenure here I have performed as a conductor in Stockholm, Helsinki, St. Petersburg, Moscow, London, Paris, Brussels etc. So then, dear Holter! Here you have what I can think of to tell you at the moment. If you can use some of it, I would be happy.

What Svendsen says is of course true, but in our opinion it is not the whole truth. When he left Norway it appears as if he in a way felt burnt out as a composer. With his keen sense of self-criticism he realized that anything he might write in the future would not measure up to his own high artistic standards. In 1883, when his wife Bergljot burned his third symphony, it appears that both the desire and the will to compose were dealt a fatal blow. To be sure, he tried to get back to work on the symphony—during the next twenty years we hear about it from time to time—but it was never completed.

Frustration over the drying-up of his spring of creativity cast a dark shadow over Svendsen's existence. During the Denmark period he increasingly withdrew into himself, seldom if ever revealing his inner thoughts to others. His artistic triumphs as a conductor could not outweigh the burdensome problems that he experienced in his work situation, his finances, and his marriage. The mounting weight of these problems eventually spelled his doom.

For Grieg, a highly emotional person who frequently expressed his feelings in passionate outbursts, Svendsen's lack of openness was hard to understand. As early as 1885 he wrote, "Svendsen is such a complex person that he will surely always be a mystery to me." There is, however, strikingly little evidence of the complexity of Svendsen's personality in his music, where light-heartedness reigns supreme. It is possible that in this area, too, he avoided expressing the darker side of his nature. While Grieg, in his compositions, ran the gamut of his highly varied emotional register, Svendsen appears to have consciously avoided doing so.

That Svendsen suddenly ceased composing had momentous consequences. The international renown as a composer that he had sought, and briefly won, became in the long run a mere mirage. At a time when people had a big appetite for engaging contemporary music, but did not have either radios or record players, an orchestra composer's fame depended entirely on his success in getting his works played at live performances. If the expected new works from his hand did not appear, in a relatively short time he would be forgotten.

Thus it was Grieg, not Svendsen, who in the eyes of the world sallied forth as the foremost representative of music from Scandinavia. Grieg had something that Svendsen lacked, namely financial security. With this as a foundation he was able, albeit with occasional interruptions, to spend the last twenty-five years of his life as an active composer and in periods of hectic inspiration to renew himself in a number of highly important works. In thousands of homes he came to be loved also for his shorter compositions—the songs and especially the *Lyric Pieces* for piano. He was also fortunate to have C. F. Peters, one of the world's leading music publishers, behind him. The Peters firm quickly recognized the market potential of Grieg's music and did much to make it known and available all over the world. Svendsen, however, had to be his own ambassador, and he had another handicap as well: except for the *Violin Romance* and the *String Octet*, his renown was tied to large orchestral works, not smaller pieces intended for the music-loving amateur.

By the time of Grieg's death, many of his works had won a firm place in the hearts of a wide audience and continue to be performed even today. When Svendsen died, his music virtually disappeared from the scene—with one single exception: the *Violin Romance*. Only in recent years has there been evidence of a renewed interest in the rest of his music.

One can also point to other reasons why things went as they did for the two composers. Grieg was throughout his life a radical who boldly challenged the conventions of his time and relentlessly went his own way. The constant struggle to explore the unknown is reflected in many works and gives his output a broad scope. Svendsen, despite some radical political views around 1870, was by nature much more conservative. His artistic outlook really was eclectic. He found his ideals during his conservatory days, and in the string octet and the first symphony he developed a style that he would retain for the rest of his life. Even in the later programmatic works the musical language remained unchanged. He never experienced the thankless fate of not being understood by his contemporaries. Having found early on a style that he was comfortable with, he never felt a need to mark out new pathways. Perhaps this very lack of a felt need for stylistic rejuvenation is one of the reasons why his music in later years has sometimes been unjustly characterized as *passé*.

Svendsen was unusually knowledgeable about the new music of his time, however, and as a conductor he regularly stuck his neck out on its behalf. In this area he clearly was progressive. It was especially the younger French, Czech, and Russian composers that he sought to promote, but contemporary German music did not capture his interest to the same degree. It is striking that he only performed symphonic works by Brahms on three occasions—despite the kinship that can be traced between the two composers, not least in their common firm anchoring in the Classical-Romantic forms. Nor does he appear to have had much interest in the music of Richard Strauss.

Even after the turn of the century there were some who regarded Svendsen as a greater composer than Grieg. The September 1, 1902, issue of *Svensk Musiktidning*, for example, stated, "No Nordic composer in our time—and few foreign ones—have handled the orchestra more brilliantly than Svendsen, and with regard to musical inspiration and inventiveness, too, he takes the prize notwithstanding the substantial musical merits of Grieg and Sinding."

There are few today who would share that view. As a composer, Grieg was undoubtedly the more gifted of the two. Nonetheless, although Svendsen eventually was overshadowed by Grieg, his best works are of such high quality that they bear comparison with anything that was composed elsewhere in the world during the years 1863–83, i.e., the period when he was most active as a composer.

The output of both composers was uneven—Svendsen's, perhaps, more than Grieg's. For Svendsen, writing music did not seem to pose any major problems regarding either form or technique, as it notoriously did for Grieg. Svendsen enjoyed gamboling about with musical elements, and he handled technical difficulties—not least regarding form—with natural ease. These qualities are reflected in life-affirming music that absolutely sparkles with freshness and vitality. Grieg, on the other hand, often wrestled nervously with the material, especially when working in the larger forms. There is in some of his music an undertone of melancholy and agonizing spiritual struggle that was quite foreign to Svendsen. "Freedom with responsibility" could stand as a motto for both Svendsen and Grieg. But while Grieg appears to have given more attention to the free expression of his musical ideas, for Svendsen the sense of responsibility to the tradition was the predominant consideration.

Grieg plumbed the depths more fully than did Svendsen and had a wider register upon which to play. This does not mean, however, that Svendsen merely skimmed the surface. There are several works in which he combined a solidity worthy of a master with a striving for perfection and an authenticity of expression in a way that commands the utmost respect and admiration.

In his symphonic works, Svendsen shines more brilliantly than Grieg as one of the great orchestra virtuosos of the Romantic period. His background as a military and orchestral musician had given him first-hand knowledge of several instruments, including both strings and winds. Thus even in his earliest works—the octet and the first symphony—he was able to handle the instrumentation with consummate skill. All of his compositions have a characteristic sonority, and according to musicians who have performed them they are exceptionally rewarding to play, adapted as they are to the capabilities of each instrument. Berlioz's effective use of the winds was an ideal for the young Svendsen, and in some of his single-movement orchestral works he became the great Frenchman's equal. With respect to the use of the strings, Mendelssohn's gossamer world of sound appears to have influenced him more than the luxuriant outpourings of Schumann and Wagner. Indeed, even when the groups of instruments are divided, the sound retains its clear and transparent character.

Norwegian folk music played less of a role for Svendsen than it did for Grieg. Except for a couple of minor works, his arrangements of folk-tune material is limited to the four *Norwegian Rhapsodies*, which were pioneer works in the genre. While a number of Grieg's works are permeated by elements derived from folk music, this is rarely the case in Svendsen's music. The most notable exceptions are the *scherzo* movements in the two symphonies.

STYLISTIC CHARACTERISTICS

With respect to *melody*, Svendsen is more diatonic than Grieg. Compared with his contemporaries on the continent, he is distinguished by his moderation in this area. In contrast to Grieg, however, his themes sometimes traverse several different keys. A typical example of this is the first subsidiary theme of the first movement of the octet (Example 3).

Purely chromatic passages in a theme are relatively rare in Svendsen's music. The exotic coloring of *Zorahayda* makes it unique in his production. Here, in Jacinta's theme (Example 11) we find some characteristic chromatic turns, clearly intended to depict Jacinta's sadness.

In fast movements Svendsen frequently uses themes consisting of broken triads, especially descending (fifth–third–tonic). Examples appear in the *String Quartet* (principal theme of the third movement), the *String Octet* (Example 3, also the principal and subsidiary themes of the *finale*), the first symphony (third movement, second theme), the second symphony (principal theme of the fourth movement), the *Festival Polonaise* (first theme of the trio), and the *Violin Romance* (the theme of the A section). Broken chords of this kind, which are often found in Norwegian dance-dance tunes, tend to give Svendsen's music a certain national tinge.

Another kind of national touch occurs when the composer occasionally—though much more rarely than Grieg—spices up his melody line with a Lydian twist (the augmented fourth above the tonic). A notable example occurs in *Norwegian Artists' Carnival* (Example 10). A melodic feature that is more characteristic of Svendsen than of Grieg is the former's unique tendency to run up to the leading tone and then go back down again without ever reaching the tonic (as in Example 2, the principal theme of the first movement of the octet).

Øivind Eckhoff (29:61) rightly points out what he calls Svendsen's "dominantizing" technique: a theme, either as a whole or in part, is moved up a fifth with small alterations, but strangely enough over a dominant chord foundation in the original key. A typical example is the principal theme in the first movement of the first symphony (Example 6). In measure 21, the theme is moved up to the dominant plane, but with a dominant seventh in

D major as the basis. Something similar happens with the subsidiary theme in the development section of the first movement of the second symphony (beginning with measure 197). A theme can have a more or less dominant cast—both in itself and in its harmonic basis—even in its original statement. This technique, which is used in the *finales* of both symphonies and elsewhere, is, however, limited to secondary themes. Treating themes in this way produces a peculiar feeling of unresolved tension: one is enroute toward something, but it is as if one can't find the right pathway and reaches the goal only by way of detours.

Svendsen's *harmony* is anchored in Vienna Classicism, with a firm tonal basis. There are, however, distinct elements of advanced Romantic coloring characterized by extensive use of chromaticism and alterations. One can, indeed, find certain features reminiscent of Wagner's style, though Svendsen was by no means an imitator of Wagner. In general one must say that he did not go beyond the harmonic vocabulary of Schumann, Chopin and Liszt.

Svendsen's use of long series of parallel diminished seventh chords is typical, but such progressions can nearly always be explained in a way consistent with functional harmonic theory. His employment of mediant relationships exhibits considerable originality. He preferred such relationships in an ascending direction and achieved quite singular results—as, for example, in the colorful sequence in *Carnival in Paris* (Example 7). The first part of the sequence goes up a minor third, then the sequence is transposed down a perfect fourth. The result is to give the passage a kind of modal tinge. Even Grieg, who loved modal touches, never used sequences in this way.

One characteristic of Svendsen's harmony—and this is also true of Grieg—is his preference for descending chromatic lines, either in the inner voices or simultaneously in one of the inner voices (occasionally an upper voice) and the bass. A very striking example of this occurs in the coda of the *Violin Romance*. In the middle of richly colored chord progressions, Svendsen frequently softens the feeling of dissonance through the use of parallel tenths, occasionally thirds and sixths.

Svendsen had a greater tendency than did Grieg to veil the chords through liberal use of suspensions, appoggiaturas and anticipations. Rarely, however, does one note anything in the way of harsh dissonance. Grieg is almost brazen in this respect. Svendsen's feeling for what sounds good often reminds one of Mendelssohn, whereas Grieg's world of sound in his later works—particularly in the *Norwegian Peasant Dances*, op. 72—anticipates Bartók.

Liberal use of modality was an idiosyncrasy of Grieg, who in this respect was far ahead of his time. Svendsen very rarely used elements drawn from the church modes. In the baptismal ceremony in *Zorahayda* there is a long, completely modal section, but it has an explicitly archaizing function, i.e., to help create a religious atmosphere.

Svendsen's *rhythms* are resilient and elegant but rarely complicated. By and large both he and Grieg keep the music within a strict, well-defined framework—restricted to a considerable degree by the "tyranny of the bar line," with strict periodic structures. One rarely finds in either Svendsen's or Grieg's music the inner rhythmic life so prominent in the works of Schumann and Brahms. Svendsen had a predilection for dotted rhythms, especially in fast movements, and he had a greater sense for hemiola than did Grieg.

The rhythmic simplicity of the music of both Svendsen and Grieg may also be to some extent a function of the homophonic character of most of their works. Svendsen, however, was a much more skillful contrapuntalist than Grieg and occasionally used polyphonic techniques with convincing virtuosity. One finds, for example, such things as ingenious, compressed *strettos* with implicit rhythmic dislocations—a practice that is almost totally foreign to Grieg. Svendsen achieves a special effect when in a very artistic way he combines two dissimilar but completely essential themes. The most striking evidences of his consummate skill in this area occur in *Festival Polonaise* (Example 9) and *Norwegian Artists' Carnival* (Example 10).

With respect to *form*, the principles of Vienna Classicism constituted the point of departure for both Grieg and Svendsen, and neither of them had any intention of blazing new paths—although they understandably could not escape from the Romantic world of ideas of which they were a part. While Grieg struggled with formal problems, Svendsen appears to have had an almost inborn, unerring feeling for the architectonic construction of a musical composition. In his works in sonata form he integrated the various parts organically in such a way as to create a well-conceived total unity. While Grieg consciously preferred a mosaic-like structure, Svendsen loved the big symphonic arch.

There was one area of form in which Svendsen did break new ground and that was in the *scherzo* movements of his symphonies. His originality here is evident in the fact that it is difficult to analyze these movements within the confines of the traditional typology. Elements of the rondo and other additive forms are combined in exciting ways with the principles of sonata form, including extensive use of development techniques and modulations to unexpected tonal regions. In general one can say that the imaginative use of development techniques characterizes virtually all of Svendsen's music. He had a superb ability to manipulate motives and themes in a sophisticated, unconstrained way.

GENRES

In the area of chamber music, Svendsen's output was significantly smaller than Grieg's. His *String Octet*, however—that surprisingly mature product of his youth—is a work of international dimensions, a composition that must be considered one of the most important chamber-music works of the Romantic era. The rest of his chamber music—with the notable exception of the *Violin Romance*—has not had the same success. His *String Quartet* deserves attention as an exciting challenge to the performers, though in originality it is by no means equal to Grieg's G-minor quartet. The *String Quintet* sounds pale and unimaginative, as do also the violin and cello concertos. The concertos are competently written, especially the one for violin, but both lack the glow of inspiration and the brilliant, innovative handling of the solo instruments that might have appealed to both performers and audiences.

In contrast to Grieg, Svendsen had no special interest in writing for the piano or the human voice. His vocal works—a dozen songs, a few simple choral compositions, and three occasional cantatas—do not in any way exhibit the sparkling eruption of originality that was Grieg's hallmark in these genres. As an opera conductor in Copenhagen for a quarter of a century, Svendsen concentrated on the human voice solely as an instrument for performers, not as a means for his own creative work.

If one looks beyond the compositions of his youth, most of Svendsen's orchestral works fall into one of four principal categories: (1) arrangements of Norwegian, Swedish, and Icelandic melodies, (2) occasional works, (3) relatively short program-music works, and (4) symphonies.

The arrangements for string orchestra of national melodies compare favorably with other similar efforts of the Romantic era. This is functional music in an effective harmonic garb, orchestrated with a touch of brilliance. More innovative than these are the four *Norwegian Rhapsodies* for full orchestra, where the composer's imagination was given freer rein.

Several of the occasional works for orchestra—*Funeral March, Coronation March, Andante funèbre,* the ballet *The Arrival of Spring* and *Prelude*—are well-written works, but they lack the stamp of originality that might have enabled them to endure. Worthy of special mention among works in this category is the brilliant *Festival Polonaise*, which is festival music of unparalleled merit.

The orchestral virtuoso is at his very best, however, in the five programmatic works. *Sigurd Slembe* provides the upbeat, and the others follow in turn: *Carnival in Paris*, *Zorahayda*, *Norwegian Artists' Carnival*, and *Romeo and Juliet*. The three works in the middle of this series are among Svendsen's finest, sparkling with inspiration from beginning to end and orchestrated with masterful skill. It is surprising—and unfortunate—that they have not long since won a permanent place in the international repertoire.

Svendsen's two symphonies constitute an outstanding achievement; indeed, some would say they constitute his highest achievement. At a time when few symphonies were being written—the period between Schumann and Brahms—these compositions stand forth as works to be reckoned with. The first symphony added something new and fresh to the genre, partly because of the specifically Norwegian coloring that it incorporates. Niels W. Gade had been a pioneer, introducing in his symphonies a Danish-Nordic tinge within the confines of a Mendelssohnian style. Svendsen, however, with his much bolder musical language, owed little to Gade. The musical expression was further intensified in his second symphony, which must be considered one of the finest Nordic symphonic works of all time. With the two symphonies, Svendsen stands as the most important symphonist in Scandinavia in the period following Gade and Franz Berwald and preceding Jean Sibelius and Carl Nielsen. In an international perspective as well, he deserves to be ranked with such other national-Romantic composers as Balakirev, Borodin and Dvořák. All drew inspiration from the folk music of their respective homelands, and all found their own paths without touching each other's circles. During his lifetime, both of Svendsen's symphonies were well received whenever they were performed. In our time they await rediscovery on the international scene.

In his best works, Svendsen appears as a composer with a pronounced profile. He succeeded in combining Classical-Romantic principles of form with features derived from Berlioz's orchestral virtuosity, elements of Wagner's chromatic harmony, and impulses whose roots lay in the folklore of his homeland. On such a foundation he created an idiom that was wholly and completely his own.

LIST OF COMPOSITIONS

Svendsen's compositions are enumerated in five lists. List A comprises completed compositions with opus numbers (opp. 1–33); list B, completed compositions without opus numbers (works 101–130); list C, arrangements of compositions by other composers (works 201–219); list D, unfinished, fragmentary, and lost compositions (works 301–308); list E, compositions about whose origin there is some question and compositions that do not fall under any of the other categories (works 401–405).

Except for list A, the compositions in each list are ordered chronologically. Svendsen's own opus list was incomplete and not altogether chronological. Later attempts to systematize the opus list have not been fully successful.

Each entry gives as much of the following information as is available: title, instrumentation, year and place of composition, date of first performance, type and present location of manuscript, year of publication, publisher and print plate number, and dedication.

The following abbreviations are used:

KBK:	Det kongelige Bibliotek, Copenhagen	instr:	instrument
		mvmt:	movement
MMCCS:	Musikhistorisk Museum Carl Claudius Samling, Copenhagen	op:	opus
		orch:	orchestra
		pl. no.:	print plate number
UB:	Universitetsbiblioteket i Oslo, Norsk Musikksamling	str:	strings
		timp:	timpani
		tr:	trumpet
2-h:	two-hands	trb:	trombone
4-h:	four-hands	var:	various
arr:	arranged, arrangement	viol:	violin
clar:	clarinet	vla:	viola
fl:	flute	ww:	woodwinds

A. WORKS WITH OPUS NUMBERS

Opus 1 *String Quartet*
Instrumentation: viol I–II, vla, cel
Composed: 1865, Leipzig
1st Performance: May 21, 1865, Leipzig
Year of pub: 1868
Publisher: E. W. Fritzsch, Leipzig, pl. no. E. W. F. 32L (C. F. W. Siegels
                 Musikalienhandlung (R. Linnemann))
Dedication: Gulbrand Svendsen

Opus 2 *Two Songs for Male Chorus*
                 (Text: King Carl XV) 1. *Till Sverige* (*To Sweden*) 2. *Aftonröster*
                 (*Evening Voices*)
Instrumentation: Men's chorus
Composed: 1865, Leipzig
1st Performance: No. 1: Oct 26, 1872
Year of pub: 1866
Publisher: Self-published by the composer; printed by Breitkopf & Härtel,
                 Leipzig, pl. no. 12277. No. 2 also published with German
                 (*Abendklänge*) and English (*Evening Voices*, trans. by Frederick
                 Delius) texts by Wilhelm Hansen, Copenhagen, 1895. Both
                 songs published for mixed chorus by Søborgs Stentrykkeri,
                 Copenhagen, year unknown.
Dedication: Carl XV

Opus 3 *String Octet*
Instrumentation: viol I–IV, vla I–II, cello I–II
Composed: 1866, Leipzig
1st Performance: Feb 24(?), 1866, Leipzig
Manuscript: 2 scores, UB. One is dated (end of 4th mvmt) Feb. 20, 1866;
                 dust cover has July 1, 1866; sequence of mvmts is I, IV, III, II.
                 The other is dated (end of 4th mvmt) May, 1866, and on the
                 inside of the dust cover July 14, 1866.
Year of pub: 1867
Publisher: Breitkopf & Härtel, Leipzig, pl. no. B 1157
Dedication: Queen Louise

Opus 4   *Symphony No. 1*
Instrumentation: orch
Composed: 1865–67, Leipzig
1st Performance: 1st mvmt: May 9, 1866, Leipzig; 2nd–4th mvmts: May 29,
               1867, Leipzig; complete symphony: Oct 12, 1867, Oslo
Manuscript: 2 orch scores, UB. One is dated July 1865 on the first page and
               Dec 1866 on the last. The other is dated Jan 21, 1867.
Year of pub: 1868
Publisher: E. W. Fritzsch, Leipzig, pl. no. E. W. F. 34L (C. F. W. Siegels
               Musikalienhandlung (R Linnemann))
Dedication: Dr. Carl F. Leche

Opus 5   *String Quintet*
Instrumentation: viol I–II, vla I–II, cel
Composed: 1867, Leipzig
1st Performance: May 17, 1867, Leipzig
Manuscript: score (just one page of 2nd mvmt), UB
Year of pub: 1868
Publisher: E. W. Fritzsch, Leipzig, pl. no. E. W. F. 66L (C. F. W. Siegels
               Musikalienhandlung (R Linnemann))
Dedication: Dr. Schüssler

Opus 6   *Violin Concerto*
Instrumentation: viol and orch
Composed: 1868–70, Paris and Leipzig
1st Performance: Feb 6, 1872, Leipzig
Manuscript: score, dated Leipzig, Jun 1870, UB
Year of pub: 1870
Publisher: E. W. Fritzsch, Leipzig, pl. no. E. W. F. 157L (C. F. W. Siegels
               Musikalienhandlung (R Linnemann))
Dedication: Ferdinand David

Opus 7   *Cello Concerto*
Instrumentation: cello and orch
Composed: 1870, Leipzig
1st Performance: Mar 16, 1871, Leipzig
Manuscript: Score, dated Nov 1870, UB
Year of pub: 1871
Publisher: E. W. Fritzsch, Leipzig, pl. no. E. W. F. 175L (C. F. W. Siegels
               Musikalienhandlung (R Linnemann))
Dedication: Emil Hegar

Opus 8   *Sigurd Slembe* ("Symphonic Prelude to Bjørnson's Play")
Instrumentation: orch
Composed: 1871, New York and Leipzig
1st Performance: Dec 12, 1871, Leipzig
Manuscript: orch score, dated Leipzig, Nov. 4, 1871, UB
Year of pub: 1872
Publisher: E. W. Fritzsch, Leipzig, pl. no. E. W. F. 195L (C. F. W. Siegels
                 Musikalienhandlung (R Linnemann))
Dedication: Dr. A. Keil

Opus 9   *Carnival in Paris* ("Episode for Large Orchestra")
Instrumentation: orch
Composed: 1872, New York, Leipzig and Bayreuth
1st Performance: Oct 26, 1872, Oslo
Manuscript: orch score, UB
Year of pub: 1877
Publisher: E. W. Fritzsch, Leipzig, pl. no. E. W. F. 340L
Dedication: Count W. Th. Seyfferth

Opus 10   *Funeral March* ("On the Occasion of the Death of King
                 Carl XV")
Instrumentation: orch
Composed: 1872, Oslo
1st Performance: Oct 26, 1872, Oslo
Manuscript: orch score, dated Oct. 1872, UB. Pub. rights were sold to Carl
                 Warmuth, Oslo, and later conveyed to C. F. Peters, Leipzig,
                 but the work has never been published.

Opus 11   *Zorahayda* ("Legend for Orchestra")
Instrumentation: orch
Composed: 1874, Oslo; revised 1879, Paris
1st Performance: 1st version: Oct 3, 1874, Oslo; later version: May 11, 1880,
                 Oslo
Manuscript: 2 orch scores, KBK and MMCCS
Year of pub: 1879
Publisher: Carl Warmuth, Oslo, pl. no. C.W. 545
Dedication: Oscar II

Opus 12   *Festival Polonaise*
                 Composed for a public ball in Oslo Aug 6, 1873
Instrumentation: orch
Composed: 1873, Oslo
1st Performance: Aug 6, 1873
Manuscript: 2 orch scores, UB. One is dated July 1873, the other is undated;
                 var orch parts, UB
Year of pub: 1886
Publisher: Carl Warmuth, Oslo, pl. no. C.W. 1132

Opus 13   *Coronation March*
                 Composed for the coronation of Oscar II and Queen Sophie
                 July 18, 1873
Instrumentation: a. janissary band; b. orch; c. piano 2-h; d. piano 4-h
Composed: 1873, Oslo
1st Performance: July 18, 1873, Trondheim
Manuscript: a^1. 2 scores for janissary band, UB. One has the inscription
                 "Jemtlands Fältjägermusikcorps," the other "5.
                 Artilleribatalions Musikcorps."
                 a^2. 2 scores for janissary band, MMCCS. One has the inscrip-
                 tion "Trondhjemske Brigades Musikcorps" and is dated June
                 1873; the other has the inscription "Marinens Musikcorps."
                 b. 3 orch scores, UB. One is incomplete and has the inscription
                 "sketch for orchestra;" the second is dated June 1873; the
                 third is undated.
                 c. piano 2-h, UB
                 d. piano 4-h, UB
Year of pub: b, c and d 1873
Publisher: Carl Warmuth, Oslo, no pl. no.

Opus 14   *Norwegian Artists' Carnival*
Instrumentation: orch
Composed: 1874, Oslo
1st Performance: Mar 17, 1874, Oslo
Manuscript: orch score with the title, *Wedding on Dovre*, MMCCS
Year of pub: 1881
Publisher: C. F. Peters, Leipzig, pl. no. 6472

Opus 15   *Symphony No. 2*
Instrumentation: orch
Composed: 1874, Oslo
1st Performance: Oct 14, 1876, Oslo
Manuscript: a. orch score dated May 1876, UB
                     b. orch score, undated drafts of third mvmt, MMCCS
Year of pub: 1877
Publisher: E. W. Fritzsch, Leipzig, pl. no. E. W. F. 350L
Dedication: Consul Dr. F. G. Schulz

Opus 16   *Humorous March* ("Purple Nose March")
Instrumentation: a. str and piano 4-h (a march based on the children's song *Ritsj,*
                 ratsj, fillibombombom)
                     b. arr for viol, cel and piano by G. Tronchi with the title *Para-*
                     phrase sur des chansons populaires du Nord
Composed: 1874, Oslo
1st Performance: Dec 13, 1874, Oslo
Manuscript: a. incomplete score pp. 7–10, MMCCS
Year of pub: b. 1916
Publisher: Skandinavisk Musikforlag, Copenhagen, pl. no. C. R. 377. See
                     also information given under the missing op 20.

Opus 17   *Norwegian Rhapsody No. 1*
Instrumentation: orch
Composed: 1876, Oslo
1st Performance: Sep 25, 1877, Oslo
Manuscript: orch score, dated Feb 10, 1876, UB
Year of pub: 1877
Publisher: Carl Warmuth, Oslo, pl. no. C.W. 291
Dedication: L. M. Lindeman

Opus 18   *Romeo and Juliet* ("Fantasia for Orchestra")
Instrumentation: orch
Composed: 1876, Oslo
1st Performance: Oct 14, 1876, Oslo
Manuscript: orch score, dated Sep 1876, MMCCS
Year of pub: 1880
Publisher: Breitkopf & Härtel, Leipzig, pl. no. B 358

Opus 19   *Norwegian Rhapsody No. 2*
Instrumentation: orch
Composed: 1876, Oslo
1st Performance: 1880(?), Munich
Year of pub: 1877
Publisher: Carl Warmuth, Oslo, pl. no. C.W. 292
Dedication: Ole Bull

(Opus 20)   There is a lacuna in the opus list at this point. In W. Altmann's
                 Kammermusik-Katalog (fifth ed., Leipzig 1942, p. 53), op 20 is
                 listed as *Skandinavische Lieder* (arr), published by W. Hansen.
                 There is, however, no such composition in Hansen's cata-
                 logues. The reference undoubtedly is to op 16, *Humorous March*.

Opus 21   *Norwegian Rhapsody No. 3*
Instrumentation: orch
Composed: 1876, Oslo
1st Performance: Jan 1879, Paris
Year of pub: 1877
Publisher: Carl Warmuth, Oslo, pl. no. C. W. 293
Dedication: Edvard Grieg

Opus 22   *Norwegian Rhapsody No. 4*
Instrumentation: orch
Composed: 1877, Oslo and Rome
1st Performance: Feb 1, 1879, Paris
Manuscript: orch score, dated Rome Dec 10, 1877, UB
Year of pub: 1878
Publisher: Carl Warmuth, Oslo, pl. no. C. W. 294
Dedication: Karl Hals

Opus 23   *Five Songs*
                 (text: F. M. von Bodenstedt, from *Mirza Schaffy*; trans. into
                 French by Victor Wilder)
                 1. *Zuleikha*
                 2. *Was ist der Wuchs der Pinie* (*What is the growth of the stone-pine?*)
                 3. *Seh' ich deine zarten Füßchen an* (*When I gaze upon your dainty feet*)
                 4. *O, wie mir schweren Dranges* (*O, how heavy is my burden*)
                 5. *Schlag' die Tschadra zurück!* (*Repulse the Tschadra!*)

Instrumentation: solo voice and piano
Composed: 1879, Paris
Year of pub: 1880
Publisher: J. Hamelle, Paris, pl. no. J. 1629–33 H. (J. Maho)
Dedication: Pauline Viardot-Garcia

Opus 24   *Four Songs*
                (text: O. P. Monrad [no. 1 and no. 2]; John Paulsen [no. 3];
                Bjørnstjerne Bjørnson [no. 4]; all trans. into French by Victor
                Wilder)
                1. *O vær lidt barmhjærtig, du susende vind* (*O show some mercy,
                howling wind*)
                2. *Birken* (*The birch tree*)
                3. *Venetiansk Serenade* (*Venetian serenade*)
                4. *Længsel* (*Longing*)
Instrumentation: solo voice and piano
                Nos. 2 and 3 were also published for piano 2-h by the composer
                (J. Hamelle, Paris).
                No. 4 was also published for piano 2-h by the composer(?)
                (Carl Warmuth, Oslo, in *Jubilæum-Album*, 1885).
Composed: 1879, Paris
Year of pub: 1880
Publisher: J. Hamelle, Paris, pl. no. J. 1611–14 H. (J. Maho)
Dedication: Professor Julius Nicolaysen

Opus 25   *Two Songs*
                (Text for no. 1: S. . . (=Johan Svendsen); trans. into German by
                Edmund Lobedanz; later also into French by Camille Benoit
                and into English by Bergljot Svendsen. Text for no. 2: F. M.
                von Bodenstedt (from *Mirza Schaffy*); trans. into Norwegian
                presumably by the composer.)
                1. *Violen* (*The Violet*)
                2. *Frühlingsjubel* (*Spring Jubilation*)
Instrumentation: solo voice and piano
Composed: no. 1: 1878, London; no. 2: 1880, Larkollen
Year of pub: no. 1: 1878; no. 2: 1880
Publisher: Carl Warmuth, Oslo; no. 1: pl. no. C. W. 412, no. 2: pl. no. C.
                W. 631
Dedication: no. 1: Alethe Due
                no. 2: Thorvald Lammers
                See also information given under Work 124, *Wergeland Cantata*

Opus 26   *Violin Romance*
Instrumentation: a. viol and orch
                 b. viol and piano
Composed: 1881, Oslo
1st Performance: Oct 30, 1881, Oslo
Year of pub: 1881 (68th printing in 1911!)
Publisher: Carl Warmuth, Oslo, pl. no. C. W. 758
Dedication: Halvard Emil Heyerdahl

Opus 27   *Two Swedish Folk Melodies*
              1. *Allt under himmelens fäste* (*Everything under heaven's firmament*)
              2. *Du gamla, du fria* (*Thou ancient, thou free*)
Instrumentation: str orch
Composed: no. 1: 1876, Oslo; no. 2: 1878, Rome
1st Performance: no. 1: Oct 14, Oslo; no. 2: Jan 29, 1881, Oslo
Manuscript: orch score, dated Rome, Mar 1878, UB
Year of pub: 1878
Publisher: Carl Warmuth, Oslo, pl. no. C. W. 334
Dedication: Morris Levett

Opus 28   *Polonaise*
Instrumentation: orch
Composed: 1882, Oslo
Manuscript: orch score, dated Jan 1882, KBK; also bears the inscription
                 "Dance on Attila's castle in act 2," which alludes to *Attila*, a play
                 by C. M. v. Scholten that had been proposed for performance at
                 the Royal Theater ca. 1908.
Year of pub: pub. posthumously in 1919 in an arr for salon orch by Nicolai
                 Hansen
Publisher: Wilhelm Hansen, Copenhagen, pl. no. 16918

Opus 29   *Wedding Cantata*
              Composed for the university festival held Oct 18, 1881, in
              honor of the marriage of crown prince Oscar Gustav Adolph
              and crown princess Sophia Maria Victoria (text: Lorentz
              Dietrichson).
              1. *Her i Pallas' hellige haller* (*Here in Pallas's sacred halls*), mixed
              chorus/orch
              2. Romance: *Og der gik dans på Bygdø gård* (*And there was a dance
              at the Bygdø estate*), women's chorus/mixed chorus/orch
              3. Recitative: *Fyrstebarn fra Neckars milde kyst* (*Royal child from*

Neckar's balmy coast), baritone solo/mixed chorus/orch
4. Aria: *Elsker det fattige land I skal værge* (*Love the poor land ye shall defend*), baritone solo/orch
5. Hymn: *Beskjærm, o Gud, det fagre træ* (*Protect, O God, the lovely tree*), mixed chorus/orch

Instrumentation: baritone solo, mixed chorus and orch
Composed: 1881, Oslo
1st Performance: Oct 18, 1881, Oslo
Manuscript: score, dated Sep 1881, UB.
                 No. 5, *Hymn*, was published for mixed chorus with a new text by Åsmund Sveen, *Du djupe jord som gjev deg mild* (*Thou deep earth*), in Norges Sangerlags korbibliotek no. 8.

Opus 30   ***Two Icelandic Melodies***
Instrumentation: str orch
Composed: 1874, Oslo
1st Performance: Oct 3, 1874, Oslo
Manuscript: orch score, UB
Year of pub: 1878
Publisher: E. W. Fritzsch, Leipzig, pl. no. E. W. F. 338L
Dedication: Carl Warmuth
                 See also information given under Work 126, *Holberg Cantata*

Opus 31   ***Ifjol gjætt' e gjeitinn*** (*Last year I was tending the goats*)
                 (Variations on a Norwegian Folk Tune)
Instrumentation: str orch
Composed: 1874, Oslo
1st Performance: Oct 3, 1874, Oslo
Manuscript: 2 orch scores, UB; one dated Aug 1874, the other undated
Year of pub: 1878
Publisher: E. W. Fritzsch, Leipzig, pl. no. E. W. F. 339L
Dedication: Bergljot Svendsen
                 See also information given under op 32, *Hymn*.

Opus 32   ***Hymn*** ("I mai, da blomst og blad sprang ud" ["In May, when flowers and leaves sprang forth"])
                 Composed in honor of the golden wedding anniversary of Christian IX and Queen Louise May 26, 1892
                 (text: Vilhelm Bergsøe)
Instrumentation: orch, mixed chorus and recitation
Composed: 1892, Charlottenlund, Denmark

1st Performance: May 26, 1892, Copenhagen
Manuscript: orch score, KBK
                  Hymn has sometimes been listed as op 31. See also information
                  given under Work 127, *Festival Cantata*.

Opus 33   *Foraaret kommer* (*The Arrival of Spring*)
                  Ballet in one act by Pietro Krohn
                  Composed in honor of the golden wedding anniversary of
                  Christian IX and Queen Louise May 26, 1892 (choreography:
                  Carl Price).
                  Nos. 1–10 are original music by Svendsen, the rest merely ar-
                  rangements of others' compositions and folk melodies. After
                  Svendsen's death nos. 1, 4, 6, 8 and 9 were arranged for piano
                  by Fini Henriques and published under the title *Hiver et
                  Printemps* (*Winter and spring*) – "Morceaux de Ballet," Wilhelm
                  Hansen, Copenhagen.
                  1. *Introduktion* (*Introduction*)
                  2. *Vinter* (*Winter*)
                  3. *Mellemspil* (*Interlude*)
                  4. *Sneflokkenes Dans* (*The Snowflakes' Dance*)
                  5. *Mellemspil* (*Interlude*)
                  6. *Vaar* (*Spring*)
                  7. *Mellemspil* (*Interlude*)
                  8. *Blomsternes Dans* (*The Flowers' Dance*)
                  9. *Insekternes Dans* (*The Insects' Dance*)
                  10. Repeat (slightly modified) of No. 1
                  11. *Fynsk Dansemelodi* (*Danish Dance Melody*)
                  12. *Jylland* (*Jutland*, a song by P. Heise)
                  13. *Islandsk Nationalsang* (*Icelandic National Anthem*)
                  14. *Der er et yndigt Land* (*There is a Lovely Land*)
                  15. *Rule Britannia*
                  16. *Nygræsk Frihedssang* (*Greek Song of Freedom*)
                  17. *Russisk Nationalsang* (*Russian National Anthem*) (the Tsar
                      Hymn)
                  18. *Slutningsdans* (*Concluding Dance*)
                  19. *Skotsk Folkedans* (*Scottish Folk Dance*)
                  20. *Russisk Folkesang* (*Russian Folk Song*)
                  21. *Engelsk Hornpipe* (*English Hornpipe*)
                  22. *Brudevalsen* (*Bridal Waltz* from N. W. Gade's ballet music
                      for *Et Folkesagn* (*A Folk Tale*))
Instrumentation: orch

Composed: 1892, Charlottenlund, Denmark
1st Performance: May 26, 1892, Copenhagen
Manuscript: a. orch score (149 pgs) in Svendsen's handwriting, dated May 7
                   "4:15 a.m.," KBK
                   b. orch score of *The Insects' Dance*, UB
                   c. orch score (200 pgs) in unknown handwriting, KBK. This
                   score differs in some respects from a; it has, among other things,
                   an extra introduction of 9 measures, an arr of an excerpt from
                   Johanne Louise Heiberg's operetta *En Søndag paa Amager* (*A
                   Sunday at Amager*), and sections with altered instrumentation.

B. WORKS WITHOUT OPUS NUMBERS

Work 101   *Anna Polka*
Instrumentation: a. piano 2-h
                   b. piano 4-h
                   c. viol and piano
                   d. orch
Composed: a. 1854, Oslo
                   d. 1858, Oslo
Manuscript: var orch parts, MMCCS, dated from June 4, 1858 to Feb 25,
                   1859; oboe, tr I–II, UB, dated June 4, 1859
Year of pub: 1883 (piano 2-h; piano 4-h; viol/piano)
Publisher: Carl Warmuth, Oslo, pl. no. C. W. 871–873

Work 102   *At the Seter* (waltz)
Instrumentation: a. piano 2-h
                   b. piano 4-h
                   c. viol and piano
                   d. orch
Composed: a. 1856, Oslo
                   d. 1859, Oslo
Manuscript: var orch parts, MMCCS, viol I dated July 7, 1859; tr I–II, UB
Year of pub: 1883 (piano 2-h; piano 4-h; viol/piano)
Publisher: Carl Warmuth, Oslo, pl. no. C. W. 874–876

Work 103   *Klingenberg Polka*
Instrumentation: orch
Composed: 1858, Oslo
Manuscript: var orch parts, MMCCS, dated from Aug 18, 1858 to June 5,
                   1859; oboe, tr I–II, UB, dated June 5, 1859

Work 104   *Bolero*
Instrumentation: orch
Composed: 1858, Oslo
Manuscript: var orch parts, MMCCS, dated from Aug 29, 1858 to June 10,
                 1859; oboe, tr I–II, UB, dated June 8, 1859

Work 105   *Catharina Waltz*
Instrumentation: orch
Composed: 1858, Oslo
Manuscript: var orch parts, MMCCS, dated from Dec 16, 1858 to June 8,
                 1859

Work 106   *Three Etudes*
                (C minor/C major; G minor/G major (*Alla polacca*); D minor/
                D major)
Instrumentation: viol I–II, vla, cel
Composed: 1859, Oslo
Manuscript: separate parts, UB, viol I dated Feb 17, 19 and 23, 1859

Work 107   *Farewell* ("Fantasia for Violin")
Instrumentation: a. viol and piano
                b. viol and str
Composed: 1859, Oslo
Manuscript: UB, viol part in a is dated July 20, 1859, piano part Aug 28,
                 1859; identified as "opus 10"
Dedication: Gudbrand Bøhn

Work 108   *Caroline Waltz*
Instrumentation: a. piano
                b. orch
Composed: 1860, Oslo
Manuscript: a. UB, dated Mar 1, 1860
                b. orch score, UB, dated May 28, 1860, also fl I and tr I–II, UB,
                dated June 1, 1860; var orch parts, MMCCS, viol I dated May
                9, 1860

Work 109   *Antonia Waltz*
Instrumentation: orch
Composed: 1861, Oslo
Manuscript: orch score, UB, dated May 27, 1861, also fl I and tr I–II, UB;
                 var orch parts, MMCCS

Work 110   *March* ("The Ninth of November")
Instrumentation: orch
Composed: 1861, Oslo
Manuscript: orch score, UB, dated July 11, 1861, also fl I and tr I–II, UB;
                  var orch parts, MMCCS

Work 111   *Elise Waltz*
Instrumentation: orch
Composed: 1862, Oslo
Manuscript: orch score, UB, dated Feb 4, 1862

Work 112   *Albertine Waltz*
Instrumentation: orch
Composed: 1862, Oslo
Manuscript: orch score, UB, dated Mar 20, 1862

Work 113   *Blomsterpike vals* (*Flower Girl Waltz*)
Instrumentation: orch
Composed: 1862, Oslo
Manuscript: orch score, UB, dated May 17, 1862, also fl I and tr I–II, UB;
                  var orch parts, MMCCS

Work 114   *Adéle Waltz*
Instrumentation: orch
Composed: 1862, Gothenburg
Manuscript: orch score, UB, dated Sep 4, 1862

Work 115   *Julie Galop*
Instrumentation: orch
Composed: 1862, Oslo and Halmstad
Manuscript: orch score, UB, dated Halmstad, Sep 19, 1862, also fl I and tr
                  I–II, UB; var orch parts, MMCCS, viol I dated Oslo July 21,
                  1871, B-flat clar dated July 20, 1871

Work 116   *Johanne Galop*
Instrumentation: orch
Composed: 1862, Oslo and Malmö
Manuscript: orch score, UB, dated Malmö Oct 28, 1862, also fl I and tr I–II;
                  var orch parts, MMCCS

Work 117   *Hedwig Waltz*
Instrumentation: orch
Composed: 1862, Malmö
Manuscript: orch score, UB, dated Dec 9, 1862

Work 118   *Guds Fred* (*God's Peace*) ("Blessed, Blessed")
             (text: B. S. Ingemann)
Instrumentation: male chorus
Composed: 1863, Lübeck
Manuscript: MMCCS, dated Feb 10, 1863

Work 119   *Ich stoß auf des Berges Spitze* (*I reached the top of the mountain*)
             (text: Heinrich Heine)
Instrumentation: solo voice and piano
Composed: 1863, Lübeck
Manuscript: MMCCS, dated Feb 12, 1863

Work 120   *Dæmring* (*Dawn*)
             (text: Chr. Molbech)
Instrumentation: solo voice and piano
Composed: 1863, Lübeck
Manuscript: MMCCS, dated Feb 14, 1863

Work 121   *March* ("Struggle Leads to Victory")
Instrumentation: orch
Composed: 1863, Lübeck
Manuscript: orch score, UB, dated Lübeck, July 13, 1863, also fl I and tr
             I–II; var orch parts, MMCCS

Work 122   *Caprice*
Instrumentation: orch with obligato solo violin
Composed: 1863, Lübeck
1st Performance: Dec 1864, Leipzig
Manuscript: orch score, UB, dated July 21, 1863

Work 123   *Norwegian Springar*
Instrumentation: orch
Composed: July 20, 1878, London
1st Performance: May 29, 1880, Oslo
Manuscript: orch score, UB

Work 124   *Wergeland Cantata*
Composed for the unveiling of the monument to Henrik
Wergeland in Oslo May 17, 1881
(text: Jonas Lie)
I. Before the unveiling: *Hver tid ejer sit Nordhav* (*Every time has its
own North Sea*)
II. After the unveiling: *En eventyrlængsel som ulmer* (*A fairytale
longing that smoulders*)

Instrumentation: baritone solo, male chorus and janissary orch
Composed: 1881, Oslo
1st Performance: May 17, 1881, Oslo
Manuscript: 2 scores, UB, both dated May 1881. The Wergeland Cantata is
sometimes listed as op 25.

Work 125   **Persian Dance**
Instrumentation: orch score
Composed: 1883, Oslo
Manuscript: orch score, UB, dated Feb 1883

Work 126   **Holberg Cantata**
Composed for the celebration of the bicentennial of Ludvig
Holberg's birth
(text: Holger Drachmann)
1. *Inledning* (*Introduction*), orch
2. *Det var hin fjerne, mørke Tid* (*It was in that distant, dark time*),
chorus/orch
3. *Han rummed sin Samtids og Fremtidens Viden* (*He fathomed the
knowledge of his day and the future*), chorus/orch
4. *Lad os ej tænke ham gammel og lille* (*Let us not think of him old and
small*), baritone solo/orch
5. *Gammel eller ung: Alle staae i Gjæld* (*Old or young: All stand in
his debt*), baritone solo/chorus/orch

Instrumentation: baritone solo, mixed chorus and orch
Composed: 1884, Copenhagen
1st Performance: Dec 3, 1884, Copenhagen
Manuscript: orch score, UB, dated Nov 1884
The Holberg Cantata is sometimes listed as op 30.

Work 127   *Festival Cantata. The Singers' Morning Greeting*
Composed in honor of the golden wedding anniversary of
Christian IX and Queen Louise May 26, 1892
(text: P. Hansen)
Instrumentation: male chorus with brass instruments
Composed: 1892, Charlottenlund
1st Performance: May 26, 1892, Copenhagen
Manuscript: piano score (with instrumental markings), UB, dated Apr 1892
The Festival Cantata is sometimes listed as op 32

Work 128   *Andante Funèbre*
Composed for the funeral of Georg A. Hindenburg June 30,
1894
Instrumentation: orch
Composed: 1894, Copenhagen
1st Performance: June 30, 1894, Copenhagen
Manuscript: 2 orch scores, KBK
Year of pub: 1895
Publisher: Wilhelm Hansen, Copenhagen, pl. no. 11565
Dedication: T. Hindenburg

Work 129   *Prelude*
Composed as *Festival Prelude* for the sesquicentennial of the
Royal Theater
Instrumentation: orch
Composed: 1898, Copenhagen
1st Performance: Dec 18, 1898, Copenhagen
Manuscript: orch score, UB, dated Dec 10, 1898
Year of pub: pub posthumously for var combinations of instruments
Publisher: Wilhelm Hansen, Copenhagen

Work 130   *Album Leaf*
Instrumentation: piano
Composed: Copenhagen
Manuscript: 2 manuscripts, MMCCS, one untitled
Dedication: GABH (Golla Andrea Bodenhoff-Hammerich)

Work 131   *Untitled Piece*
Instrumentation: viol and piano
Manuscript: MMCCS, which also has some sketches of the work

C. ARRANGEMENTS OF WORKS BY OTHER COMPOSERS

Work 201   *27 Pieces* (by various composers)
                  (Exercises in instrumentation)
Instrumentation: viol I–II, vla, cel
Composed: 1858–62, Oslo
Manuscript: complete parts, UB, dated from Aug 15, 1858 to Apr 2, 1862

Work 202   **Johann Strauss the Younger:** *Bouquet Waltz*
                  ("Sträusschen")
Instrumentation: viol I–II, double bass, fl, cornet I–II, trb
Composed: 1861, Oslo
Manuscript: orch score, UB, dated Jan 24, 1861

Work 203   **Joseph Lanner:** *Marie Waltz*
Instrumentation: viol I–II, double bass, fl, cornet I–II, trb
Composed: 1861, Oslo
Manuscript: orch score, UB, dated Jan 24, 1861

Work 204   **Johannes Steenberg:** *Minuet*
Instrumentation: orch
Composed: 1866, Connewitz
1st Performance: Oct 12, 1867, Oslo
Manuscript: orch score, UB, dated June 11, 1866

Work 205   **Robert Schumann:** *Faschingsschwank aus Wien*
Instrumentation: orch
Composed: 1866, Connewitz
Manuscript: orch score, UB, dated July 19, 1866

Work 206   **Franz Liszt:** *Hungarian Rhapsody No. 2*
Instrumentation: orch
Composed: 1866, Leipzig
1st Performance: Oct 12, 1867, Oslo
Manuscript: orch score, UB, dated Oct 19, 1866

Work 207   **Karl von Radecki:** *Andantino et Adagio*
Instrumentation: str
Composed: 1868, Leipzig
Manuscript: orch score, UB, dated Jan 1868

Work 208   **Franz Schubert:** *Divertissement à la Hongroise*
Instrumentation: orch
Composed: 1869, Paris
Manuscript: orch score, UB, dated Oct 26, 1869

Work 209   **Franz Liszt:** *Hungarian Rhapsody No. 6*
Instrumentation: orch
Composed: 1871, New York
1st Performance: Oct 26, 1872, Oslo
Manuscript: orch score, UB, dated July 6, 1871

Work 210   **Richard Wagner:** *Träume* (from the *Wesendonck songs*)
Instrumentation: str, ww, horn
Composed: 1872, Darmstadt
1st Performance: Oct 26, 1872, Oslo
Manuscript: 2 orch scores, UB, one dated Apr 16, 1872, the other dated
                 June 1894, Copenhagen
Year of pub: 1893
Publisher: Schott & Söhne, Mainz, pl. no. 25758

Work 211   **Robert Schumann:** *Abendlied*
Instrumentation: str orch
Composed: 1872, Darmstadt
1st Performance: Oct 26, 1872, Oslo
Manuscript: 2 orch scores, UB, one dated Apr 18, 1872, the other undated
Year of pub: 1887
Publisher: Carl Warmuth, Oslo, pl. no. C. W. 1321

Work 212   **Franz Schubert:** *Andante sostenuto*
                 (2nd mvmt of piano sonata in B-flat major)
Instrumentation: orch
Composed: 1872, Donndorf by Bayreuth
Manuscript: orch score, UB, dated May 31, 1872

Work 213   **Ole Bull:** *Sæterjentens Søndag* (*The Shepherd Girl's Sunday*)
Instrumentation: str orch
Composed: 1872, Oslo
1st Performance: Feb 18, 1873, Oslo
Manuscript: orch score, MMCCS, dated Rome, Mar 1878
Year of pub: 1878
Publisher: Carl Warmuth, Oslo, pl. no. C. W. 335
Dedication: Captain Alexius Ræder

Work 214   **Robert Schumann:** *Träumerei*
Instrumentation: str orch
Composed: 1872(?), place unknown
Manuscript: orch score, UB

Work 215   **Alessandro Stradella:** *Kirke-Arie* (*Sacred Aria*)
Instrumentation: str orch
Instrumentation: 1874, Oslo
Manuscript: orch score, UB

Work 216   **Jacques Halévy:** *Il va venir*
                 (from the opera *Jødinnen* (*The Jewess*))
Instrumentation: solo voice, str, ww, horn I–II, timp
Composed: 1876, Oslo
Manuscript: orch score, UB, dated Mar 21, 1876

Work 217   *Foraaret kommer* (*The Arrival of Spring*) (ballet music)
                 The work includes a number of arrangements of the composi-
                 tions of others and of folk melodies. For detailed information
                 see op 33.

Work 218   **Edmund Neupert:** *Foran Slaget* (*Before the Battle*)
Instrumentation: orch
Composed: 1895, Copenhagen
1st Performance: Nov 21, 1896, Copenhagen
Year of pub: 1895
Publisher: Wilhelm Hansen, Copenhagen, pl. no. 11746

Work 219   **J. P. E. Hartmann:** *Funeral March*
                 Composed for the funeral of sculptor B. Thorvaldsen in 1844
Instrumentation: organ, gong, B-flat cornet, 3 trb, tuba
Instrumentation: 1898(?), Copenhagen
Year of pub: 1898
Publisher: Wilhelm Hansen, Copenhagen, pl. no. 2068. Svendsen's name
                 does not appear on the published score but is mentioned in an
                 advertisement in *Musikalisches Wochenblatt* 1898, p. 527.

D. UNFINISHED, FRAGMENTARY, AND LOST COMPOSITIONS

Work 301   *Axvalla March*
Instrumentation: janissary band
Composed: 1858, Oslo
Manuscript: 2nd B-flat clar part, UB, dated June 1858

Work 302   *March* (E-flat major)
Instrumentation: janissary band
Composed: 1858, Axvalla, Sweden
Manuscript: 2nd B-flat clar part, UB, dated July 1858

Work 303   *Reveille*
Instrumentation: janissary band
Composed: 1858, Oslo
Manuscript: 2nd B-flat clar part, UB, dated Sep 2, 1858

Work 304   *Song* (without text)
Instrumentation: solo voice and piano
Composed: 1872, Oslo
Manuscript: MMCCS, dated Nov 8, 1872
Dedication: Bergljot Svendsen ("à sa petite Bergljot")

Work 305   *Gyldenlak* (*Gillyflower*)
Undated sketch of a setting for solo voice and piano of a text by
Henrik Wergeland, UB

Work 306   *Zwei Könige sassen im Orkadal*
Undated pencil sketch of a composition for string quartet and
recitation, with very unclear text, UB

Work 307   *Den sörjande* (*The mourner* ("Swedish Folk Melody"))
An arr for string orch that was played at Svendsen's concert of
his own works in Oslo Oct 14, 1876, but then disappeared.
When *Two Swedish Folk Melodies*, op 27, was published in
1878, *The mourner* was replaced by *Du gamla, du fria* (*Thou
ancient, thou free*)

E. MISCELLANEOUS

Work 401   *Waltz*
Instrumentation: viol solo
Composed: Oslo
Manuscript: 3 copies, UB, none in Svendsen's handwriting. A notebook
                 with dances from Sandsvær has the following inscription on this
                 waltz: "Composed in the 1850's by Johan Svendsen."

Work 402   *Hun er søfd, hun er rød* (She is sweet, she is red)
                 (text: Chr. Winther)
Instrumentation: solo voice and piano
Manuscript: UB, in a collection of songs transcribed by H. C. Albrechtsen.
                 This song has as 1st verse a version composed by Kjerulf, as 2nd
                 verse a version composed by Johan Svendsen. Svendsen's origi-
                 nal version has not been found.

Work 403   *Andantino Quasi Allegretto* (theme with three variations)
Instrumentation: str orch
Manuscript: score, UB (written partly on the back of Work 214 and partly
                 on two loose pages). The composer's name is not given but the
                 score is in Svendsen's handwriting. The piece presumably was
                 used in the tableau *Jagt på Højfjeldet* (*A Hunt in the Mountains*)
                 (*Calm - Andantino*), see below *From Mountain and Fjord*.

Work 404   *Dance* (untitled)
Instrumentation: piano
Manuscript: MMCCS. The piece is 16 measures long, in E major, and has
                 the character of a Norwegian *springar* (a dance tune in 3/4
                 time).

Work 405   *Piano piece* (untitled)
Instrumentation: piano
Composed: Jan 8, 1888
Manuscript: Photocopy UB. The piece consists of 8 measures in D minor.

From Mountain and Fjord

A festival presentation Feb 13, 1882 in Christiania Theater, with tableaus by K. Bergslien, texts by L. Dietrichson and music by J. Svendsen. According to newspaper announcements the presentation included the following numbers:

a. Prologue

b. *Prelude* (orch)

c. Tableau: "From the Winter Fisheries"

Storm (Tempest – Allegro)

d. Tableau: "A Hunt in the Mountains"

Stille (Calm – Andantino)

e. Tableau: "A Peasant Wedding"

Springdans (same as a *springar*; see information given under Work 404)

f. *Epilogue*

BIBLIOGRAPHY

The bibliography includes the most important primary and secondary sources regarding Svendsen and his music. The sources for musical reviews and the like are not listed here but are given when cited in the text of the book.

1. Aumont, Arthur (ed.): *Dansk Teater-Aarbog*, annual volumes for the years 1889/90–1908. Copenhagen, 1890–1908.
2. Aumont, Arthur: *Det Kongelige Teater 1874/75–1888/89*. Copenhagen, 1889.
3. Balzer, Jürgen (ed.): *Carl Nielsen i hundredåret for hans fødsel*. Copenhagen, 1965.
4. Bang, Oluf: *Eyvind Johan-Svendsen*. Copenhagen, 1947.
5. Behrend, William: "Den nordiske Musikfest i København 1888." *Tilskueren.* Copenhagen, 1888, pp. 594–611.
6. Behrens, Carl: *Erindringer: Mennesker og Begivenheder*. Copenhagen, 1937.
7. Benestad, Finn: "Johan Svendsens fiolinkonsert." *Norsk Musikkgranskning*, Yearbook for 1956–58. Oslo, 1959, pp. 209–265.
8. Benestad, Finn and Dag Schjelderup-Ebbe: *Edvard Grieg: The Man and the Artist*, trans. William H. Halverson and Leland B. Sateren. Lincoln, 1988.
9. Beyer, Harald: "John Paulsens utrykte bind erindringer: 'Aftnerne i Arbiensgade hos fru Susannah Ibsen.'" *Edda*, Oslo, 1943, pp. 42–43.
10. Bird, John: *Percy Grainger*. London, 1976.
11. Bjørnson, Bjørnstjerne: "Hr. Kapelmester Halvorsen." *Morgenbladet*. Kristiania, May 7, 1908.
12. *Bjørnstjerne Bjørnsons brevveksling med danske. Vol. II.* Ed. by Øivind Anker, Francis Bull and Torben Nielsen. Copenhagen/Oslo, 1953.
13. *Bjørnstjerne Bjørnsons brevveksling med svenske. Vol. III.* Ed. by Øivind Anker, Francis Bull and Örjan Lindberger. Oslo/Stockholm, 1961.
14. Bonnén, Helge: *P. E. Lange-Müller*. Copenhagen, 1946.
15. *Borgerskapsbevilgningen i Christiania*. In Riksarkivet, Oslo.
16. *Brockhaus, F. A. (Die Firma F. A. Brockhaus)*. Anonymous publication by the publishing company. Leipzig, 1872.
17. Brockhaus, Heinrich: *Reisetagebuch aus den Jahren 1867 und 1868*. Leipzig, 1873.

18. Brøgger, Kr. Fr.: *Trekk av kammermusikkens historie her hjemme.* Oslo, 1943.
19. Bull, Jacob B.: "Johan Svendsen." *Folkebladet.* Kristiania, 1908, pp. 289–291.
20. Bull, Jacob B.: "Johan Svendsens mor." *Aftenposten.* Kristiania, July 10, 1911.
21. Bülow, Hans von: "Skandinawische Concertreiseskizzen." *Allgemeine deutsche Musik-Zeitung,* vol. 9, 1882.
22. Børretzen, Odd: *Berus Eder.* Oslo, 1985.
23. *Carl Nielsens Breve.* Ed. by Irmelin Eggert Møller and Torben Meyer. Copenhagen, 1954.
24. *Dansk Teater-Aarbog.* Ed. by Arthur Aumont. Annual volumes for the years 1889/90–1908. Copenhagen, 1890–1908.
25. The Royal Theater's correspondence files and play evaluations. Housed in Det danske Rigsarkiv, Copenhagen.
26. Dolleris, Ludvig: *Carl Nielsen. En Musikografi.* Odense, 1949.
27. Eckhoff, Øivind: "Johan Severin Svendsen," in *Cappelens musikkleksikon,* vol. 6, pp. 225–231. Oslo, 1980.
28. Eckhoff, Øivind: "Johan Svendsens symfoni nr. 1 i D-dur—et tidlig vitnesbyrd om vesentlige trekk ved hans egenart som komponist." Unpublished M.A. thesis. University of Oslo, 1965.
29. Eckhoff, Øivind: "Noen særdrag i Johan Svendsens instrumentalstil." *Festskrift til Olav Gurvin,* ed. Finn Benestad and Philip Krømer. Drammen/Oslo, 1968.
30. Eggert Möller, Irmelin and Torgen Meyer (ed.): *Carl Nielsens Breve.* Copenhagen, 1954.
31. Ekman, Karl: *Jean Sibelius.* Helsingfors, 1935.
32. Elvestad, Sven: "Johan Svendsen i Norge. En Samtale paa Toget." Interview in *Aftenposten.* Kristiania, Nov. 20, 1907.
33. Ende, Hans von: "Johan Severin Svendsen." *Musikalisches Wochenblatt.* Leipzig, March 31 and April 7, 1871.
34. Fabricius, L. B.: *Træk af dansk musiklivs historie.* Copenhagen, 1975.
35. Falkenberg, Carl Fredrik: "Paolo Sperati (1821–1884)." Unpublished M.A. thesis. University of Oslo, 1984.
36. Friis, Niels: *Det kongelige kapel.* Copenhagen, 1948.
37. Friis, Niels: *Det kongelige teater.* Copenhagen, 1947.
38. Fønss, Johannes: "Johan Svendsens Betydning for Det kongelige Teater." Article in *Social-Demokraten.* Copenhagen, October 3, 1940.
39. Gandrup, Victor: "Johan Severin Svendsen 1840–1940." *Dansk Musiker-Tidende.* Copenhagen, Sept. 16, 1940, pp. 273–281.
40. Gandrup, Victor: "Johan Svendsen." *Danmark.* Copenhagen, 1946, pp. 262–265.
41. Gandrup, Victor: Notes concerning Johan Svendsen, in Musikhistorisk Museum Carl Claudius Samling, Copenhagen.
42. Gandrup, Victor: Unpublished draft of a Svendsen biography, in Musikhistorisk Museum Carl Claudius Samling, Copenhagen.

43. Godske-Nielsen, Sv.: "Nogle Erindringer om Carl Nielsen." *Tilskueren.* Copenhagen, 1935, pp. 414–430.
44. Gottschalksen, Carl: *En glad Musikants Dagbog.* Copenhagen, 1920.
45. Gradman, Peter: "Erindringer om Johan Svendsen." *Berlingske Aftenavis.* Copenhagen, Sept. 28, 1940.
46. Gran, T. O.: *Sandsværs saga II. Personalhistorie.* Kristiania, 1913.
47. Greni, Liv: *Rikard Nordraak.* Oslo, 1942.
48. Grinde, Nils: *A History of Norwegian Music,* trans. William H. Halverson and Leland B. Sateren. Lincoln, 1991.
49. Grinde, Nils: "Johan Severin Svendsen." *Norsk biografisk leksikon.* Oslo, 1966.
50. Grønoset, Rise: "Min far elsket det land han aldri fikk tid til å besøke." Interview with Sigrid Johan-Svendsen in *Østlendingen.* Elverum, Dec. 22, 1965.
51. Grønvold, Aimar: *Norske Musikere, Første Række.* Kristiania, 1883.
52. Gurvin, Olav: "Litt frå Johan Svendsens dagbok på Islandsferda 1867." *Norsk Musikkgranskining,* Yearbook for 1937. Oslo, 1938, pp. 51–56.
53. Gurvin, Olav: Notes concerning Johan Svendsen, in the manuscript collection of the University of Oslo library.
54. Gurvin, Olav: Unpublished draft of a Svendsen biography, in the manuscript collection of the University of Oslo library.
55. Hagtun, Erik: "Studenterorkesteret. Universitetets symfoniorkester, tidligere Studentersamfundets orkester. En historisk oversikt 1826 til 1987." Unpublished M.A. thesis. University of Oslo, 1987.
56. Hammerich, Angul: "Johan S. Svendsen." Article signed "A. H." in *Illustreret Tidende.* Copenhagen, Oct. 22, 1882.
57. Hansen, Peter: *Den danske Skueplads. III.* Copenhagen, 1896.
58. Hauch, Gunnar (ed.): "Breve fra Johan Svendsen." *Samtiden.* Oslo, 1913, pp. 481–512.
59. Henriksen, Alf Henrik: "Musikalsk virksomhet ved Christiania Theater fra 1850 til 1877." Unpublished M.A. thesis. University of Oslo, 1983.
60. Henriques, Fini: "Et Par Mindeord." *Gads danske Magasin.* Copenhagen, 1911, pp. 609–610.
61. Hetsch, Gustav: "Johan Svendsen og hans franske musikervenner." *Aftenposten.* Oslo, Sept. 4, 1934.
62. Holm, Emil: *Erindringer og Tidsbilleder I.* Copenhagen, 1938.
63. Huldt-Nystrøm, Hampus: *Fra munkekor til symfoniorkester.* Oslo, 1969.
64. Jessen, Peter: *Dengang i femti- og sexti-Aarene.* Kristiania and Copenhagen, 1912.
65. Johansen, Lars and Vilhelm Bartholdy: *Fem taktstokkens mestre.* Copenhagen, 1957.
66. Johan-Svendsen, Eyvind: "Min Far." *Berlingske Tidende.* Copenhagen, Dec. 31, 1944.
67. Jullien, Adolphe: "La musique en Norvège." *Le Ménestrel.* Paris, Oct. 10, 1873.
68. Kjerulf, Axel: *Hundrede År mellem Noder.* Copenhagen, 1957.

69. Kjerulf, Axel: *Kongelig Majestæts Musikanter.* Copenhagen, 1952.
70. Kjerulf, Charles: "Johan Svendsen." *Teatret.* Copenhagen, 1907–08, p. 35.
71. Kjerulf, Charles: "Johan Svendsen fylder halvfjerds." Article in *Politiken.* Copenhagen, Sept. 30, 1910.
72. Kjerulf, Charles: "Johan Svendsen i København." *Af Dagens Krønike II.* Copenhagen, July–December 1889, pp. 296–300.
73. Kjerulf, Charles: "Musiken i 1892." *Politiken.* Copenhagen, Jan. 9, 1893.
74. Kjerulf, Halfdan: *Halfdan Kjerulf. Av hans efterladte papirer 1831–1868, I–II.* Ed. Vladimir Moe. Kristiania, 1917–18.
75. Kortsen, Bjarne: *Johan Svendsens cellokonsert op. 7. En analyse.* Bergen, 1970.
76. Krog, Eli: *Lek med minner.* Oslo, 1966.
77. Kvarstein, Helene: "Johan Gottfried Conradi 1820–96." Unpublished M.A. thesis. University of Oslo, 1984.
78. Kaartvedt, Alf: *Frederik Stang og Georg Sibbern. Den politiske korrespondanse mellom Frederik Stang og Georg Sibbern, I–III.* Oslo 1956/1970/1976.
79. Larsen, Karl: "Monumentet for Johan Svendsen." Article in *Politiken.* Copenhagen, Jan. 22, 1931.
80. Leicht, Georg and Marianne Hallar: *Det kongelige Teaters repertoire 1889–1975.* Copenhagen, 1977.
81. Løken, Haakon: "Johan Svendsen og Nordmændene." *Norske Intelligentssedler.* Kristiania, May 1, 1908.
82. Løvstad, Theodor: "Ungdomsminder. I. Johan Svendsen." *Orkestertidende,* no. 2. Kristiania, 1892, pp. 5–6.
83. Meyer, Torben and Frede Schandorf Petersen: *Carl Nielsen: Kunstneren og Mennesket.* Copenhagen, 1947/48.
84. Monrad, O. P.: "Lidt om Johan Svendsen før hans Københavnertid. I–II." *Musik.* Copenhagen, 1920, nos. 2 and 3.
85. Neiiendam, Robert: *Det kongelige Teaters Historie, IV–VI.* Copenhagen, 1927/1930/1970.
86. Neiiendam, Robert: "Det realistiske Teater." *Teatret paa Kongens Nytorv 1748–1948.* Copenhagen, 1948, pp. 175–216.
87. *Nielsen, Carl. Breve.* Ed. Irmelin Eggert Møller and Torben Meyer. Copenhagen, 1954.
88. *Nielsen, Carl. Dagbøger og brevveksling med Anne Marie Carl-Nielsen 1–2.* Ed. Torben Schousboe. Copenhagen, 1983.
89. Nielsen, Carl: "Johan Svendsen." *Politiken.* Copenhagen, Sept. 30, 1900.
90. Nielsen, Carl: "Tale til Johan Svendsen ved 'Dansk Tonekunstnerforenings' Fest efter Jubilæumskoncerten den 12. November 1907." *Tilskueren.* Copenhagen, 1908, pp. 42–45.
91. Nielsen, Carl: "Til Johan Svendsens Ære." Interview in *Politiken.* Copenhagen, Jan. 23, 1931.

92. Nielsen, Thorvald: "Nogle personlige erindringer." *Carl Nielsen i hundredåret for hans fødsel.* Ed. Jürgen Balzer. Copenhagen, 1965.

93. Paulsen, John: *Erindringer. Sidste Samling.* Copenhagen, 1903.

94. Paulsen, John: "Johan Svendsen fortæller." *Verdens Gang.* Kristiania, May 1, 1908.

95. Paulsen, John: *Mine Erindringer.* Copenhagen, 1900.

96. Ravn, O. E.: "Johan Svendsen." *Levende musik, III.* Copenhagen, 1944, pp. 1–15.

97. Reinecke, Carl: "Meine Schüler und ich." *Neue Zeitschrift für Musik.* Leipzig, June 15, 1911, pp. 373–375.

98. Rosenfeld, Leopold: "Johan Svendsens norske Komponistgage." *Dannebrog.* Copenhagen, April 27, 1908.

99. Sandvik, O. M. and Gerhard Schjelderup: *Norges Musikhistorie I–II.* Kristiania, 1921.

100. Schart, Carl: *VIII Norske Slaatter for Hardingfele.* Bergen, 1865.

101. Schiørring, Nils: "Johan Severin Svendsen." *Dansk Biografisk Leksikon.* Copenhagen, 1983.

102. Schiørring, Nils: *Musikens Historie i Danmark,* vol. 3. Copenhagen, 1978.

103. Schjelderup, Gerik: *Gerhard Schjelderup. En norsk operakomponists liv og virke.* Oslo, 1976.

104. Schjelderup-Ebbe, Dag: *Edvard Grieg 1858-1867.* Oslo and London, 1964.

105. Schjelderup-Ebbe, Dag: "Sibelius og Norge." *Suomen Musiikin Vuosikirja 1964-65.* Helsinki, 1965, pp. 80–90.

106. Scholten, C. M.: *Dengang. Spredte Billeder fra svundne Tider.* Copenhagen, date of publication not given.

107. Schousboe, Torben (ed.): *Carl Nielsen, Dagbøger og brevveksling med Anne Marie Carl-Nielsen. 1–2.* Copenhagen, 1983.

108. Schulerud, Mentz: *Norsk kunstnerliv.* Oslo, 1960.

109. Seligmann, Hugo: "Johan Svendsen." Article in *Politiken.* Copenhagen, Sept. 28, 1940.

110. Sommerfeldt, W. P.: "Musiklivet i Christiania da Ole blev født. En Dagbog fra 1875." *Festskrift til O. M. Sandvik.* Oslo, 1945, pp. 223-58.

111. Stolpe, Steinar: "Johan Svendsens norske rapsodier op. 17, 19, 21 og 22." Unpublished M.A. thesis. University of Oslo, 1971.

112. Stortings dokumenter (National Assembly documents) from 1868–69, 1874, 1875, 1885, 1886, 1908 and 1909. These documents are housed in the archives of Stortinget in Oslo.

    a. Supplement to the Stortinget's summary of minutes for 1868–69. No. 179.

    b. Stortings forhandlinger (proceedings) 1868–69, Indstilling S. No. 85.

    c. Supplement to the Stortinget's summary of minutes for 1874, no. 116, which also includes *Musikalisches Wochenblatt*, Leipzig, for Jan. 2, 1874, with an unsigned article about Grieg, and for March 31 and April 7, 1871, with articles about Svendsen written by Hans von Ende.

    d. Stortings forhandlinger (proceedings) 1874, Indstilling S. No. 131.

    e. Stortingstidende 1874, pp. 886–888.

    f. Stortings forhandlinger (proceedings) 1875, St. prop. No. 1 A.

    g. Stortings forhandlinger (proceedings) 1875, Indstilling S. No. 101.

    h. Stortings forhandlinger (proceedings) 1885, Document No. 117.

    i. Stortingstidende 1885, pp. 1449–60.

    j. Stortings forhandlinger (proceedings) 1886, pp. 1891–93.

    k. Stortings forhandlinger (proceedings) 1908, part 6 a, Indstilling S XXVI, p. 23.

    l. Stortings forhandlinger (proceedings) 1909, part 6 a, Indstilling S XXVI, p. 42.

113. Svendsen, Johan: Articles (untitled) from Paris dated respectively Dec. 6, 1879 and March 1, 1880, signed "Quintus Octavus." *Nordisk Musik-Tidende*. Kristiania, Jan. and April, 1880.

114. Sævik, Rolf: "Johan Svendsens symfoni i B-dur, op. 15." Unpublished M.A. thesis. University of Oslo, 1970.

115. Tofft, Alfred: "Til Fjelds. En Rejse-erindring." *Berlingske Aftenavis*. Copenhagen, June 30, 1911.

116. Venzoni, Joh.: *Aus dem Tagebuch eines Gesanglehrers*. Leipzig, 1879.

117. Wagner, Cosima: *Die Tagebücher, I–II*, ed. Martin Gregor-Delling and Dietrich Mack. Munich, 1976–77.

118. Wenzel Andreasen, M.: *Kongens musikanter*. Copenhagen, 1983.

119. Whistling, Karl W.: *Der Musikverein Euterpe zu Leipzig 1824–1874*. Leipzig, 1874.

120. Wieth-Knudsen, K. A.: "Johan Svendsen som Komponist." *Tilskueren*. Copenhagen, 1908, pp. 525–538.

121. Wulfsberg, Sæmund: "Komponistens datter på Sandsværbesøk." *Lågendalsposten*. Kongsberg, July 10, 1964.

The following articles and interviews, which are unsigned or published under a pseudonym, are listed in chronological order.

122. "Johan Severin Svendsen." Unsigned article in *Skilling-Magazin*. Christiania, April 29, 1871.

123. "Two Afternoons with Svendsen, the Composer." Unsigned article in *Watson's Art Journal*. New York, Aug. 12, 1871.

124. Unsigned article about Johan Svendsen in *The Cincinnati Commercial*. Cincinnati, Sept. 22, 1878.

125. "Johan Severin Svendsen." Unsigned article in *American Art Journal*. New York, May 8, 1880.
126. "Hvem skal være Kapelmester?" Unsigned article [by Charles Kjerulf] in *Dagsavisen*. Copenhagen, Oct. 20, 1882.
127. "Johan Svendsen." Unsigned article in *Svensk Musiktidning*. Stockholm, May 1, 1883.
128. "Hr. Joh. Svendsen og Kapellet." Unsigned editorial in *Avisen*. Copenhagen, Oct. 18, 1884.
129. "Huru Svendsen öfvar in." Article signed "Bis" in *Nordisk Musik-Tidende*. Kristiania, May 1886.
130. "Johan Svendsen i Kjøbenhavn. En trofast Nordmand." Unsigned article in *Verdens Gang*. Kristiania, Oct. 22, 1907.
131. "Johan Svendsen." Unsigned article in *Aftenposten*. Kristiania, Nov. 24, 1907.
132. "Hos Johan Svendsen." Unsigned interview in *Aftenposten*. Kristiania, Sept. 30, 1910.
133. "En Kunstens Stormand fylder 70. Paa Fødselsdags-Visit hos Joh. Svendsen." Interview signed "Témoin" in *Dannebrog*. Copenhagen, Oct. 1, 1910.
134. "Johan Svendsens Død." Article signed "Anker" in *Politiken*. Copenhagen, June 15, 1911.
135. "Johan Svendsens Minde hædres. Hakon Børresen om den norske Komponists Betydning for Danmark." Interview signed "Haagen" in *Nationaltidende* (evening edition). Copenhagen, Jan. 21, 1931.
136. "Johan Svendsen. Og hans livs eventyr. Et besøk hos fru Juliette Svendsen." Interview signed "Per B. S." in *Urd*. Oslo, October 7, 1933.
137. "En genial Kunstner og hans Skæbne!" Interview with Juliette Svendsen, signed "Finn," in *Politiken*. Copenhagen, Sept. 15, 1940.
138. "Johan Svendsen. Dr. med. Gades erindringer fra den tid han spilte som 'dilettant' i Svendsens orkester." Unsigned article in *Morgenbladet*. Oslo, Sept. 30, 1940.

INDEX OF COMPOSITIONS

INDEX OF PERSONS

The index includes the individuals mentioned in the text in pp. 1–378. Names occurring only in the List of Compositions or the Bibliography are not included.